Sport in the Global Society

General Editors: J.A. Mangan and Boria Majumdar

A SPORT-LOVING SOCIETY

Sport in the global society
Edited by J.A. Mangan and Boria Majumdar

The interest in sports studies around the world is growing and will continue to do so. This unique series combines aspects of the expanding study of *sport in the global society*, providing comprehensiveness and comparison under one editorial umbrella. It is particularly timely, with studies in the aesthetic elements of sport proliferating in institutions of higher education.

Eric Hobsbawm once called sport one of the most significant practices of the late nineteenth century. Its significance was even more marked in the late twentieth century and will continue to grow in importance into the new millennium as the world develops into a 'global village' sharing the English language, technology and sport.

A Sport-Loving Society

In a time of unprecedented political and economic transformation, the middle classes of Victorian and Edwardian England became principal players in a new social order. Nowhere did their culture, values and identity gain clearer expression than in their sports, and their influence is still felt in the way we organise, play and think of sport today.

A Sport-Loving Society presents a selection of groundbreaking essays from *The International Journal of the History of Sport*, the journal which has helped to define the field of sports history over the past three decades. These essays explore the role of the social institutions and issues of the Victorian and Edwardian periods in shaping the sports of the English middle classes, including:

- education
- the emancipation of women
- religion
- culture and class
- diplomacy and war

In presenting the work of prominent cultural historians, this book demonstrates the value of sport as a vehicle for the study of wider social change.

Professor J.A. Mangan is former Director of the International Research Centre for Sport, Socialisation and Society at the University of Strathclyde, UK. He was founding Chairman of the British Society of Sports History and founding editor of *The International Journal of the History of Sport*. He is author of the acclaimed *Athleticism and the Victorian and Edwardian Public School* and has written and lectured extensively on sport, culture and society.

A Sport-Loving Society

Victorian and Edwardian middle-class England at play

Edited by J.A. Mangan

Routledge
Taylor & Francis Group

LONDON AND NEW YORK

Caw

First published 2006
by Routledge
2 Park Square, Milton Park, Abingdon, Oxon OX14 4RN

Simultaneously published in the USA and Canada
by Routledge
270 Madison Ave, New York, NY 10016

Routledge is an imprint of the Taylor & Francis Group

© 2006 Routledge

Typeset in Baskerville by
Newgen Imaging Systems (P) Ltd, Chennai, India
Printed and bound in Great Britain by
TJ International Ltd, Padstow, Cornwall

British Library Cataloguing in Publication Data
A catalogue record for this book is available
from the British Library

Library of Congress Cataloging in Publication Data
    A sport-loving society : Victorian and Edwardian
middle-class England at play / edited by J.A. Mangan.
        p. cm. – (Sport in the global society)
    Includes bibliographical references and index.
    1. Sports – Great Britain – Sociological aspects.
    2. Sports – Great Britain – History. 3. Middle class –
    Recreation – Great Britain – History. I. Mangan, J. A.
    II. Series.
    GV706.5.S7355 2005
    306.4'83'094109034–dc22   2005018701

ISBN10: 0–7146–5245–8 (hbk)
ISBN10: 0–7146–8229–2 (pbk)

ISBN13: 978–0–7146–5245–0 (hbk)
ISBN13: 978–0–7146–8229–7 (pbk)

Contents

PART VI
Sport, war and diplomacy

Contributors

William J. Baker is a historian at the University of Maine and author of a biography of Jesse Owens and a general history of sport in the Western world. He is currently working on a study of sport and religion.

Derek Birley now deceased, was Vice-Chancellor of the University of Ulster and author of the attractive trilogy *Sport and the Making of Britain* (1993), *Land of Sport and Glory* (1995) and *Playing the Game* (1995) published in the series International Studies in the History of Sport edited by J.A. Mangan and published by Manchester University Press.

Eric Halladay now deceased, was Rector of Grey College at the University of Durham and author of *Rowing in England: A Social History* published in the series International Studies in the History of Sport edited by J.A. Mangan.

Colm Hickey, Headteacher of St Thomas More R. C. School, a specialist sports college in Wood Green, London, was educated at Blackrock College, Dublin and Colfe's Grammar School, London. He trained as a teacher at Borough Road College and holds a Master's Degree in History of Education from the University of London, Institute of Education and an MBA in International School Leadership from the University of Hull. His PhD, completed in 2001, dealt with the impact of athleticism on elementary education. He has published several articles on the history of sport and is currently co-authoring with J.A. Mangan, *Soccer Schoolmasters*, dealing with the contribution of elementary schoolteachers to the evolution and development of association football in Britain.

Mike Huggins is a Lecturer at St Martins College, Lancaster. He has published widely on the history of sport, most recently, with Jack Williams *Sport and the English 1918–1939* (Routledge, 2005). His *Flat Racing and British Society 1790–1914* (Frank Cass) was awarded the Sports History Book Award of 2000 by the North American Association of Sports Historians.

John Lowerson is Research Reader in History at the University of Sussex. He has published extensively on the social and cultural history of leisure in modern Britain. His principal works are *Sport and the English Middle Classes, 1870–1914* (Manchester University Press, 2003) and *Amateur Operatics, A Social and Cultural History* (Manchester University Press, 2005).

J.A. Mangan is Emeritus Professor and former Director of the International Research Centre for Sport, Socialisation and Society, University of Strathclyde. He is the author and editor of many books, founding editor of the series Sport in the Global Society, founding and Executive Academic Editor of *The International Journal of the History of Sport* and founding Chairman of the British Society of Sports History. He also founded the journals *Sport in Society, Soccer and Society* and *The European Sports History Review*. His *Athleticism in the Victorian and Edwardian Public School* and *The Games Ethic and Imperialism* have been internationally acclaimed. He is a Fellow of the Royal Historical Society.

Kathleen E. McCrone has written extensively on women, education, sport and emancipation and is the author of the highly acclaimed *Sport and the Physical Emancipation of English Women 1870–1914* and on this topic, contributed to the innovatory *From Fair Sex to Feminism: Sport and the Socialization of Women in the Industrial and Post-Industrial Eras* edited by J.A. Mangan and Roberta J. Park.

Callum McKenzie was a doctoral student under Professor J.A. Mangan at the International Centre for Sport, Socialisation and Society, Strathclyde University. He has contributed to several collections in the series Sport in the Global Society. At present he is working on a monograph with Professor Mangan provisionally entitled *Blooding the Martial Male; Hunting, Militarism and the Imperial Officer* to be published in the series in 2007.

Martin Polley is Senior Lecturer in Sport at the University of Southampton. He is the author of *Moving the Goalposts* (Routledge, 1998) and *A–Z of Modern Europe since 1789* (Routledge, 2000), and editor of the five-volume reader *The History of Sport in Britain 1880–1914* (Routledge, 2003).

Series editor's foreword

The West is a name for a subject, which gathers itself in discourse but is also an object constituted discursively; it is, evidently, a name always associating itself with those regions, communities and peoples that appear politically or economically superior to other regions, communities and peoples (Naoki Sakai, 1998).[1]

This Western superiority, despite recent neglect of the community by scholars, was largely a handiwork of the Victorian and Edwardian middle classes, the first truly global community. *A Sport-Loving Society* brings this cardinal truth back to the forefront of academic scholarship. In fact, *A Sport-Loving Society* has many virtues but candour has primacy.

Going through *A Sport-Loving Society* feels like walking through a historical archive: you might be interested in a few things and not in others, but virtually everything is of great value. It tells you among other things how central the middle classes were to the British imperial consciousness. As argued by Tony Mangan in his introduction, in Empire, Christian clergymen like Tyndale Biscoe took the gospel of god and the gospel of games to its most distant corners and far beyond: Missionaries (products of the public school system) took cricket to the Melanesians, football to the Bantu, rowing to the Hindu, athletics to the Iranians with a firm intent: to create a universal Tom Brown.[2]

This statement by Mangan reflects a chain of thought characteristic of all his scholarship. In fact, he has always been at his most charismatic when writing about the middle classes and the public school code, such as in his magnificent tome-Athleticism in the Victorian and Edwardian Public School.[3]

How real is this story? It would be unfair to say anything less than to call *A Sport-Loving Society* fascinatingly cohesive and surprisingly candid. The forte of this book is its sweep – an examination of the Victorian and Edwardian middle class in all their facets: their morality, their religion, their discipline and the enmeshing of all of these with sport. *A Sport-Loving Society* is thus as much a study of the fashioning of a British global identity, as it is the study of the Victorian and Edwardian middle classes.

Much of what has been written on the middle classes of late is quintessentially critical. This book is equipped to sidestep misery. It also takes a step further – bring the middle classes back in their true element. Therein lies the true virtue of *A Sport-Loving Society*.

The editor has left all future scholars with a challenge: to blend with grace, generosity and completeness the significant moral, social and cultural contributions of the middle classes into a seamless story and bring back to life those across the entire community who gave determined birth to the games ethic, nurtured it with sustained affection and so helped bring it to its present popularity.

May I ask Tony Mangan to take the lead in fulfilling this challenge.

Boria Majumdar
Series Editor
Sport in the Global Society

Notes

1 Quoted by Dipesh Chakrabarty in *Provincializing Europe: Post Colonial Thought and Historical Difference* (Princeton, 2000), p. 3.
2 Mangan, Introduction, p. 6.
3 First published in 1981 by Cambridge University Press, this classic was reprinted by Frank Cass in 1998.

Middle-class memorials

La mode de l'athlétisme est devenue générale; tout le monde est converti. La toute l'Angleterre veut se faire des muscles, il redoute l'obésité comme une humiliation et le combat comme un fléau.

Baron Pierre de Coubertin
L'Éducation en Angleterre: Collèges et universités
(Paris: Hachette, 1888, p. 37)

By 1900, games, sports…had become more highly organized and team-oriented than at any time in the past. The main authors of this development were the urban middle class who were guided and inspired by public-school practices, so that sport was seen to have crucially important social and moral attributes.

Harry Hendrick
Images of Youth (Oxford: Clarendon Press, 1990, p. 137)
By permission of Oxford University Press

'We must thank the English people because they invented all modern sports.'

Juan Antonio Samaranch
Quoted by Mihir Bose, 'Inside Sport',
The Daily Telegraph (11 December 1999, p. S6)

Introduction
Complicated matters

J.A. Mangan

> The truth is too simple; one must always get there by a complicated route.
>
> George Sand[1]

In his review of Peter Gay's *Schnitzler's Century: The Making of Middle Class Culture 1815–1914*, published in 2002, Noel Malcolm wrote of Gay's 30-year struggle that it was a battle for acceptance fought on several fronts in the face of psychological rather than physical resistance: 'against the traditional Lytton Stracheyish attitude to the Victorians [and Edwardians]; against the modern politicised historiography which condemns them for capitalism and imperialism; and most importantly of all, against sheer neglect, at a time when everyone wanted to study women's history, black history and labour history, and no-one was interested in the respectable middle classes'.[2] Earlier Peter Bailey had sung from the same seditious hymn book: 'the reconstruction of the historic class cultures . . . remains on the agenda. Here the obvious deficiency is the still marked lack of attention to the middle class compared to . . . the workers'.[3] or as he expressed it on another occasion: 'Nearly everybody, it seems, has taken to heart [Marx's] warning against patronizing the lower orders and has set out to rescue yet more of them from the enormous condescension of posterity.'[4]

As Mike Huggins remarks trenchantly in *A Sport Loving Society*, 'All of us should know better.'[5] Without doubt 'the middle classes have suffered "a bad press" in some academic quarters'.[6] Apologists for other classes have set about them or set them aside. It is now time for a revisionist reassessment in the interests of balance, accuracy and impartiality, and time to break free from an intellectual headlock.

The contribution of the English middle class remains 'inexcusably undervalued and underappreciated'.[7] There is historical virtue, especially for historians of sport, in expressing greater interest in sport and the Victorian and Edwardian middle class; the historian of sport should make a special effort to be virtuous, at least in this regard. There has been far too little interest in pressing the merits of investigation.

There have been, of course, occasional sustained excursions into the world of middle-class sport, notably the recent *Reformers, Sport, Modernizers: Middle Class*

Revolutionaries[8] and the earlier *Sport and the English Middle Classes 1850–1914.*[9] *A Sport Loving Society*, hopefully, will further contribute to remedying a habit of relative neglect. It arose from discussions with the greatly missed and greatly respected Frank Cass, who, with his usual sharp eye for gaps in academic coverage, requested a collection of past IJHS articles on the subject of the 'missing middle class' in the historical study of sport.

In meeting his request, two things should be made clear: to echo, but rework, John Lowerson's words in the introduction to his lucid, nuanced and balanced *Sport and the English Middle Classes 1850–1914*, there is no intention in *A Sport Loving Society* to produce *A Making of the Sport of the English Middle Classes* but rather to cover significant aspects of their involvement in the making of modern sport. There is, however, a deliberateness in the *emphasis* on the English: the 'patriotism' is judicious.

Surely few would argue with the assertion that much of modern sport owed most to the English in the mid-nineteenth century, due to the pragmatism, enthusiasm and energy of the increasingly influential middle class and that in the forty-four years after 1870 this English middle class whole-heartedly embraced and endorsed this new fashion. The English mostly led; others mostly followed. As a consequence, sport became part of the culture of the emerging middle class and a community anxious to define its own position in a rapidly changing world characterised by amorphous changes, multiple innovations, sensuality and sobriety.[10]

With admirable comprehensiveness, Lowerson discerns five interwoven themes associated with this development: a complex differentiation which created criteria for demarcation; the emergence of popular sport which made it an arena for entrepreneurship; new notions of disposable assets, principally time, space and income; extensive voluntarism; increased opportunities allowing wide involvement; all resulting in the creation, intended and unintended, of 'implicit, often shadily sketched, codes of values'.[11] It was not all innovation. There was, of course, continuity and discontinuity, delicately handled by Lowerson in his scrupulous manner.[12] *In nuce*, there was a new pluralism of roles, forms, expectations and actions.[13]

In short, the English middle class was to be found in the vanguard of the Victorian and Edwardian 'sports revolution' which in time had such extraordinary global consequences – political, cultural, economic, aesthetic, emotional and spiritual. And a revolution was precisely what it was. It was wholly unlike anything that preceded it: 'sport, in its modern, organised, commercialised and extensive form, was truly an "invention" of the Victorian and Edwardian age'.[14] And much of this invention was the product of middle-class education, leisure and affluence.

It was an invention that was adopted as well as adapted, reconstructed and resisted throughout the world.[15] It coexisted with other parallel inventions but eventually in a variety of evolved forms it took over the world. There is more fact than fiction in Sir Charles Tennyson's mid-1950s grandiose title in *Victorian Studies* referring to the middle classes: 'They Taught the World to Play.'[16] Victorian and Edwardian middle-class sport was a cultural invention that became a cultural 'chameleon' adjusting to ever-changing global conditions and circumstances.

In sport then, as in much else, the Victorian and Edwardian period was a great revolutionary age 'an age in which Britain did more to change the world than she has ever done before or since.'[17] Middle-class revolutionaries were to the fore in sport and frequently led from the front in all manner of activities and in all manner of places. In this confident charge, they were in sport, as in other things, far from perfect. Their sport could be exclusive, patronising and ethnocentric:

> Victorians often did the right things for the wrong reasons and the wrong things for the right reasons. They made their mistakes…and with their successes they left to succeeding generations a legacy of many social and spiritual problems…They have been called 'giants with a limp' and lame giants the Victorians may well have been, but limp and all, their strides were still the strides of giants[18]

and not only in intellectual and material progress and legislative reform, but also in cultural innovation in which sport had an important place. Consequently, 'they have left their mark not only on England, but in some degree on Western and Westernized civilisation everywhere'.[19]

Nevertheless, to put *A Sport Loving Society* in perspective, a caveat, implicit in all that has been written earlier, is required. A great deal more research is necessary before our understanding of one of the most impressive and relatively neglected Victorian and Edwardian innovatory agencies is even adequate. There are still sizeable gaps in the analytical landscape. Delineation of even main features is still required.[20]

Striped blazers, be-ribboned boaters and Fortnum and Mason hampers in jolly boating weather complete with a hay-harvest breeze are secure images in what was an insecure age in religion, politics and economics. The Victorian and Edwardian middle class in its complex composition faced its share of challenges and changes. These were mirrored in sport. Two illustrations make this point: the slow advance of women in the face of conventional gender obstinacy and the lengthy struggle against self-serving amateurism.

It is a truism to declare that to define the Victorian and Edwardian middle class with precision is far from simple. There has been a great deal of debate: 'Nobody has ever found a definition which is short, satisfactory and watertight. To attempt to evolve one is to be lured into an almost interminable study of the social sciences and the result, while probably failing to satisfy the expert, would certainly weary the layman.'[21]

Thus, there is merit in following John Stuart Mill: 'It is not part of the design of this treatise to aim at metaphysical nicety of definition, where the ideas suggested by a term are already as determinate as practical purposes require.'[22]

In the pursuit of practical purposes, there appears to be general agreement on three things: that the rise of the middle class was one of the most remarkable phenomena of the Victorian era[23], that the term was widely used by 1850[24] and that the middle class was an indefinable kaleidoscope embracing everyone from entrepreneur to skilled worker.[25] Effectively it was a series of shifting social layers characterised by both conflict and collaboration, with increasing *rapprochement* from the 1880s on,[26] as a consequence of, among other things, the steady expansion of professionalism and the continuous growth of the 'melting pot' public schools.[27] In time,

> …this amorphous mass of people, who formed between a fifth and sixth of the population, controlled the destiny of a country whose future was to depend heavily on the quality of its professional men. This indeed was the age of the professions, proclaimed by the roll call of organisations they formed, such as the Royal Institute of British Architects (1834), the Institute of Mechanical Engineers (1847) or the British Medical Association (1856). These bodies reflected the needs of an increasingly complex society which called for more doctors, lawyers, apothecaries, civil engineers, architects, and many other specially qualified people to meet its needs.[28]

These professionals – the core of the middle class – are prominent in *A Sport Loving Society* for this reason. From them, more often than not, came the men and women, who, it is suggested,[29] whatever the contribution of others, played a disproportionate part in the evolution of modern sport, as innovators, participants, organizers and administrators.

There is considerable truth in the assertion that the legislators of Victorian sport were often the products of public school and university, that grounds, clubs and equipment were often paid for, and fees and wages paid by, businessmen, that period sport; like commerce, industry and politics, was controlled by capitalists and landlords and that the quest for respectability itself (the hallmark of middle-class status) expressed itself in the exuberant manner in which sport was projected by many of the middle class as a source of Anglo-Saxon greatness.[30] They are not the whole of the middle-class story, and they are even less the whole of the whole story, but they are a significant part of the story.

Ascent of the ladder of social mobility between and within classes to professional status was achieved by a number of means including education, family connection, money, talent and the shared membership of an organization or institution.[31] Successful ascent depended on the status of gentleman 'and much agony attended the definition.'[32] However, by the 1880s, by general agreement, a gentleman was someone educated at a public school. This still allowed scope, of course, for 'layer and shift' as generations competed for higher-status schools. With the advent of athleticism in the schools, this agreement had considerable direct and indirect consequences for modern sport by way of public school example, influence, inspiration and imitation.

Confident assertions such as this are bemusing: '…many middle class men most closely involved in the promotion of working class sport had little contact with the public school games ideology and little sympathy with the behavioural values it sought to inculcate'.[33] In the present state of knowledge how can anyone be so sure? Evidence is hardly extensive. And indeed, what recent evidence there is would appear to go some way to contradicting this assertion.[34] And what precisely does 'little contact' with the public school games 'ideology' mean? There are many kinds of contact, some obvious, others less obvious. Have they all been fully considered?

Subtlety should be the spur. It goes without saying, of course, that great care should be taken to avoid simplistic subscription to widespread hegemonic impact, 'downward diffusionism' and overemphasis on stability. The reality was more complex. Nor should it be overlooked that investigation is certainly needed into the growth of modern sport, that goes beyond class and penetrates 'neighbourhood, workplace, town, region, religion and nation'.[35]

Nevertheless, those who press the case for large-scale rejection of the influence of public school innovation in the rise of modern sport, need to demonstrate a wider vision and greater subtlety. Here is a case in point:

> ...the re-shaping of late-nineteenth century working-class culture is the consequence neither of hegemony nor of convergence – the common culture thesis – but of an independent response at an individual (male) as much as a class level; nor is this a culturalist victory wrested from the dominant class, but a demonstration of the British ideology of live and let live, of separate and largely self-sufficient class worlds.[36]

Accuracy is better served by this more balanced observation:

> The public schools were central to the development of the rhetoric of the gentleman amateur and *much else* [emphasis added] that was to characterize much of British and imperial sport for several generations thereafter. Yet their role has been largely underplayed, largely through the contagion of cultural condescension. The over-emphasis on working-class sport by some key practitioners, and the *collective myopia* towards the middle-class contribution this entails in sport history circles has tilted sports history downward to its detriment in terms of making a more accurate, complete and substantial contribution to social and cultural history.[37]

Certainly there was independent action and autonomous innovation but this can be stressed too strongly and with insufficient regard for the complexity of the processes of diffusion, direct and indirect, short term and longer term, positive and negative. The following statement only hints at a reality which still awaits its subtle analyst:

> ...the public schools enjoy an 'invisible empire'. Those who miss the direct environment of the public schools may sense it later at the universities, while it is a curious tribute to the hypnotic power of the public school tradition that

its atmosphere, if in a somewhat sensational guise, has been purveyed for many years to a fascinated clientèle of lower middle class youth by convivial juvenile magazines such as *The Magnet*.[38]

A single telling example of this invisible influence is sufficient to make the point:

> The public school house system, compulsory team games, playing fields, cups and cup ties, leagues and league tables...spread throughout the public school world. This gave a major boost to the systematization, re-organisation and regulation of modern sport, in which former public schoolboys and staff played an important role...throughout the world.[39]

By the 1880s, athleticism was firmly in place in the public school system. Middle-class ideological solidarity,[40] as far as it was achieved and as far as it existed, was advanced, as R.J. Morris argues, by a transformation of the public schools involving a formidable culture of collective responsibility by an elite defending its privileges.[41] He argues that this was the product of evangelism. However, by the last quarter of the nineteenth century, this relative solidarity was also promoted by the consolidation within the public school system of the ideology of athleticism, with its consequences in one form or another (still, incidentally, far from adequately explored and exposed,[42] which spun a moral, hedonistic and utilitarian web across the world. To be satisfactorily subtle, it should be appreciated that athleticism and evangelism meshed on occasion at home and abroad and fully incorporated the ethnocentric vices and virtues of Victorian and Edwardian middle-class England – a state of affairs no better exemplified than in the person of Cecil Earle Tyndale-Biscoe.[43] He was the personification of three complementary and contradictory period ideologies: Muscular Christianity, Social Darwinism and Evangelism.[44] In fact, he was one of many! Without doubt, 'the relationship between period sport and religion was very close'. Not least because so many clergymen were public school headmasters.[45] Others were simply Muscular Christians. In England, these professional men founded 'an extraordinary number of cricket and soccer clubs.... The Lancashire clergy, for example, played a pivotal role in the development of soccer in that county, and almost a quarter of urban soccer clubs appear to have been built by religions leaders!'[46] In Empire, Christian clergymen like Tyndale-Biscoe took the gospel of God and the gospel of games to its most distant corners and far beyond: 'Missionaries took cricket to the Melanesians, football to the Bantu, rowing to the Hindu, athletics to the Iranians'[47] with a firm intent: to create a universal Tom Brown.

To hone the arguments of Morris further, while undoubtedly the North and South represented different cultural milieux as he states, in terms of middle-class values[48] they were far from isolated from each other. The public schools, as much as, if not more than, the voluntary societies were a potent means of cultural integration, through, for example, athleticism and its various offshoots. The case for the role of the public school system as a middle-class consolidatory cultural matrix has been made over and over again by social commentators[49] not merely in terms of its direct influence but also its indirect influence through grammar school, elementary school, church and club.

It was associated and diffused social values, styles and networks, certainly not all but certainly some associated with public school athleticism, which gave the middle class its greatest coherence.[50] Perhaps Roger Scruton makes a shrewd observation:

> Enchantment is a personalising force: it endows objects, customs and institutions with a moral character, so that we respond to them as we respond to one another. The English were more than normally alert to this and filled their lives with local forms of membership. Indeed they related more easily to clubs, regiments, schools and teams than to human beings.[51]

While Eric Hobsbawm has remarked,

> 'The institution of old boys, which developed from the 1870s on, demonstrated that the products of an educational establishment formed a network which might be national or international, but it also bonded younger generations to older. In short, it gave social cohesion to a heterogeneous body of recruits. Here... sport provided much of the formal cement [emphasis added].[52]

Hobsbawm, of course, saw only part of the picture: sport was also an agent of militarism, an instrument of imperialism and a source of moral hegemony. To say this, it must once again be made very clear, is *not* to overlook, dismiss or marginalize regional, local and sectional freedom of action in terms of adaptation, adjustment, assertion and rejection, but to request an adequately comprehensive consideration of the forces of change in the middle-class world of Victorian and Edwardian England.

Industrialization, commercialism, urbanization and technology drove this engine of change and there emerged, as already noted, ever-increasing numbers of professionals. They became, again as already noted, a large and influential group. They populated and dominated the public schools. The growth of their power and influence led to subscription to a view of hard work as a moral virtue and 'increasingly middle class influence on society led to this idea becoming formally interlocked with the moral and social code of the nineteenth century'.[53] Within the public school system the secular moral values of hard work were transferred from classroom to playing field; this was the educational rationalization for athleticism. However, if complexity was a feature of the composition of the middle class, it was also a feature of middle-class athleticism and its associated constellations, patterns and trends. For many in many schools, in institutional actuality if not intention, athleticism was as much sensual escapism as moral indoctrination and a form of necessary control as much as virtuous stimulation.[54]

The power of ideologies should never be underestimated: 'ultimately it is the question of values that lies at the heart of history, the values which drove people to act, which shaped and transformed institutions... and underpinned communities, families and individuals'.[55] Equally, it is necessary to be aware of the ability of individuals and groups to coexist casuistically with useful ideological principles and practices without sincere subscription, serious commitment and with subversive intentions.[56] In all these regards, the part middle-class sport and its multiple manifestations played in the evolution of modern global sport has barely been explored. In further exploration, open-minded appreciation of the fact that ideologies influence action in many ways – overtly and covertly, directly and indirectly, crudely and subtly, narrowly and widely and, not least, negatively as well as positively will bring rich analytical rewards, especially if a close rather than a wide mesh analytical 'net' is employed and a willingness to follow the unexpected turns and twists of the 'quarry' is demonstrated.

In *A Sport Loving Society* Huggins and Lowerson especially, provide a good start, and Huggins' assertion is a good one to end with: 'Historians need to move away from what is currently relatively narrow, crude and coarse-grained analysis and begin to open up Victorian middle-class sport to a far wider base of historical and cultural investigation'.[57]

Notes

1 George Sand quoted in *The Oxford Book of Aphorisms* chosen by Edward Gross (Oxford: OUP, 1987), p. 228.
2 *See* Noel Malcolm's review of Peter Gay, *Schnitzler's Century: The Making of Middle Class Culture 1815–1914* (London: Allen Lane, 2001) in *The Sunday Telegraph*, 18 November 2001, p. 17. Throughout this Introduction reference will be made to 'the middle class' not the 'middle classes' following Roy Strong: '...by 1850 the terms "middle class" and "working class" had become the accepted way of referring to the various strata of society' in Roy Strong, *The Story of Britain: A People's History* (London: Pimlico, 1996), p. 439.
3 P.C. Bailey, *Leisure and Class in Victorian England: Rational Recreation and the Contest for Control 1830–1885* (London: Methuen, 1987), p. 17.
4 P.C. Bailey, 'Leisure, culture and the historian: reviewing the first generation of leisure historiography in Britain', *Leisure Studies*, Vol. 8 (1989), 114.
5 *See* Prologue, Mike Huggins, 'Second-Class Citizens? English Middle-Class Culture and Sport, 1850–1910: A Reconsideration', p. 11.
6 *See* the Preface by J.A. Mangan, in J.A. Mangan (ed.), *Reformers, Sport, Modernizers: Middle Class Revolutionaries*, London: Frank Cass, 2002.
7 Ibid.
8 John Lowerson, *Sport and the English Middle Classes 1870–1914* (Manchester: MUP, 1994).
9 Ibid., preface, p.viii.
10 Ibid., Introduction, p. 1. For a good example of English influence on Scottish middle-class innovations in sport, see J.A. Mangan, 'Missionaries to the Middle Classes,' in Heather Holmes (ed.), *Scottish Life and Society: Education: A Compendium of Scottish Ethnology* (East Linton: Tuckwell Press in association with the European Ethnological Centre, 2000), pp. 415–34.
11 Ibid.
12 Ibid., p. 2. Neil Tranter makes it clear that this continuity did not always fare well in the new revolution: 'there were numerous examples of sports which decreased rather than increased in popularity.... It would be quite wrong to suppose that the history of sport in the late nineteenth and early twentieth century Britain was one of general continuous expansion.' Neil Tranter, *Sport, Economy and Society in Britain 1750–1914*

(Cambridge: CUP, 1998), p. 14. This comment from F.M.L. Thompson also should not be overlooked: 'The countryside was swept clear of many of its traditions and popular amusements in the face of public opinion and legislation inspired by class.' F.M.L. Thompson, *English Landed Society in the Nineteenth Century* (London: Routledge and Kegan Paul, 1963), p. 283.

13 Bailey, *Leisure and Class*, p. 121. I have lightly adapted his analysis.

14 Tranter, *Sport, Economy and Society in Britain*.

15 J.A. Mangan, Prologue: 'Britain's Chief Spiritual Export: Imperial Sport as Moral Metaphor, Political Symbol and Cultural Bond', in J.A. Mangan (ed.), *The Cultural Bond* (London: Frank Cass, 1992), pp. 7–9.

16 Sir Charles Tennyson, 'They Taught the World to Play', *Victorian Studies*, Vol. 2 (March, 1959), 211–22.

17 A comment by Charles Dawson in Herbert Tingsten, *Victoria and the Victorians* translated and adapted by David Grey and Eva Leckström Grey (London: George Allen and Unwin, 1972), p. 552.

18 Ibid.

19 Ibid.

20 To offer merely one glaring example, the sport of the lower middle class still requires its definitive analyst. Other omissions include religious sects and sport, technology and sport, sex, sexuality and sport, and period sports journalism.

21 Roy Lewis and Angus Maude, *The English Middle Classes* (Bath: Cedric Chivers Ltd., 1973), p. 13.

22 Ibid.

23 Paul Adelman, *Victorian Radicalism: The Middle Class Experience 1830–1914* (London: Longman, 1984), p. 1.

24 Strong, *The Story of Britain*, p. 439.

25 Ibid., p. 434.

26 Martin Pugh, *State and Society: British Politics and Society, 1870–1992* (London: Arnold, 1994), p. 89.

27 J.A. Mangan, *Athleticism in the Victorian and Edwardian Public School: the Emergence and Consolidation of an Educational Ideology* (London: Frank Cass edition, 2000). See also S.G. Checkland, *The Rise of Industrial Society in England 1815–1855* (London: Longmans, 1964), pp. 292–3. Checkland, as so many others, misunderstands the complexities of athleticism but his general approach to growth and change in the public school system is broadly accurate and his recognition of its role as a 'melting pot' is sound.

28 Strong, *The Story of Britain*, p. 434.

29 Bearing in mind the present state of knowledge on this point, this statement is considered to be a working hypothesis and not an unassailable conclusion.

30 Keith A.P. Sandiford, 'The Victorians at Play: Problems in historiographical methodology', *Journal of Social History*, Vol. 15 (1981), 275–9. This article remains one of the most constructively provocative comments on Victorian sport.

31 Strong, *The Story of Britain*, p. 445.

32 Ibid.

33 Tranter, *Sport, Economy and Society*, p. 50.

34 Colm Hickey and J.A. Mangan, *Soccer's Missing Men: Schoolteachers and the Spread of Association Football* (London: Routledge, forthcoming), *passim*. There is extensive evidence that professional teachers had a substantial impact on the early development of association football – school, amateur and professional. See also Colm Kerrigan, *Teachers and Football: Schoolboy Association Football in England 1885–1915* (London: Routledge Falmer, 2005), *passim*.

35 Huggins, 'Second Class Citizens', p. 26.

36 *See* Bailey, *Leisure and Class*, p. 15.

37 Huggins, 'Second Class Citizens', p. 35.

38   Lewis and Maude, *The English Middle Class*, p. 22.
39   Huggins, 'Second Class Citizens', p. 17.
40   It must always be recognised and acknowledged that in practice, in the words of
     C.J. Morris, 'middle class ideology contained a number of competing, often contradic-
     tory strands, such as evangelicalism, political economy and utilitarianism. Other strands
     were represented by Smiles' concern with household suffrage and self-fulfilment; and
     by Attwood's assertion that liquidity and maintaining economic activity were more
     important than monetary stability.' C.J. Morris, *Class, Sect and Party: The Making of the
     British Middle Class, Leeds 1820–1850* (Manchester: MUP, 1990), pp. 12–13.
41   Morris, *Class, Sect and Party*, p. 330.
42   'Regression and Progression,' Introduction to the New Edition of Mangan, *Athleticism*,
     pp. xxvii–xiix.
43   See J.A. Mangan, *The Games Ethic and Imperialism: Aspects of the Diffusion of an Ideal*
     (London: Frank Cass edition, 1998), Chapter 7.
44   For a discussion of complementary and competing period school ideologies, see
     J.A. Mangan, 'Social Darwinism and upper-class education in late Victorian and
     Edwardian England', in J.A. Mangan and James Walvin (eds), *Manliness and Morality:
     Middle-class Masculinity in Britain and America, 1800–1940* (Manchester: MUP, 1987),
     pp. 135–59.
45   Sandiford, 'The Victorians at Play', p. 277.
46   Ibid.
47   Mangan, *The Games Ethic and Imperialism*, pp. 174–5. For merely one illustration of
     'beyond', see J.A. Mangan, 'The Early Evolution of Modern Sport in Latin America:
     A Mainly English Middle Class Inspiration?' in J.A. Mangan and Lamartine P.
     DaCosta (eds), *Sport in Latin American Society: Past and Present* (London: Frank Cass, 2002),
     pp. 9–42.
48   Morris, *Class, Sect and Party*, p. 325.
49   This comment is typical: 'In the public schools, reorganized upon lines laid down by
     Arnold, the middle classes and the gentry were gradually welded together . . . .' in Lewis
     and Maude, *The English Middle Classes*, pp. 58–9. Of course, it was also on lines laid
     down by later headmasters! See Mangan, *Athleticism, passim*.
50   A point made by Jonathan Barry in his review article, 'The Making of the Middle
     Class', *Past and Present*, Vol. 145 (1994), 205.
51   Roger Scruton, *England: An Elegy* (London: Chatto & Windus, 2000), p. 13.
52   E.J. Hobsbawm, *The Age of Empire, 1875–1914*, p. 179 quoted in J.A. Mangan,
     'Epilogue: The history of modern European sport as a history of modern European
     ideas', in *Reformers, Sport, Modernizers*, p. 254.
53   Janet Roebuck, *The Making of Modern English Society from 1850* (London: Routledge and
     Kegan Paul, 1973), p. 11.
54   Mangan, *Athleticism, passim*.
55   Mark Mazower, *Dark Continent: Europe's Twentieth Century* (London: Allen Lane, 1998), p. xv.
56   For a discussion of these attitudes *see* Mike Huggins and J.A. Mangan (eds), *Disreputable
     Pleasures: Less Virtuous Victorians at Play* (London: Routledge, 2004), *passim*.
57   Huggins, 'Second Class Citizens', p. 36.

Prologue: setting the scene

Second-class citizens? English middle-class culture and sport, 1850–1910: a reconsideration

*Mike Huggins**

From the second half of the nineteenth century onwards English middle-class sport increasingly functioned as a powerful cultural bond, moral metaphor, and political symbol. It had a major impact on recreational culture, career access and the formation of class cultures and relationships. Yet, as J.A. Mangan has point-edly remarked, discussion of the huge contribution of the middle classes 'to national and world sport as a political, cultural and social entity' and, more broadly 'to British, imperial and global culture' is, with a few notable exceptions, either consciously neglected, or inappropriately unfashionable.[1] Currently their contribution is inexcusably undervalued and under-appreciated. Its manifesta-tions constantly receive ritual reference yet frequently are not carefully considered or enterprisingly explored. All of us should know better.

The reasons are partly historical. Leisure historiography has a provenance as an offshoot of labour studies, and the 'new' social history of the 1960s, fed by the boom in sociology, moved away from a focus on middle-class 'high' culture towards attempts to recreate the world of the Victorian working classes, exploring the world of leisure in an industrial society, the more ordered and 'rational' recre-ations and its more commercialized popular leisure. Amongst historians of sport the resonances of this over-preoccupation with working-class experience can still be felt in terms of their research agenda. A recent review of issues in sports his-tory sees it as still largely and narrowly 'glued to working-class experiences', with the 'snobbish ethical codes' and 'sporting investment' of the middle classes often depicted as their only contribution to sport.[2] Such forms of inverted snobbery have meant that middle-class Victorian leisure and sport have received only lim-ited attention in recent decades. Scholarly overkill of one group has been coupled with neglect of another. The middle classes have been made second-class citizens.

Some historians recognize this. Recently Peter Bailey, one of the scholars who has been most assiduous in his explorations of the Victorian world of leisure, has

Originally published in *The International Journal of the History of Sport*, 2000, 17(1), pp. 1–35. http://www.tandf.co.uk/journals

argued that scholars' preoccupation with working-class experience has meant that there 'has been too little attention to the leisure history of other classes', although recently there has been some exploration of more private forms of their 'domestic, familial and sexual sensibilities', and the distinctive process of their 'making'.[3] The distinguished cultural historian Jeffrey Richards makes a similar point: 'while the working classes have received close attention, the middle classes, their values and life styles have been comparatively neglected'.[4] Richard Holt, amongst the most influential of recent writers, has likewise recognized that 'the aversion of researchers to the bourgeoisie' has meant thin coverage of their sports. Indeed his own interests, like those of most other sports historians, have lain more in the field of working-class sports, and this has contributed to a myopic view of the sporting field.[5] While the origins of modern organized sport have been recognized as middle-class inspired, the major debate among sports historians has been about the way in which this culture of athleticism and club development spread amongst the *working classes*. Most have favoured a simplistic downwards social diffusionist process, although others have pointed to the failure to give weight to the many other factors which helped to determine the way in which organized sport spread, and stressed the ways in which working-class sports could be self-initiated.[6]

It is high time that sports historians began to put the Victorian middle classes under the same detailed scrutiny to which working-class participation in sport has been subjected. Cultural historians, most particularly the highly prolific and influential J.A. Mangan, have performed this task in the context of middle-class education, investigating the origins of manliness, the games ethic in the public schools, its diffusion into other areas of education in Britain and abroad, and the links with imperialism and militarism. Education, of course, lay at the heart of British culture and the athleticism of the Victorian and Edwardian public school has fully merited the close scrutiny it has received. But the task of exploring middle-class sporting culture still needs to be addressed more completely in the field of *post-education*.

The middle classes were a highly significant group within the English population, and although estimates vary, there is some agreement that by the 1870s there was a total of over 1,500,000 families and the total was rising thereafter.[7] More importantly, their social position and influence were extremely high in proportion to their numbers. Yet even in the few cases where middle-class sport *has* been explored, the previous stress on 'high' middle-class culture still has its echoes. John Lowerson's *Sport and the English Middle Classes 1870–1914* (Manchester, 1993), which is by far the most complete and authoritative analysis thus far of this middle-class adult sporting life, gave a much-needed boost to the field. But his decision to pay most attention to those more *exclusive* new middle-class sports which developed in late Victorian and Edwardian England, such as golf, tennis, or cycling, meant that those still popular *cross-class* sports which survived from an earlier period, such as racing, boxing and wrestling, or coursing, together with middle-class playing and spectatorship of football, rugby and other *team games*, were comparatively neglected. As a result we still know far more about middle-class involvement in more exclusive sports, and their apparent quest for ethical or cultural purity.[8] This is curious, since sport was contested cultural space, an arena where ideas about class, gender and ethnicity were articulated, debated and developed. The exploration of the complex ways in which sport developed *within* the middle classes therefore, is important, but is as yet oddly neglected.

Even though the development of particular sports cannot be explained solely in class terms, historians from a range of standpoints have largely conducted their studies of sport with the use of class analysis as their defining investigatory approach.[9] In the linked area of cultural studies class has been even more central, and by the 1970s it had come to dominate discussion of Victorian leisure and sport, largely employing the twin themes of 'social control' and Gramscian notions of 'cultural hegemony', alongside relatively unsophisticated mechanisms of class differentiation.[10] The over-simplistic and reductionist application of 'social control', and the stereotyped class interests it portrayed, ignored the complexity of motives and divisions of interest within social groups, and the concept of hegemony has generally proved more fruitful. But there are complexities even here, and different sports have very different patterns of social involvement in terms of spectatorship and participation. Moreover, even if sports are to be seen as playing a part in battles for position in establishing particular levels of hegemony or counter-hegemony, there are problems in matching up the often very different chronologies and geographies of development of different sports, linking them with putative agents of control and finding actual evidence of hegemonic 'negotiation' in particular cases. For the most part empirical research has focused on working-class experience of sport rather than on the specific details of how control 'from above' might have been exercised historically by middle-class hegemonists.[11] There is as yet insufficient empirical research to support the theoretical debate about the utility of the hegemonic approach, which has been subjected to strong critical attack from a number of sociologists, largely from across the Atlantic.[12]

The hegemonic approach has led to a narrowing of focus largely upon the tensions and arguments concerned with what is generally described as 'middle-class', 'amateur' sport, and its apparent social exclusiveness, usually contrasted with supposedly 'working-class' sports such as professional soccer, conceptualized as zones of negotiated control, and such taken-for-granted bifurcation pervades much recent writing.[13] In reality, however, few sports were purely 'amateur', purely 'middle class' or purely working-class in membership while the flexibility of sporting governing bodies varied quite considerably. In both professional football and in cricket, for example, the classes mixed as players, the working-class professional was somewhat differently treated in each, and both classes watched. In terms of the debate about professionalism too, this was not necessarily a middle-class reformist versus working-class argument. Dave Russell argues strongly that in football the amateur/professional debate was partly an intra-middle-class conflict, with the more provincial, non-public school educated much more likely to argue for professionalism than the public school élite.[14] In rugby, although it could be argued that the 1895 split was based on middle-class anxieties about the nature of working-class participation, it also reflected different attitudes within the middle classes. The leading figures in the organization of the breakaway Northern Rugby Football Union were mostly middle class but had a background and outlook 'with a lack of real commitment to amateurism'.[15]

In terms of broader leisure studies, where in recent years the concept of 'leisure cultures' has received increasing attention, historians have explored the ways in which differential types of leisure and the values embodied in them are linked to social class and class consciousness. Amongst the most influential work has been that of Hugh Cunningham, who argues strongly that class boundaries were often reproduced in leisure. His tentative model identifies six different, albeit loose and shifting leisure cultures, including 'the leisured classes', 'urban middle-class culture', 'skilled artisan culture', 'working-class reformist culture', 'rural popular culture', 'urban popular culture'.[16] His taxonomy has been extremely useful in leisure studies, and although sport is treated as a part of leisure, and not as a central feature, it is clear that each of his categories has links with particular types of sports praxis. The picture Cunningham paints of undifferentiated middle-class culture needs critical examination with regard to sport. In Cunningham's model there is a single, unified group culture which he calls 'urban middle-class culture', characterized by a 'seriousness of approach', and exclusivity in environments which were 'in accordance with the canons of respectability'. Sporting activity was only one aspect of this leisure culture, but an important one, and Cunningham pays it due attention, largely following what now appears conventional wisdom in sports history.

This conventional wisdom might be broadly synthesized along the following lines. In the eighteenth century sport expressed many of the values of the urban gentry but by the nineteenth century the middle classes were examining all sports to see if they met evangelical and dutiful purposes, and sociability for a time shifted towards domesticity. There was an elevation of 'rational recreation' and a denigration of the sheer physical enjoyment of some activities. A number of sports, such as cockfighting or bull-baiting became disapproved of. From the mid-nineteenth century public schools began to transform the nature and purpose of sport. Here, an ideology was developed which legitimated sport as helping keep order and discipline, encouraging team spirit, fostering qualities of leadership, taking minds off sex, grooming them for imperial service or other future professions and occupations or even preparing pupils for war.

A separate but related strand of more overtly hegemonic ideology was developed to emphasize the role of sports in recreating men for work. Sports were seen as 'improving' of body, health and character. Sport was re-conceptualized as a competitive struggle within agreed parameters. Its 'respectable' credentials led to some exclusion of non-middle-class participants, initially through rules, and then later through cost and locational factors. Social exclusion led both to the growth of amateurism, which affected the competitiveness of some teams, and to working-class concerns over the lack of recompense for playing sport. Social changes, especially the growth in disposable assets of time, space and income, led to the emergence of commercial sport entrepreneurs, to the widespread creation of voluntary sports organizations, and to deeper involvement in sports across a wide range.

Holt, an articulate synthesizer and communicator of this view of Victorian middle-class sport, has suggested that the main debate is whether it was a new development based on recently imbibed values of competitiveness and rational administration, or whether innovations drew upon old ideas of honour and chivalry, or whether it was a combination of the two.[17] This assumes, rather than proves, that middle-class sport was characterized by such values. The reality was more complex, with a much wider range of values permeating middle-class sport over the course of its evolution.[18] There is still a need for greater subtlety of analysis.

Such assumptions are premised on a monolithic view of middle-class culture. Models of middle-class involvement with leisure and sport thus far have been insufficiently comprehensive and precise, largely due to insufficient empirical research. Sports historians have moved to the stage of producing broad works of synthesis somewhat prematurely in relation to many aspects of middle-class sporting life. There is still a lack of the more detailed and painstaking analyses of primary source material which would have provided a sharper focus. To bring middle-class sport back into such focus, we need first a better general recognition and understanding of the types of social pressures which contributed to the patterns of conformity suggested by the current model of middle-class sport outlined above. These are covered briefly in the first section of this essay. We also need to recognize some of the ways in which such an 'ideal schema' of middle-class sport is still flawed: in terms of limited source utilization, the failure to recognize internal fragmentation within the middle classes, the problems of periodization involved in viewing Victorian and Edwardian sport as a single unit, and the still neglected importance of regional and local sporting identity, and these are covered in section two of this article. We should begin to accept too that 'middle-class respectability' was never particularly strong, even amongst the middle classes, despite the massive scale of church building in the second half of the nineteenth century. In reality the clear pressures for convergence, coming often from social contexts such as the domestic arena were often balanced by divergent tendencies, pulling middle-class sportsmen, and to a lesser extent middle-class sportswomen, in different directions. The mixed membership of many clubs, the complex social working out of sporting 'respectability', the very significant middle-class group which enjoyed less respectable sporting activities and the sporting leisure contexts where less respectable behaviour was much more common are given their due weight in sections three and four.

I

There were certainly pressures for middle-class sport to be respectable, rational, and improving, and such pressures came from a variety of socializing agencies and institutional organizations, not least the home, the school, churches and the workplace, although historians need to keep alert for the limits to such pressure, and the current gaps in our knowledge. Space does not permit a full exploration of the range and extent of such pressures, and the following discussion therefore concentrates on the two key agents of socialization into sporting middle-classness, the home and the school. In so doing one should not underestimate the role of the church and other religious organizations, the 'muscular Christianity' exertions of vicars and priests, or the role of employers in, for example, the creation of sports clubs, although all need to be explored in more detail. It should be said, however, that once churches attempted to impose unacceptable ideological constraints on sports clubs such evidence as we have suggests they were usually resisted and avoided.[19] Outside a minority of large concerns, most employers made only a modest contribution to the organization of works teams and other recreational activities.[20] There is still much to research here.

Middle-class morality and class relationships were managed and controlled as much in the domestic context as at school, at work or in leisure, although given the many middle-class autobiographies and biographies we know very little indeed about the way sporting attitudes were developed in the home and this is an area which really needs to be extended. In the wider context of class attitudes, the limited feminist research carried out seems to indicate that despite or because of the emergence of separate spheres for men and women, it was women, with their more constant domestic presence, who largely acted as social gatekeepers, and this aspect of gender roles is an under-researched factor in relation to sport.[21] Such a role was strengthened both by social maternalism and by that strand in nineteenth century feminism which saw women as the natural guardians of the moral order.[22] At home many women played a considerable role in managing and controlling class relationships, elaborating the subtleties of social distinction, and defining the boundaries and internal divisions of middle-class life. Their contribution to the drawing up of the rules of morality, propriety and decorum is as yet unclear, but they are likely to have exercised considerable control and influence over their menfolk in the home, and schooled the early behaviour of their children almost everywhere. This might involve defining appropriate protocols for what children could or could not legitimately do, and the acceptability or non-acceptability of the other children whom they met and with whom they might play. Women were active in purchasing the trappings of respectability. We are far less clear about the extent to which they supported the involvement of their children in sport. Much writing about women's domestic role has been feminist in origin and sport has been too little stressed, although this has been in part a reaction against the trivialization of women's position in earlier writing. The role of fathers, who might, when available, teach their children their first sporting skills, provide equipment, or take them to sporting events as spectators, also needs far greater consideration than it has been given at present, as does the importance of parental expectatations outside the context of the public school. The regulation of family activities, often in a context of fear of local disapproval, was a product of the mores by which families lived in the middle-class suburbs.

But even here, the rise of social feminism in the domestic context and the pressures on males to behave in appropriate ways inside the home, may have engendered its own reaction. Eric Dunning, drawing in part on American work, sees the 'great sports boom' as creating a sphere of life where 'true manliness could be instilled in boys by *men*', so that 'organised sport became a primary masculinity-validating experience', and thus played a key role in the formation of male middle-class identity.[23] Some initial work has been carried out but this is an interesting avenue for more exploration.[24]

In terms of the growth of athleticism in the upper-middle-class public schools we are on surer ground. Athleticism was 'the most telling' of all influences on British sporting culture.[25] Mangan's pioneering work on its complex development has been hugely significant in extending our understanding of the roots of 'fair play', 'manliness' and 'sporting' play, and the range of ways in which cultural conditioning took place.[26] It was not a simple process, since in these public schools communities there were a range of ideologies concerned with sport, linking boys, parents and staff, differently emphasized at different schools. The ideology of 'fair play', for example, was initially developed in the context of the reform of public schools from the mid-nineteenth century, the need for social control, order and containment of what sometimes were clearly sometimes brutal and frequently brutalized pupils, with a tendency to occasional revolt. The public school house system, compulsory team games, playing fields, cups and cup ties, leagues and league tables were a reaction to this, and soon spread throughout the public school world. This gave a major boost to the systematization, re-organization and regulation of modern sport, in which former public schoolboys and staff played an important role, not just in Britain, but throughout the world.

Success at games was linked with high institutional status. Masters soon developed a code of sporting conduct to support this approach and ensure constructive involvement, playing to the rules, subordinating the individual to the needs of the team, stressing social integration and character training. As Mangan shows, 'fair play' was 'cultivated carefully as a practical tool' and 'a means of ensuring *controlled confrontation* in the physical struggles on the new playing fields'.[27] Its emphasis however was very much on winning, albeit winning within the rules, and there was an equally firm belief in the futility, not the moral usefulness, of failure. Indeed, there was acute status tension and competition within and between schools with regard to games. A more complex concept of 'manliness' stressed victory (within the rules), aggression, ruthlessness, and yet courtesy towards and compassion for the defeated. 'Athleticism' involved 'virtuousness, indulgence and expedience', and embraced 'idealism, casuistry and opportunism'.[28] Such values were at times very uneasy bedfellows, but in disentangling them a more complex reality emerges than a simple juxtaposition of competitiveness and rational administration against chivalry and honour in middle-class sport.[29]

Although the public schoolboy certainly took his sporting myths, rituals and symbols of belonging with him into the adult world, the actual numbers involved were relatively small, although disproportionately powerful, especially in founding clubs. In Cornwall, for example, ex-public school boys were linked to the founding of clubs at Redruth and Camborne.[30] What we currently lack is any data on the geographical diffusion of ex-public school boys, and it is highly likely that they settled in disproportionate numbers in the south. Most links could only be indirect. It was young apprentices, led by the athlete Walter George, who was apprenticed to a chemist, who played a key role in founding Worcester Rugby Football Club in 1876, and we know little of the influences on them.[31] Many men closely involved in the development of team sports in northern England had not gone to public schools, so their contact with any form of public school sporting ideology is not easy to define. Of the team members of soccer clubs entering the FA Cup in the north-east in the period 1876–84/85 (Tyne, Middlesbrough, Redcar, and Sunderland) whose education can be identified only two were ex-Clarendon public schoolboys, although a number went to grammar schools.

By a process of what has been termed 'reverse social osmosis' athleticism also penetrated the late nineteenth-century grammar schools, and here again Mangan's work has been significant.[32] We still need to know much more about the extent to which elementary schools absorbed much of the same rhetoric and practice, although as C. Hickey's recent research indicates, the London training colleges for elementary teachers were soon using the same material with their trainees.[33] Battersea Training College students were drawn from across the country and took athleticism with them to their appointments. But there was significant regional variation. In football, while St Peter's College at Saltley, Birmingham was playing football in the early 1870s, in the north-east it was only in the mid-1880s that St Bede's Training College in Durham had a football team. In the elementary schools it was only at the end of the century that the ideology of athleticism was effectively diffused. Lack of time and lack of facilities had to be overcome, and boys went home each day. As a result the nature of the athleticism developed there was later and somewhat different from that of the public schools.[34]

Although the 'sports boom' and its consequences was essentially a male phenomenon, the influence of the home, public school, college and university was also important on women's sport, which was almost entirely upper- and middle class during this period.[35] C. Parratt has pointed out that the middle-class female participation in sport outside the context of the home was more than many historians have supposed, and was particularly significant in educational contexts, although in both range and type of sports it offered little real challenge to the ideology of sporting masculinity, and had only limited impact on gender roles.[36] Some valuable work has shown how in the public schools, Swedish gymnastic exercises were first to be introduced, followed by an increasing number of individualistic and team sports, often organized in inter-house and inter-school competition.[37] But its wider impact was limited. A much smaller, and possibly far less typical, proportion of middle-class females experienced such élite education. Even here the status of school sport came well below that of academic subjects for most girls and their teachers. And besides, not all girls took part regularly.[38] In schools below this level opportunities were even more rare. In female adulthood therefore, diffusion of sporting attitudes was slower to enter broader middle-class culture, and most sporting participation was recreational, social, casual and gentle throughout the late Victorian period. Robust, physical and energetic sporting activity was limited to a tiny minority. The competitive, institutionalized and formalized structures needed to boost women's sport were largely a product of the twentieth century, with only rare exceptions such as golf, tennis or hockey. Here too, we still know more about the elite clubs and national organizations, competitions and governing bodies, than we do about the actual membership and participation rates of more local sports clubs or of informal sporting activity.

The power of the forces of ideological rhetoric coupled with the practical pressures of the playing field were considerable, and of central importance to our understanding of sporting culture. They eased the transition of many schoolboys accustomed by habit and indoctrinated by education into the adult sporting world. Even the ornate surface trappings of athletic success, blazers, badges, and strips were often carried on to new sports clubs, transferred along with mannerisms and expectations, the potent symbols of a corporate class culture. Mangan also makes clear, however, that in the public schools there was often 'an ideology for public consumption and an ideology for personal practice: in a phrase Muscular Christianity for the consumer, Social Darwinism for the constrained'.[39] Muscular Christianity, with its morbid fear of sin, was meant to fill boys' lives with regimented activity, and ensure that all their waking lives were purposeful, although its specifically religious impact was limited. Mangan sees too that 'various ideologies co-existed in the public schools. They overlapped, even fused on occasion, but certain of their elements were discrete and even contradictory.'[40] However, the direct impact of such ideologies on wider society should not be over-emphasized. Actual numbers of public school leavers were quite small, while not all boys absorbed and accepted the rhetoric. The athletic heroes, the 'bloods', the athletes and 'hearties', the 'remnants' and 'aesthetes' experienced the ruthlessness of the system of winners and losers in different ways. Some only learned about exclusion, others may have reacted against it. At Eton, for example, the cult of athleticism was not wholly dominant. A small group of Socratic teachers who believed that athletic prowess simply inculcated ruthless egotism and forced pupils to submit to arbitrary standards of judgement, cultivated an ideology of intellectualism and independence, fostered a cult of love, truth and beauty, and opposed 'manliness'.[41] At Marlborough the (somewhat later) *The Heretick*, published by a small but daring 'high aesthetic' band, had a cover showing a 'crop haired, square jawed, wide-shouldered athlete' surrounded by taunting pixies, and unsurprisingly attacked athleticism in its pages.[42] Such anti-sports subcultures, resistant to the internal adjustments most schoolboys made, were to play their own role in elite society in the twentieth century. The marginal nature of such protests, however, suggests that the cultural cloning process was powerful, although much more work is needed to see if protests against athleticism were part of a wider pattern at this time.

By the 1880s the cloning process clearly played a role in producing an increasingly unified and standardized educational élite, and a new ideologically powerful concept of the English gentleman-amateur in aspects of English sport such as cricket, but it is much less clear what degree of *consensus* it had overall *even* in middle-class society itself. Was it as all-pervasive as is sometimes inferred, especially beyond the public school? How effective were the efforts of propagandists, publicists and active proselysizers? How far was it a rhetorical strategy, like the condemnation of working-class character, or public espousal of evangelical attitudes? How far was it reality? These are important questions, yet they have still to be addressed.

What happened when boys left public school? What exactly was the role of the Universities? After all, at Oxford and Cambridge during the period of élite masculinity, individualistic participation in field sports such as hunting and shooting survived and flourished, and could be seen by some as complementary to, and by others in direct competition with team games. This stress on field sports was a continuation of their similar role in the making of masculinity in the public school system, where they had provided another form of social training for a minority of upper-middle-class youth, drawing on an older, more conservative tradition of masculinity based on rural and country gentleman ideals, and coloured by traditional pastoral mythology. Field sports aided the process of cultural assimilation, and conveyed an alternative sense of social superiority.[43] Here again we see the complexity of sporting masculinity, with two public school and university masculinities existing side by side. Only a *minority* of public school boys went on to university, and we know insufficient about the proportion from a middle-class background. It may be that field sports were more appealing to the upper-class groups, and to social climbers, and athleticism to those with less wealth.

But the chronology of the ways in which the ideology of athleticism took hold in the universities was also complex. It was first legitimized, encouraged and sustained in colleges like Trinity and Jesus at Cambridge or Brasenose and Balliol at Oxford, where there were supportive dons, and T.J. Chandler has argued that it took the period from 1880 to 1900 for it to reach the smaller colleges and halls, although he provides little supporting evidence.[44] As Mangan shows, it was 'never as dominant in the universities, and varied in intensity from college to college and from period to period, but it became woven tightly into the social and educational fabric'.[45] From the universities, some sportsmen went back to the more élite schools as teachers, to pass on their belief in games for physical and moral well-being.

The late Victorian games cult in the public schools was soon linked to militarism, patriotism and imperialism, as a number of revisionist writers have demonstrated.[46] How far the existence of the British empire, the pressures it created and the responses it demanded helped to consolidate and reinforce the spread of athleticism and militaristic manliness both in the schools and in more widespread general middle-class aspirations, actions and responses needs further exploration. Current research evidence does not tell us how extensive the process of militarization through sport was. It certainly existed in the more supportive cultural contexts of metropolitan London, and schools like Marlborough, Clifton or Cheltenham. Equally it could be found further afield in the imitative schools of Scotland, or those of the British empire, as Martin Crotty's recent Australian work has shown.[47] But its spread into the adult world is yet to be demonstrated.

II

As we have seen, there are dangers in holding onto an uncritical belief that these social pressures for convergence resulted in a single middle-class leisure culture in practice even in the schools, while the extent and form of ideological implementation beyond homes, schools and universities in wider middle-class society have also not yet even begun to be adequately explored. Such ideologies *informed* aspects of people's lives. They did not *dictate* them.[48] Ideologies such as the 'games ethic' or 'respectability' were a highly flexible means of transmitting values and so capable of being adapted to the uses and desires of a range of groups with different end results, and were responsive to changes in wider society. As one cultural historian has strongly argued, 'the analyst of ideological proselytism and its cultural consequences should confront...the nature of interpretation, assimilation and adaptation, and the extent of resistance and rejection by the proselytised'.[49] But we need more recognition that the proselytized were not just the working classes but also many amongst the middle classes themselves. We need to move beyond the simplistic assertions of ideological impact. We need more analytic exploration and evaluation, based far more firmly on empirical evidence than is at present the case.

Cunningham's preliminary model of middle-class sporting leisure, whilst undoubtedly useful, still has a number of deficiencies. Firstly the model is largely driven by source availability. It was easier for historians to assess the moral revolution of evangelicalism and its impact on the working classes than its real impact upon the middle classes. Such supposed 'middle-class respectability' was censorious but it was much more prone to be used to interfere with the leisure of other classes than to attack the sports of the middle classes themselves. We know more about its application to attempts to abolish 'cruel' sports amongst the working classes; or to attack other sports which were not seen as uplifting and improving, such as horse-racing, than we do about the way in which members of the middle classes in the early and mid-Victorian period actually behaved outside church. But this is because Liberal nonconformist papers in particular gave prominence to the fulminations from pulpit and platform or to (often in reality poorly attended) public meetings. Such meetings were carefully staged and manipulated to 'demonstrate' public backing and help what might be a vociferous minority appear the moral majority. So we may well have exaggerated both the status and influence of sporting respectability, and the reformist attacks on sports.

The sheer dominance of the rhetoric, coupled with the easy accessibility of the 'moral imperialist' records and writings of sabbatarians, the temperance movement, the later anti-gambling associations, the religious groups, and other such cultural and philanthropic associations can lead historians to believe that such views were all-pervading in lived experience.[50] A good example is the opposition to horse-racing which led for many years to the widespread acceptance amongst leisure and sports historians that racing was virtually without middle-class support, whereas more detailed research has demonstrated that the middle classes played a central role.[51]

There were certainly attempts by reformist groups to use the three strands of religious instruction, education, and the encouragement of appropriate patterns of leisure on the working classes. Yet how deep the penetration of such 'moral imperialism' actually went even within the working classes is unclear, especially given the counter-tensions of social exclusivity. This was probably even more problematical amongst the middle classes themselves, given the discontinuities, divisions and rivalries that plagued reformist groupings, and different views and values related to the idea of moral fitness for social and political leadership. If one major future influence on global sport was the activity of middle-class groups attempting to establish what they saw as appropriate habits and patterns of sport right across the class structure, we need both to broaden our range of sources, and exploit existing ones much more creatively, to check this, and assess their impact.

Although there were church and chapel sporting organizations, most middle-class sporting associational forms were male, secular, and totally independent of any church, and were often undocumented. Here again ease of source availability has led the agenda. We know more about sport in the public schools, with their upper-middle-class pupils, than we do about sport in the provincial grammar schools which had pupils from other middle-class backgrounds as well as some working-class pupils. We also know much more about the institutionalized and/ or commercialized larger-scale forms of sporting activity, the professional clubs, the enclosed race meetings, or the county cricket clubs. As a result, as Clarke and Critcher have pointed out, there has been a marginalization of the unorganized and the informal.[52]

As the impact of secularism increased later in the period the balance was increasingly in favour of often temporary and much smaller sports clubs. Such smaller clubs, by their very nature, did not always leave records, and need careful tracing. By the last quarter of the nineteenth century too, the most puritanical reformers were largely irrelevant; increasingly out of touch with middle-class public opinion. In racing, for example, there were very rare evangelical attacks on meetings or against credit betting by those who could afford it, and the agenda increasingly shifted to attacks on off-course working-class betting.[53]

Secondly, and more importantly, the middle classes, like the working classes, should not be seen as a uniform, unified group, as F.M.L. Thompson and others have pointed out.[54] In his meticulous and carefully nuanced studies of football Mason showed clearly that just 'as there was no monolithic middle class, so there was no monolithic middle-class attitude to football'.[55] So there should be no temptation in discussion of late nineteenth century sport to rely on a simplistic separation of supposedly working-class and middle-class sport. Cunningham's reminder of the complexity of attitudes to leisure and the associated social divisions amongst the working classes is itself a useful corrective to this. But amongst the middle classes too, there were major differences in both income and status, and at the level of those who earned between £100 and £300, a group which covered some two-fifths of middle-class households in the 1880s, the choice might well have been between the paraphernalia of sporting gentility and a second servant.[56] The middle classes were riven by divisions. Some of these were horizontal divisions; of incomes, of geography, and even of religion. There was also the further (and very important) vertical fracture between the business and professional classes.

At the upper end some clearly thought it natural to enjoy themselves and were buying large estates, often of over a thousand acres, and founding landed families, emulating upper-class pursuits, and were merging with the fringes of high society, although the debate on the extent of gentrification continues. Others of similar disposition combined active involvement in business with upper-class sports. Some of the more prosperous industrialists and merchants were amongst the most enthusiastic hunting, shooting, yachting and racing participants. Businessmen were a significant source of hunt secretaries, whilst the *Field* estimated that they composed about two thirds of mounted hunt followers.[57] The banker Meyer Rothschild (1818–74) formed a pack of staghounds as early as 1839, whilst the mid-century growth of the fashionable sport of deerstalking meant that high prices were soon being paid for Scottish deer forests. The purchase of grouse shooting estates by businessmen was becoming common by the 1850s. In racing the growth of upper-middle-class business penetration was such that both Meyer de Rothschild and his nephew Leopold (1845–1917) became members of the highly select Jockey Club. Equally emulative of upper-class leisure were some of the upper professional groups, especially those educated at the public boarding schools and endowed grammar schools.

By contrast there were others amongst the middle classes, sometimes equally wealthy, who should be seen more as an urban élite in sporting terms. Their interests did not lie alongside those more rural sports of the 'leisured classes'. Some, often the more religious, thought that only leisure which improved the soul and mind was appropriate, and rejected sporting culture in its entirety. These were the most reformist of middle-class members in their attitudes, and were often the most vociferous in the press, which can lead to an overestimation of their importance and impact. Others, equally religious, saw sport as an opportunity for the exercise of muscular Christianity, sometimes teaching team sports to, and playing with the working classes, in an attempt at the promotion of cross-class contact and understanding. Some of the early football and rugby teams were founded by just such individuals, and other examples can be found throughout the 1880s and 1890s. This is a major area for further work. Their contribution has never been fully recognized and assessed. Yet others again, more secular in their approach, thought it natural to enjoy themselves, and were more prone to the pursuit of pleasure and personal gratification in their sports as in other aspects of leisure. This more hedonistic group have been effectively ignored in current historiography.

Another group, at the lower end, the 'petty bourgeoisie' of small shopkeepers, school teachers, clerks and white-collar workers, had more in common with the upper working-class in their sports, even if their dress, speech and housing might be different. Little research on their sporting involvement has been carried out on this group, apparent historiographic failures both as heroes of the class struggle and villainous capitalists.[58] The limited research carried out has portrayed petty bourgeois culture as tightly exclusive in many of its attitudes, with an identity based on an obsessive pursuit of status and respectability.[59] How far this applies to sporting participation is less clear since status and respectability were often set more in the Pooteresque and paterfamilian context of marriage, family life and work and the pressures these created to construct a complex and shifting masculine identity.[60] This has implications for sport, where participants were often the younger unmarried, and these could be less socially exclusive in their pursuits. Outside of work times, as a recent revisionist article shows, they sometimes compensated for the greyness of their working lives with displays of peacock masculinity and subversiveness. They were a marginal group, with all the tensions that entailed, 'between conformity and dissent, pretension and insecurity, caution and confidence, the puritan and the bohemian, prudery and rudery'.[61] Until the increased residential segregation of the end of the century they often lived in or on the margins of working-class areas. Their marginal income put sports such as golf, shooting or hunting beyond their reach, and they were more likely to play team sports, together with tennis.[62] They were the backbone of many of the church, mechanics' institutes, YMCA or other urban petit bourgeois and artisan sports clubs, as they would be later in the Clarion movement with its cycling clubs. This group could, for example, be found in many of the socially mixed football and cricket urban sides of the north-east. Clerks, teachers, and commercial travellers were all to be found in the Middlesbrough, Sunderland and Newcastle football sides of the 1880s, even after semi-professionals were introduced. Overall, such divisions suggest that the urban middle classes were divided in their attitudes even to the sporting activities of their own class.

Thirdly, there has been a tendency to describe the Victorian and Edwardian sporting 'revolution' as a continuum, especially amongst historians of working-class sport wishing to emphasize a social control thesis, although in fact there has as yet been little empirical research to underpin the thesis itself.[63] There are concealed problems here with periodization since towards the end of the nineteenth century the middle classes were expanding at a rapidly increasing rate which has real implications for potential clubability. Linked to this expansion Harold Perkin has argued that, although the middle classes were themselves fragmented, from the 1880s there was a widening inequality gap between them and the working classes at the zenith of class society, and classes became more sharply differentiated.[64]

Around this time broader social and cultural factors such as the rise of socialism and a perceived renewed political working-class threat, growing social unrest, the impact of social Darwinism, and, especially at the end of the century, the resurgence of nationalism and jingoism, also had their impact, although this was by no means uni-directional. There was renewed religious activity, especially in London. Some churchmen, for example, set up missions in the slums, or specific sports clubs and encouraged sport, and middle-class organizations such as the Boys' Brigade, the Church Lad's Brigade or the Young Men's Christian Association, or university settlement workers increasingly used sport both as counter-attractions and means of social discipline from the later 1880s.[65] Other middle-class sportsmen were drawn towards social exclusivity, and new definitions of middle-class masculinity, as was also the case in Australia.[66] Overall there was a greater emphasis on separateness, the reassuring familiarity of social homogeneity, and the reassertion of prestige and the 'amateur' principle at this time, even amongst the lower-middle-class groups. The larger numbers of the middle classes in urban areas also meant that clubs and teams could now be more easily exclusive. Prior to the 1880s this had been much more difficult to achieve, even had it been wished.

But by then there were also other tensions pulling the middle classes in different directions. There was the growing secularism of society, with the 1880s seen as 'the golden age of secularism'.[67] The increased sporting apostasy and Sunday sport of the end of the century contrasted with the efforts of 'muscular Christian' vicars.[68] Sunday sport was a movement led by the middle classes in the 1880s and 1890s, when increased use of rivers and roads, the seaside, croquet lawns, tennis courts and golf courts reveal a growing indifference to the demands of sabbatarians.[69] The 1880s and 1890s also saw a renewed opposition to betting and gaming amongst a minority but vociferous middle-class anti-gambling group, alongside an increasing recognition by an increasingly class-sensitive House of Lords of the potential bias in attacking 'popular' sporting interests, and a growing middle-class betting public.[70] There were also the changing attitudes to animal suffering reflected in the attempted legislation on the predominantly middle-class and upper-class sport of pigeon-shooting, or the intra-class debates about field sports in the 1890s.[71] The 1880s and 1890s also saw the intra-class debates about professionalism. In football, as Mason notes, vocal opposition to aspects of the professional game grew stronger in some but not all middle-class circles.[72]

Equally, we need to examine the chronology of the influence of the public-school inspired 'games ethic' much more closely. It was only by c.1880 that the ethic dominated the British public school system.[73] The sheer weight of exemplar material which Mangan cites is far heavier at the very end of the nineteenth century and afterwards, as the diffusion process gained more momentum, and the grammar schools took up the ideology with wide enthusiasm only from the 1880s. Widespread diffusion into the elementary schools came later still. As just one index of the increasing pace of diffusion at elementary level, school football, only three elementary school football associations appear to have been formed before

1890, but thereafter there was rapid growth.[74] The earlier stages of education are potent with possibilities for further work to establish the chronology and rate of diffusion more precisely.

Fourthly, it is worth reminding ourselves both that social class as a single explanatory category has come under attack from proponents of the 'linguistic turn', and of the growing complexity of analysis offered by work on identity, sexuality and ethnicity. Patrick Joyce has argued that people possessed a spectrum of collective identities not only of class, but also of neighbourhood, workplace, town, region, religion and nation, and that these can involve shared values and perspectives which cut across class.[75] Sport is a major vehicle in producing the populist discourses in which these are identified. The moves to postmodernist and post-structural thinking have meant that the study of identities ranging from varied associational forms, or the complexity of local, regional and national loyalties, to 'imagined communities' has become increasingly common. In recent work on sport and identity in the north of England, Hill and Williams emphasize this point strongly.[76] Not just class, but also gender, generation, religion, urban space or territory, language, the use of power, education and ethnicity help to determine social and cultural allegiances in complex ways. Though commonalities created by the world of work, material existence and resulting social position, were still often the strongest, differences in consumption and life within the middle classes also need more consideration. All these complex elements now need to be linked more precisely to the forces making for class cloning and sporting conformity.

It should also be stressed that a sense of regional and local identity was sometimes stronger than class identity, and here the rich complexity of regional variation needs to be far more emphasized.[77] In terms of the relationship of sports to hegemonic struggles, many sports were shaped by groups whose interests were rooted in class privilege and class exclusiveness, and who were largely located in London and the south. National organizations and their bureaucracies were usually located there. Current research on the English middle classes is dominated by the experience of London suburbanites.[78] Yet regional variation can be seen, for example, in the firmer support given to the ideology of amateurism in London and the south-east, compared to that given in the north of England, and tensions between London and the provinces were often critical in the development of many sports, such as rugby, and, for a time, football. The headquarters of organizations such as the Football League and the Northern Rugby Union were located in the north. Different local practices in angling reflected a similar pattern.[79] There were complex processes at work here. Hegemonists now need to explain exactly how and why in England, unlike America, it was the south which won. How was it able to exploit cultural, social, political and educational power to form the new structures of British sport?

We need to remember here, that public school culture was anti-commercial and anti-industrial, far more at home in London or the Empire than with the urban communities of Leeds, Manchester, or Newcastle. The more hard-nosed businessmen, manufacturers, brewers, teachers or solicitors involved in the northern team games had different attitudes, and a rich complexity of motives for their involvement. There certainly appears to have been a far less deferential attitude in parts of northern England. The strength of many of the most strongly amateur organizations with a social control bent, such as the Amateur Athletic Club (which excluded mechanics and artisans), the Rugby Union Football Association or the Amateur Rowing Association, was largely in London and the south-eastern part of England. In the north a different attitude can be detected, for example in the attitude of the Northern Counties Athletic Association, which had a much wider membership. Attitudes to professionalism were much more positive in the north, and this can be particularly seen in soccer. In the early and middle 1880s, when local rivalries were strong, and many powerful sides were still composed of a mixture of middle- and working-class players, it was football committees who decided whom to select, when to import and whether to pay them.

Here the role of the middle classes in club organization, as also in rugby (union and league), was central. In almost all identifiable cases, these northern and midland committees who decided to move towards professionalism were composed of middle-class ex-players; teachers, bank officials, clerks. At Sunderland, the former player Rev. Hindle, the vicar of Eppleton, was a main spokesman for the club in its early semi-professional days in 1886–87, and another ex-player James Alan, a local teacher, the treasurer; while by 1887–88, when the team was 'renovated' and the club was well known in the region for its quite deliberately concealed professionalism, the *Northern Review* claimed that 'to make it above suspicion [the General Committee] includes two clergymen and two local preachers', while two shipbuilders and a coal owner took the main offices.[80]

We now need to explore why it was that beliefs and attitudes of such groups were far less influential on a national canvas. This would have given British and world sport a different direction. What were the processes of committee selection, representation, sociability, agenda construction and political interaction that effectively marginalized such views?

III

For many men pleasure was still a major objective, and so supposed Victorian values were characterized by hypocrisy, compromise and extension. As a whole variety of recent research has demonstrated, most middle-class participation in and spectatorship of sport was done in the pursuit of pleasure, although pleasure too needs more careful examination.[81] It involved words like 'enjoyment', 'amusement' and 'excitement', but also potentially contradictory elements like companionship and individualism or competition and co-operation. It could also mean the excitements of gambling or escape from the stifling social mores of the home and work environment. A large part of middle-class respectability, as with working-class respectability, was located in anxiety at knowing themselves to behave otherwise in certain contexts.[82] Some of the class got pleasure out of sports through stretching the confines of morality; by watching and participating in less respectable sports, bending of the rules in others, convivial drinking after events, or gambling upon them.

Three key points are important here. Firstly, most writers uncritically see middle-class sport as 'respectable' in character, without exploring the nature of that respectability in practice. Lowerson, for example, sees the middle-class sports ethic as 'grafted on to the virtues of Work, Punctuality, Thrift and Respectability'.[83] But the line between 'respectable' and 'rough' was not a sharp divide, but a continuum, and one which sometimes transcended class divisions in a sporting context, just as it did with regard to visits to prostitutes, drinking or betting. Bailey's notion of the calculated performance of different social roles in different social contexts is important here, and needs more application to sport, especially in the fragmented milieu of urban life, where some sports events happened well away from more respectable suburban terraces and lawns.[84]

Secondly, even though spectatorship at many events was socially zoned, and some sports were socially exclusive, it is quite clear that some cross-class mixing still occurred at many sporting events. It is possible to overstress the working-class nature of crowds. The *proportion* of middle-class spectators certainly dropped at professional football matches over the period, for example, but it is quite possible that *numbers* of middle-class spectators actually rose, and not just in the grand-stand. Their numbers may actually have reflected accurately their proportion in the male population, or even been above it, given the general absence of unskilled men in crowds. Even in London, West Ham's move to a more middle-class loca-tion improved crowd numbers, while at Ibrox in 1902, admittedly for an inter-national match, casualties on a standing terrace included clerks, commercial travellers, a colliery manager, and other clearly middle-class spectators.[85]

Thirdly, there existed a very significant middle-class group which enjoyed less respectable activities associated with some sports, and in certain leisure contexts less respectable behaviour was much more common amongst such cultural hedo-nists. Such contexts included, as we shall see, particular points in the life cycle, certain occupational groups, certain associational forms, certain locations, and the world of the imagination. The complex inter-relationships of male middle-class society created 'layered identities' in sport, as in other aspects of cultural life.[86]

The easy generalizations about and academic stereotypes of middle-class Victorian leisure and sport therefore need to be examined extremely critically. As early as 1979 Geoffrey Best argued that in looking at all Victorian recreations, notions of social class are less useful than what he called 'respectable' and 'non-respectable' activities.[87] As leisure began to restabilize over the second half of the nineteenth century it was also increasingly fragmented. People pursued their plea-sures amongst various communities of place and interest. People were divided about leisure, as they were about religion, but not primarily on class lines. Best did not see respectability as the prerogative of any one class, let alone the Victorian middle classes. Many sports, or the activities associated with them, were ambiguous, seen as respectable by some, and not by others. Where, for example, should we locate the blatant cheating involved in the running of many flat race and or national hunt horses, of which so many were owned by the middle classes, to gain prize money or suit the betting book? What about the antics of players like cricket's W.G. Grace, out to influence umpires or referees? Then too, the 'expenses' which he and others took from their games were often far higher than the professionals' wages.[88] In both rugby and soccer old boys' sides often demanded high expenses on tours of the provincial north. The Corinthians supposedly demanded £150 a match in the 1880s.[89] How are we to view the constant disputes over goals, appeals against results, and complaints about referees that characterized the 1870s and early 1880s when rugby and football games were still predominantly middle class in the south and socially mixed only to an extent in the north? Collins points out the violence, argumentiveness and gamesmanship of the ex-public school boy sides of the 1860s and 1870s.[90] Unexpected defeat was by no means always taken well by middle-class 'amateur' sides. The rhetoric, that the result was supposedly of little matter, was different to the reality. Rather than absolute obedience to the authority of the referees, there was constant challenge. Rather than respecting the spirit of the law, as 'amateur' apologists claimed, there was often an appeal to the letter of the law, as can be seen in the surviving minute books of county associations or the Football Association itself. This exposes some of the ambiguities of the notion of 'fair play', the supposed virtues of amateurism and of the need to play a game for its own sake, once school was left behind.

What about the drinking that was often associated with sports, even when members were predominantly middle class? This was common by spectators at some cross-class sports events such as race meetings, and even cricket grounds often had drinking facilities. At Lords in mid-century there was constant selling of various sorts of liquor and tobacco, at the Tavern and around the ground. Drinking could also be by participants. In the north-east, for example, a report of the Stockton Cycling Club's last meet of the season in 1888, at the seaside resort of Redcar included references to many toasts, and the imbibing of 'whisky punches', prior to riding home.[91] Working-class 'hooliganism' was thus transformed into middle-class 'manliness'. At the conclusion of team games of association football and rugby, visiting teams were usually 'hospitably' or 'sumptuously' entertained, and smoking concerts with music and strong drink were a common feature of cricket, rugby, football and even early harrier club dinners by the late 1870s. At Stockton Cricket Club dinner in 1888, 'high jinks generally prevailed' but the 'solids and liquids were the best of all'.[92] The role of the public house is a commonplace in discussions of working-class life, yet *middle*-class team use of pubs for changing rooms, meetings and celebrations is yet to be fully explored.

What about the widespread betting on horse-races amongst the middle classes? Some were members of sporting clubs where bets were exchanged. Sporting tobacconists, cigar shops or hairdressers were also relatively safe social venues where bets could be made and payout was fairly certain. Some early music halls also provided betting opportunities. A Liverpool 'free and easy' for example, was a 'betting meet' which was full of 'apparently respectable men'.[93] Subscription betting rooms could be found in London, York, Sheffield and other cities as early as 1850, allowing middle-class punters to bet on credit, and by the 1860s the 'self made men', including employers, manufacturers and clerks described betting at the Post Office Hotel in Manchester also had the choice of placing bets at office premises run by bookmaking firms or via commission agents by post.[94] After prosecution of London commission agents in 1969, major commission agents moved, first to Scotland, and after the 1853 Betting Houses Act was extended to Scotland, to France and the Netherlands.[95] By the 1870s growing numbers of credit bookmakers were emerging in the major towns. It is unclear how many middle-class men used street bookmakers, although as many of the recorded bets in the 1870s and 1880s cited in court cases were of figures in excess of two shillings it seems likely that some did. This is another difficult area, since the police rarely prosecuted middle-class men for drink offences, and the same may well be true of gambling offences. Even so, occasional prosecutions certainly show some middle-class betting.[96]

The notion that most sports club membership was exclusively middle class is also problematic. Middle-class sporting characteristics and activity did not always equate with this model. This can be seen in the tension between attempts at period exclusivity and the competing period ideology of social inclusivity; in the realities of the necessity to make up effective teams in team sports where numbers of potential participants were low; in the socially mixed nature of many crowds; and in the significant middle-class investment in the professional forms of more proletarian sports such as football or horse racing. Moreover it is clear that some middle-class sportsmen wanted to test themselves against the strongest of opposition, rather than hide away in middle-class enclaves playing inferior opponents.

It is certainly true that some middle-class organizations and clubs made great efforts to restrict contact with their social inferiors, achieving this either by explicit rules excluding occupation, blackballing systems of election to membership, or by excessively high entry or subscription levels.[97] But this was more rare than historians have portrayed. A commonly presented argument in some mid and late-Victorian sports promoters' or club presidents' speeches was that sport could be a type of social cement, embodying community values, with upper and lower classes meeting together in mutual enjoyment.[98] It supposedly broke down class barriers and prejudice and 'had a beneficial effect in cementing good feeling between the classes'.[99] Others saw it as contributing to social stability by providing a more 'rational' alternative to more disruptive activities. Some clubs with a predominantly middle-class membership did make attempts to recruit manual workers while others were always socially mixed.[100] Only at the end of the Victorian period, however, as the boundaries between classes were increasingly threatened, was the main emphasis on class division perpetuated through sporting organization, and 'horizontal comradeship' became more dominant amongst some club membership.

Some clubs and sports were undoubtedly bastions of exclusivity. Recent Scottish research has shown how in the second half of the nineteenth century in terms of participation in sport there was little cross-class association in golf, fox-hunting, croquet, or lawn-tennis which were almost exclusively composed of upper and middle-class men and, increasingly, women.[101] Such sports were largely confined to the upper-middle classes, largely through cost and access criteria. But not all the middle class felt threatened by the working-class presence. By contrast both the Scottish middle and working classes took part in cricket, whilst bowls and angling were much more clearly cross-class, and there were middle-class partici-pants in the sports of football, athletics and quoits. We now need English research on a regional basis on similar lines.

Where the number of potential middle-class members was low, it must have been very difficult to form exclusive yet effective teams. In Middlesbrough, for example, the attempt to run a more exclusive town cricket club from the 1870s onwards, meant that it was consistently unsuccessful against teams from smaller towns in the region who had recruited a more socially mixed playing membership to help achieve success.[102] Most football, rugby, athletic, and bowls clubs in the north-east of England contained a mixture of working and middle-class players from the 1870s to the 1890s, although it was more usually the middle-class play-ers who went on to hold office. In the north-west, with its traditions of trade, com-merce and professionalism there was also quite significant social mixing in some sports, and members of team sports clubs were usually socially mixed.[103] Even in rowing, that bastion of amateurism, many northwest clubs had by the 1880s legit-imized membership even for labourers and those 'in and about boats' and had joined the National Amateur Rowing Association rather than the more elitist Amateur Rowing Association.[104] We need to know much more about sports clubs than we do currently, although Wigglesworth's work, based on the records of some hundred sports clubs, is a useful first step.[105] It is still a matter of some debate whether clubs were primarily a feature of the last quarter of the century or whether the process of club formation was already well underway by the third quarter.[106]

Evidence for exclusivity in terms of sporting spectatorship is even less strong. Grandstands at football or rugby matches, or at athletics contests or racemeetings were socially zoned only by price and not by class. Where we have lists of atten-ders in the grandstand, and there are times when these are available, we see them peopled by a mixture of classes. In racing, press lists of attenders in the grand-stand, reports of accidents, and criminal prosecutions all show how truly cross-class attendance was. At Manchester in 1867 the grandstand contained 'a great many who regard themselves as the aristocracy from a monetary and cottonian point of view'.[107] Bookmakers, touts and trainers with working-class origins used the stand too. Grandstands were exciting and dangerous, and there were some-times complaints of unruliness, swearing and shouting, and even fights in the stand. Many MPs, councillors, aldermen, and JPs could be found at all meetings. As one solidly anti-racing paper sadly recognized in 1866, the 'greater portion of society' appeared to actively support the races.[108] Lists of shareholders in surviving joint stock grandstand and racecourse companies set up from the 1860s, or the range of other commercial sports companies analysed by Wray Vamplew, likewise show that the majority of their membership were in middle-class occupations.[109] Where local authorities became involved in race meetings, as at Doncaster, York or Chester, we see a similar pattern. At Nottingham the corporation took over the course following the Nottingham General Enclosure Act of 1845. Racing was managed by a committee composed of corporation members and profits were devoted towards the improvement of the meetings and for the purpose of other general public recreation. Although there was an attempt by some reformist councillors in 1856 to end one of the two meetings this was fought off.[110]

IV

Right through the period it is possible to identify a range of *leisure contexts* where respectability's hold was potentially much less strong than in the home, the workplace or the church and chapel. Such contexts included certain points in the life cycle, some occupational groupings, certain locations and associational forms, and the reading of some types of literature. I have written about these 'leisure contexts' at some length elsewhere, and will give only very brief examples here.[111] Sports have not as yet been analysed in such ways, although a wide range of sources allow their exploration. These sources range from newspaper and sporting magazine material, and institutional sources such as sports club minutes, to more private sources such as diaries and memoirs. So what follows provides tantalizing hints and raises questions rather than providing answers.

But sports were certainly influenced by such leisure contexts. Indeed, sporting venues were themselves a key locational context, especially in terms of attendance or participation in less respectable sports such as cock-fighting, ratting, or pugilism; less respectable behaviour as a participant or spectator in sports such as football, cricket, or racing; or in becoming involved in betting on sporting results.

Middle-class respectability was stronger in the home and neighbourhood, where social pressures on conformity could be exerted. *Punch*, that barometer of middle-class attitudes, values and occupations, made the point in a number of cartoons and captions. An 1871 text provides an illustration:

> Major Blazer – 'But you won't object to your daughters coming to *our* races, Mrs Hoodwink? Quite a private affair and close to home'.
> Mrs Hoodwink – 'Ah! That is it, Major. I should not mind so much if it were not *in their own neighbourhood*'.[112]

So some sporting venues or major sporting events offered liminal *locational* contexts where the shackles of respectability could, at least for a while, be laid aside. The Epsom Derby provides a useful illustration, with *The Times* admitting that it attracted many people 'who stick closely to their business and propriety for the rest of the year...many a habitually decent family', and 'foolish young men of the middle classes', and 'men of business in provincial towns', whilst military men arranged leave.[113] The poet and bank clerk William Allingham, a friend of Tennyson and Carlyle, made a special visit to Epsom to see the Derby in 1868.[114] Recent research on racing has revealed that descriptions of race meetings throughout Britain show middle-class men drinking in booths and also sometimes associating with prostitutes there.[115] Respectable opposition to betting, both on and off course, similarly seems to have had little effect. On the course the middle classes were major patrons both of the credit bookmakers in the ring and of ready-money bookmakers. For middle-class women, who also enjoyed a bet in the grandstand, the bet was often a pair of gloves, and made with a male in their own social circle. Off-course Derby sweeps at prices from £1 a ticket upwards were a regular feature of newspaper advertisements by the mid-1840s, and by the mid-1870s *The Times* claimed that even clubs which forbade card play fostered Derby sweeps.[116]

As recent research has demonstrated, the more liminal nature of the seaside gave early opportunities for middle-class female participation, mixing between the sexes and courtship in a sporting context. Resorts also provided fertile ground for many of the earlier middle-class women's sports clubs.[117] The remote mountains were another such context. Upper-middle-class climbers in the Alps from the 1850s often exhibited a fairly wild informality at odds with their respectable lives, as did the professors, teachers, businessmen, doctors and lawyers who developed the sport of rock-climbing in the later nineteenth century in north Wales or at Wasdale Head in the Lake District, while mountain and rock climbing also attracted small numbers of women.[118]

There has been little historical interest in life-cycle determinants in sport, yet cross-class mixing at matches, spectator misbehaviour and betting may well have been more common at certain times in the *life cycle*, especially amongst middle-class teenagers, younger unmarried males, and older men whose families had grown up. One of the more powerful images and major concerns in mid-Victorian literature was the unmarried male, enjoying more free time and play than his elders.[119] The increased use of the word 'spree', for the notion of being away from the constraints of home or workplace, reflects the commonality of the activity. We need to explore this further in terms of sports. In terms of participation in sport students provide a good example. Students at military colleges, together with students of law and medicine, stood out from their mid-century contemporaries, working hard and playing hard, with abuse of policemen and riotous behaviour after school matches, middle-class 'high spirits' and 'manliness' rather than working-class delinquency.[120]

Such boisterousness and enjoyment of violence amongst the middle classes was variously tolerated, endorsed and even embraced, even by those who would have strongly disapproved if such behaviour had been by working-class youths. At the annual Eton versus Harrow, a regular part of the solidarity ritual was the clash between younger supporters in front of the grandstand at the end of the match, an approved exhibition of manly 'virility'.[121] By the end of the nineteenth century The National Sporting Club had a 'respectable' middle-class membership enjoying the spectacle of working-class men fighting, in clear opposition to organized evangelical Christianity.[122]

As we have seen, some young middle-class men also betted. Such betting was often learned in the middle-class home and then continued at public school. As late as 1900 the head of Harrow admitted that many pupils bet, although this was 'less than formerly'.[123] Betting 'victims' tended to be 'inexperienced youths of all classes', according to a range of anti-betting pamphlets.[124] Unsurprisingly, given their background, university students from Cambridge were often attenders at Newmarket races.[125]

Some middle-class sons of wealthy middle-class parents, who had not had to work for their money, were prone to get into debt through injudicious betting. Some of the latter references in the newspapers were a reflection of the moral panic about betting which emerged for a range of reasons in the 1880s.[126] Middle-class betting was not new at this time. Like working-class betting it had been growing from the 1840s. But the increased focus on working-class betting created concern about middle-class betting too. The constant generational accession of young middle-class males to new sporting freedoms and forms was always likely to throw up some cases of excessive betting. Much of the moral-panic press writing about sports-related issues such as association football injuries was likewise linked to such factors.

For those who attended public schools, and accepted the conformist ideology, middle age could generate potential problems in terms of sporting culture. C. Dewey suggests that old Etonians could end up as sports 'bores' and that 'men brought up to believe that games were the only thing worth living for, ran out of things to do in early middle age. Some of them became professional spectators; others wasted their lives in "a meaningless round of trivial distractions", in billiards and bridge; a few sank into "vice".'[127] Dewey's findings may or may not be capable of extrapolation to wider society, and this is yet another area where research is still needed.

The sports clubs themselves were key *associational* leisure forms, and have been insufficiently analysed in this light. Instead there has been an over-concentration on membership, rules and regulations, and annual general meetings. Sport and sociability run close, and sports historians have not yet explored the sociability aspects of middle-class sports clubs in any real detail. Even in the more middle-class-dominated 1870s football and rugby teams playing away from home were wined and dined, sometimes stayed away overnight and went out on the spree. Touring matches may have been arranged as much for this reason as to raise funds or to strengthen playing experience by meeting strong opposition. Most sports clubs, even the most exclusive, had evening functions where members met and drank together. The activities – club dinners, songs and doggerel – seem to have been opportunities for letting off steam and fairly riotous behaviour.

It may well be that some *occupational groups* were more prone to escaping the shackles of respectability in sport, or more happy to mix socially, especially when living away from home. Clearly then as now students seem to have needed relief from the pressures of study, and in Oxford, Cambridge and London misbehaviour associated with student sport was relatively common. Clerks are another significant group, especially in the anonymity of large urban areas. Teachers, who had to be models of probity in the classroom, played a major role in spreading football in many of Britain's regions, almost always playing in socially mixed sides.

Finally, it is worth exploring the interaction between the proliferation of sports journalism and its readers. Most sports journalists were themselves middle class, and their role in constructing, disseminating and mediating an ideological discourse related to the construction of sporting identity, or in exploiting angst, appetite or aspirations, has yet to be examined in any detail. Equally, can we begin to tease out the readership and authorship of particular journals and sports columns in social class terms? Did the middle classes, in looking at them, 'read' the texts in different ways to the working-class readership? Did their imaginative liminality provide vicarious excitement, fellowship, participation or belonging? Much sports journalism was written in ways that allowed the 'expert' reader to read between the lines. It employed transactional codes that allowed a variety of interpretations, respectable and less respectable. Sporting 'knowingness', the techniques of observing hints, silences and coded references in journalistic texts, that allowed one to 'read' the implications, fill in gaps, and complete the circuits of meaning was important here. In descriptions of races, for example, a knowing, well-informed and superior reader could recognize which horses had not been fully stretched, had been held back, in ways which would be opaque to his or her uninitiated friends. To what extent were the middle classes creators of and participators in this secret world?

V

Sport in the Victorian period has always been a matter of historiographic debate. In the 1970s the early academic historians of sport were generally agreed that during the first decades of the nineteenth century a once thriving sporting working-class culture declined through the impact of urban industrialization. More recently this view has been subjected to criticism, and it has been argued that by focusing too narrowly on the most brutal and turbulent working-class sports, the very different experience of other working-class sports, for which clear evidence of decline is either entirely lacking or less than conclusive, has been overlooked.[128] This article has argued that a similar narrowness of focus and an over-simplicity of analysis has characterized much of the historiography on middle-class sport covering the period from the 1850s to the late 1890s. Most sports historians have continued to show some embarrassment in treating the topic. The role of the middle classes was central to the development of the late Victorian 'sports boom'. The public schools were central to the development of the rhetoric of the gentleman amateur and much else that was to characterize much of British and imperial sport for several generations thereafter. Yet their role has been largely underplayed, largely through the contagion of cultural condescension. The over-emphasis on working-class sport by some key practitioners, and the *collective myopia* towards the middle-class contribution this entails in sports history circles has tilted sports history downwards to its detriment in terms of making a more accurate, complete and substantial contribution to social and cultural history.

Sport constitutes a large part of leisure culture and during the Victorian period was differentiated primarily by class. But with regard to sport the urban middle classes were not a single undifferentiated group, as they have too often been presented. Beyond those who simply saw sport as irrelevant there were horizontal divisions within the class. The interests of those at the top lay more with 'high society', and the complex and changing nature of middle-class relationships with the aristocracy remain to be disentangled in sporting terms. There were middle groups whose income allowed a wide variety of sports to be played and watched, and the 'petty bourgeoisie' whose sporting links were sometimes more downwards. Vertically those espousing a more hedonistic approach and the more serious, recreational and 'respectable' sporting group can also be located at points along a continuum. Both vertically and horizontally much more research still needs to be done if we are to have a clearer and more subtlely nuanced picture. The socializing forces which drew the middle classes together need to be set more clearly against the tensions of fragmentation. And what of the, largely but not exclusively English, middle-class contribution to the origins of modern sport and the modern 'global village'?

We need more recognition of complexity, diversity, adaptation and projection as well as the shifting nature of class. We also need a clearer understanding both of change over time and historical specificity in terms of middle-class culture. We need more provincial case studies of middle-class influence or its lack on specific clubs, organizations, sports and sporting events, especially in terms of the school background of participants. We need to start to analyse and explain the continuities and discontinuities in the development of middle-class sports more clearly, drawing out the cross-currents and countervailing trends of specific sports and different locations. Finally, the key role of the English middle classes in the creation of an international sports culture of immense power, wealth, status and influence can only be properly grasped if the origins of that role in late Victorian England are made clear. Historians need to move away from what is currently relatively narrow, crude and coarse-grained analysis and begin to open up Victorian middle-class sport to a far wider base of historical and cultural investigation.

Notes

* An earlier version of this paper was read at the British Society of Sports History conference at Eastbourne in April 1999 and gained from discussion there. I would like to thank Professor J.A. Mangan of Strathclyde University, Professor J.K. Walton of the University of Central Lancashire, and my colleagues Dr P. Brett and H. Telfer for their helpful comments and support during the preparation of this article, although none should be held responsible for its contents. All italics in the paper are mine, and not those of authors quoted.
1 J.A. Mangan, Introduction to the new edition *of Athleticism in the Victorian and Edwardian Public School* (London, 2000).

2 J. Lowerson, 'Opiate of the people and Stimulant for the Historian? – Some Issues in Sports History', in W. Lamont (ed.), *Historical Controversies and Historians* (London, 1998), p. 209.

3 P. Bailey, 'The Politics and Poetics of Modern British Leisure', *Rethinking History*, 3, 2 (1999), 151.

4 J. Richards, personal comment.

5 R. Holt, 'Sport and History; the State of the Subject in Britain', *Working Papers in Sport and Society*, 3 (1994/5), 5. Holt's highly readable book *Sport and the British: A Modern History* (Oxford, 1989) is a work of synthesis, heavily reliant on selective published research and so largely shaped by the same paradigms.

6 N. Tranter, *Sport, Economy and Society in Britain 1750–1914* (Cambridge, 1998), pp. 26–31, summarizes and provides references for this debate. He sees the diffusionist model as 'too restricted to be acceptable'.

7 J. Lowerson, *Sport and the English Middle Classes 1850–1914* (Manchester, 1993), p. 6 for figures and references. H. Perkin, *The Rise of Professional Society* (London, 1989) gives more detail on middle-class numbers.

8 Such approaches, although very useful, have been largely in the context of single sports, such as rowing. See, for example, E. Halliday, *Rowing in England: a Social History* (Manchester, 1990) which he subtitled 'The Amateur Debate', and N. Wigglesworth, *A Social History of English Rowing* (London, 1992).

9 The studies of (*inter alia*) angling, rugby and football in T. Mason (ed.), *Sport in Britain: A Social History* (Cambridge, 1989) move beyond a simple and deterministic social class approach.

10 For discussion of hegemony see J. Hargreaves, *Sport, Power and Culture: A Social and Historical Analysis of Popular Sports in Britain* (Oxford, 1986), and J.M. Golby and A.W. Purdue, *The Civilisation of the Crowd – Popular Culture in England 1750–1900* (London, 1984) p. 13. A good example of hegemonic ideas applied in a more global context is B. Stoddard, 'Sport, Cultural Imperialism and colonial Response in the British Empire', *Comparative Studies in Society and History*, 30 (Oct. 1988), 649–73, a curiously neglected article. For a critique of the usefulness of social control theories see R. Hay, 'Soccer and Social Control in Scotland 1873–1878', in R. Cashman and M. McKernan (eds), *Sport: Money, Morality and the Media* (Kensington, New South Wales, 1984), pp. 223–47.

11 M. Hewitt, *The Emergence of Stability in the Industrial City: Manchester 1832–67* (Aldershot, 1996), p. 158 argues that middle-class groups were 'establishing alternatives' to working-class activities, which were 'incorporating recreation into an overly respectable lifestyle', or 'tightening middle-class control and proscription' of other elements in mid-nineteenth century Manchester, but does not examine the process itself, concentrating on working-class experience.

12 For a flavour of the debate see J. MacAloon, 'The Ethnographic Imperative in Comparative Olympic Research', *Sociology of Sport Journal*, 9 (1992), 104–30; J. Hargreaves and A. Tomlinson, 'Getting There: Cultural Theory and the Sociological Analysis of Sport in Britain', *Sociology of Sport Journal*, 9 (1992), 207–19; W.J. Morgan, 'Hegemonic Theory, Social Domination and Sport: The MacAloon and Hargreaves–Tomlinson Debate Revisited', *Sociology of Sport Journal*, 11 (1994), 309–29.

13 It is understandable that ease of organization and the need to address dominant themes within the historiography force many sport overviews into this mould. R. Holt, *Sport and the British*, for example, has a chapter on 'Amateurism and the Victorians' followed by 'Life in the City: Working-class Communities'. N. Wigglesworth, *The Evolution of English Sport* (London, 1996) has chapters on Amateurism and Professionalism.

14 D. Russell, *Football and the British* (Preston, 1997), p. 27.

15 P. Greenhalgh, 'The Work and Play Principle: The Professional Regulations of the Northern Rugby Football Union, 1898–1905', *International Journal of the History of Sport*, 9, 3(1992), 359.
16 See H. Cunningham, 'Leisure and Culture' in F.M.L. Thompson (ed.), *The Cambridge Social History of Britain 1750–1940 Vol 2, People and Their Environment* (Cambridge, 1990).
17 R. Holt, 'Sport and History', 14. C.p. M. Girourard, *The Return to Camelot; Chivalry and the English Gentleman* (Yale, 1981) and J. Lowerson, *Sport and the English Middle Classes.*
18 Mangan, *Athleticism, passim.*
19 T. Mason, *Association Football and English Society 1863–1915* (Brighton, 1981), p. 25 provides a range of football examples from the 1870s and 1880s; Lowerson, *Sport and the English Middle Classes*, p. 84, a rugby example. Holt, *Sport and the British*, p. 139, argues that 'muscular Christians' among the clergy were 'less common than many suppose'.
20 In the Northumberland coalfield, for example, the role of the mine owners was only minimal. See A. Metcalfe, 'Football in the Mining Communities of East Northumberland 1882–1914', *International Journal of the History of Sport*, 5, 3 (1982), 269–91.
21 E. Langland, *Nobody's Angels: Middle-Class Women and Domestic Ideology in Victorian Culture* (Cornell, 1995).
22 J. Lewis, *Women in England 1870–1959: Sexual Divisions and Social Change* (Hemel Hempstead, 1984), pp. 83–97.
23 E. Dunning, *Sport Matters: Sociological Studies of Sport, Violence and Civilisation* (London, 1999), p. 224.
24 J.A. Mangan and J. Walvin (eds), *Manliness and Morality: Middle-Class Masculinity in Britain and America* (Manchester, 1987).
25 J. Horne, A. Tomlinson and G. Whannel, *Understanding Sport: An Introduction to the Sociological and Cultural Analysis of Sport* (London, 1999), p. 8.
26 The work done by J.A. Mangan, in a wide range of books and articles is seminal here. Amongst the most accessible are J.A. Mangan, *Athleticism in the Victorian and Edwardian Public School* (Cambridge, 1981), a landmark study, and J.A. Mangan, *The Games Ethic and Imperialism* (Harmondsworth, 1985).
27 J.A. Mangan, 'Sport in Society; the Nordic World and Other Worlds', in H. Meinander and J.A. Mangan (eds), 'The Nordic World', special issue of the *International Journal of the History of Sport*, 14, 3 (1997), 181.
28 Mangan, *Athleticism*, p. 9.
29 A critique of Holt's analysis is developed in the new introduction to J.A. Mangan, *Athleticism.*
30 A. Seward, 'Cornish Rugby and Cornish Identity: A Socio-Cultural Perspective', *The Sports Historian* 18, 2 (1998), 82–3.
31 J. Bromhead, 'Sporting Bathers at Droitwich Spa', *British Society of Sports History Newsletter* 9 (1999), 32.
32 J.A. Mangan and C. Hickey, 'English Elementary Education Revisited and Revised; Drill and Athleticism in Tandem', *European Sports History Review*, 1 (1998), 71; J.A. Mangan, 'Grammar School and the Games Ethic in the Victorian and Edwardian Eras', *Albion* 15, 5 (Winter 1983), 313–24. See also J.A. Mangan, 'Imitating their Betters and Dissociating from their Inferiors; Grammar Schools and the Games Ethic in the Late Nineteenth and Early Twentieth Centuries', *Proceedings of the 1982 Annual Conference of the History of Education Society of Great Britain* (Leicester, 1983).
33 C. Hickey, 'Athleticism and the London Training Colleges' (Ph.D. thesis, IRC333, University of Strathclyde, forthcoming).
34 Mangan and Hickey, 'English Elementary Education', pp. 74–89.
35 For succinct overviews of the current state of the field with useful bibliographies see Tranter, *Sport, Economy and Society*, pp. 78–93; Lowerson, *Sport and the English Middle Classes*, pp. 203–20.

36 C.M. Parratt, 'Athletic Womanhood: Explaining Sources for Female Sport in Victorian and Edwardian England', *Journal of Sport History*, 16, 2 (1989), 140–57. For the influence of the Victorian home see J. Hargreaves, 'Victorian Familism and the Formative Years of Female Sport', in J.A. Mangan and R.J. Park (eds), *From Fair Sex to Feminism: Sport and the Socialization of Women in the Industrial and post-Industrial Eras* (London, 1987), pp. 130–44.

37 K.E. McCrone, 'Play up! Play Up! And Play the Game! Sport at the Late Victorian Girls' Public Schools', in Mangan and Park (eds), *From Fair Sex to Feminism*, pp. 97–129; K.E. McCrone, *Sport and the Physical Emancipation of English Women 1870–1914* (London, 1988), pp. 85–93.

38 McCrone, *Sport and the Physical Emancipation of English Women*, pp. 85–93.

39 J.A. Mangan, 'Sport in Society: The Nordic World', p. 178.

40 Ibid.

41 C. Dewey, 'Socratic Teachers': Part I – The Opposition to the Cult of Athletics at Eton 1870–1914', *International Journal of the History of Sport*, 12, 1 (1995), 51–80.

42 Mangan, *Athleticism*, p. 216.

43 J.A. Mangan and C. McKenzie, 'The Other Side of the Coin: Masculinity, Victorian Field Sports and English Elite Education', *European Sports History Review*, 2 (1999), 62–85.

44 T.J. Chandler, 'Games at Oxbridge and the Public Schools 1830–1880: The Diffusion of an Innovation', *International Journal of the History of Sport* 8, 2 (1991), 174.

45 J.A. Mangan, 'Lamentable Barbarians and Pitiful Sheep: Rhetoric of Protest and Pleasure in Late Victorian Oxbridge' in T. Winnifrith and C. Barrett (eds), *Leisure in Art and Literature* (Warwick, 1986), pp. 130–54. See also S. Rothblatt, *The Revolution of the Dons: Cambridge and Society in Victorian England* (Cambridge, 1968).

46 J.A. Mangan, 'Duty Unto Death: English Masculinity and Militarism in the Age of the New Imperialism' in J.A. Mangan (ed.) 'Tribal Identities: Nationalism, Europe and Sport' special issue of the *International Journal of the History of Sport*, 12, 2 (1995), 10–38 provides a detailed discussion and references.

47 J.A Mangan, *The Cultural Bond: Sport, Empire, Society* (London, 1992); J.A. Mangan, 'Braveheart betrayed? Cultural Cloning for Colonial Careers', *Immigrants and Minorities*, 17, 1 (1998), M. Crotty, 'Making the Australian Male: the Construction of Manly Middle-Class Youth in Australia 1870–1920' (Ph.D. thesis, University of Melbourne, 1999), 106–33.

48 See the discussion in A. Blake, *Reading Victorian Fiction* (1989), Ch. 2.

49 J.A. Mangan, *The Cultural Bond: Sport, Empire, Society*, p. 4.

50 For 'moral imperialism' see R.J. Morris, *Class, Sect and Party. The Making of the British Middle Class* (Manchester, 1990), p. 232.

51 For a discussion of this point see M. Huggins, 'Culture, Class and Respectability: Racing and the English Middle Classes in the Nineteenth Century', *International Journal of the History of Sport*, 11, 1 (1994), 19–41.

52 J. Clarke and C. Critcher, *The Devil Makes Work – Leisure in Capitalist Britain* (London, 1985), pp. 49–50.

53 M. Huggins, *Flat Racing and British Society 1790–1914* (London, 2000), Ch. 8.

54 F.M.L. Thompson, *The Rise of Respectable Society: A Social History of Victorian Britain 1830–1900* (London, 1988), pp. 265–72.

55 T. Mason, 'Football and the Workers in England 1880–1914', in R. Cashman and M. McKernan (eds), *Sport: Money, Morality and the Media* (Kensington, NSW, 1981), p. 264.

56 For discussion of middle-class structural complexity see Lowerson, *Sport and the English Middle Classes*, pp. 6–12.

57 R. Carr, *English Foxhunting* (London, 1986), pp. 154, 157.

58 See P. Bailey, 'White Collars, Grey Lives? The Lower Middle Class Revisited', *Journal of British Studies*, 38 (July 1999), 276–7.

59 See the essays in G. Crossick (ed.), *The Lower Middle Class in Britain* (London, 1997).

60 For example, J. Hammerton, 'Pooterism or Partnership? Marriage and Masculine Identity in the Lower Middle Class', *Journal of British Studies* 38 (July, 1999), 291–321.
61 Bailey, 'White Collars, Gray Lives?', p. 289.
62 For the financial and opportunity costs of middle-class sporting involvement see Lowerson, *Sport and the English Middle Classes*, pp. 12–17.
63 For example, J. Hargreaves, *Sport, Power and Culture: A Social and Historical Analysis of Popular Sports in Britain* (New York, 1986), pp. 26–86.
64 Perkin, *The Rise of Professional Society*, Ch. 2 and 3.
65 Holt, *Sport and the British*, p. 138. C. Booth, *Religious Influences Series* (1902), Vols. 1, p. 102; 2, p. 88; 3, p. 82; 6, p. 73 is a good source of such examples of religious sporting activity.
66 See Crotty, 'Making the Australian Male', pp. 48–105. Holt, 'Sport and History', p. 3, has noted the 'ethnocentric tendency' of much British sports history and there is a need for much more work on cultural comparisons with the middle classes elsewhere. See also Mangan, *The Cultural Bond*, Prologue.
67 J.R. Moore, Freethought, Secularism, Agnosticism: The Case of Charles Darwin', in G. Parsons (ed.), *Religion in Victorian Britain Vol. 1, Traditions* (Manchester, 1988), p. 275.
68 Lowerson, *Sport and the English Middle Classes*, pp. 268–77.
69 J. Lowerson, 'Sport and the Victorian Sunday: The Beginnings of Middle-class Apostasy', *British Journal of Sports History*, 1, 2 (1984), 202–20.
70 Huggins, *Flat Racing*, Ch. 3 and 8.
71 M.A. Kellet, 'The Power of Princely Patronage: Pigeon Shooting in Victorian Britain', *International Journal of the History of Sport*, 11, 1 (1994), 63–85; Lowerson, *Sport and the English Middle Classes*, pp. 36–7.
72 Mason, 'Football and the Workers', pp. 254–62.
73 Mangan, 'Braveheart Betrayed?', p. 193.
74 Birmingham, not London, was the most active association, and had a challenge shield for schools in the 1884/5 season. A South London Schools FA. was formed in 1885. See T. Mason, *Association Football*, p. 85.
75 P. Joyce, *Visions of the People: Industrial England and the Question of Class 1848–1914* (Cambridge, 1991).
76 J. Hill and J. Williams (eds), *Sport and Identity in the North of England* (Keele, 1996), p. 2.
77 For an attempt to show how north-eastern sporting identity had its own unique variations when compared with Hill and Williams' more general work on northern sporting identity see M.J. Huggins, 'Sport and the Social Construction of Identity in North-East England 1800–1914', in N. Kirk (ed.), *Northern Identities: The Construction of Identity in Northern England from 1800 to the Present* (Aldershot, 1999), pp. 132–62.
78 Even with a strong regional component to Lowerson, *Sport and the English Middle Classes*, a count of place-name references in its index shows strong metropolitan dominance, forced on it in large part through use of current historiography.
79 See for example the complexities of the apparent north-south debate over dry-fly fishing; Lowerson, *Sport and the English Middle Classes*, pp. 46–7.
80 *Northern Review*, 31 Dec. 1887.
81 Tranter, *Sport, Economy and Society*, pp. 52–4. Eric Dunning has always emphasized that the pleasurable excitement of sport was a major dynamic. See N. Elias and E. Dunning (eds), *The Quest for Excitement* (Oxford, 1986).
82 On the ambiguities of respectability see P. Bailey, 'Will the real Bill Banks stand up? A role analysis of mid-Victorian working-class respectability', *Journal of Social History*, 12 (1979), 346.
83 Lowerson, *Sport and the English Middle Classes*, p. 2.
84 P. Bailey, *Popular Culture and Performance in the Victorian City* (Cambridge, 1998).
85 Mason, *Association Football*, pp. 156–7.

86 For use of the concept of 'layered identities' see H.L. Malchow, *The Social and Political World of the Victorian Businessman* (London, 1991), p. 8.

87 G. Best, *Mid-Victorian Britain 1851–1875* (London, 1979), pp. 218–49.

88 E. Midwinter, *W.G. Grace: His Life and Times* (London, 1981), p. 156, suggests his income would have made him a modern millionaire.

89 Russell, *Football and the British*, p. 23.

90 T. Collins, *Rugby's Great Split: Class, Culture and the Origins of Rugby League Football* (London and Portland, OR, 1998), p. 16.

91 *Northern Review*, 13 Oct. 1888.

92 *Northern Review*, 15 Dec. 1888.

93 J.K. Walton and A. Wilcox, *Low Life and Moral Improvement in Mid-Victorian Liverpool* (Leicester, 1991), p. 49.

94 *Free Lance*, 25 May 1868, gives details of the Post Office Hotel betting rooms. For the Talbot in 1850 see Sylvanus, *The Byeways and Downs of England* (London, 1850), p. 124. For subscription betting rooms in Commercial Street Sheffield see *Doncaster Gazette*, 15 Aug. 1845.

95 D. Itzkowitz, 'Victorian Bookmakers and their Customers', *Victorian Studies*, 32, 1 (1988), 7–20.

96 In Hull, for example, five clerks, and a shopman, cashier, butcher, tailor, joiner, engineer and jeweler were amongst those fined for betting in 1884. *Beverley Guardian*, 7 June 1884.

97 The growth of exclusivity from mid-Victorian times is covered in Wigglesworth, *The Evolution of English Sport*, pp. 94–6. For athletic examples see J. Crump, 'Athletics', in Mason (ed.), *Sport in Britain*, p. 51.

98 P. Bailey, *Leisure and Class in Victorian England* (London, 1978), p. 23; Tranter, *Sport, Economy and Society*, pp. 37–8.

99 J.C. Shaw, the president of the Sheffield Association, claimed the Sheffield team, which was a mixed one of 'gentlemen of the middle class and working men' fulfilled this function. See T. Mason, *Association Football*, p. 252.

100 Tranter, *Sport, Economy and Society*, p. 43.

101 N. Tranter, 'The Social and Occupational Structure of Organized Sport in Central Scotland in the Nineteenth Century', *International Journal of the History of Sport*, 4, 3 (1987), 301–14.

102 M.J. Huggins, 'Leisure and Sport in Middlesbrough 1840–1914', in A.J. Pollard (ed.), *Middlesbrough: Town and Community 1830–1950* (Stroud, 1996), p. 138.

103 The Blackburn Olympic side which won the 1883 FA Cup, although seen as a 'plebian' side by some, contained a clerk, a licensed victualler and a dentist. Mason, *Association Football*, p. 54.

104 N. Wigglesworth, 'A History of Rowing in North-west England', *British Journal of Sports History* 3, 2 (1986), 153.

105 Wigglesworth, *The Evolution of English Sport*.

106 Tranter, *Sport, Economy and Society*, pp. 23–4.

107 *The Free Lance*, 15 June 1867.

108 *Middlesbrough Weekly News*, 17 Aug. 1866.

109 W. Vamplew, *Pay Up and Play the Game: Professional Sport in Britain 1875–1914* (Cambridge, 1988).

110 R.A. Church, *Economic and Social Change in A Midland Town; Victorian Nottingham 1815–1900* (London, 1966), pp. 212–13.

111 M.J. Huggins, 'More Sinful Pleasure? Leisure, Respectability and the Male Middle Classes in Victorian England', *Journal of Social History*, 23, 3 (2000), 585–800.

112 *Punch*, 24 June 1871.

113 *The Times*, 4 June 1874; *The Times*, 6 June 1874.

114 H. Allingham and D. Radford (eds), *William Allingham, a Diary 1824–1889* (London, 1907), p. 181.

115 Huggins, *Flat Racing*, Ch. 3.

116 *The Times*, 4 June 1874.

117 A.J. Durie and M.J. Huggins, 'Sport, Social Tone and the Seaside Resorts of Great Britain c.1850–1914', *International Journal of the History of Sport*, 18,1 (1998), 173–87.

118 Lowerson, *Sport and the English Middle Classes*, p. 55; A. Hankinson, *The First Tigers* (London, 1972), *passim.*

119 Bailey, *Leisure and Class*, p. 71.

120 For the life of one medical student see S. Taylor, *The Diary of a Medical Student During the Mid-Victorian Period 1860–1864* (Norwich, 1927).

121 Mangan, *Athleticism*, p. 144.

122 G. Deghy, *Noble and Manly: The Story of the National Sporting Club* (London, 1956).

123 Huggins, *Flat Racing and British Society*, p. 59.

124 For example, A Chester tradesman, *Chester Races: Do They Pay? Indirect Gain and Loss* (Chester, 1865).

125 See for example the report on the trap accident to four Cambridge 'collegians' at the conclusion of racing in April 1883, *Newmarket Journal*, 28 April 1883. Earlier in the century the banker Joshua Crompton wrote to his son at Jesus College warning against racing, claiming racing had been the 'ruin of half' of your young men'. M. Ashcroft (ed.), *Letters and Papers of Henrietta Matilda Crompton and her Family* (Northallerton, 1994), p. 5.

126 D. Dixon, *From Prohibition to Regulation; Bookmaking, Anti-gambling and the Law* (London, 1991).

127 Dewey, 'Socratic Teachers', p. 52.

128 For a summary of the debate see Tranter, *Sport, Economy and Society*, pp. 3–12.

Part 1

Sport and schools

Chapter 1

The other side of the coin

Victorian masculinity, field sports and English elite education

J.A. Mangan and Callum McKenzie

The morality of field sports[1] and their purpose in élite education were contentious issues during the nineteenth century. Field sports now symbolised aristocratic privilege and sustained the traditional code of the gentleman in a period when middle-class sensibilities were reconstructing his image and redefining his masculinity on games fields. Field sports, therefore, were no longer unproblematic. The situation had become more complicated. Thomas Arnold's rejection of field sports during his headship at Rugby, for example, aimed at curtailing perceived anti-social behaviour. Although he succeeded in minimising the boys' poaching in the vicinity of the school, Arnold's efforts to reshape youthful sensibilities, however, faced a number of difficulties. The pervasiveness of the rural masculine ideal of the huntsman, and the associated moral imperatives of the country gentleman, not to mention his accustomed pleasures, remained strong throughout the nineteenth century and indeed long after.[2] This ideal found expression in literature, art and custom and represented for many an appropriate social training for middle- and upper-class boys. Furthermore, by the age of the New Imperialism killing wildlife for sport by the young had become part of an ideological conflict in which racial superiority, ethnocentric assertion and manly aggression were given priority over the Christian virtues of consideration, compassion and gentleness. This chapter considers the evolving relationship between masculinity, field sports and élite education during the nineteenth century and discusses field sports as both *complementary to, and in competition with* team games, in the making of period élite masculinity.

Setting the scene: field sports before the era of athleticism

Before about the 1850s, there is no evidence to suggest that field sports took place in any organised way at the public schools. The rural location of some schools

Originally published in *The European Sports History Review*, 2000, 2, pp. 62–85.
http://www.tandf.co.uk/journals

meant that their pupils were free to roam without restriction through the countryside during leisure hours. In the winter at Winchester, for example, badger-hunting was a favourite sport. Huntsmen were hired to keep badgers and pro-vided terriers and dogs.[3] Winchester was described as a 'sporting school, in a very sporting county', where many of the boys hunted in the holidays.[4] At this time, too, 'not a few boys kept guns for hare and partridge shooting'.[5] Other activities at Winchester included bird-shooting, nesting, duck-hunting and beagling, but the most common and popular of all was 'toozling' or chasing and killing birds with hand thrown stones in the hedgerows. There were variations on this. One pupil spent all his free time killing squirrels and birds with a catapult, a practice which he later felt was useful for creating proficiency in other pastimes such as racquets, cricket, tennis and big-game hunting![6] At Harrow, one 'toozler' wrote in his diary,

> went out shooting over Hedstone fields and having no sport, put down the gun and found a Joe Bent in Hedge adjoining private road, which was killed after a splendid run by M. Tufnell. Found a robin in same hedge, which, after an exceedingly brilliant run, was killed by Mr Torre. Had an animated run with Joe Bent. Home by Church Fields. NB Game plentiful but blackbirds wild. First eggs taken, Mistle Thrushes.[7]

Bird-nesting was a widespread hobby.[8] The boys of Wellington College were occasionally lectured by Charles Kingsley on the manly merits of bird-nesting.[9] Pupils at Marlborough during this period also enjoyed the largely unrestrained hobbies of taking birds eggs from nests, as well as trespassing and poaching game. In addition, in the vicinity of the college, rabbits and squirrels were at constant risk from the 'squaler', a small cane with a lead head thrown with uncanny accu-racy by some Marlborough boys.[10] Frogs fared no better when hunted by the Marlborian 'barbaric tribe' which 'collected in gangs to beat frogs with sticks in the wilderness and filled buckets with their bodies'.[11] Eton too provided many opportunities for the reluctant scholar to decimate local wildlife. Some students kept ferrets at 'Fishers' and hunted rats in the hedgerows; 'Nimrod's' autobio-graphy notes how recreations such as rat-catching and rabbit and badger taking provided certain Eton scholars with the necessary skills for subsequent careers as Masters of Foxhounds.[12]

Poaching by public school boys at this time did not carry the stigma of dishonour. On the contrary, boys identified as poachers were often lauded by their peers.[13] Poaching by the sons of the aristocracy and gentry not only won public esteem, it provided excitement, hazard, entertainment and useful experience. Some, like Joby Minor, 'the most artful poacher in Eton', graduated in time to the respected position of kennel huntsman to the Eton Beagles in the 1860s.[14] Sir John Dugdale Astley (1828–94) chased deer and poached pheasant eggs in Home Park while at Eton, fully 'enjoying the excitement of dodging the gamekeeper'.[15] Poaching by upper-class boys, of course, was not born of necessity, nor was it an act of social resentment. It demonstrated a healthy sense of boyish daring, privileged resistance to conformity and the right to upper-class licence. Poaching as a marker of bravado, non-conformity and freedom lingered on into the twentieth century. In fiction, Rudyard Kipling's schoolboy heroes in his *Land and Sea Tales for Scouts and Guides*[16] were capable rabbit ferreters and had the 'poaching instinct', while in life, boys at Eton prior to the Great War were still poaching large amounts of game. Between October 1908 and July 1910, for example, six friends at Eton poached 2,260 head of game.[17]

Arnold, manliness and middle-class morality

For many mid-Victorians, Thomas Arnold was a focus for the desire for moral reformation.[18] His objective, at least according to C.L.R. James, was the development of a public-school system which provided a meeting place for the moral outlook of the dissenting middle classes and the athletic instincts of the aristocracy.[19] Perhaps. What is more certain is that within any alleged compromise between the aristocratic and bourgeois conceptions of culture, however, there was no place for field sports. Character-building was the main purpose of Arnold's Rugby, in which education was firstly an ethical and only secondly an intellectual process.[20] One aim, as is well known, was the creation of Christian gentlemen as the 'champions of righteousness especially selected to combat the ever watchful forces of evil'.[21] To this end Arnold wanted to reduce the difference in lifestyles between the middle and upper-middle classes.[22] His ambition was moral embourgoisement – downwards. The luxury and privilege of the 'sporting squire' without responsibility, and his associated recreational and social excesses, was anathema to Arnold.[23] Arnold's perception of the Christian gentleman was not that of the old chevalier, jealous of his paramilitary honour but otherwise indifferent to morality, but that of a new gentle gentleman, competing not in duels undertaken or foxes killed, but in consideration for others.[24] Field sports, a prominent part of this older culture, were considered by him as a feudal anachronism and at odds with his civilising mission for young gentlemen. Arnold's objections to field sports certainly derived from his evangelicism, a Christian doctrine which was antithetical to killing wildlife for sport, with its stress on moral earnestness and compassion for the weak. Masculinity for many of the aristocracy and gentry, on the other hand, still manifested itself in military prowess, and in codes of honour based on medieval chivalric martial values, in which field sports were essential training. The life of the feudal élite, of course, had been dominated by the essentials of war, hunting and the tournament, the latter two being preparation for the first.[25] This domination, with the exception of the tournament, had by no means disappeared by the first half of the nineteenth century.

For his part, Arnold thought all field sports a 'waste of time'. At Rugby, he was determined to secure their abolition. If Arnold's vision was to be realised, in his view he needed to abolish those recreations which reinforced cultural divisions and boundaries and traditional, unacceptable practices. Consequently, on arrival he attempted ruthlessly to end the former licence to roam the countryside at

Rugby: in 1833 Arnold expelled six boys for fishing in the Avon, the local river, after complaints from a local landowner.[26] Then hunting became the target. It had been common practice prior to Arnold's arrival for boys to hire cottages from local countrymen for hiding dogs and sporting equipment. The use of dogs and guns were now forbidden and keeping to bounds firmly enforced.[27] He went further, actually destroying packs of hounds kept by the boys.[28] By edict, and by appeals to local farmers and landowners, Arnold gradually curtailed the traditional sports of hunting, shooting and fishing. According to Charles Kingsley, fishing was the sport of sports for those overworked businessmen, professional men, barristers, statesmen and merchants, who sought mental relaxation to ease the strain of excessive occupational pressure.[29] This argument did not work with Arnold. Even angling, that restrained, leisurely rural activity, was denied the boys. In a nutshell, Arnold's opposition to field sports of all kinds, was driven by idealism, pragmatism and humanitarianism.[30]

Arnold's deliberate efforts to exclude the landed aristocracy from Rugby formed part of his crusade against field sports.[31] It is interesting that between 1800 and 1850, the proportion of boys at Rugby from titled families never exceeded between five and seven per cent in any decade.[32] Subsequently the post-Arnold opposition to field sports was facilitated by the substitution of readily acceptable alternatives, such as cricket and football.[33] These were part of an emerging and increasingly powerful educational ideology, namely athleticism, incorporating tests of manliness and character formation without the need to kill animals or exhibit prowess on a horse.[34] Circa 1850, various headmasters brought about organisational and disciplinary reform in their schools.[35] These included an increase in indirect surveillance by the headmaster and assistant masters over the boys' recreational activities and pastimes,[36] a practice which contrasted with the earlier unrestricted freedom which allowed, among other things, shooting, beagling and ferreting.

Competence at team games now for many became the supreme expression of masculine moral excellence.[37] The result was the arrival of a process by which the public schools after the 1860s, increasingly produced a unified and standardised English educational élite,[38] and formulated a new concept of the English gentleman in due course nowhere better exemplified than in the image of the ex-public school cricketer, A.W. Hornby[39] or his superior at the 'game for gentlemen', C.B. Fry.[40]

These educational developments took place as Britain underwent at least some material embourgeoisement, involving a partial amalgamation of the established upper class and the rising middle class.[41] However, another social development was also taking place. Where the new commercial, industrial and business class sought assimilation with larger landowners, field sports were one expression of class parity. They were a form of recreational conspicuous consumption that demonstrated comparable, or ever superior wealth, especially when linked to the expensive honour of Master of Hounds. Arnold had a lonely victory. Field sports were not abandoned in the public school system at the onset of athleticism. The *two* means of making masculinity now coexisted. And it would certainly be an over-simplification to suggest, therefore, that boys from well-established landed families pursued field sports at school, whereas those from industrial middle-class families did not. Well before 1850, cotton and ironmasters, for example, were buying land for sporting purposes, indeed as early as the late eighteenth century.[42] The new man of wealth sought to become part of the existing establishment by buying land and playing by the rules of existing landed society; few families, it has been argued, held out for long against its leisured, bucolic delights.[43] The acquisition of a landed estate was one of the criteria for the upward rise of the socially ambitious.[44] By about 1800, it had become common practice to transfer wealth from commercial enterprises to moneyed interests and then to landed estates.[45] Field sports were popular amongst the new men of commerce and industry, despite the opposition to killing wildlife by leading Dissenters during the early nineteenth century.[46] Furthermore, the 1831 Game Reform Act quickened the pace of democratisation in field sports. Not only the upper middle classes could 'sport', according to one authority, but also the 'blacksmith, the butcher, the hog jobber, the fisherman and the cadger…all have certificates'.[47] By mid-century, new money was being used to support fox-hunting. According to a number of contemporary hunting authorities, the middle classes were firmly established in the hunting field. These included 'the *pater familias*, respectable householders and responsible vestrymen, churchwardens and other parish administrators; attorneys, country bankers, doctors, apothecaries – the profession of medicine has a special aptitude for fox-hunting – maltsters, millers, butchers, bakers, innkeepers, auctioneers, graziers, builders, retired officers, judges home from India, barristers who take weekly holidays, stockbrokers, newspaper editors, artists and sailors'.[48] The erosion of class boundaries and the rise in the popularity of field sports was linked then to the increased earning capacity of the business and professional classes. *The Saturday Review* even suggested that the radical movement against field sports, which began in the 1840s, was now ineffectual because 'sport could not be represented as peculiar to the aristocracy, as all men like to shoot, and men in trade bought estates and became game preservers'.[49] The gradual erosion of social barriers in field sports was noted by the old Etonian, Charles Milnes-Gaskell, who asserted that all classes who had any leisure or money to spare could participate in field sports. He added, sadly, 'it is humiliating to be obliged to acknowledge that in spite of all the additional facilities afforded in this country for the pursuit of a scientific or artistic career, the average Englishman's conception of a leisured life is undoubtedly a life spent in the enjoyment of sport. The Englishman who has the means will spend those means on racing, hunting, fishing or shooting.'[50]

Arnold's well-meaning reforms, then, were taking place at a time when field sports were becoming as much the recreation of the business and the professional middle classes as of the aristocratic class.[51] This trend continued into the late nineteenth century.[52] In 1851 the population of England and Wales was 17,927,609 with 28,950 game licences issued; by 1866, 43,231 licences had been sold; the number of gun licences sold per thousand males in England confirmed the rise in participation: 9.7 in England and Wales, 7.8 in Scotland; by 1891, this had risen to 11.37 and 8.8 respectively.[53] In the light of this evidence, it is tempting and reasonable to suggest that class boundaries and their respective codes of masculinity were becoming increasingly blurred. Nevertheless, while the 'gradual emergence of the bourgeoisie as the ruling class . . . their growing control of major institutions, and the consequent spread of their values through society' was particularly evident in games and athletics,[54] and despite the 'bourgeoisification' of aristocratic culture through these games, at Eton and Cambridge in particular, field sports remained powerful symbols of upper-class masculinity. And one other manifestation of the pursuit of a class 'caste mark' should be noted, the desire of the 'nouveau riche' to educate their sons at public school and university. Its relevance will be seen shortly.

Bastions of resistance, inclusion and exclusion: Eton and Oxbridge

Aristocratic refugees from Arnold's Rugby with their too frequent enthusiasm for field sports, were frequently advised that Eton would provide a more suitable education.[55] And there was sense in this. Field sports played a distinctive and influential part in Eton life throughout the Victorian period. In part, this reflected the social composition of the school, which contained about 20 per cent of boys from titled families in every decade during the first half of the century,[56] but it also reflected a keenness on the part of the *nouveau riche* on entry to display a hard-won caste mark. And it also reflected a propensity by both groups to cling tenaciously to a long-standing Etonian tradition.

Hunting at Eton College possessed a long history. From the seventeenth century onwards, Eton boys hunted, sometimes with rams as quarry.[57] The Founder, in fact, had stipulated that no scholar, fellow, chaplain or other minister of the College should keep dogs, nets for hunting, ferrets, falcons or hawks. These rules, however, seem to have been broken at will.[58] However, the Eton College Hunt, founded in the late 1850s by boys from the shires, familiar with and keen on field sports, represented a departure from past defiant and less formal modes of hunting, by virtue of the tacit approval given to it by the school authorities. The Oppidan Hunt, a separate group, began on 19 January 1858 with the formation of a beagle pack,[59] initiated by 'a manly country-loving boy, versed in the etiquette of hunting and devoted to a healthy open-air life, who loved horse and hound, and who spent every moment of daylight cultivating the instincts of a clean, country bred Englishman'.[60] Contemporaries recalled that this first pack of beagles was led by two influential senior pupils, Valentine Lawless and Eyre William Hussey, who had already attained high positions within the College, the latter being the Captain of the Boats[61] and the former being a member of Pop. The inspiration for a College Hunt clearly came from the desire to perpetuate the practices of the country gentleman in this school for gentlemen. Membership was open to all on payment of an annual subscription. It should not be overlooked that almost at the very moment when athleticism was establishing itself formally within the public school system, hunting too, at least at Eton, was also establishing itself with similar formality!

When Dr Goodford[62] resigned in 1861 at the prospect of the publication of the Report of the Clarendon Commission,[63] the new Headmaster, Dr Balston,[64] did not enforce the school rules against hunting. The then Captain of the Boats, Valentine Lawless, was invited to meet Dr Balston to discuss the question of 'Lower Boys frequenting Tap', which was a private room in a public-house beyond Barnes Bridge. Here, boys were prone to drink large quantities of beer and took part in customs such as 'drinking the Long Glass'. Dr Balston proposed that, in return for Lawless' assistance in keeping Lower Boys away from 'Tap', he would withdraw the rules against dogs in College, and authorise and recognise the Beagles Club. There was logic in Balston's offer, since field sports were widely seen as an antidote to degeneracy. 'What is a youth,' one observer enquired, 'without his shooting and his hunting, his gloves and his foil? – an inflation of tobacco and beer, of vice and folly. And what's a man without his recreation? – a miracle of inaptitude, of infir-mity of purpose, and incapable of action'.[65] In *The Young Sportsman's Manual* of 1867, one writer insisted on the superior moral status of the manly field sportsman, asserting that most sporting writers were united against mixing the pleasures of the field with alcohol. 'There was no place,' he argued, 'for drink in the field, covert or moor.'[66] At the meeting between Dr Balston and Lawless, clearly a deal was struck and beagling was officially sanctioned by the College, although there was some resistance, at least for a little time, in some official quarters. The *Eton College Chronicle* reported briefly in 1864 that 'our only regret is that the authorities do not seem well-disposed towards this fine and invigorating exercise'.[67] The exercise appeared to prove invigorating. In its first month, there were about one hundred pupils out following the pack. The Eton College Beagles, incidentally, were entirely financed, administered and organised by the boys. The construction of new expen-sive kennels on College land in 1872, for example, was wholly financed by them[68] and had an educational rationale. The development of appropriate masculinity was considered to be closely linked to self-reliance. The Public Schools Commission Report of 1864 alluded to the 'freedom of public school life', which promoted 'independence and manliness of character'. Goodford himself was described as 'unmeddlesome',[69] and argued that 'English gentlemen should not be excessively manipulated and shaped by the school'.[70] In Goodford's action there was not only purpose, there was precedent. In 1866, judicious action by the boys at Eton had resulted in an amalgamation between the Oppidans and Collegers[71] to strengthen the Hunt against the local farmers, some of whom were reluctant to allow meetings to trample their crops.[72] This was smiled upon by the authorities. The capacity of Etonians to successfully organise and administer hunting was one expression of a confident and competent masculine identity.[73]

The relationship between the Hunt and adjacent farmers deteriorated steadily in the 1860s. The successful management of conflict, which might require a superior attitude towards others, was an essential component of period upper-middle-class masculinity. In consequence, the continuation of the Eton College Hunt became a contest of wills. The first mention of school field sports in the *Eton College Chronicle* on 14 May 1863 had noted that local farmers had asked in 'a good-natured' manner for Eton gentlemen not to cross the young corn. *The Chronicle* opined that to accede to their request was a good idea as the farmers by and large were very helpful with regard to the Hunt, especially in finding hares.[74] This sound advice appears to have been ignored. By the mid-1860s it was reported that the Beagles had had a poor season owing to 'the extreme perversity of some farmers, who own the best land about the place. We cannot see what possible harm a few boys running over ground could possibly do to crops, and compensation is easily and readily obtainable.'[75] Difficulty with local farmers is also recorded in the boys' hunting journals. Clearly the farmers had persisted in their complaints, and the boys in their dismissal of them. The fact that the local farming community felt able to do so reflected developments at a national level. By the 1860s, the capability of farmers to organise and improve their position was improved by the establishment of new farmers' clubs and associations. In August 1865, *The Field* remarked that such local groups were intent on publicising the issue of landlords' sport, a sure sign of farmers' growing self-confidence.[76] Local assertion was no doubt a consequence of this. In contrast to the period before the 1850s it is notable that Eton's young sportsmen now preferred negotiation rather than confrontation when dealing with the local farming community.[77] One Master of the Beagles, H.B. Creswel, noted in the *Hunt Diaries* that 'great care should be taken with regard to certain farmers, or my successor will get into serious trouble which may lead to the abolition of the Hunt'.[78] There can be little doubt that farmers' growing self-assertion nationally was reflected locally.

In the mid-1860s the Public Schools Commission found that intellectual standards were unsatisfactory at Eton and the other 'Great Schools'.[79] This fact, together with the growing popularity and significance of organised games as well as the formal acceptance of the Eton College Hunt during this decade, resulted in debates about education at Eton, and indeed at the other public schools. Nevertheless, athleticism went from strength to strength. During the 1860s, for example, there was a gradual admission of Collegers into Oppidan school sports in general: the lower club and lower college were now allowed into cricket, and athletics, a development which was seen as an extension of their privileges.[80] By the turn of the century these changes had become consolidated. For most boys games playing became *de rigueur*. In 1898, it was recorded that:

There are fifty fives courts where before there was one; twenty games or thereabouts of cricket as against three; compulsory football for every house four or five times a week; to say nothing of beagles and athletic sports in the Easter Term, and rowing and bathing daily through the summer. There are house colours for football and school colours for football, cricket, rowing, racquets; there are challenge cups, senior and junio....[81]

The Hunt, however, remained strong in the face of major changes in sport at the school. A.J. Pound, the first Master of the combined hunt in 1866 was 'thoroughly honest and straightforward', if intellectually below average. This was no liability. His virtues[82] were ordered correctly. Pound was fondly remembered as a spartan and spirited youth, frequently arranging to be early at the 'Saying Lesson, so as to be away from school at seven-thirty a.m., breakfasting on beer and biscuits, and hunting until eleven a.m.'[83] Prestige allocated to huntsmen was enhanced by their knowledge of, and interest in, sporting literature rather than Greek or Roman Classics, a practice not always condemned by the school.[84] Popular public school heroes and their many admirers, of course, preferred energetic sports to sedentary classwork, since all but the most material forms of intelligence were considered effeminate.[85] Etonians with no fondness for Greek and Latin, as noted earlier, were praised for their manly rowing and poaching.[86] At Eton, those who rejected the river, track or pitch could legitimately take part in ratting, poaching or fox-hunting. The distinguished Eton headmaster, Edward Warre[87] was concerned about the manliness of boys who were excessively academic, and was convinced that strenuous exercise was the panacea for associated youthful deficiencies.[88] He was reassured that Eton 'possessed in itself the antidote to effeminacy'.[89] It comes as no surprise, therefore, that Warre supported the Hunt. This antidote, in his view, *included* field sports.

The Trinity College Foot Beagles at Cambridge, like the Eton Hunt, was under the control of Matthew Arnold's 'barbarians', the unintellectual sons of country gentlemen. For these Beaglers, field sports were their preference, for both social and educational reasons. As with school pupils and beaks, so with students and dons. Both combined to make a success of the College Beagles. William Edward Currey,[90] for example, took the lead in setting up the Beagles in 1867, combining the duties of College don and Master of the Beagles, while W. Rouse-Ball[91] was an enthusiastic supporter of the Beagles as well as a loyal Fellow of the College. Field sports at Cambridge, of course, had long been a counter-balance to scholarship. One foreign visitor in 1602 noted that students 'perhaps keep more dogs and greyhounds that are so often seen in the streets, than they do books'.[92] Student preference for field sports over learning was again noted in the late eighteenth century.[93] In the 1740s, Francis Coventry noted of Magdalene College that wealthy fellow-commoners and noblemen were indulged in by tutors who hesitated to oppose the inclinations of gentlemen. The allure of preferments and benefices in the gift of titled families ensured that the dons allowed students to substitute hunting parties for lectures much as they pleased. Privilege and patronage eroded the authority, power and control of the school beak and the university don.[94] Generations of Cambridge undergraduates, therefore, had been noted sportsmen, who raced at Newmarket, shot throughout Cambridgeshire, and avoided lectures and chapel whenever possible. The pleasures of point-to-point and partridge shooting were frequently accompanied by heavy drinking and riotous behaviour, and the rights of local owners of land received little sympathy.[95] In passing, it might be noted that things were no different at Oxford. Local farmers and huntsmen were resentful of irresponsible undergraduates who paid little attention to crops or more heinously to the proper treatment of hounds,[96] while the famous George Osbaldestone, hunted for three days a week at Brasenose during the early nineteenth century and kept two hunters;[97] Captain John White, educated at Eton and Christ Church, hunted regularly on his three hunters and, after a catalogue of falls and broken bones, stupidly or bravely or perhaps both, he rode 'harder than ever'.[98] Christ Church, according to one observer writing in 1890, was open to anyone who 'could eat, drink and hunt, play cricket and punt'.[99] Not always, it appears. In 1885 the Dean of Christchurch wrote to Lord Bathurst in some exasperation, suggesting that his eldest son should find a more convenient hunting box for the following season than the 'House'.[100] Nevertheless, at the turn of the century, Christ Church, New College, Magdalene and Exeter all had their own beagle packs. And despite intermittent moral objections to hunting, Christ Church Beagles were formally supported by College Amalgamation Club subscriptions.[101]

In the last quarter of the nineteenth century, Cambridge had the reputation over Oxford of giving even more latitude to sportsmen and placing even less emphasis on learning.[102] Old Etonians were the leading figures in the halcyon years of the Trinity Foot Beagles from the late 1870s to the early 1880s, when Lord Yarborough, Watkin Wynn, W. Warton, E. Mesey-Thompson and Rowland Hunt among others, 'graduated with the degree of Master of Foxhounds'.[103] Of course, some managed to combine classwork with 'fieldwork'. J.W. Larnach, educated at Eton and Trinity College, Cambridge, was a case in point. At Cambridge he hunted regularly with the Cambridgeshire and Fitzwilliam and raced at Newmarket. *Baily's Magazine* noted approvingly that immediately prior to his finals he raced during the day and worked through the night.[104]

Nonetheless, it is true to say that at Cambridge in the whole of the second half of the nineteenth century many students had little interest in serious study. Only 44 per cent of undergraduates took honours courses between 1850 and 1906,[105] and many who took the ordinary degree never bothered to graduate. Magdalene illustrates well both the licence and the laxity which too frequently prevailed at Cambridge throughout the nineteenth century.

During the 1860s, Magdalene became the sanctuary for those unruly and ill-disciplined students rejected by other colleges.[106] Under the Mastership of Latimer Neville,[107] described as a 'thoroughgoing opponent of academic progress', Magdalene became a 'pleasant residential sporting club for the well-to-do or more or less well-descended young men'.[108] Superior social position demonstrated by access to field sports, particularly the costly activity of hunting, enabled students from the older landed families to set themselves apart. In this way they could, and did, flaunt an older tradition of masculinity, and distanced themselves from their inferiors. The growth of the public school system and the expansion of the ancient universities increasingly brought the commercial and professional middle classes into close proximity with the established landed classes in the second half of the nineteenth century.[109] Eton and Oxbridge, for example, were by this time receiving an ever-increasing number of solidly middle-class entrants.[110] Field sports at Eton and Oxbridge, therefore, could be manifestations of social demarcation which heightened self-perceptions of superiority based on cultural heritage.[111]

No Cambridge college projected this self-perception more completely than Magdalene. Magdalene in the 1860s, it was observed, was occupied by 'decent chaps devoted to horse and hound, but unfortunately, there were also in residence a few undergraduates, mostly sons of monied parvenus from the north of England, who exhibited a cheap imitation of these very creditable gentlemen... They tried to liken themselves to country gentlemen, and succeeded in looking like stableboys.'[112] According to contemporaries, hunting and riding were the most notable features of Magdalene at this time, when five or six couples of hunters were regularly to be found waiting at the College gate.[113] Between about 1850 and 1904, an undergraduate at Magdalene was allowed to count two nights towards his term if he was in college before 11 p.m. and did not leave before 6 a.m. on the following morning. This arrangement was intended to control the large number of Magdalene men who hunted two or three days a week with the Fitzwilliam Hunt or the Oakley, often staying overnight in Bedford. Absence from Chapel or Hall entailed the payment of fines, although when racing was on at Newmarket, Hall was cancelled.[114] In fact, the restrictions were pointless. Undergraduates frequently broke curfews and college regulations in order to pursue hunting.

After 1850, success on the games field, as already noted, was increasingly evidence of a proper masculinity. However, many undergraduates who hunted at Cambridge saw themselves as a male élite. They had no wish to embrace the fashion for modern sport – in any form. One member of the Beagles put this well:

> the truth is that we were extremely, almost morbidly, sensitive of being regarded as having any connection with any form of athletics, and the appearance of a stray member of the 'Hare and Hounds', a paper-chasing athletics club, set all our defensive bristles erect in half a minute. He might be a magnificent runner and keep with the hounds all the way, but we would observe that he knew nothing of skirting, or of saving himself by any knowledge of the shifts of the hunted hare: his running was fine running, but it wasn't running to hounds, so he was felt to be no sportsman and therefore to merit no trophy. Beagling is hunting...the exercise of running was a subordinate consideration.[115]

The historian of the Trinity Foot Beagles, F.C. Kempson, stated bluntly that athletic contests, based on Hellenic morality, were an inferior way of establishing masculine and moral identity, and that in contrast, hunting, beagling and steeple-chasing were clear evidence of the natural superiority of the 'barbarian' character with his masculine qualities of efficient organisation, control and negotiation.

The appearance of a critique of hunting in the *Cambridge Review* in 1912, hardened Kempson's suspicions that middle-class athletics were not only inferior activities but the antithesis of virtuous field sports, which remained rightfully in the control of the country gentleman. He regretted the fact that the ancient universities were now under the control of the middle classes. The true sportsman, he asserted, matched himself *against* nature, and pursued no reward unlike the modern multi-coloured blazered and scarved game-playing 'blue'. To emphasise this point, dress for hunting was tweed jacket, breeches and a soft cashmere scarf. In this way, the values of the new 'blood' preoccupied with colours, and the old sportsman honouring tradition, were pointed up.

Of course, in reality *both* games, athletics or rowing, and field sports enabled pupils at school and students at university to display their unquestionable masculinity to their respective admiring peers. Some excelled in one masculine world. H.M. Mesey-Thompson at Eton, for example, won the hurdles and the mile in 1863, the steeplechase in 1864, was also a top school oarsman and basked in the glory of being an 'all-round' athlete. Some bridged the worlds of the two masculinities. Rowland Hunt, who was at Eton between 1871 and 1877, won the steeplechase, 'with consummate ease' for two consecutive years, and was revered for his versatility, 'a wonderful runner, excellent shot, fearless rider and good fisherman'.[116] In addition, Hunt was one of the best exponents of the Eton Football Game, was keeper (Captain) of the Field Game, won the School Diving and House Racquets trophies and was in the School Shooting Eleven. Furthermore, he was Master of the Beagles in 1876. In due course, he went up to Magdalene, Cambridge. There, he never 'wasted much time in attending lectures, chapel or Hall; he did pass Part I of the 'Little-Go'[117] which satisfied his aspirations for academic honours'.[118] In short, while games, athletics and rowing with their intense inter-college rivalries based substantially, if not completely, on public school habits, clearly predominated at Cambridge during the late nineteenth century, hunting still found staunch support in a few quarters within the university. For some, killing wildlife for sport fitted easily into the fabric of a university experience, which produced 'tastes, inclinations, even vices which were positive and virile'.[119] It was reported that while there were hardly any ladylike men in the University, there was not a single one at Magdalene. The tendency was to the manly rather than to the effeminate.[120] Charles Kingsley, obsessed with manliness, was a passionate apologist for Magdalene manners. University education, he asserted, was not the prerogative of scholars but of *men*, 'bold, energetic, methodic, liberal-minded, magnanimous'.[121] For his part, he looked back fondly on his undergraduate days at Magdalene as spent largely in 'drink, horses, gambling, cards, prize-fighting, fishing and poaching; the keeping of horses and dogs, the latter inside college itself....'[122] The merits of such masculine behaviour in Kingsley's typically romantic opinion, of course, lay in the moral message: killing wildlife for sport promoted a love of nature. This in turn produced the ideal naturalist 'gentle, courteous, sympathetic to the poor, brave and enterprising, patient and undaunted, reverent and truthful, selfless and devoted – he would aspire to the ideal of chivalry'.[123] Others, equally famous, were no less committed to college custom. Arthur C. Benson[124] spent a good bit of his time at Magdalene in the company of his gun. Most Saturdays he was out shooting with his two siblings, Fred and Hugh Benson. This trio of sportsmen were described as a 'happy band of brothers'.

Interestingly, despite caste differences between 'Beaglers' and 'Bloods' both groups had become, to varying degrees, bound by the imperatives of 'fair play'. The Trinity Foot Beagles and the Eton College Hunt were created in the mid-nineteenth century, a significant time in the application of utilitarian values in the form of compulsory and regulated team games. This new code of conduct, contrary to the claims of Pierre de Coubertin,[125] was not the instinctive behaviour of upper-class youth, but depended on the acquisition of new attitudes through the medium of sport, towards self-control and self-discipline. Many of the public school 'hooligans' were taught the new virtues of 'fair play' on new school playing fields. The hunting clubs for their part, at Eton and Cambridge in turn shifted from the uncontrolled to controlled killing of wildlife, regulated by a tight sporting code. Of course, there is some truth, even if it is far from the whole truth, in the suggestion that the late nineteenth century concept of 'fair play' was in part a continuation of subscription to the older aristocratic chivalric tradition of honour, decency, style and manners.[126] Consequently, upper-class sporting periodicals of course, such as *Baily's Magazine*, never abandoned the belief that traditional landed families retained a superiority which incorporated a sense of decency and style. It paraded an impressive set of exemplars. John Poyntz Spencer, educated at Harrow and Trinity College, Cambridge in the 1850s, Master of the Pytchley Hounds, for example, inspired *Baily's* to write: 'we believe that sport of every kind is calculated to promote generous and manly impulses, and to strengthen a character for honesty and chivalry which has usually been considered a national peculiarity of Englishmen'.[127] H. Wentworth Fitzwilliam, from a family of churchmen, soldiers and statesmen, country gentlemen and sportsmen, also, in *Baily's*, view, embodied the necessary attributes of traditional manhood, being 'a true and courteous gentleman, quiet in demeanour, a sportsman, but not a sporting man'.[128] His social class credentials were impeccable. Like most of his family before him, he was educated at Eton, then Trinity College, Cambridge. There, he became Master of the Drag-Hounds and hunted regularly with the Fitzwilliam hounds. According to *Baily's*, the Duke of Bedford, clearly of unquestioned pedigree, who was educated at Westminster and Cambridge in the early nineteenth century, was a 'bold and elegant rider, whose leading quality was his sense of justice'.[129]

A belief in the superiority of aristocratic tradition in the eyes of at least some, is clearly revealed in the fact that when between the 1850s and 1860s, sport at Eton was being transformed from unregulated recreation to a regulated system of rowing, cricket and football house competitions,[130] an *Eton College Chronicle* editorial of 1864 suggested that all school athletics should be organised by the newly created *Master of the Beagles* not by the long established Captain of the Boats! Articles on sport within the influential *Chronicle*, incidentally, were usually sequenced as 'Beagles, Fives, Athletic Sports and Rowing'.[131]

Of course, hunting at Eton and Cambridge after the 1860s did not reflect an untrammelled continuation of noble aristocratic demeanour, but an amalgam of newly acquired sporting codes and traditional customs. Hunting was an evolving sport. The attitudes, procedures, language and dress code of both hunts at both places did respond to change and changed. However, association with historic codes of conduct enabled pupils at Eton and Cambridge to adopt an attitude of superiority based on past privilege. They acquired confidence from a legacy of class confidence. When evangelical pressures 'civilised' the public schoolboy, producing a new regard for playing games under new rules, there was a knock-on effect on the hunting field and an appropriate rationalisation. Respect for the quarry now heightened the intrinsic manliness of hunting. And, as a by-product, the application of fair play to the Hunt tended to produce a more compassionate morality. Several members were ousted from the Hunt, for example, during the 1860s because they complained of poor sport[132] by which they meant over-regulated killing. During the early years of the Eton College Hunt, its moral code did not exclude the hunting of 'bagged' or released quarry, either fox or hare, usually obtained from Leadenhall Market. However, the hunting of 'bagged' hares was later used to question the manliness required of this form of hunting.[133] With the development and regulation of the Hunt only wild hares were used for sport. New codes of conduct after the 1860s reflected the notion that wild animals were the proper quarry of a *manly* sport.[134] In this way the enthusiast for field sports joined the enthusiast for team games in the pursuit of a proper period masculinity.

It should not be overlooked, of course, that in pursuit of manliness at least three ideals coexisted, sometimes in harmony and sometimes in disharmony, at Eton – and certainly at King's College, its finishing school[135] for Etonians, at Cambridge. To record this is to introduce a timely and appropriate note of complexity into the Victorian middle- and upper-middle-class making of masculinity. To borrow a useful term from Christopher Hibbert[136] and redefined here for the purposes of this chapter, after 1850 there was the increasingly influential and popular phenomenon of 'Bloodism', the product of athleticism, in conjunction with the celebration of the athlete of the games field as an iconic representation of all that was virtuous in the period public school male. There were cynics and critics of 'Bloodism', of course, but they were heavily outnumbered.

There was also, to borrow a term from Siegfried Sassoon, 'Loderism' which he coined in celebration of his friend Norman Loder[137] (Dennis Milden in *The Memoirs of a Fox-Hunting Man*). At late Victorian Eton Loder 'did little but hunt with the beagles'.[138] After Cambridge, where he did not get a degree, he 'spent most of his life on the hunting field as master of various packs'.[139] And on his death in 1940, he was described as 'the perfect knight of the saddle, a gallant English gentleman'.[140] Loder, 'the very picture of an English sporting gentleman',[141] represented for Sassoon a way of life of the county set that was 'healthy, decent but animal and philistine'.[142]

There was also 'Socratism' preached *and* practised by a small number of masters and their protégé pupils. They were opposed to the tyranny of games, rejected its associated 'manliness and all its works'[143] and in slightly 'furtive subcultures' (they would have needed to be at least on the part of pupils)[144] they 'proclaimed the importance of "love, truth and beauty"'.[145]

Socratism, very much a minority movement, is not the concern here. It has been interestingly discussed elsewhere,[146] but its existence should be noted in order to provide depth and breadth to Victorian masculinity at Eton and Cambridge, and elsewhere.

Conclusion

Thomas Arnold at Rugby stressed Christian manliness as a means of improving English gentlemen. Arnold was concerned that 'the sturdy rough and tumble manliness of the games field and the poaching expeditions could easily lend itself to the lawless tyranny of physical strength'.[147] For Arnold, therefore, games were 'subordinate to moral and religio-political goals',[148] whilst field sports, because of their privileged associations and connotations and heartless brutality were to be proscribed. Arnold advocated the shortest route possible from boyhood to manhood by way of a moral maturity achieved by acquiring the compassion of Christ.

Shortly after Arnold's death, other headmasters, in contrast, asserted that muscular manliness was to be admired and encouraged. However, while increasingly this came to be demonstrated on the games field, Eton and Cambridge, in particular, remained true to field sports in the belief that they still made the man. This conservatism is illustrated in part by Beagle Club social and dining evenings, where behaviour often descended into accepted mayhem, in imitation of the robust hunting behaviour of their elders.

Horace Hutchinson wrote of his experiences at Eton in the first half of the nineteenth century that 'the education of future sportsmen begins with the first stone thrown from childish fingers at a confiding sparrow, and is continued with the use of that series of boyish missile weapons which leads up to the adult dignity of the gun'.[149] He concluded that, as boys, 'we never had a moment's doubt as to our ambition: the killing, skinning and stuffing, or the capturing, caging and taming of every wild thing that came our way'.[150] By the second half of the nineteenth century this was only half the story, or less than half the story. The making of élite masculinity had moved for many, but not for all, from the hunting field to the playing field. Two popular public school and university masculinities of 'Bloodism' and 'Loderism' (one more popular, one less popular) now existed side by side, sometimes in cooperation and sometimes in confrontation. One has attracted quite considerable attention; the other should not be overlooked – hence this chapter. *Both* jointly helped create an imperial ethnocentric sense of a superior English masculinity summed up perfectly by one historian of the hunting field:

Lord Granby was in many respects the type of Englishman formed by our school life and our sports; and if the type is commoner now, as it undoubtedly is, than was the case in the eighteenth century, that is one of the results of the ideals in school life and in sport being to raise all training, mental and bodily, to the level of the higher classes, rather than to bring down the higher to the level of the lower. Every Englishman, as Mr Rudyard Kipling has told us in verse and prose, is an aristocrat when among an inferior race; and from the rare insight Kipling has into the many-sided character of our national life, that great genius has risen to be the laureate of England, and the English as formed by the hunting field, the cricket pitch, and the football ground.[151]

Notes

1 The term field sports is used here as a generic term for the killing of game under the Game Laws, and other birds and wild life, such as vermin, which were not included in these laws. For a discussion of game laws as social conflict in England see H. Hopkins, *The Long Affray* (London, 1985), and H.L. Knight, 'The Game Laws in the Nineteenth Century, With Reference to Reform' (PhD thesis, University of Missouri, 1945).

2 Witness the current furore over foxhunting in response to Tony Blair's pledge to abolish it (July 1999), which in part is heir to this tradition.

3 A. Clark, 'When We Middle-Aged Fogeys Were Boys', *Baily's Magazine*, 33 (Jan.–June 1879), 147–8.

4 Ibid.

5 Ibid.

6 Felix (pseudonym), 'How to Become a Good Big Game Shot', *Baily's Magazine*, 86 (July–Dec. 1906), 273–4.

7 H.J. Torre, 'Harrow Notebook 1832–1837' (HSA). For a further description of 'toozling' see *Harrow Association Record* (1907–12), p. 29. See also J.A. Mangan, *Athleticism in the Victorian and Edwardian Public School: The Emergence and Consolidation of an Educational Ideology* (Cambridge, 1981), pp. 18–21, 273. *Athleticism* has been reprinted by Frank Cass with a new introduction by the author and additional introductions by the distinguished cultural historians Jeffrey Richards and Sheldon Rothblatt.

8 Bird-nesting seems to have preoccupied many an 'errant scholar' at certain schools. E.P. Rawnsley of Uppingham noted with some regret bird-nesting had become unfashionable amongst boys by the early twentieth century, in W.R. Rawnsley, *Highways and Byways in Lincolnshire* (1922), pp. 86–7. See also 'Schoolboys as they were', *Blackwoods Magazine*, 159 (Jan. 1896), 606–12.

9 Mrs Charles Kingsley (ed.), *Charles Kingsley: Letters and Memories of His Life*, Vol. 2 (London, 1877), pp. 163–4.

10 A.C. Bradley, *A History of Marlborough College* (London: John Murray, 1893), pp. 106, 126. See also Mangan, *Athleticism*, pp. 18–21.

11 A. Burns (ed.), *A Victorian Schoolboy: Tom Brown's Schooldays, from the Letters of Thomas Harris Burns, 1841–1852*, quoted in J. Chandos, *Boys Together: English Public Schools, 1800–1864* (Oxford, 1984), p. 150. See also Mangan, *Athleticism*, pp. 18–21.

12 C.J. Apperley, *The Life of a Sportsman* (London, 1905), pp. 76–7. See also Gerald Lascelles, *Baily's Magazine*, 83 (Jan.–June 1905), 421.

13 Chandos, *Boys Together*, pp. 149–50, 341–2.

14 Letter by A. Turner in A.C. Crossley (ed.), *A History of the Eton College Hunt* (Eton, 1922), p. 10.

15 Sir John D. Astley, *Fifty Years of My Life*, Vol. 1 (London, 1894), p. 13.

16 R. Kipling, *Land and Sea Tales for Scouts and Guides* (London, 1923), pp. 162, 269, 270.

17 T. Card, *Eton Reviewed: A History from 1860 to the Present Day* (London, 1994), p. 50.

18 G. Himmelfarb, *Victorian Minds* (London, 1968), p. 2802.

19 C.L.R. James, *Beyond a Boundary* (London, 1969), p. 164.

20 A.P. Stanley, *The Life of Thomas Arnold* (1844, 1910), p. 60; see also J. *Gathorn-Hardy, The Public School Phenomenon* (London, 1977).
21 A. Whitridge, *Dr Arnold of Rugby* (London, 1928), p. 133.
22 T. Arnold, *Miscellaneous Works* (London, 1845), letter 6, pp. 1967.
23 A.P. Stanley, *The Life and Correspondence of Thomas Arnold* (London, 1901), p. 554, and Arnold, *Misc.*, letter 2, p. 176.
24 H. Perkin, *Origins of Modern English Society* (London), p. 298.
25 L. Gautier, *Chivalry* (London, 1959), pp. 9–31. See also, J. Strutt, *The Sports and Pastimes of the People of England* (London, 1801), reprinted (ed. J.C. Cox) (London, 1901), p. 4.
26 T.W. Bamford, *Thomas Arnold* (London, 1960), p. 159.
27 J. Gathorn-Hardy, *Public School*, pp. 72–3.
28 N. Wymer, *Dr Arnold of Rugby* (London, 1953), p. 119.
29 F.G. Aflalo, 'The Infinite Variety of Sports', *Baily's Magazine*, 94 (July–Dec. 1910), 28–9.
30 Letter from C. Vaughan to L.A. Tollemache, quoted in L.A. Tollemache, *Old and Odd Memories* (London, 1908), pp. 126–7.
31 A.W. Merivale, *Family Memorials* (London, 1884), p. 330.
32 T. Bamford, 'Public Schools and Social Class, 1800–1850', *British Journal of Sociology*, 12 (March 1961), 225.
33 F. Dunning and K. Sheard, *Barbarians, Gentlemen and Players* (Oxford, 1979), p. 77.
34 See Mangan, *Athleticism*, Chs 3, 4.
35 Ibid.
36 Ibid.
37 Lord Berners, *A Distant Project* (London, 1964), p. 23.
38 D. Newsome, *Godliness and Good Learning* (London, 1961), p. 197.
39 See E. Grayson, *Corinthian Casuals and Cricketers* (London, 1983).
40 See C. Ellis, *C.B: the Life of Charles Burgess Fry* (London, 1984).
41 See H. Perkin, *The Origins of Modern English Society* (London, 1969), p. 269.
42 E.P. Thompson, *The Making of the English Working Class* (London, 1963), p. 218.
43 E.L. Jones, 'Industrial Capital and Land Investment: The Arkwrights in Herefordshire', in E.L. Jones and G. Mingay (eds), *Land, Labour and Population in the Industrial Revolution* (London, 1967), p. 51.
44 D. Rapp, *Economic History Review*, 2nd Series 27 (1974), p. 380.
45 C. Shrimpton, *The Landed Society of Essex in the Late Eighteenth Century* (London, 1977), p. 1.
46 F.M.L. Thompson, *The Rise of Respectable Society, 1830–1900* (London, 1988), p. 270.
47 *Sporting Magazine*, 132 (Nov. 1858), 317.
48 Anthony Trollope, *British Sports and Pastimes* (London, 1867), 75.
49 'The Game Laws', *Saturday Review*, 31, 2 (April 1871), 481.
50 C. Milnes-Gaskell, 'The Country Gentleman', *Nineteenth Century*, 10 (Sept. 1882), 460–3.
51 *The Times*, 10 Oct. 1865, 10.
52 See R. Jeffries, *The Gamekeeper at Home* (London, 1878), p. 45. Also R. Jeffries, 'Defence of Sport', *Baily's Magazine*, (April–Oct. 1885), 323 and P.A. Graham, *The Revival of English Agriculture* (London, 1899), p. 94.
53 Quoted in B. Martin, *The Great Shoots* (London, 1988), p. 19.
54 Dunning and Sheard, *Barbarians, Gentlemen and Players*, p. 306.
55 See J.R. de Honey, 'The Victorian Public School 1828–1902' (DPhil, thesis, Oxford, 1969), pp. 20–1.
56 Bamford, *Journal*, p. 225.
57 Remaines of J. Aubrey, 1688, quoted in H. Salt, *Memories of Bygone Eton* (London, n.d.), pp. 241–6.
58 A.C. Crossley, *The History of the Eton College Hare Hunt* (published privately, 1922), p. 2.
59 Oppidan Hunt. The term Oppidan referred to 'non-scholars', who were not King's Scholars, usually residing in the town with a landlady (College Archivist).
60 'The Diaries of Edward Charrington', in Crossley, ch. 1.

61 Both positions were highly prestigious and indicated institutional success, popularity and status. Valentine Lawless, later the fourth Lord Cloncurry, was at Eton from 1850 to 1858. He rowed in the VIII in 1857 and 1858 and also played in the Oppidan Wall Game and Field Games teams in 1857. He was elected to Pop (the Eton Society) in 1856. Eyre William Hussey was at Eton from 1853 to 1858. He rowed in the VIII in 1857 and 1858. Thanks are extended to Mr P. Hatfield, College Archivist, Eton College for this information.

62 Dr Charles Old Goodford (1812–1884), Headmaster 1853–1862, Provost 1862–1884.

63 Clarendon Commission, *Report of Her Majesty's Commissioner. Appointed to Enquire into the Reserves and Management of Certain Colleges and Schools and the Studies Perused Therein with an Appendix and Evidence*, 1864.

64 Dr Edward Balston (1817–91). He was educated Eton, then went to King's College, Cambridge, where he was a Fellow from 1839 to 1850. He was an Assistant Master at Eton from 1840–60, Fellow 1860–62, Headmaster 1862–68 and Vicar of Bakewell, Derbyshire 1869–91.

65 A. Clark (The Gentleman in Black, pseudonym), 'School Life: its Sports and Pastimes', *Baily's Magazine*, 2 (Oct.–April 1861), 370–1.

66 J. Carleton, *The Young Sportsman's Manual* (London, 1867), pp. 51–2. See also 'Modern Sport', *Baily's Magazine*, 28 (Dec.–June 1875–6), 274–81.

67 *The Eton College Chronicle*, 24, 28 (Jan. 1864), 60.

68 *Eton College Hunt Diaries*, Vol. 2, 1863–73.

69 G.W. Cornish (ed.), *Extracts from the Letters and Journal of Willian Cory* (Oxford, 1897), pp. 59–60.

70 E.G. Mack, *Public Schools and British Opinion since 1860* (New York, 1941), pp. 24–5.

71 Collegers was the term for 'King's Scholars' who resided at the College itself.

72 *Eton College Hunt Diaries*, Vol. 2, 1863–73.

73 As will be shown, many Etonians took these skills on to Cambridge. See F. Kempson, *The Trinity College Beagles* (London, 1913).

74 *The Eton College Chronicle*, 32 (May 1863), 4.

75 *The Eton College Chronicle*, 55 (April 1866), 217.

76 *The Field*, 26 (Aug. 1865), 131. See also P. Self and H.J. Storing, *The Stale and the Farmer* (London, 1962), p. 37; J.A. Scott-Watson and M.E. Hobbs, *Great Farmers* (London, 1937), p. 111.

77 *The Eton College Chronicle*, 55, 26 (April 1866), 217.

78 *Eton College Hunt Diaries*, Vol. 4 (1888–9), p. 21.

79 See Mangan, *Athleticism*, p. 106.

80 Crossley, *Hunt*, p. 24.

81 L. Ford, *Essays in Secondary Education* (London, 1898), p. 289, quoted in Mangan, *Athleticism*, p. 68.

82 At this time Spartan qualities were more highly valued than Athenian values in the public schools.

83 Crossley, *Hunt*, p. 14. The 'Saying Lesson' involved constant oral repetition of a text or task.

84 Letter by A. Turner in Crossley, *Hunt*, p. 8. A.J. Pound was a King's Scholar 1859–1867. Later he went on to Exeter College, Oxford. After working as a lawyer, he became Stipendiary Magistrate in British Guiana, 1867–77. (This information from Mrs P. Hatfield, Archivist, Eton College.)

85 See Mangan, *Athleticism*, for a wider treatment of this notion.

86 'George Osbaldestone', *Baily's Magazine*, 2 (Oct.–April 1860–1), 295.

87 See C.R.L. Fletcher, *Edward Warre* (London, 1922), pp. 64–5.

88 Ibid.

89 Quoted in E. Warre, in *Boy's Own Paper*, 17 (Sept. 1898), 10.

90 William Edward Currey, MA, Master of Magdalene, 1862–5.
91 W. Rouse-Ball, Assistant Master of Trinity College, Cambridge, 1859–63.
92 See 'Diary of the Journey of Philip Julius, through England, 1602', in G. von Bulow and W. Powell (eds), *Transactions of the Royal Historical Society*, n.s., vi (1892), p. 35.
93 H. Gunning, *Reminiscences of the University Town and County of Cambridge from the year 1780* (Cambridge, 1854), pp. 40–2.
94 Francis Coventry, *The History of Pompey the Little* (Cambridge, 1978 edition), pp. 179–9.
95 See A.C. Croome, *Fifty Years of Sport at Schools and Universities* (Oxford, 1913), pp. 174–86.
96 See *Sporting Magazine*, 63 (Dec. 1823), 110.
97 E.D. Cumming (ed.), *Squire Osbaldestone: His Autobiography* (London, 1927), p. 10 and R. Onslow, *The Squire* (London, 1980).
98 'Captain John White', *Baily's Magazine*, 4 (Dec.–June 1862), 271.
99 'Lays of Modern Oxford', Sports and Pastimes at the Universities, *Baily's Magazine*, 53 (Jan.–June), 364–5.
100 Quoted in L. Edwards, *Famous Foxhunters* (London, 1932), p. 77.
101 Letter from F.W.M. Cornwallis to F. Kempson in *Trinity Foot Beagles*, p. 36. And see, 'Oxford and Cambridge Sports Histories', *Baily's Magazine*, 89 (Jan.–June 1908), 101–11.
102 Cambridge University Archives, Magdalene College, C/SAD/1, no iii, letter from Richard Neville, 5 Dec. 1910.
103 Henry J. Haines, Letter to *Baily's Magazine*, quoted in Kempson, *Trinity Foot Beagles*, p. 102.
104 'J.W. Larnach', *Baily's Magazine*, 75 (Jan.–June 1901), 398–9. Of course, it was not uncommon for even the highly intelligent to leave the ancient universities without a degree. Evelyn Waugh, John Betjeman, Alan Pryce-Jones and Roger Hollis all left Oxford without degrees as late as the 1920s. See W.J. West, *The Truth About Hollis* (London, 1989), p. 15.
105 R. Hyam, *A History of Magdalene College* (Cambridge, 1992), p. 201.
106 W. Everett, *On the Cam: Lectures on the University of Cambridge* (London, 1866), pp. 18, 151.
107 Latimer Neville, Rev., 6th Baron Braybrooke (1827–1904). He was educated at Eton and Magdalene. Fellow of Magdalene 1849, Vice Chancellor of Oxford University 1859–1861, Rector of Heydon, Herts, 1851–1902, Rural Dean of Saffron Walden 1879–1897. In 1902 he succeeded to the title of 6th Lord Braybrooke.
108 'The Appanage of Audley End', *Spectator*, 23 (Jan. 1904), 1201.
109 A. Briggs, *Victorian People* (London, 1965), p. 152.
110 See W.B. Gallie, *An English Public School* (London, 1949).
111 See Mangan, *Athleticism*, p. 142.
112 S. Sproston, *College Magazine*, Cambridge, 3, 4 (1910), 65–9,108–10.
113 A. Edgecumbe, 'Magdalene College, Cambridge: A Retrospect' (unpublished ms, Magdalene College, Old Library), 2.
114 Ibid, p. 3.
115 Kempson, *Trinity Foot Beagles*, pp. 172–3.
116 Crossley, *Hunt*, Ch. 2.
117 Little-go. This was the preliminary examination taken by all undergraduates.
118 Rowland Hunt was a supreme example of the highly regarded all-round athlete. See Kempson, *Trinity Foot Beagles*, pp. 104–5 and 'Rowland Hunt' *Baily's Magazine*, 59 (Jan.–June 1893), 145.
119 'Magdalene in the sixties', *Magdalene College Magazine* (March 1910), 106.
120 Ibid.
121 Letter to Mrs Scott, in Mrs Charles Kingsley (ed.), *Charles Kingsley, Letters and Memories*, Vol. 2 (London, 1877), p. 198.
122 O. Chadwick, 'Kingsley at Cambridge', *Historical Journal*, 18 (1975), 305–6.
123 Charles Kingsley, *Glaucus: or the Wonders of the Shore* (London, 1855), p. 43.

124 J. Edgcumbe, 'Magdalene College, a Retrospect'. See also, D. Newsome, *On the Edge of Paradise, A.C. Benson the Diarist* (London, 1980), pp. 184–5.
125 See J.A. Mangan, 'Coubertin and Cotton: European Realism and Idealism in the Making of Modern Masculinity', Proceedings of the First Conference of the European Society for Sports History (Rome, 1996), *passim*.
126 R. Holt, *Sport and the British: A Modern History* (Oxford, 1993), p. 364. For a fuller and more subtle discussion of 'fair play', see J.A. Mangan, 'The Nordic World and Other Worlds', in Henrik Meinander and J.A. Mangan (ed.), *The Nordic World: Sport in Society* (London, 1997), pp. 180–3.
127 'John Poyntz Spencer', *Baily's Magazine* (Dec.–June 1862), 273.
128 'H. Wentworth-Fitzwilliam', *Baily's Magazine*, 489 (1888), 231.
129 'The Duke of Bedford', *Baily's Magazine*, 1 (1860), 51.
130 Newsome, *Godliness*, pp. 224–5.
131 For one example of many, see *Eton Chronicle*, 27 Sept. 1864.
132 See, for example, *The Journal Book* (1867).
133 J. Brinsley-Richards, *Seven Years at Eton (1857–1864)* (London, 1883), pp. 90–1.
134 See, for example, Eton College Hunt, 1–4, *Diaries*, 1899–1906, p. 83.
135 For a good part of the nineteenth century King's College was the Cambridge College for Etonians, while 'the Ancient Universities' in the words of Noel Annan were 'little more than finishing schools for public schoolboys', see Mangan, *Athleticism*, p. 122.
136 Christopher Hibbert, *No Ordinary Place: Radley College and the Public School System 1847–1997* (London, 1998), p. 195.
137 Jean Moorcroft Wilson, *Siegfried Sassoon, The Making of a War Poet* (London, 1995), pp. 111–12.
138 Ibid., p. 111
139 Ibid., p. 112.
140 Ibid., p. 111.
141 Ibid.
142 Ibid., p. 112.
143 Clive Dewey, 'Socratic Teachers: Part 1 – The Opposition to the Cult of Athleticism at Eton 1870–1914', *International Journal of the History of Sport*, 12, 1 (April 1995), 51.
144 Ibid.
145 Ibid.
146 Ibid. See also Part II, *IJHS*, 12, 3 (1995), 18–47.
147 Dunning and Sheard, *Barbarians, Gentlemen and Players*, p. 78.
148 N. Vance, 'The Ideal of Manliness', in B. Simon and I. Bradley (eds), *The Victorian Public School* (Dublin, 1975), pp. 1–7.
149 H. Hutchinson, 'The Sportsman at School', *Badminton Library*, 1 (Aug.–Dec. 1895), 614.
150 Ibid., 629.
151 T.F. Dale, *The History of the Belvoir Hunt* (London, 1899), p. 40.

Chapter 2

English elementary education revisited and revised

Drill and athleticism in tandem

J.A. Mangan and Colm Hickey

In a relatively recent article, Stephen Humphries surveyed the current ideological battleground between liberal orthodoxy and Marxist revisionism.[1] In his view, the liberals maintain that the growth of state education was democratic and progressive in both intention and effect. Their Marxist critics argue that this argument fails to set the evolution of state education realistically within a wider framework of social and political mandates. Most importantly, they maintain, such a view fails to acknowledge the bureaucratic response to demands for class control derived from a view of state schooling as a means to maintain and sustain capitalist society.

Two criticisms can be made of the revisionists: they exaggerate the importance of a minority of legislators who were concerned with notions of class control and, as a corollary, they adopt a point of view advanced by Gwyn Williams in which he argues that it was virtually impossible for the working class to resist the dominant culture or to generate independent ideas and actions.[2] This consideration of the ideology of athleticism in selected London elementary schools before the Great War advances an argument that is less simplistic and which reflects more complex working-class reactions and responses to their schooling.

The Education Act of 1870 made provision for the establishment of local school boards throughout England and Wales. They were to be responsible for the organisation of elementary education in their area. Such School Boards quickly mushroomed all over the country. This essay will concentrate on London. Elections for the London School Board were held on Tuesday, 29 November 1870. Its area of responsibility was to be the same as the existing Metropolitan Board of Works, a grand total of 114 square miles. London was divided into ten administrative districts: City, Southwark, Chelsea, Greenwich, Lambeth, Tower Hamlets, Hackney, Westminster, Finsbury and Marylebone. The number of representatives for each area depended on its size and the elections held were significant in two respects: they used the secret ballot and women were allowed to stand

Originally published in *The European Sports History Review*, 1999, 1, pp. 63–91. http://www.tandf.co.uk/journals

as candidates: two were elected, Miss Emily Davies, the female emancipationist, and Dr Elizabeth Garrett (later Garrett-Anderson), the first woman doctor. The task facing the Board was enormous. London's population was 3,265,005. There were 681,000 children aged between three and thirteen. Some 97,307 were educated at home or attended schools which charged more than 9d. per week, taking them out of the social class for whom elementary schools were meant to cater. Another 9,101 were officially classed as 'inmates of institutions'. Then there were children who were too young to attend school, working at home or abroad, ill, disabled or ineligible for other reasons.[3] This left 454,783 to be educated by the Board.

Faced with this vast undertaking what, therefore, were the aims of the members of the London School Board? David Rubenstein identifies three main points of view held by the board members.[4] The main preoccupation of the Conservatives was to maintain the status quo. Many Conservatives were suspicious of popular education, believing that if the mental horizons of the working class were enlarged they might get ideas above their station and this would subvert the existing social order. The Conservatives, says Rubenstein, 'initially at least [were] opposed to compulsory education, to free elementary schools, and to advanced, or higher grade elementary schools. That they contributed to the introduction of these reforms indicates that their tactics changed in response to pressure; the ends, however, remained constant'.[5] The Conservatives, Rubenstein further asserts, were particularly concerned with the level of the School Board Rate and the position of Anglican schools believing that church schools would 'encourage both working class docility and lower rates'.[6] They also opposed higher grade schools. Lord George Hamilton, a conservative who was to become Chairman of the London School Board in the 1890s, observed that the function of the School Board should be:

> To give the children of the working mass a sound, a compact and a thorough education in those subjects which children during the limited time they were at school could master . . . What ought to be resolutely fought was any attempt to grasp a secondary system of graded education and applying it to the education of the School Board. Such an education . . . would be bad for the children, bad for the teachers and worse for the ratepayers.[7]

The Liberals, although sharing similar social backgrounds to the Conservatives, looked at things rather differently. Liberals and Socialists comprised the Board's Progressive faction. 'The Liberals', states Rubinstein, 'believed that a well-educated working class was an aim desirable in itself. But additionally, it was also an important means of securing economic advance and social mobility'.[8] E. Lyulph Stanley, vice-chairman of the London School Board and a prominent member of the Progressives, declared at the time:

> We want our lower classes to be educated . . . We want them in the schools and in the homes to learn the self respect of citizens, to feel their responsibility as voters, to have the self restraint, the thoughtfulness, the power of

judging and weighing evidence, which should discipline them in the exercise of the great power they now wield by their industrial combinations and through their political action.[9]

For their part, the Socialists, while broadly in sympathy with the Liberals, were often prepared to advance what were often unpopular ideas with the Board. The Rev. Stewart Healam, for example, demanded that board school education should make children discontented 'with the evil circumstances that surround them...not indeed with that state of life into which it shall please God to call them, but with that evil state into which anarchy and monopoly has [*sic*] forced them, so that by their own organised and disciplined effort they may lead fuller lives... in a more beautiful world'.[10]

The Board was dominated by the Progressives. As mentioned earlier, their aims were the provision of good basic education, the creation of an educational ladder and the 'civilising' of the working classes. The first two of these aims it can be said were widely achieved. The last one is contentious for it raises a whole host of issues concerning the relationship between working-class culture and values of the consumers – the children, and middle-class culture and values of the providers – the School Boards. Physical Education provides an excellent example of how the School Boards approached what in their view was the mutually supportive needs of their children and society and will be the focus of this chapter.

Peter McIntosh believes that the introduction of military drill into the curriculum of Board schools in 1871, which attempted to ensure 'attendance at drill under a competent instructor for not more than two hours a week and twenty weeks in the year', was designed mainly as a disciplinary measure. He writes:

Four features of this administrative measure are noteworthy. First it was permissive legislation, and no obligation was put upon any school to provide physical education. Secondly, physical education was permitted for boys only... Thirdly, the permitted physical education took the form of military drill. The Education Department made arrangements with the War Office for instruction by drill sergeants at the rate of sixpence a day and a penny a mile marching money... Fourthly, the main purpose of this drill was disciplinary. The exercises in the words of the Committee's *Report*, 'would be sufficient to teach the boys habits of sharp obedience, smartness, order and cleanliness'. The fact that the Franco-Prussian War had broken out in the year preceding the issue of the new code may have been partly responsible for the strong military flavour of the regulations.[11]

McIntosh's explanation for the absence of organised games (increasingly popular, of course, in the private schools of the privileged) from the curriculum of Board schools is that it was a widely held view that drill was most suitable for the working classes and games were most suitable for the middle and upper classes. Matthew Arnold appears to have held this view. He endorsed the need for physical education in the elementary school, but advocated gymnastics rather than games because if boys worked long hours then gymnastics would be better for their health than games. 'It suggests', writes McIntosh quite reasonably, 'that he assumed that there should be one type of physical education for the ruling class and a different one for the masses.'[12] This view, in fact, was made explicit by Wallace MacLaren, who in a preface to a new edition of his father's [Archibald] book on Physical Education in 1895, asserted:

> On the one hand we have to deal with the upper and middle classes, in fact with all that large class who are sent to private and public schools or training colleges for their education, and proceed to the army, to the universities or to business life. On the other side is the still larger class of those whom the nation still educates, a class which the subject of gymnastics may be thought to touch more nearly, in as much as, after an early age, they have little or no time for recreation like those socially above them, and the gymnasium is therefore to them a vital source of health.[13]

He went on to claim that the physical requirements of the two classes were in themselves distinct, and should be dealt with from altogether different standpoints.[14]

McIntosh paints a bleak picture of games provision in elementary schools in the early twentieth century:

> In 1900 and again in 1906 organised games received tardy recognition as a possible means of physical education and were officially allowed by the Board to be a suitable alternative to Swedish drill or physical exercises. The hard realities of the situation prevented a very large number of children from benefiting from this innovation of policy. As recently as 1895 Her Majesty's Inspector for the Metropolitan Division had estimated that there were 25,000 school children within a mile of Charing Cross who had no playground at all and very few playgrounds worth the name were to be found in the whole of London.[15]

Thus he gives the clear impression that at this time physical education in the shape of games was virtually non-existent in elementary schools, that the schools had very poor facilities and that games were seen by the Board as either unnecessary or unsuitable for elementary school children. As will be shown below, non-existence was not necessarily the case. For one thing playgrounds were not park playing fields! The absence of games has been exaggerated both prior to and after 1900.

The formal introduction of games came about, according to McIntosh, through the appointment of officials to the Board of Education who believed strongly in their educational value: 'Fortunately for physical education Robert Morant, an ardent Old Wykehamist, who became Permanent Secretary of the Board of Education, was as keen on the physical welfare and physical development of children as he was on administrative tidiness.'[16] The man directly responsible for the inclusion of games in curriculum time, according to McIntosh, was A.P. Graves, HMI, who had written an article in the *Contemporary Review* in 1904, in which he deplored the way in which school playgrounds were so little used and called for the introduction of games into elementary schools. Graves subsequently met Augustine Birrell who had succeeded Lord Londonderry as Head of the Board of Education. Birrell told his Chief HMI, E.G.A. Holmes, to discuss the matter with Graves. He did. In 1906 organised games, namely cricket, hockey and football, were introduced in school hours. There were other crucial reasons rather than a failure to utilise unused space why games were seen as desirable for elementary pupils. The Board now accepted that discipline, *esprit de corps*, and fair play could be acquired through the games field, with the result that a new conception of the content of public elementary education now became *de rigueur*.[17]

McIntosh's explanation for the introduction of games into the elementary school when they arrived, is supported by H.C. Barnard:

> Health education should be not merely palliative, or even preventative, but still more positive. The increasing realisation of this fact has been shown by the development of all kinds of physical activity, designed not merely to strengthen the bodies of pupils, but also as an integral part of the 'education of the whole man'. Here again something is due to the influence of Morant.[18]

McIntosh has neatly summed up the developments in physical education in the years leading up to the First World War in a classic exposition of liberal orthodoxy.

> Between 1900 and 1914 physical education in elementary schools had taken great strides forward. Military drill persisted in many places as a legacy from the past, but military training as official policy had been left in the ditch, and armed with the 1909 syllabus of which nearly 100,000 copies were sold within a year of its publication, inspectors, organisers, and teachers marched along the road to therapeutic physical training. Some even had visions of a more liberal physical education beyond.[19]

McIntosh's belief that the disparity of games provision was a reflection of priorities in society has wider support: 'Games, ostensibly the main means of transmitting the concept of fair play, and until 1900 denied by the state to the elementary school [and afterwards not greatly encouraged there] were part of a definition of selective education, but more than that they were evident symbols of the disparate dispensation of national resources among the classes.'[20]

The general view is that the physical education received by children in elementary schools in curriculum time after 1872 and before 1906 was drill. After 1872, drill, of course, had proved to be a contentious issue. Initially, it was seen as a desirable part of the curriculum. David Smith, for example, has pointed out that 'concentration on drill would obviously be approved by the militarists, and by others who believed that physical training should complement an instrumentary education. They saw the result, the acquisition of the physical equivalent of literacy, as paying dividends in better and more obedient workers, servants and soldiers.'[21] Smith also makes the point that militarists argued that as the upper and middle classes financed elementary schools through the rates, it was only reasonable that the state should obtain a return in the form of drill as basic military preparation. They further argued that discipline would improve: 'A basic belief in the effectiveness of the transfer of training encouraged the view that the way to civilise the street arabs and hooligans was to drill them into habits of instant obedience, a training held to be eminently suitable for the character of the recipients.'[22]

In London, the School Board, presumably acting on this belief, in 1872 appointed Regimental Major William Sheffield as Drill Master on a salary of £2.10.0d per week. Sheffield organised courses in drill for serving teachers who became qualified to teach drill in Board schools. Sheffield died in 1888 and the Board then appointed two men – Allan Broman from Sweden, who had been trained in what was known as the Swedish system of gymnastics, and Thomas Chesterton to oversee the implementation of an 'English' system of drill.

Chesterton's English 'system' was, in fact, little more than a reworking of existing military drill exercises with references to military words and phrases omitted. Indeed Chesterton admitted that much of his system was unoriginal: 'I do not, in any way claim to have originated the whole, the classification and adaptation being the chief points claimed as original.' He continued that his 'system' was 'compiled after the careful and practical test of the whole of the methods taught on the Continent in which I was guided by the experience of twenty years gained in teaching physical culture in all its branches.'[23] Chesterton explicitly stated that his system was not military in flavour. He wrote:

'The various systems in vogue on the Continent, though their primary object is undoubtedly an educational one, have another object in view – viz the laying of a foundation for future military service under a system of conscription.... Hence any Continental system built on these lines is unsuitable for adoption in its entirety in this country.[24]

This assertion was quite specious. Although Chesterton maintained that his system was not military in origin and nature, he was later forced to admit that in fact it was! When he gave evidence on his own system to The Royal Commission on Physical Training (Scotland) 1903, he stated that 'Military drill is indispensable in securing discipline and a ready response to orders', yet he then went on to say that 'It is erroneous to suppose ... that the system is a military one although all the exercises contained in the military system are contained therein.' Questioned by one of the Commissioners as to why, if he claimed that his drill was for children, he sometimes referred to it as military drill, he answered weakly:

Well, we will call it drill if you like. It is based on military lines ... In my book I do not call it 'military drill'; I call it 'drill and military exercises', but the drill that I teach is solely military drill, but I leave out the word military. It is advisable in many cases to do so.[25]

Chesterton's duplicity on this point is very probably due to the fact that the London School Board did not allow military drill to be taught directly in its schools. Indeed, the Board of Education had insisted since 1895 that 'the higher grant for Discipline and Organisation will not be paid to any school in which provision is not made for instruction in Swedish or other drill or suitable physical exercises'.[26]

However, the reality as distinct from the theory was made clear in 1901. A committee established to look at the curricula of Training Colleges commented:

> All the systems that are in use at the present time are founded on the army system, but each local instructor wants to make a book to sell; it is a laudable desire; and so he pads it up with a certain amount that is merely exhibition or decorative or amusing, adds pictures and music until the book will sell for three shillings or whatever the price may b.... .[27]

This distinction between reality and theory, incidentally, is overlooked by Richard Holt, the historian of British sport, in his too slight pronouncements on drill in English elementary education.[28] In addition, he fails to appreciate the commitment to drill, military or otherwise, among politicians, educationists and others at this time.

Chesterton, incidentally, firmly believed in the value of games. In his book *The Theory of Physical Education* published in 1895, he provided the classic Victorian justification for playing games:

> In addition to developing bodily powers, boys' games exercise a powerful influence in forming individual character. They promote good temper, self-control, self-reliance, endurance, patience, courage under defeat, promptness and rapid judgement. Mutual goodwill and the advantages of co-operation are taught by the companionship associated with the performance of games. Much of the success in after life may be attributed to the qualities developed in boyhood, by the healthy, spirited games of school life.[29]

Athleticism, as it was now very well known, was an ideology born and nurtured in the public schools,[30] which by a process of 'reverse social osmosis' steadily permeated the late nineteenth-century and early twentieth-century grammar schools which increasingly emulated the upper middle-class public schools and attempted to distance themselves from the public elementary schools.[31] The explanation, as discussed earlier, for the extensive official non-adoption of athleticism by the elementary schools is that the acquisition of the playing fields necessary for the ideology to flourish fully was beyond the means of the schools and that funds were denied them – as they certainly were – by the state for playing fields after 1872, as a reflection of priorities in public education.

A rather dramatic description of these priorities is provided by Humphries adopting a position 'similar to that of the emerging revisionist school of Marxist

sociologists and historians who during the past decade have challenged the
method and metaphor upon which the orthodox literature on youth has been
based'.[32] Humphries maintains that the state elementary schooling system 'was
not designed to impart literacy, skills and knowledge as ends in themselves.
Instead learning was conceived as a means to an end – it made the pupil more
amenable to a socialisation process, through which his or her character and future
lifestyle might be shaped.'[33] He endorses, in short, the classic education for social
control thesis. He does concede wisely that games were introduced into elementary schools after 1906 but argues that 'the inclusion of games and sports in the
school curriculum was justified in terms of their encouragement of a corporate
spirit and their development of the physical strength and moral fibre of working
class youth – thus contributing to imperial success and stability'.[34]

In short, with the proletariat controlled in the Metropolis, the natives were to
be controlled in the colonies – and the elementary schools were to be part of the
process. While there is some truth in this, it is hardly the whole truth. In fact it is
a considerable simplification.[35]

At the outset, the term athleticism requires definition. In what is widely recognised
as the most authoritative study of the subject, it is described as:

> Physical exercise... taken, considerably and compulsorily, in the sincere
> belief of many, however romantic, misplaced or myopic, that it was a highly
> effective means of inculcating valuable instrumental and impressive educa-
> tional goals: physical and moral courage, loyalty and cooperation, the capacity
> to act fairly and take defeat well, the ability to command and obey.[36]

Of course, games had a multiplicity of functions, including control, pleasure,
recreation and fitness, but the primary educational purpose was moral – the
inculcation of the qualities outlined above.

This was true also of athleticism in elementary education. This is hardly
surprising. After 1906 the introduction of athleticism into the elementary schools
was state pedagogical policy and this policy was in the hands of public school educated state officials. In addition, for some decades earlier the London (and other)
teacher training colleges had increasingly embraced this public school ideology
and their products left these institutions imbued with a sense of the moral value
of team games and took this moral conviction into the elementary school.[37]

Thus when reference is made below to the introduction and assimilation of
athleticism into elementary education earlier than 1906, this is neither casual, nor
unfounded, nor surprising. It has however, been substantially overlooked. If the
complex nature of drill and full significance of drill in the elementary school have
been carelessly dismissed by at least one historian of sport,[38] generally the presence prior to 1906 of the influential philosophy and practice of athleticism has
also been casually ignored. While it is true that records of elementary schools are
in short supply in contrast to those of the public schools, happily sources are being
discovered which ensure that the pedagogical history of elementary education is

being slowly re-written. Perhaps even more to the point, the presence of the ideology of athleticism in the teacher training colleges is now being revealed along with the presence of public school educated staff who brought their educational precepts and practices to these institutions and widened their pedagogical rationale and activities. Furthermore, the Cross Commission of 1888 lent its weight, both directly and indirectly, to the espousal of athleticism in the Training Colleges – and thus the elementary schools. The ideology faced many difficulties in these schools and it is unlikely that it had the same powerful impact as in the public schools. The reasons for this are obvious and will be set out later, but the point is that the ideology existed, was promulgated and was absorbed in the schools.

Athleticism, therefore, as is now well established, was initially an upper- and middle-class means of coercing and controlling and cajoling large numbers of boys in public schools in the mid-nineteenth century.[39] Once, however, control had been achieved it evolved into an educational rationale to sustain imperial masculinity.[40] In this process, and in time, the ideology spread to the teacher training colleges. How far, and in what ways, did it permeate the elementary schools of England and the hearts and minds of working-class boys? The difficulties in answering these questions are readily apparent. The amount of documentary, or other archival material that has survived is fragmentary and limited and the material that does survive tends to be a bland record of special events that took place during official school hours like the anodyne one-lined entry 'the School Manager visited today'.[41] Furthermore, days often go unrecorded. In addition, extra-curricular activities are not always recorded in School Log Books. Finally, the overwhelming evidence that does survive tends to have been written by those who were involved in the delivery of education: HMIs, School Board Managers, Headmasters or those who compiled Official Reports and Commissions. This poses an obvious problem. How is it possible to find out how athleticism was received by the children themselves?

There is one thing that can be asserted with confidence: athleticism in the public schools and grammar schools of England and Wales between 1870 and 1914 was not the same as athleticism in elementary schools in London between 1870 and 1914. There are a number of basic reasons for this. Perhaps the most important is that public schools were independent of state control. If a headmaster wanted to introduce athleticism in his school he had far more latitude to do so than an elementary school headmaster answerable to his Manager, the School Board and the Board of Education, who laid down precisely which subjects were to be taught in his school. Then elementary schools dealt with children from the ages of five or six to 14, whereas public and grammar schools contained children from 11 to 19. Many public schools and some grammar schools had a boarding element: elementary schools did not. There is the matter of facilities and their expense: public schools were wealthy schools for wealthy people; grammar schools were comfortable schools for children of comfortable people; elementary schools were schools for children of poor people. Finally, the matter of facilities affected staff as well as pupils – staff at public schools and many at grammar schools would have had the privilege and advantage of an 'Oxbridge' games – playing education while elementary school teachers would have spent one or two years at a far less privileged residential training college. However, despite these considerable differences, athleticism was so pervasive and dominant an ideology that it was adapted to suit the conditions of the elementary schools and did bring new values and ideals into these schools while at the same time having these ideals and values modified by working-class experience.

Athleticism in the elementary schools, this enquiry suggests, went through a number of recognisable phases. The first involved the pioneering efforts of a number of influential headteachers who acted as proselytisers for this new ideology before as well as after 1906. The second involved a period of reinforcement which saw the expansion of schools sports and games organisation. The third saw the growth of a muted rhetoric which sustained the ideology, the fourth and final phase produced the official recognition and legitimisation of the ideology through the inclusion of games playing in the formal curriculum. Of course, it must be appreciated that there was often overlap between these stages.

One point should be laboured. While it is difficult to be precise about when games playing began in the schools and while it is clear that games were not officially allowed in curriculum time until 1906. It is also quite clear that elementary schoolboys were playing games under teacher supervision certainly as early as 1885! Of course, even before this date boys were playing team games outside of school time. F.H. Spencer, for example, who was born into a working-class family in Swindon in 1872, recalled that he had become 'boy secretary of a home-made cricket club which played or attempted to play less primitive cricket'.[42]

The men who were responsible for the introduction of athleticism as an educational ideology into the elementary schools of England before and after 1906, had themselves been exposed to it in their training colleges. In London the early pioneers of this ideology included W.J. Wilson of Oldridge Road Board School, Balham, and J.G. Timms of Rosendale Road Board School, Lambeth. W. J. Wilson is arguably the most significant of this pair. In 1885 he established the South London Schools' Football Association. Wilson used *The Schoolmaster*, the official newspaper of the National Union of Teachers, to promote the Association and to encourage schools to become affiliated. By 1888 the Association had both a senior and junior section and Wilson politely issued their 'invitation' to the Annual General Meeting: 'all teachers [Board and Voluntary] in South London, interested in our popular winter pastime, are kindly requested to attend'.[43]

The following year saw two significant developments. The first was a match between South London Schools and Chatham Schools in Chatham with the money raised going to the Orphanage Fund of the NUT, and the second was the printing of a pamphlet 'How to Start and Manage a Football Club', which was distributed at the Annual General Meeting of the Association. The success of the Association can be seen from the fact that by 1891 sixteen schools were regular members as Table 1 shows.

Table 1 South London Schools Football Association 1890–91[44]

	Played	Won	Drawn	Lost	Points
Seniors					
Nunhead passage	10	9	0	1	18
Oldridge Road	10	7	1	2	15
Hasselrigge Road	10	5	1	4	11
Goodridge Road	10	5	0	5	10
St Mary's Balham	10	2	2	6	6
Belle Ville	10	0	0	10	0
Juniors					
St Mathews Brixton	18	17	1	0	35
Hackford Road	18	14	1	3	29
Eltringham Street	17	11	3	3	25
Bellenden Road	17	10	1	6	21
Priory Grove	18	8	5	5	21
Upper Kennington Lane	18	8	1	9	17
Heber Road	18	5	3	10	13
Springfield	18	6	1	11	13
Southwark Park	18	2	0	16	4
St Thomas	18	0	0	18	0

Wilson proved to be both an energetic Association secretary and a successful headmaster. His school, Oldridge Road, opened on Monday, 26 June 1882 with 85 boys. As a games enthusiast Wilson was soon organising a series of fundraising events for his school teams. He established a regular feature of an evening's entertainment at which the proceeds went to the sports fund. For example, the Log Book for 16 November 1888 reads: 'The Children's Operetta of Golden Hair was repeated on Wednesday for the third time in aid of the funds for the school sports. The first performance was in aid of the Teachers Orphanage and Benevolent Fund. The proceeds of the concerts amounted to over £42.'[45] Wilson's efforts were appreciated by his local Board Manager, W.J. Rogers. In the Government Report of 1888 he noted: 'Cricket, Football and Swimming Clubs exist in connection with this school to the obvious benefit of the boys.'[46]

Whatever else he was, Wilson was certainly an enthusiast. Almost any and every sporting and athletic competition was entered with alacrity and generally no little success. For example, for the Annual Drill Competition at the Albert Hall, Wilson closed the school and entered his boys who 'obtained 89 marks out of 100'.[47] Swimming and drill were both part of the curriculum and regular drill displays were given to parents and friends. Against this background of a commitment to swimming and drill in curriculum time and athletics, cricket and football as extra curricular activities, numbers soared. In October 1891, 456 boys were in attendance with an average attendance rate of 90 per cent; in March 1892, 538 boys had an average attendance rate of 93 per cent. In October 1890, he wrote, 'Every week I am refusing children, who apply for admission, unless they have passed Standard II. The reason for this is that Standards I and II are overfull and as all the rest of the school is nearly full I have no room for these fresh applicants.'[48]

Wilson was driven by a threefold desire to improve the health and fitness of the boys, teach them to enjoy games playing for its own sake and to develop in them a competitive spirit. In an article in *The Schoolmaster*, of the South London Schools' Football Association it was claimed:

> South London Teachers give up a lot of their time to teaching the young idea the art of 'leather hunting'. All matches are played on Saturday mornings, so the attendance of the teachers means the sacrifice of a good portion of the weekly holiday...Mr Wilson who is an enthusiastic lover of manly sports is never so happy as when his boys secure a victory, and they have won laurels not only in South London, but at Sheffield, Chatham and elsewhere'.[49]

Wilson was undoubtedly a dedicated and dynamic headmaster. He was a tireless and devoted active member of the influential South London Schools' Football Association – the first elementary schools' football association in the world. However, to what extent was Wilson typical as an elementary school head-master? This is not known at this moment but he was not alone. It is possible to chart athleticism's progress in the London elementary school by providing a fuller picture of its growth in another school, Rosendale Road, in Lambeth.

Rosendale Road was designed by the London School Board's own architect, Thomas Jerram Bailey. Plans for the construction of an elementary school of 238 boys, 238 girls and 277 infants were approved by the Board on the 29 July 1897. The school was officially opened in 1898 in time for the autumn term, although it was housed in temporary accommodation until the permanent buildings were ready on 8 January 1900. Its first headmaster was John Goddard Timms, who had been trained at Borough Road College from 1883 to 1885. When he gradu-ated he was appointed to Paradise Road Board School, Peckham, where he remained until becoming the Headmaster, first of Priory Grove in 1888, and subsequently Rosendale in 1897.

Timms was a conscientious and devoted headmaster. In 1902 the Board's Inspector wrote that:

> The headmaster has made reports not only in each subject, in each class, but on each subject for each child in addition to ordinary numerical results. This elaboration, however, has not prevented him from doing much actual teaching. No Head Teacher have I oftener found teaching a class.[50]

He was also committed to the ethos easing its way down from public school to elementary public school. From the earliest moments, games played an important role in the life of the school. In the first year the Manager's Annual Report noted, 'considerable attention has been paid to cricket and football'.[51]

The earliest surviving Log Book for the school begins in 1903. It is replete with references to games. Between 24 and 29 June, for example, there are five entries relating to games and sports activities, and a detailed and comprehensive record of what had happened during the week. To provide a flavour of Timms' commitment to the period ideology of athleticism these entries require to be quoted in full:

24/06/03 School closed for the South London School Sports. The athletics of the school are flourishing. The Football championship of the South London Schools was nearly secured this season as the boys were the runners up and only succumbed after a good struggle in the final match to a much heavier and stronger team. The boys were winners of the East Lambeth Division section and had a fine record of wins in the football league competition securing medals from the association. The boys were trained by Mr Mingay and in every way did the greatest credit to him and the school. Great pains were taken by the master in securing every benefit possible for the boys from the exercise....

The cricket club and class organisation in connection with it is in a most flourishing condition and the interest taken by the staff all round is most gratifying.

In each classroom a smaller club is organised and the younger boys are looked after by Mr Huggins and Mr Hill, while in the upper divisions Mr Boait has charge of, and is responsible for, the training of the school team being warmly assisted by Mr Mingay. The boys are playing successfully and a miniature league has been formed in the school with the greatest success. The club is over 120 strong and is doing great work among the boys.

The athletics... are also in a successful state and for the South London Schools Festival, the school entered this year 120 competitors from 7 years of age to over 14. The boys have been trained for the past few months and their practices in the evening have been much enjoyed. The Head Teacher who has this year personally undertaken the training of the boys has been heartily assisted in every direction by Mr Boait, Mr Mingay, Mr Huggins and Mr Hill, the latter two masters being present at the sports to look after the boys. The boys easily secured the championship of the South London Schools gaining 90 points in the competition against the next highest 62 points and bringing up their wins to four out of the last five years.

26/06/03 The children who competed in the sports festival were photographed on this day after the close of the afternoon session.

29/06/03 An outing to Ashstead Woods was decided upon for Saturday July 18th as a reward to the competitors at the sports and to commemorate the winning of the championships at sports.[52]

In 1906 the Board of Education permitted, as noted earlier, games to be played in curriculum time. What was seen by McIntosh as a progressive measure was similarly viewed by members of the London County Council. The Day Schools Sub-Committee reported to the LCC on 29 November 1906: 'We are of the opinion that the educational value of organised games is becoming so generally recognised that the Council should be asked to give its authority for their introduction into schools and to make some provision for the expenditure in connections therewith.[53]

Rosendale Road took up games playing in school time enthusiastically. On 21 September 1906 Timms recorded:

> The Head Teacher and his assistant supervised the games and kept those poorly equipped physically, or by nature, encouraged. One boy Shambrook was in an unfit state to strip and had his parents communicated with. The scholars appeared to receive great freshness and benefit from these games and thoroughly enjoyed themselves.[54]

A week later Timms noted that an assistant master, Mr Bartlett, took the boys 'in an excellent match of football with properly laid out ground poles, flags etc. and with sides and captains of each team appointed'. With the result that, 'At 4.20 the scholars were brought back looking bright and fresh and having thoroughly entered into the games.'[55] In October HMI Graves visited the school. The Log Book read: 'From 3 p.m. a section of the school took organised games for the lessons on the timetable and under the supervision of their masters the scholars went into the playing fields and played matches in football. His Majesty's Inspector watched the games proceeding under the instruction of the masters.'[56]

Timms had an influence beyond Rosendale. He was a committee member of the influential South London Schools' Football Association and a man whose advice on sport was widely sought. By 1913 he was contributing to a number of sports conferences and events. On 1 December, for example, the Log Book recorded:

> Visit by Head Teacher to various schools in North Lambeth in connection with organised games to be played in the Archbishop's Park on the afternoons of 8th, 9th, 11th and on one of the mornings; also on the morning of Friday 12th December.[57]

How was Timms able to develop games so successfully in his school? The answer is that he used coercion, rewards and rhetoric to instil into the boys a belief that games were rewarding both physically and morally.

Discipline at Rosendale Road historically had been severe. In his autobiography, *A Cab at the Door*, Victor S. Pritchett, the writer and critic, has recalled rather less than objectively, with a sharp polemic style, and perhaps sour grapes, his school days at Rosendale:[58]

> Discipline was meant to encourage subservience, and to squash rebellion – very undesirable in children who would grow up to obey orders from their betters. No child here would enter the ruling classes unless he was very gifted

and won scholarship after scholarship. A great many boys from these schools did so and did rise to high places; but they had to slave and crush part of their lives, to machine themselves so that they became brain alone. They ground away at their lessons, and, for all their boyhood and youth and perhaps all their lives, they were in the ingenious torture chamber of examination halls. They were brilliant, of course, and some when they grew up tended to be obsequious to the ruling class and ruthless to the rest, if they were not tired out. Among them were many who were emotionally infantile.[59]

However, even Pritchett recognised that under Timms the situation gradually changed:

> A reaction against this fierce system of education had set in at the turn of the century. Socialism and the scientific revolution – which Wells had described – had moved many people. New private schools for the well-off were beginning to break with the traditions of the nineteenth century and a little of the happy influence seeped down to ourselves.[60]

Pritchett is making an important distinction here between the harsh attitudes that existed in many elementary schools in the late nineteenth century and the more 'liberal' outlook increasingly found in the twentieth century. Interestingly, he picks out for special praise the new progressive system of active tutorial work employed in his class by Mr Bartlett, the keen football coach and trainer.

> The other teachers hated him and it; we either made so much noise that the rest of the school could hardly get on with their work, or were so silent that teachers would look over the frosted glass of the door to see if we had gone off for a holiday. Mr Bartlett . . . by some strange magnetism he could silence a class almost without a word. He never used the cane. Since we could make as much noise as we liked, he got silence easily when he wanted it.[61]

Pritchett's account of a more relaxed school is certainly borne out by official statements. The Annual Report of the Inspectors in 1906, for example, commented that, 'Every effort by organised games and by many other means, is made by the staff to maintain a beneficial influence over the scholars outside the ordinary school work.'[62] Such accounts, of course, provide difficulties for historians following Humphries' committed Marxist standpoint. He sees working-class children as being in constant conflict with the teachers:

> The most potent and persistent opposition of working-class children to schooling, however, occurred in the classroom itself. Their enforced confinement in institutions which had little to offer apart from rote learning, rigid discipline and training in manners and morals which were often alien and meaningless, led to a constantly antagonistic atmosphere. . . . This non-cooperative and

sometimes openly hostile behaviour of many children, together with the large size of classes and the inadequately trained or equipped teachers, combined to produce a potentially dangerous conflict situation. Elementary schools attempted to resolve this conflict by tightly regulating the learning situation and by resorting to the traditional authoritarian methods of fear, punishment and physical violence.[63]

Humphries is perhaps too handicapped by Marxist views, by inflexible notions of class and control and dominant and subordinate groups. He is perhaps too quick to present elementary schools and elementary teachers in stereotypical ways. In truth there was variety in London's elementary schools, a fact acknowledged by Pritchett who is surely more accurate in his first-hand analysis.

There were and are good and bad elementary schools in London. They are as nearly as much created by their districts and their children as by their teachers. The children at Rosendale Road, which was a large school, were a mixture of working class and a few middles with a few foreigners and colonials – Germans, Portuguese, Australians, French and one or two Indians. It was a mixed school.[64]

One thing is certain – Rosendale did not fit neatly into Humphries' neat stereotypic paradigm. This is made even clearer by what follows below.
Games evolved successfully in Rosendale through a system of rewards for athletic success. Teams were regularly photographed with an often beaming headmaster[65] and outings for successful teams were arranged. Humphries, predictably, is wary of reading too much into the participation of boys in school sport. In his view, although children may have been enthusiastic, this was because 'Many children clearly welcomed games lessons...as a relief from the monotony of the school routine,'[66] but so do children everywhere! This was even more true in the public schools. Humphries is quick to point out that even where children competed in large numbers their 'enthusiastic participation in school sports did not imply automatic development of the specific character traits intended by the school authorities'.[67] Of course, it did not! Only the naive would claim this. Humphries also takes the jaundiced view that the fact that boys embraced the games cult only served to 'illustrate not only the internalisation of the public school ethos by a working-class boy, but also the process by which the corporate and competitive spirit and the hierarchical control that infused school sports, was reproduced in deference to social superiors.'[68] He quotes an elementary school educated man from Bristol:

I was proud of the school, I used to play football for the school. On Friday afternoons we would 'ave school assembly and whoever was picked for the team, their name was called out and you had to march to the front. The teacher would give you out your 'shirties' as we used to call them. No football knickers or nothing like that...We'd play in the park...The teachers would arrange the teams...We had our own colours, green shirt, 'St Giles for honour, for loyalty, for courage, for courtesy. Play up, play fair, play the game.' When I left school they had one of the finest teams in England.[69]

Is this experience all bad? Perhaps Humphries should reflect a little more deeply and less prejudicially. There is at least one powerful reason to recommend this: games playing, whether it was cricket or football, was not possible within the school curriculum until 1906. Therefore, all training was done in the evenings and all matches were played out of school time and this realistically meant Saturday mornings for St. Giles and all the other schools. Those elementary school children who played games did so in their own leisure time voluntarily and enthusiastically, wholly before, and partially after 1906, and not as a release from the monotonous school curriculum or as an act of deference to social superiors. As remarked earlier, elementary school athleticism, of necessity, was expressed in different ways than in the public and grammar schools.

Athleticism in the elementary school as in public and grammar schools developed its own supportive rhetoric. If Rosendale's Log Book is anything to go by, praise for those selected for sporting competitions – the elementary school 'bloods' – found full expression. And Timms established a Social Club which acted as an Old Scholars Club:

Meeting of the Social Club and Guild and Reunion of Old Scholars. A successful meeting was held with the sanction of the Board on the evening of Wednesday 24th February from 7.30–9.30 p.m. and was attended nearly 200 past and present scholars of the school.[70]

Then in December 1904 Timms founded a school magazine:

The first issue of the school quarterly magazine 'Rosebuds' on this date. The programme of the scholars entertainment being printed with it as a supplement and the magazine itself containing a list of school honours, prizes, medal and certificate winners. The Head Teacher places on record his great appreciation of the services and loyal work and co-operation of the members of his staff in organising and bringing to a successful issue the entertainment and distribution of prizes.[71]

Unfortunately no copy of the magazine survives. However, we do have a single copy of another school's home-produced magazine for 1893, *The Bellenden*, the magazine of Bellenden Road Board School. The magazine was produced by the boys of Standard VI and edited by them and is full of articles about the South London Schools' Sports, and it contains this enthusiastic if ungainly verse:

The Sports

The sports were something lovely
And went off jolly fine
  I hope that they will be repeated
Many and many a time
They cannot be praised too highly
For I'm sure nothing could have been
so highly interesting
For competition was so keen
  Everyone wanted a prize of course
But everyone cannot win
Somebody must be beaten
And to loose [*sic*] is not such a sin
  You fellows are'nt [*sic*] half artful
If there's a chap you want to beat
Take him to the refreshment bar
And stand a jolly good treat
  And when he wants to run
He'l have a pain in his back
And then you'l win the race
Which will be quite exact
  And then if you win a marble clock
Or a nice little watch and chain
You won't need to ask a Policeman
When the time is wanted again
  The prizes were really handsome
But I think that all our mothers
Ought to have raced for the sunlight soap
Presented by Lever Bros.[72]

    If anything illustrates the difference between public school and elementary public school athleticism it is this exceedingly clumsy verse. The central theme of the poem is how to beat an opponent by 'artful' means and win useful prizes! Such sentiments are not normally found in the doggerel in public school magazines in which 'fair play' is celebrated.

    A further way in which the rhetoric of athleticism was sustained was through school songs. In his autobiography Pritchett recalled one dramatic match:

    The school was beaten by Effra Road Higher Grade – boys stayed until fifteen there and were heavier than we were – on a frosty morning, near the railway arches, one to nil. It was a desperate game. The assistant teacher came with us and sang the school song on the touchline, in his weak, Cockney voice. Roses was pronounced 'Rowsis'.

> Roses on the ball, Roses on the ball,
> Never mind the half back line
> The Roses beat them every time.
> Give the ball a swing
> Right over to the wing,
> Roses, Roses, Roses on the ba-a-ll.[73]

Boys, of course, were also influenced by what was said in school lessons and assemblies were especially important. In class they were encouraged to write, stories and verses about games. But whether it was in school time or on Saturday mornings they were nevertheless under teacher supervision. Accordingly, it may be argued – it certainly is by Humphries – that their behaviour was influenced, even determined, by teacher expectations, and then once free from them they would reject the values of the adults. Such a view, again of limited insight, ignores the powerful effect that the public schools' games cult had on young boys through weekly comics and magazines.[74]

Undoubtedly, the two most popular boys' weekly comics were *The Gem* and *The Magnet*, both of which contained stories of life in an imaginary English public school, Greyfriars. The stories about the school were written by Frank Richards, who was born in Ealing on 8 August 1876. His real name was Charles Harold St John Hamilton, but he came to use, and to regard his pseudonym, as his real name. Richards did not go to a public school and in some respects Greyfriars was rather idiosyncratic – in one respect, discussed below, deliberately so. By 1905, after having had a number of stories accepted by various boys' newspapers, he was invited to write for a new newspaper, *The Gem*. He was so successful that he then was asked to contribute to another paper *The Magnet*, and it was in this paper that on 15 February 1908 Greyfriars School and Billy Bunter were born.

In his book *Happiest Days*, Jeffrey Richards analyses the importance of these two papers in shaping and influencing schoolboy reading and behaviour.[75] A number of features stand out about life in Greyfriars. In the first place games are not compulsory and there are no cadet corps, chapel nor houses.

> Most interesting of all, perhaps, is the fact that the Greyfriars boys play association football and not the rugby so integral to the public school ethos. This clearly points to the intended audience of non-public school boys, for whom soccer was the chief sport, an assumption reinforced by the presence in *The Magnet* of a regular soccer column where readers' queries were answered by the Linesman or the Old Ref.[76]

These papers exerted a powerful influence upon the boys of Rosendale Road. Pritchett relates how he was offered them by a friend of his: 'One page and I was entranced. I gobbled these stories as if I were eating pie or stuffing...The Japanese-looking boy was called Nott. He had a friend, called Howard, the son of a compositor. *The Gem* and *The Magnet* united us. We called ourselves by Greyfriars' names and jumped about shouting words like Garoo.'[77] For Pritchett's father, however, the discovery that Victor was reading these papers was an horrific experience:

'Good godfathers', said my father not touching the pile...'I give you your Saturday penny and this is what you're doing with it. Wasting the money I earn. I suppose you think you're so superior because you have a father who has his own business and you spend left and right on muck like this....' 'A man is known by the company he keeps' said my father. And getting up...he threw the whole lot onto the fire.[78]

George Orwell more or less agreed with a reviewer in the *Times Literary Supplement* of 1938 when he wrote that public schoolboys read them till about the age of 12 years; boys at cheap private schools for several more years, but they were certainly read by working-class boys as well.[79] How right he was! *The Gem* and *The Magnet* remained firm favourites at Rosendale Road and other London elementary schools. These weeklies helped shape positive attitudes to the previously middle-class games cult in a way that was very seductive. Coercion, rewards and rhetoric; these then were effective ways in which Timms and his staff promoted athleticism at Rosendale, but as noted above, there were a variety of other factors at work which created the adapted athleticism of the elementary school. As already noted facilities and time were not as readily or fully available to elementary schools as they were to secondary schools – public or grammar.

In passing it should be noted that it was due to the influence of men like Timms that there was a rapid growth in the number of elementary schools football associations well before 1906, as Table 2 shows.

Finally, it should also be noted that there was one further powerful means by which the ideology of athleticism was promoted in the elementary school: diffusion. One influential diffusionist was George Sharpies. He was born in Bolton in 1856, and educated as both a pupil and pupil teacher at Holy Trinity National School. In 1875 he entered St. John's Teacher Training College, Battersea. A brilliant scholar he was Latin prize man in both years at college. He was also one of the top twenty prize men in the country in Mathematics, gaining the Committee of Council on Education prize for Euclid in 1876. After leaving college he became Head of All Saints Church School in Bolton and in 1879, Headmaster of Pikes Lane Board School. By 1881 he had been appointed Organising Master and Inspector of Board Schools in Bolton. In 1883 he moved across the Pennines and was appointed Headmaster of the Spring Grove Board School in Huddersfield. Five years later he became Headmaster of Leeds Central Higher Grade Board School before returning to Lancashire to take up the headship of Waterloo Road Board School, Manchester. Sharpies, incidentally, was an excellent footballer. Apart from representing college he also played for Eagley F.C.

Table 2 Foundation of Elementary Schools'
Football Associations

Year of formation	Association
1886	South London Schools FA
1887	
1888	Sheffield Schools FA
1889	
1890	Manchester Schools FA
	Birmingham Schools FA
	Liverpool Schools FA
	Nottingham Schools FA
	West London Schools FA
1892	Brighton Schools FA
1893	
1894	Leyton Schools FA
	Reading Schools FA
	Newcastle Schools FA
	Sunderland Schools FA
	Leicester Schools FA
1895	Northampton Schools FA
	Leeds School FA
	Oldham Schools FA
	Cardiff Schools FA
1897	Blackburn Schools FA
1898	Hull Schools FA

and ultimately Bolton Wanderers, captaining them in 1882. He retired from playing in 1885 having represented Lancashire and subsequently became a football league referee. Sharpies had no doubt about the value of games, believing that the growth of elementary schools' football 'has done more for the real well-being of the boys of this country than all the drill and callisthenics exercises yet introduced'.[80] He spread the ideals of athleticism widely as a 'roving' headmaster.

Athleticism then gradually developed in the elementary schools of England and Wales from 1870 onwards. Again, the point must be laboured, once more, athleticism in these schools was not the athleticism of the public and grammar schools. The reasons for this have been well rehearsed and do not require detailed repetition. The way in which the ideology could be delivered, of necessity, was different. The twin problems of lack of time and lack of facilities had to be over-come, and they were up to a point. When government regulations proscribed games in school time schools promptly played them after school or on Saturday mornings – a legacy that still survives today. If schools lacked their own playing fields they simply took to the nearest park. The teachers negotiated for facilities with representatives of the Royal Parks, the Archbishop of Canterbury and with local park wardens or philanthropic private individuals.

By the time of the First World War, physical education in English elementary schools had undergone a radical transformation. Originally introduced into the school timetable as military drill and intended as a means of instilling discipline, drill had moved first towards a 'non-military' variety and finally, been assimilated in the early twentieth century, into a physical education programme reflecting a holistic view of education. In particular, team games, which were not allowed originally in the school curriculum or in school time, saw their significance reassessed until they were formally introduced into the curriculum in 1906.

While the elementary schools were still denied the games facilities typical of both public schools and grammar schools well into the twentieth century, in fact, by virtue of staff commitment, training college experience and pupil enthusiasm, the English elementary schools well before the twentieth century in some instances, as illustrated here by London Board Schools, had embraced the philosophy and practice of the upper middle-class ideology of athleticism. Drill and games went in tandem. If it is unacceptably casual to dismiss drill in the elementary school as a rudimentary exercise for elementary school children, and to fail to be aware of the significance of, and support for, military drill in the late nineteenth and early twentieth centuries,[81] it is equally casual to view the elementary schools as locations simply for the practice of drill-military or 'non-military'. This is to fail to recognise the role of teacher training colleges in the diffusion and dissemination of athleticism in Britain and its empire,[82] and to fail to be aware of the proselytising efforts of its products at home and abroad. W.J. Wilson and J.G. Timms, and in time others, some known and some as yet unknown, are ensuring that the history of English elementary schools is being both revisited and revised.

Notes

1 S. Humphries, 'Hurrah for England: Schooling and the Working Class in Bristol 1870–1914', *Southern History*, 1 (1979), 171–207.
2 Gwyn Williams, 'The Concept of Egomania in the Thought of Antonio Gramsci', *Journal of the History of Ideas*, 21 (1960), 586–99.
3 For a full account of the establishment of the London School Board see S. Maclure, *One Hundred Years of London Education* 1870–1970 (London, 1970).
4 David Rubenstein, 'Socialization and the London School Board 1870–1904: Aims, Methods and Public Opinion', in P. McCann (ed.), *Popular Education and Socialization in the Nineteenth Century* (London, 1977), pp. 231–64.
5 Ibid., pp. 239–40.
6 Ibid., p. 240.
7 *The Times*, 25 November, 1891, 7, quoted in Rubenstein, p. 243.
8 Rubenstein, 'Socialization', p. 242.
9 E. Lyulph Stanley, *Our National Education* (London, 1899), pp. 139–40 quoted in Rubenstein, 'Socialization', p. 243.
10 D. Rubenstein, 'Annie Beasant and Stewart Headlam: the London School Board Elections of 1888', *East London Papers*, 13 (Summer 1970), 10–11.
11 P. C. McIntosh, *P.E. in England since 1800* (2nd edn) (London, 1968), p. 109.
12 P. C. McIntosh. 'Games and Gymnastics for Two Nations in One', in P.C. McIntosh (ed.). *Landmarks in the History of Physical Education* (London, 1981), p. 202.

13 Ibid., p. 202.
14 Ibid., p. 202.
15 Ibid., p. 209.
16 McIntosh, *P.E.*, p. 145.
17 Ibid., pp. 146–7.
18 H. C. Barnard, *A History of English Education from 1760* (2nd edn) (London, 1961), p. 226.
19 McIntosh, *P.E.*, pp. 168–9.
20 J.A. Mangan, 'Imitating their Betters and Dissociating from their Inferiors: Grammar Schools and the Games Ethic in the Late Nineteenth and Early Twentieth Centuries', *Proceedings of the 1982 Annual Conference of the History of Education Society of Great Britain* (Leicester, 1983), p. 22.
21 W. D. Smith, *Stretching their Bodies* (London, 1974), p. 88.
22 Ibid., p. 90.
23 T. Chesterton, 'Physical Education under the School Board for London', in M.E. Sadler (ed.), *Special Reports on Educational Subjects* (London, 1898), p. 188.
24 Ibid, p. 188.
25 *Royal Commission on Physical Training* (Scotland, 1903), p. 154.
26 McIntosh, *P.E.*, p. 118.
27 PRO *Committee on Training Colleges Courses of Instruction*, 1901, 1, p. 184. Ed 24 68B.
28 See Richard Holt, 'Contrasting Nationalisms: Sport, Militarism, and the Unitary State in Britain and France before 1914', in J.A. Mangan (ed.), *Tribal Identities: Nationalism, Europe, Sport* (London, 1996), p. 90. Holt states that elementary school drill was brief, basic and by no means uniformly practical. He reveals no awareness of the considerable efforts made by politicians, educationalists and others to promote drill, of the extensive debate on drill and the types of drill for years in the late nineteenth and early twentieth century or of the careful and systematic programmes attempted by educational agencies throughout England at this time. In contrast, for a thorough, detailed and careful consideration of the topic, see Alan Penn, *Targeting the Schools: Drill, Militarism and Imperialism* (London: Cass, 1999), *passim*.
29 T. Chesterton, *The Theory of Physical Education* (London, 1895), pp. 94–5.
30 See J.A. Mangan, *Athleticism in the Victorian and Edwardian Public School. The Emergence and Consolidation of an Educational Ideology* (Cambridge, 1981 and Falmer, 1986).
31 See Mangan, 'Imitating their Betters'.
32 S. Humphries, *Hooligans or Rebels? An Oral History of Working Class Childhood and Youth, 1889–1939* (Oxford, 1981), p. 2.
33 Ibid., p. 31.
34 Ibid., p. 41.
35 See J.A. Mangan, *The Games Ethic and Imperialism* (London, 1986) for a more complete analysis of the role of games in British Imperial purpose. See also J.A. Mangan, 'Prologue: Britain's Chief Spiritual Export: Imperial Sport as a Moral Metaphor, Political Symbol and Cultural Bond', in J.A. Mangan (ed.), *The Cultural Bond: Sport, Empire, Society* (London, 1992), pp. 1–9.
36 Mangan, *Athleticism*, p. 9.
37 See C.F. Hickey, 'Athleticism and the London Training Colleges: the Proletarian Absorption of an Educational Ideology, 1870–1920' (unpublished PhD thesis, University of Strathclyde, 2001).
38 Holt, 'Contrasting Nationalisms', *passim*.
39 Mangan, *Athleticism, passim*.
40 See Mangan, *The Games Ethic and Imperialism, passim*, and J.A. Mangan, 'Duty unto Death: English Masculinity and Militarism in the Age of the New Imperialism', in J.A. Mangan (ed.), *Tribal Identities*, pp. 10–38.
41 A large number of school Log Books covering this period are housed in the Greater London Record Office. They await systematic and thorough examination.

42 F.H. Spencer, *An Inspector's Testament* (London, 1938), p. 31.
43 *The Schoolmaster*, 34, 29 September 1888, p. 388.
44 *The Schoolmaster*, 39, 21 March 1891, p. 541.
45 Greater London Record Office (hereafter GLRO), Oldridge Road School Log Book EO/DIV9/OLD/LB/1, 16 November 1888.
46 Ibid., 15 March 1889.
47 Ibid., 30 June 1891.
48 Ibid., 3 October 1890.
49 *The Schoolmaster*, 39, 16 May 1891, p. 872.
50 Annual Report of Board Inspector, Rosendale Road School, 1902.
51 GLRO Annual Report of Board Manager, Rosendale Road School, EO/PS/12/R40/1, 1897.
52 GLRO Rosendale Road School Log Book, EO/DIV8/ROS/LB/1, 24–29 June 1903.
53 GLRO, *London Council Education Committee Minutes*, 2, 28 November 1906, p. 3628.
54 GLRO Rosendale Road School Log Book, 21 September 1906.
55 Ibid., 28 September 1906.
56 Ibid., 26 October 1906.
57 Ibid., 1 December 1913.
58 V. S. Pritchett, *A Cab at the Door* (New York, 1967). Pritchett was born into a lower middle-class family in Ipswich in 1900. His father was an unsuccessful salesman and the family was constantly in debt. To avoid creditors and landlords the family was always on the move to the extent that by 1911 Pritchett had moved house 18 times and he had lived in Woodford, Palmers Green, Balham, Uxbridge, Acton, Ealing, Hammersmith, Camberwell, Bromley and Dulwich. After Rosendale Pritchett entered Alleyns Grammar School in 1914 from where he drifted into the leather trade before moving to Paris in 1921 subsequently becoming an author, academic and critic.
59 V. S. Pritchett, *A Cab at the Door*, p. 103.
60 Ibid., p. 103.
61 Ibid., p. 104.
62 Annual Report of Board Inspector Rosendale Road School, 1905.
63 Humphries, 'Hurrah for England', p. 190.
64 Pritchett, *A Cab at the Door*, p. 102.
65 The Greater London Record Office houses an extensive collection of photographs of all aspects of life in Elementary Schools.
66 Humphries, *Hooligans or Rebels?*, p. 41.
67 Ibid., p. 42.
68 Ibid.
69 Ibid.
70 GLRO Rosendale Road School Log Book, 24 February 1904.
71 Ibid., 12 December 1904.
72 GLRO The Bellenden, June 1893.
73 Pritchett, *A Cab at the Door*, p. 128.
74 See Jeffrey Richards, *Happiest Days: The Public Schools in English Fiction* (Manchester, 1988), and P. W. Musgrave, *From Brown to Bunter* (London, 1985).
75 Jeffrey Richards, *Happiest Days*.
76 Ibid., p. 277.
77 Pritchett, *A Cab at the Door*, p. 110.
78 Ibid., p. 113.
79 George Orwell, 'Boys' Weeklies', *Horizon*, 1, 3 (1940), 174–200. quoted in Musgrave, *From Brown to Bunter*, p. 230.
80 George Sharpies, 'The organization of games out of school for the children attending public elementary schools in large industrial centres as voluntarily

undertaken by the teachers', in *Special Reports on Educational Subjects*, 2 (London, 1898), pp. 159–84.

81 See Holt, 'Contrasting Nationalisms', but see also the discussion of Holt's shallow consideration of drill in the English elementary school in J.A. Mangan. 'Sport in Society: The Nordic World and Other Worlds', in Henrik Meinander and J.A. Mangan (ed.), *The Nordic World: Sport and Society* (London, 1998), pp. 189–91.

82 See Colm Hickey, 'Athleticism and the London Training Colleges', especially chapters 4, 5 and 6, and J.A. Mangan and Colm Hickey, 'A Pioneer of the Proletariat: Herbert Milnes and the Games Cult in New Zealand', in J.A. Mangan and J. Nauright (eds), *Sport in Australasian Society: Past and Present* (London: Cass, 2000), pp. 31–48.

Part II

Sport, universities and colleges

Chapter 3

'Oars and the man'

Pleasure and purpose in Victorian and Edwardian Cambridge

*J.A. Mangan**

In the year of Victoria's Diamond Jubilee, Hedley Peek, the journalist and author, announced to the English-speaking world through the medium of the *Fortnightly Review* that the past 15 years had witnessed one of the most remarkable revolutions in popular taste to spread throughout Great Britain and Ireland, not to mention many other countries. Sport of various kinds had become 'not only the ruling passion of the people, but well nigh the chief topic of conversation'.[1] With greater perception, he would have appreciated that he had witnessed not merely a recreational but an educational evolution. It was not simply social inclination that had changed, but educational fashion. This change in fashion was neither casual nor spontaneous. The 'mania' he remarked upon had been introduced deliberately into the upper-class educational system. There it became known as 'athleticism', and was eventually considered as an unfortunate obsession with physical activities, especially team games. By 1897, it was a feature of life in both the public schools *and* their 'finishing schools', the Universities of Oxford and Cambridge, for mostly the same reasons.

These reasons have been discussed in *Athleticism in the Victorian and Edwardian Public School*.[2] While not excluding Oxford and Cambridge, this study, of course, concentrated on the upper-class schools. Here the intention is to redress the balance a little; to investigate the 'mania' in a Cambridge college where its hold was especially strong; to argue that, as in the schools, the same forces of hedonism, casuistry, pragmatism and idealism were at work. Perhaps most usefully, since the originality now lies in the evidence rather than in the argument, my intention is to add further to our knowledge of a significant aspect of recent social history – athleticism in the ancient universities. Its consequences were potent. 'Oxbridge' was the matrix[3] of this hugely influential moralistic ideology – disseminated enthusiastically by alumni throughout the public, state and colonial school systems of Motherland and Empire. The ramifications of ethical inspiration were even more widely dispersed. It is far from notional to suggest that the activities

Originally published in *The British Journal of Sports History*, 1984, 1(3), pp. 245–271.
http://www.tandf.co.uk/journals

characteristic of the rivers and playing fields of late nineteenth-century Oxford and Cambridge were load-bearing supports underpinning the moral structure of British and imperial society. Attitudes, relationships and administrations owed much to the ethical imperatives of the playing fields.

Numerous vignettes of sporting moments on the Cam, the Isis, Parker's Piece or Christ Church Meadow exist in reminiscences and memoirs yet much remains to be discovered about the process of ideological propagation within the Oxford and Cambridge colleges. Who were the exponents, adherents and propagandists inside the system and why did their predilections, enthusiasms and shibboleths prevail? Conversely, who were the heretics, debunkers and opponents and why were they relatively ineffectual? Generalities regarding some of these questions, occasionally inaccurate,[4] are available but there is a need for studies in depth and detail if a proper understanding of the evolution and diffusion of a phenomenon which has effected the whole of the English-speaking world to a greater or lesser extent, is to be achieved. This paper marks a beginning. It focuses on Jesus College, Cambridge between 1875 and 1914. Jesus, as we shall see, had a hand in the propagation and dissemination of this powerful and pervasive Victorian and Edwardian ideology.

Life in late nineteenth-century Oxford and Cambridge revolved around a public school 'nodus of prejudices and predilections'.[5] This was scarcely to be wondered at: 'the average undergraduate was merely…the average public schoolboy transferred to conditions affording him rather greater scope for his essentially schoolboy impulses'.[6] Consequently as William Baker has written: In a manner never before or since duplicated, late-Victorian and Edwardian university life was an extension of the English public school. It was a sporting life, centred not so much around horses and hounds as around the river, the cricket pitch, and the football field'.[7]

The athletic relationship between school and university, of course, was cyclical;[8] in this way the 'mania' was mutually sustained and reinforced. On its inception in the universities, however, it had a mixed reception. There were cautious advocates. A contributor to *Blackwood's Magazine* in 1866 wrote with hesitant approval of passion excited by athletic contests which 'has become, to the vast majority of the undergraduates, the great interest of the academical year'.[9] Things had got to such a pitch, he argued, that it was now a matter of some doubt as to whether matters of the mind could hold out 'before the popular glories of the palaestra'. There were outright enthusiasts. A writer in the *Contemporary Review*, a little later, laid stress on university sports as 'being a main element in teaching a youth to fulfil his baptismal vow by keeping his body in temperance, soberness and chastity'.[10] Others were sardonic. T.H. Huxley remarked about the same time: 'When I think of the host of pleasant, monied, well-bred young gentlemen, who do a little learning and much boating by Cam and Isis, the vision is a pleasant one; and, as a patriot, I rejoice that the youth of the upper and richer classes of the nation receive a wholesome and manly training, however small may be the modicum of knowledge they gather, in the intervals of this, their serious business.'[11] Some attempted a carefully judicious assessment of events. Hippolyte Taine expressed admiration for the 'Oxbridge' cultivation of muscle but felt obliged to deprecate the consequent neglect of the mind.[12] *Punch* was wilfully injudicious in its view of a muscular enthusiasm shared by Freshmen and Fellows.

Who cares a hang for a first in Greats
And Academic glory,
Dull bookworm, come and see the sights
and shut *de Oratore!*
Learn what a thing a man might be
And think to win a pewter
More splendid than a first, like me your Tutor.[13]

Whether enthusiasts or critics, no one disputed the state of affairs. It would not be too exaggerated an act to adapt the words of Mark Pattison, the lugubrious Rector of Lincoln College, Oxford, and remark that for many at Oxford and Cambridge, the colleges were boarding schools in which the elements of rowing were taught to youths.[14] Activities on river and playing field eventually became so pressing that the hour of dinner in college was moved back 'from 3 o'clock to 4 o'clock and then to 5 or even later', and eventually 'the timing of cricket matches to begin at 12 noon effectively cut down the lectures which could be attended to one per morning'.[15] It can be stated with little fear of contradiction that

> memories of Oxford and Cambridge throughout the second half of Victoria's reign were frequently those of 'idle years of cricket, fives, racquets and billiards', when work weighed lightly on the conscience and the river and the games field engrossed many students. One disillusioned Uppingham scholar found Cambridge minds of the time 'not in reality much occupied with...lofty themes' and eyes of the time 'if open at all, more likely to be fixed on some vision of Cam or Thames than on the deep flowing river of Thought'.... 'The Reign of Athletics is at hand', an astonished undergraduate reported back to Stonyhurst in 1896.[16]

With touching loyalty, A.C. Deane boasted that late-Victorian Cambridge was certainly more idle than Oxford. And in *Times Remembered*, with a fitting economy of effort, he borrowed from A. A. Milne a description of the Cambridge undergraduates of the period which, he asserted, caught them to perfection: 'Life, for us, was..."rather a rag" and at twenty to be most enjoyed'.[17] His point is reinforced by the fictional Cambridge heroes of E.F. Benson,[18] drawn from his own experiences and depicted in *The Babe B.A. and David of Kings*. In the literary fashion of the time both novels celebrate innocuous pleasures. They are lightweight idylls of leisurely breakfasts, jolly companions, 'footer' and boating. They accurately depict the more innocent aspects of the pleasant lives of well-off, well-fed and well-contented upper-class young men, who, when the fancy took them, splashed in Byron's Pool, rowed energetically past Romsey Weir or sprinted on Parker's Piece. By the twentieth century, as a consequence of an unabated enthusiasm and an increasing provision for exercise, Charles Tennyson was provoked to comment that

> the mechanism of work at the University is as nothing compared with the vast machinery of play.... Cambridge life still shows traces of that fundamental principle of British education, the belief that while limitless exercise is essential to the production of a sound body, a sound mind can only be produced by a studious and deliberate inactivity. One is not, therefore, surprised to find sport of all kinds carefully and elaborately organised.[19]

When considering the philistine appetites of Tennyson's undergraduates it is well to be aware of those with more epicurean tastes, who have written in some number of the intellectual feast placed before them by learned late nineteenth-century academics of the Cambridge colleges. The autobiographical reminiscences of sober, earnest and able intellectuals bear witness to a Cambridge that gloried in learning. G.P. Gooch, for example, remembered of Victorian Cambridge that, 'For a young man with a healthy appetite there was an almost bewildering choice of fare among the lectures or courses of distinguished visitors'.[20] Many of Gooch's contemporaries would have taken issue with him over his definition of 'a healthy appetite'. The Jesuan don, Foakes Jackson, has left this desolate description of the response to two of the most distinguished late nineteenth-century university lecturers, Lightfoot and Wescott: 'The behaviour of the audience was not edifying. The virtuous attended and took notes, the studious devoted themselves to their own subjects, and read books bearing on them, the frivolous read novels, the utterly profane played surreptitious games of cards, the rest slept.'[21]

The caveat of Rowland Prothero therefore, is not to be lightly discarded: 'Life at the University has been too exclusively described in the autobiographies of men whose subsequent careers were only the fruition of their brilliant triumphs at school and college. Both in boyhood and youth, they belonged to that distinguished minority who made the fullest use of their educational opportunities.'[22] This is a point of substance. There were, in reality, three Cambridges: predominantly of the mind, predominantly of the body and of both mind and body. In short, there were reading men, rowing men and men who attempted both. All three types persisted throughout the Victorian and Edwardian eras. W.E. Heitland recalled that, in the 1860s, 'the quiet reading men...often went for long walks in the country...[they] meant close companionship and exchange of views, and were in truth, a valuable part of the varied processes that made up university training'.[23] The longevity of this lifestyle is well illustrated by the experiences of Stanley Eddington who, as a hard-working and reserved undergraduate at Trinity College in 1902, could not afford time for football or cricket but enjoyed strenuous walks with a fellow undergraduate of like persuasion.[24] In contrast to such inoffensive exercises, non-reading men who, according to Heitland, were many in his day, did not have enough harmless amusements as analgesics against the pain of occasional contemplation. They despised walking: 'the exercise was too humdrum to suit youths with no ideas to exchange and prone to intellectual rest.'[25]

Intellectual Cambridge has been described by Leonard Woolf, who wrote of his *Seelenfreundshaft* with Lytton Stratchey, Saxon Sidney-Turner and Thoby Stephen at the time of the Boer War: 'We were intellectuals...with three genuine and I think, profound passions: a passion for friendship, a passion for literature and music [and]...a passion for what we called the truth.'[26] In search of absolutism these sceptics certainly got more genuine pleasure from the close scrutiny of George Moore's *Principia Ethica* than from a careful examination of the state of the wicket at Fenners. In brutal contrast to these purists, there was Leslie Stephen's 'Rowing Man' in *Sketches by a Don*:

> He resided at the University for, say, 800 days, excluding Sundays and vacations. Of those he passed 790 on the river; and during nine of the remainder he was laid up by a sprain caused by his exertions. The remaining day, which he wasted in lionising his mother and sisters, he will regret as long as he lives. Years afterwards he will date events by the University races of that time. The Crimean War, he will say, broke out in the year of 'the eighteen-inch race' – i.e. the race when Oxford beat Cambridge at Henley by that distance.... Every morning, he was up at seven o'clock, and took his tub after half an hour's trot. His breakfast, according to a superstition not yet extinct, was raw beef-steak; his supper was oatmeal porridge. He measured his wine (except on occasional jollifications) with the careful eye of a gaoler distributing an allowance. He did not smoke, for fear of injuring his wind. The only ornaments in his room were cups or 'pewters' won on the river. His dress always included the colours of his boat-club. His library consisted chiefly of the 'Boating Almanac' and the back numbers of 'Bell's Life'. His conversation varied only by referring at one season to the sculls, and at another to the 'fours'.[27]

There were those in fact as well as in fiction who managed to live in both worlds. Robert Elsmere, the well-adjusted Oxford undergraduate, in Mrs Humphrey Ward's book of the same title, whose 'athletic instincts...were always fighting in him with is literary instincts',[28] had his Cambridge counterpart in reality. On entering Trinity College in 1870, Walter Leaf found to his surprise that although he was never a fine oarsman he was 'at least a fair average'. And so it was that he found himself admitted 'into two quite different college sets: the rowing men and the reading men'. His heart was mostly with the latter.[29] Others, like F.W. Lawrence, who went up to Trinity in 1891, also seemed to balance brains and brawn without undue strain and combined high intellectual achievement with moderate athletic success.[30] They were the exceptions. Reading men and rowing men, in fact, coexisted uneasily. The hearties tended to be irreligious and overbearing, while the intellectuals tended to be holy or affected. Cecil Earle Tyndale-Biscoe described Corpus Christi in the 1880s as the Angel and Devil College, 'for it was divided into two opposite sets...the pious and the rowdy'.[31] Things changed little even after the Great War, and T.C. Worsley wrote of the Cambridge of 1926: 'The division between athletes and aesthetes was...absolute. There was a clear choice and I surrendered abjectly. I could pride myself after two years at University that I had never opened a book, apart from the set books for the Classical Tripos: and even these were shamefully neglected...I virtually abandoned lectures altogether and did such work as couldn't be absolutely avoided.'[32]

Arnold Lunn wrote in his autobiography *Come What May* that there were colleges at both Oxford and Cambridge which perpetuated 'the public school athletocracies', and considered himself exceedingly fortunate to enter Balliol College in 1907 at a time when it 'shared something in common with Periclean Athens'.[33] Cambridge, too, had its Athenian shrines of high culture among Barbarian loci of tones muscle. King's College, to the great delight of E.M. Forster, 'was civilised and proud of its civilisation. It was not sufficient glory to be a Blue there, nor an additional glory to get drunk'.[34] To Esme Wingfield Stratford, King's was 'the intellectual College *par excellence*', an institution devoted to 'education, religion, learning and research'. And it was no respecter of persons. It would be discreetly conveyed 'to the most magnificent of undergraduate bloods or the doughtiest of athletes' that failure to conform to the standards of the college meant removal to one where those kinds of talents were better appreciated. King's had little time for 'the type of youth who comes up from a public school with no other object than to squander three or four years in the pursuit of athletic honours and a good time...with just the minimum of study required to scrape through the examination for a pass degree. What, in fact, books about University life love to describe as 'the average undergraduate'.[35]

Yet even in this rarified atmosphere of intellectual endeavour, the crude excesses of the hearty were not unknown, and the contemptuous ridicule of the intellectual by the muscular was not uncommon. Intellectuals were known disparagingly as 'knaves' and the commonplace antagonism between reader and rowdy found ready expression. 'There was a mutual opposition between a comparatively conventional and athletic majority, and a minority of self conscious intellectuals, with a tendency on each side to run defiantly to extremes.'[36] Shane Leslie's clear recollection of King's men, circa 1904, was that they were 'very hearty in groups'; there was careful discouragement of effeminacy. It was during his time that a third-year man was actually discovered using a hot-water bottle: 'This was considered a disgrace to the college, and Hope-Jones challenged its owner to run the quarter mile round the front court on a wintry dawn. It was agreed that the challenger should run stark while the challenged wore as much clothing as he wished. The race was won by the less encumbered party and the offending hot-water bottle was duly confiscated and sent to Doctor Barnardo with the compliments of the Provost, the Fellows and Scholars of the college.'[37] Of course, in dons like Augustus Austin Leigh[38] and Walter Headlam[39] King's could boast the staunchest of philathletes. Leigh was 'renowned for his great sympathy for athletic sports of every sort'. Headlam, for his part, by virtue of athletic enthusiasms earned an obituary in *The Sporting Life*.

The antithesis of King's was Jesus – an alleged haven of hearties and a reputed repository of muscular addiction. Few things depict better the similarity between the Victorian and Edwardian public school and Jesus than the College magazine of the period, *The Chanticlere*. In the main it is hearty, philistine, considerably taken up with athletics and preoccupied with the associated issues which so greatly concerned the English public schoolboy of the period – athletic heroes, successes and regalia.[40] In 1889, the editors of *The Chanticlere*, with a certain perspicacity and some irony, amused themselves by speculating on the eventual fate of the volume which they had produced: 'We can picture the joy of some learned professor of English on finding this priceless treasure, a relic of the remote past. Aided by this work he will prove that the Universities of the ancient English were really devoted to athletic pursuits.'[41]

Whatever the learned professor's conclusions regarding the universities, he would not have been too awry in coming to such conclusions about Jesus. As the magazine reveals, the undergraduates gave much thought, effort and time to athletics. The first number devoted 18 of the 28 pages to boating, cricket, rugby, soccer, athletics and lawn tennis. In the second number, the news that yet another attempt was to be made to resuscitate the College Debating Society provoked the clearly rhetorical question, 'Is the slander true that we care for nothing and excel in nothing but athletics?'[42] A little later *The Sporting Times* attracted attention when it was disclosed that it 'is generally torn in two one hour after it has arrived, so eagerly do men dispute the proud privilege of reading that high class paper'.[43] In contrast *The Nineteenth Century, Saturday Review* and *Spectator* lay untouched between their boards!

In October of 1886 the lament of a discontented intellectual with a taste for epigrams was published for general delectation: 'once a small college of tasteful students, now a large body of rowing athletes.'[44] The statement was a little harsh. The editors for the Easter Term of 1887 were correct: ' "the old order changes, giving place to new". We are no longer Head of the River and we have a College Debating Society.' There was also a society to discuss political, social and economic matters – the Cranmer Society (established as early as 1897) – and within two years there was a literary and philosophical society – the Coleridge Society.[45] These cultural endeavours gave the editors confidence a little later to remark of a Jesus Fellow of the early part of the century, that 'in a sterner age when athletics were then unknown as a serious pursuit', he was a typical Jesus man possessed of 'the spirit of athleticism tempered with learning, which has since been characteristic of so many distinguished members of our College'.[46] Content contradicted compliment. While the Debating Society found difficulty attracting support, a college meeting held to debate the desirability of a blazer for members of the Jesus College Athletic Club 'was a large one and many men spoke'. The proposition was carried by a substantial majority.[47]

As in the magazines of the public schools, former alumni in the Empire wrote of their staunch attempts to maintain the essential aspects of an English heritage despite tropical downpours flooding the wicket; they tempted the adventurous: 'a swift bowler of the type so well known of Jesus of late is badly wanted here';[48] letters requested improved facilities of the right sort: 'racquets and five courts, a cinder path, a gymnasium ... and everything else which would help to render happy the life of the athletic scholar';[49] and 'athletic scholars' received fitting prominence in death. H.E. Rhodes, whose gallantry in abandoning a cricket match and, quite untrained, taking the place of a sick colleague in the winning boat of 1876, was 'so intimately associated with the athletic history, and particularly the rowing history of the college, that his death could not be passed over in silence'.[50] Again, as in the public school magazine of the period, the plaintive demands of editors desperate for print and the disenchanted comments of the disgruntled occasionally surfaced. In 1894 one long-suffering editor wondered dejectedly 'when a literary contribution had last been sent in for the delight of the overworked staff',[51] and shortly before the Great War, a brave if anonymous voice was raised in protest against the tone of the place which at the time, in the opinion of one long-lived Jesuan don, was 'a place of senseless and brutal rowdyism' and not unlike 'an ill-disciplined public school'.[52] 'Mother of Seven', the complainant, found a great deal wrong with the callous imposition of a way of life modelled on the 'perfect' undergraduate who 'will swear – but not too often, . . . will keep chapel – but not too many, . . . will work – but not too much [and] the more games he plays, the nearer will he approach perfection [attaining] the apotheosis by representing the University and gaining his "Blue" '.[53] Sporting doggerel of a cheery moralistic nature so familiar to the reader of the *Harrovian*, *Lorettonian*, *Uppingham Magazine* and similar products, also appeared in *The Chanticlere*:

O batsman play the game, or a 'duck' will blot your fame;
Don't shiver when the umpire sings out 'PLAY!'
But be wary, wise, and ready; play 'em straight and true and steady.
And watch the ball and gently feel your way.[54]

Perhaps the clearest evidence of institutional priorities is the meticulous listing of the athletic talents of newcomers to the college:

Freshmen 1893[55]

Beck, A.C.T.	Ford, E.B., Hastings
Breakey, H., Eliock[a]	Harries, O.W., Bury St Edmunds
Bower, G.F., private	Harvey, Winchester
Brydone, P., Lancing[b]	Lucas, R., Cheltenham
Busby, G.H., Repton[b,c]	Maclaren, W.V. St C., Merchiston Castle
Chapman, W.T., Loughborough[b,c]	Maddison, J.R.S., Durham
Coode, A.T., Fauconberge, Beccles[b,c]	Marriott, H.S., Bradfield
Dickson, A.C., Rossall	Sadler, H., Durham[d]
Exton, G.G., Oundle[a]	Sedgwich, J.S., Lancaster[a]
Siddons, A.W., K. Edward's, Birmingham[a,c]	Thorburn, K.D.S.M., Wellington[a,c]
Skrimshire, H.F., Gresham[c]	Turner, W.G., Chatham House[a]
Stevens, H., Beaumont[b]	Walton, H.G., Newcastle
Swanson, A.W., Loretto[a]	Whitty, R.F.L., Felsted[b,c]
Thompson, W., Ripon[a,c]	Wigram, G.E., Bradfield
	Woolston, Wellingboro[b,c]

Notes
a denotes 1st XV Rugby colours.
b 1st XI Association.
c 1st XI Cricket.
d First boat.

In the light of such things, it seems reasonable to suppose that the typical Jesus undergraduate of the late nineteenth century would have had much in common with B.H. Stewart who matriculated in 1893 and graduated in 1896. Stewart opened his short book of *Reminiscences*[56] with this categorical statement: 'To anyone who should pick up this little booklet.... I feel under an obligation to state that it is concerned mainly with sport – touching lightly on cricket, football, running, swimming, rowing, gymnastics, golf, tennis and boxing with chess, billiards and cards thrown in.'[57] He added unnecessarily, 'all my life sport has been and still is – a passion with me'.[58] He measured his degree of contentment at the university exclusively in terms of his athletic accomplishments and activities. He underwent the obligatory period of 'compulsory rowing' as a freshmen, became an enthusiastic but indifferent cricketer, won a worthy 'blue' at soccer and became an efficient President of the Jesus College Athletic Club. He took full advantage of the opportunities available 'in the most sporting College in Cambridge'[59] and ended his brief and breezy memoirs with a sententious homily for the young reader, on games as a training for life which set three years of hedonism in proper moral perspective:

And if you're beaten – well, what of that?
Come up with a smiling face.
'Tis no disgrace to be knocked down flat,
But to lie there, that's disgrace.
The harder you're knocked, the higher you bounce,
Be proud of the blackened eye
It isn't the fact that you're licked that counts,
But *how* did you fight – and why?[60]

Stewart's typicality is underlined by the contrasting nature and experiences of Mark Sykes[61] who resided at Jesus at about the same time. Sykes was worthy, serious 'and held firmly to high principles'. It is hardly surprising, therefore, to discover from his biographer, Shane Leslie, that he had little in common with his own College. 'Jesus was a medieval foundation which in the course of modern progress had passed from the housing of religious women to the production of...highly trained oarsmen.'[62] To add insult to injury Sykes had no liking for the river: 'He was one of those of whom it might be said that they neither toiled nor did they spin up and down the green and scented courses of the Cam.'[63] He devoted himself to his Eastern travels, theatricals and journalism and inevitably gravitated away from Jesus toward King's, the undisputed centre of intellectual affairs. To King's men he was a curious acquisition. 'Jesus men, remarked Leslie, 'were seldom called into King's circles unless to improve the sytle of a racing crew.'[64] However, he quickly won the respect of, and was at ease with, an Olympian academic of the stature of Montagu James. He was not missed at Jesus. The college Grandees were the athletes. For the most part they defined reality, set the tone, determined the values, coerced the unwilling and disciplined the recalcitrant. In the light of these comments it is attractively straightforward to argue that the ethos of Victorian and Edwardian Jesus was essentially the product of hearty public schoolboys with hearty period enthusiasms, who danced to their own tunes despite the feeble piping of despairing dons. It is hardly so simple. Such an argument explains much but not all. The recorded enthusiasm of the dons requires the closest scrutiny.

Throughout the later period of Victoria's reign Jesus was in the charge of two former (and unrelated) assistant masters of Lancing College, H.A. and E.H. Morgan, who during their time at the school strongly encouraged the rise of athleticism with its attendant machinery of colours and compulsion.[65] They were typical athletic pedagogues of the period[66] and their school experience was to be valuable to them as College Fellows. Both were able, enthusiastic and committed athletes and only moderate academics. Their propensities greatly influenced the ethos of the college and transformed its standing. This was just as well. By the 1850s the college had fallen on hard times. In 1849 George John Elwes Corrie had been elected Master. It is customary to portray him as an 'Evangelical High Churchman equally opposed to Dissent and Popery',[67] with pronounced conservative inclinations in political, and social and educational matters. His qualities are summarized on his memorial tablet in the College Chapel – 'Votis, Studiis, moribus Christo devotissimus'. They do not seem to have had much appeal. Corrie's early years as Master witnessed a 'disastrous drop' in admissions which continued until shortly before the appointment of H.A. Morgan as Tutor in 1864. The immediate rise in numbers is attributed in part to the interests and efforts of Morgan, and the cause of its continuation was obvious to the College historian, Arthur Gray, writing in 1902: 'It was in the decade of the "seventies" that the College sprang into...athletic prominence...it was not unnaturally, accompanied by a great rise in the number of undergraduates.'[68] It was, in fact, in 1875 that Morgan's efforts came to fruition and the Jesus College boat 'attained the proud position of Head of the River'.[69] The college moved quickly from sixth to third largest after Trinity and St John's.[70] Growth, of course, was due in part to a general expansion of the university after the Act of Parliament in 1871 by which religious tests for all degrees except Divinity were abolished,[71] but the fame of Jesus oarsmen was the main reason. Jesus retained the Head of the River for 11 years. The college now enjoyed an athletic pre-eminence which, in the words of Gray writing with period enthusiasm at the turn of the century, comprised 'its greatest glory in modern times'.[72]

Towards the end of the 1870s, as a result, the 'inflow of freshmen became phenomenal'.[73] Additions to the college structure made in 1870 had to be extended. Further extensive additions resulted in the 1880s. As in the case of some modern American universities, there were tangible returns to be gained from sporting prowess. This is underlined by the fact that the same phenomenon of expansion occurred in 1904 when the legendary Steve Fairbairn[74] returned to coach the Jesus boats. He was informed by the then Tutor F.J. Foakes-Jackson that 'the position of the College boat on the river was an index of the prosperity of the college'.[75] As College successes on the river mounted, Foakes-Jackson informed him that he was refusing two men a day as there was no room for them. At least one motive for condoning athletic excess was pecuniary. Yet college prosperity through athletic success could not be guaranteed. Despite continued victories on the river, by the time the new buildings were completed in the 1880s numbers had fallen by one-third from 216 in 1880 to 147 in 1884. Paradoxically athletic dominance brought both popularity and unpopularity. Regardless of the enthusiasms of the time, the concentration on rowing was overdone. In the opinion of the latest historian of the college: 'There can be little doubt that the decline in numbers was due to over-emphasis on rowing at Jesus during Corrie's later years, coupled with the rowdiness and idleness of many of the rowing men.'[76] In view of what was acceptable, the licence must have been considerable. To the modern eye some recorded behaviour seems almost ochlocratic. It comes as no surprise to learn that the ringleaders came from the first and the pre-eminent of the social clubs, the Rhadegund Society for the leading athletes, established in 1874.[77] About this time even H.A. Morgan felt obliged to remark that, 'The College is becoming nothing but a boat club, and it will do it much good if the boat comes down'.

The two Morgans in conjunction with Corrie ushered in 'high and palmy days' in which ' "the Master", "the Tutor" and "the Dean" formed a great triumvirate in the history of their own or any other College'.[78] Their accord on matters of educational principle was, in fact, closer than would seem to be the case from a reading of both histories of the college published in 1902 and 1962 respectively. In both, the impression given of Corrie is of a crusty, anchoritic 'student of many of the bye-paths of theological research'.[79] It is suggested that Corrie loathed rowing men, harbouring a resentment towards them not unlike Swartwout's 'Aesthete' in his *Rhymes of the River* who beseeched his bosom companion:

Pray, Cyril, do not read the *Field*,
Nor seek for any detailed knowledge
Concerning those great louts who wield
An oar for 'Varsity or College;
I don't see why my breast should swell
With pride of those whose only function
Is to defeat the men who dwell
On t'other side of Bletchley Junction.[80]

Yet Morgan himself acknowledged the influence of Corrie in the process of transforming Jesus into a college of the river and the games field. Corrie, wrote Morgan, approved 'vigorous, manly recreations' and frequently watched his boys playing cricket and football. He also supported the athletes. Percy M. Thorton, in a little-known description of the origins of Jesus athletics in the early 1960s, wrote that he desired 'to place on record how generously and enthusiastically the late venerable and beloved Master of Jesus, Dr. Corrie, supported the athletics, frequently coming to see the sports on Jesus Close'.[81] In fact, Corrie saw the same ethical qualities in sport as did thousands of his contemporaries. He might have had mysogynic objections to the camp followers, who, he alleged, followed the boats along the banks of the Cam, but he saw moral worth in the efforts of the oarsmen. He was judicious in his praise and opportunistic with his advice. He remarked on the occasion of the College becoming Head of the River in 1875 that a position had been won in 'which could not have done without courage and self-denial and he trusted that they would carry their qualities into after life'.[82] Later the same day, out of chance meeting with a group of excited undergraduates he created the opportunity for a further brief homily: 'I am very glad that you have done so well on the river. I hope you do as well with your books as you have done with your oars.'[83]

There are many similarities between the rise of games – cult in the public schools and the universities not least in the support it received from those in authority. This legitimatized, encouraged and sustained it. At Jesus, Corrie helped lay the foundations but the two Morgans were pillars of institutional support who ensured the eventual image of Jesus as a college for athletic toughs. Both acquired awesome but rather different reputations. At the same time of his death in 1912, H.A. Morgan was described in *Blackwood's Magazine* as 'a don of the old school – a sportsman and a gentleman'.[84] Charles Whibley, the composer of these literary obsequies for this pronounced philathlete, announced that the College in which Morgan had resided for over half a century was peculiarly his own creation:

> He filled it with undergraduates, and then endowed it with a soul – a soul of energy and patriotism. He gave to one and all a just cause of pride in their College, and warmed their courage at the fire of his own enthusiasm. In all sports – . . . he took the keen and intimate interest of one who had practised them . . . . For half a century he encouraged the College boat by his voice and presence; he watched its rise and fall upon the river with the stern enthusiasm of a general watching his army in the field, and his enthusiasm was rewarded by so long a list of victories as has never been claimed by any other College in the world.[85]

The Jesuan 'General' it seems chose his 'army' with care: his students were selected in his own image. Charles Hose, for example, on seeking entrance to the College in 1882 was closely interrogated by Morgan about his athletic record.[86]

While Morgan wholly lacked the intellectual ability of his close friend Leslie Stephen, he almost matched him in his enthusiasm for physical exercise. Walking was a great passion and strenuous walks of anything up to 30 miles[87] were undertaken with colleagues in the Cambridgeshire countryside during term time, while in the vacations the Alps frequently beckoned.[88] In the summer of 1862, with a casualness of purpose typical of the amateur gentleman of the period, having nothing better to do, he went with Stephen on an expedition to Switzerland and unostentatiously achieved the first crossing of the Jungfrau-Joch – as late as 1925 still considered a hazardous undertaking.[89] When mountains were not available to tire them, and cultural interests drew them to Vienna, Prague, Dresden and

Berlin, Stephen and Morgan would get exercise by racing back to their hotel by different routes. And they got not merely exercise. Stephen wrote: '... great judgement and discrimination were required to decide whether or not it would be advantageous to dash down some narrow street or not'.[90] Henry Jackson, who eventually became Regius Professor of Greek at Cambridge, throws an interesting light on Morgan's limitations, Stephen's versatility and the Jesus ethos, in a letter written in 1904 to Stephen's distinguished biographer F.W. Maitland: 'You may be surprised to hear that in the late sixties I knew well the roistering crew which assembled at Jesus. Stephen was quite at home there; but I always knew that there was another Stephen, of whom Morgan, and Co. knew nothing.'[91]

Rowing was Morgan's great love – seemingly for moral as well as sensual reasons: 'athletics were too much for self-glorification, another pot for this or that, and so on, till [a man] has a row of silver pots or cups. Boating was the ideal, no pots or personal rewards, all for the honour of the College and the University.'[92] Morgan's own rowing feats were impressive. He rowed in the Jesus College boat for ten years and coached the college boats for many years after that, becoming a well-known figure riding on his white horse Gehazi along the tow-path shouting instructions to 'the boat with the red and black oars'.[93] He held the record for the number of 'eight-oared' races on the Cam – over 100, and his daughter in an untypically boastful attempt to place this considerable feat in proper perspective, wrote 'in endeavouring to surpass this record another oarsman rowed sixty-eight races and died'.[94]

Throughout the whole of his life Morgan remained an enthusiast for the river. Even in the most extreme of circumstances his support for the Jesus boat was assured. Apparently at death's door with fever in 1875, when Jesus went Head of the River for the first time, the whole College stood silently under his window. It slowly opened and 'a stick on which was suspended his straw hat with the Jesus ribbon was waved slowly up, and down'. Perceptive students, we are told, dated his recovery from that moment.[95] In his passion for the boats he was as prone to rationalization as any other zealot pursuing his own interests. It was remarked of him by Canon John Domett Nairne, a student during his period as Tutor, that he 'encouraged men to take up rowing, not merely because he knew it promoted their bodily and moral health but because it interfered less than anything else with their work'.[96] He clearly chose to disbelieve the well-known university axiom of the time: 'He who runs may read but he who rows simply cannot.'[97]

Morgan's love of rowing and of Cambridge coalesced around the practical matter of facilities. He was acutely conscious of the fact that from 1861 to 1869 Oxford won the Boat Race nine years in succession and it occurred to him 'that Cambridge might possibly be labouring under a disadvantage of having to undergo constant practice on a shallow river, whereas Oxford had the advantage of deeper water'.[98] The matter was of such importance to him that he incessantly worried all those interested in university rowing until in 1868 a meeting was held in his rooms at Jesus and funds were promised for improving the river. Eventually a subscription list was opened in London and Morgan had the pleasure of placing

Queen Victoria herself at its head. The Queen donated £100 and the Prince of Wales £50. The work of deepening and widening the Cam was completed in 1870. Cambridge won the next five races in succession! Morgan's pragmatism in such smatters naturally embraced his own College. In 1885 he donated a clock turret to the College boat clubhouse erected in 1882. And in 1901, together with the Fellows, he purchased the freehold of the site for the benefit of the club.

Morgan's interest in sport was not restricted to the river. It is not widely recognized that it was not just Leslie Stephen, long reputed to be the creator of the inter-varsity athletics sports, but in addition, a number of Jesus fellows including H.A. Morgan, who won over the hostile university authorities to the idea of 'fresh inter-University competitions of a non-intellectual nature' and made it possible for Percy M. Thornton, an undergraduate from Jesus, and C.B. Lawes, an undergraduate from Trinity, to visit Oxford University early in 1864 to make arrangements for the first inter-university athletics meeting which took place later in the same year on Christ Church cricket ground.[99] It seems that Morgan kept some sense of perspective on matters of sport. In the Jesus archives there are a set of untidy scribbled notes for his annual speech to Freshmen. While he warned them to avoid debt, drink and doing nothing, he also warned them against being pressed into too many clubs and making their sports the business of life. Work was the real thing they had come for.[100] How far this introductory set of admonitions represented simply lipservice to official orthodoxy is impossible to ascertain. What is ascertainable is that in these obsecrations and in his own style of life Morgan first as Tutor and later as Master was more like a glorified public school headmaster than a distinguished university scholar. The transformation in late nineteenth-century Cambridge discerned by Heyck,[101] from intellectual torpor to intellectual originality, did not appear to include the Master of Jesus. He chose the intermediate position of earnest decent don. He was cast more in the mould of John Hardy than Charles Appleton.[102] In this regard he was ideally suited to Jesuan undergraduates proclivities.

Edward Henry Morgan was a more controversial figure than his namesake. He aroused strong passions. He was described by one Jesus undergraduate, who took a very pronounced dislike to him, as: 'an enormous man, over six feet in height, with a stomach and feet to match, a closely trimmed red beard, and a voice like a bull – one of Nature's bullies'.[103] Elsewhere he was compared in aspect to those massive warriors 'who from their northern homes sallied out to harry and destroy their feebler men'.[104] He was an ardent devotee of sport. *Granta* reported in May 1890: 'he fostered esprit de corps in every pursuit; he encouraged the genuine athlete; ... Such a man at the head of affairs soon effected a change in a College that had grown somewhat sluggish, and the consequence is that at the present day Jesus men have increased in numbers to such an extent as to require and possess new College buildings and ... [are] to be found in the front rank of every branch of athletics.'[105] Others were less convinced of his merit, seeing his rise to prominence as a malign ascendency and believing that he played the role of Coryphaeus with enthusiasm. Brittain and Gray in their history of Jesus remark: 'There can be little doubt that the decline in numbers was due to an over-emphasis on rowing at Jesus during Corrie's later years coupled with the rowdiness and idleness of many of the rowing men and the acquiescence of the Dean, E.H. Morgan.'[106] Morgan's propensity to turn a blind eye when it suited him is revealed in Stewart's *Reminiscences*. He recalled that S.M.J. Woods,[107] a double blue in his first year and 'too priceless to lose' always got his way with Morgan.[108]

Brittain returned to the theme of Morgan's disastrous influence in his autobiography *It's a Don's Life*, attributing both the restless reformation and reckless iconoclasm of Arthur Gray, Master from 1912 to 1940, to the need 'to administer an antidote to ... [and] smash the idol of Red Morganism'.[109] The antipathy Morgan could attract to himself is sharply revealed in a long-lived reaction and a tasteless anecdote respectively, both described by Brittain. He wrote of Arthur Gray: 'To the end of his life he could always be roused to wrath by any mention of the repugnant name. Anyone who did not know might have thought that Red Morgan's enormities had been perpetrated a few weeks previously, whereas he had been dead for forty years.' Brittain recounted of Morgan that on the death of a colleague at Lancing, he swiftly organized a subscription for the widow, ensured that a substantial sum was donated and then promptly married the lady.[110]

It is clear that Morgan was a man to be feared rather than loved. He found few lions in his path and those he quickly tamed. Master and Fellows apparently were all terrified of him.[111] One of them, however, summoned up enough courage to compose the following disrespectful verse which gives a fair idea of Morgan's autocratic majesty!

Red Morgan: I am the tutor, bursar, butler, dean:
              I rule the College with imperial sway
              The very Master owneth me supreme,
              The Fellows tremble and my rule obey.
Chorus: The Czar of Russia and our gracious Queen
              Are not so potent as our noble Dean.[112]

H.A. Morgan's daughter, in her book about her father, recounted with delicate malice several of his stories about 'the noble Dean' – none of them to his advantage. She, herself, wrote euphemistically of E.H. Morgan that he possessed 'a vigorous and resolute personality combined with a masterful will'.[113] Clearly she shared her father's antipathy towards him.

Despite the systematic removal of Morgan memorabilia under Gray, there remain clues in the Jesus archives to the extent of Morgan's absorption in sport. He was a philathlete of extreme persuasion. His Jesus scrapbook, for example, is filled with telegrams dispatched to him from various scenes of Jesuan sporting success – Lords, Henley and elsewhere, reporting famous victories on the Thames or informing him of the doings of men in the University cricket match. For the rest, it includes records of work done for the University Cricket, Boating and

Athletic Clubs and meetings of the famous Isthmian, Queen's or Leander sports clubs of which he was a proud member.[114] Perhaps the clearest indication of excessive zeal and disproportionate involvement is an entry entitled 'Muscular Education' in *Punch*, the merciless recorder of the extravagances of the English gentleman, in which he appears under the opaque pseudonym of R.E.D. Horgan of Jesurum College, Cambs., as a referee for an exciting new preparatory school where boys are trained 'to the real requirements of modern life' (rowing, cricket, football, swimming, racquets, boxing, hockey, billiards, poker, nurr and spell) in preparation for the great public schools and universities. Extras at this utilitarian establishment (for which there was an additional charge) included reading, writing and arithmetic.[115]

Morgan made practical contributions to the development of the sporting ethic in late nineteenth-century Cambridge. He was for many years treasurer of the leading university athletic clubs, and in addition played a major role in organizing the subscription fund for the purchase of Fenner's Cricket Ground in March 1892, when it became available from the Master and Fellows of Gonville and Caius College.[116] He performed similar functions for Jesus athletics, auditing the annual subscriptions and promoting the development of athletic facilities. In this regard, whatever personal failings he may have had, 'the Dean' as he was usually styled, was considered by many of the time to be 'an admirable type of...muscular Christian'.[117] Morgan's personality and predilections ensured his dominance of Jesus for much of the last quarter of the nineteenth century. There can be little doubt that his values prevailed in the College and, in effect, if H.A. Morgan was a glorified headmaster with a taste for sport, E.H. Morgan was a glorified games-master with an obsession for it. He had much in common with the archtype of the species – 'the Bull' of Sherborne, drawn so effectively by Alec Waugh in his famous *Loom of Youth*.[118] In contrast to the other Morgan, his motives appear to have been more hedonistic than moralistic. Certainly no records of moral arguments for sport have survived.

In their schoolmasterly efforts to nurture the bodies and to a lesser extent the minds of their charges, the Morgans received steady support from dons of far less athletic ability but just as much enthusiasm. The most quietly persistent was J.C. Watt[119] who spent an undistinguished lifetime at Jesus rather like a 'varsity Mr. Chips', greatly endearing himself to the undergraduates in large part because he 'knew all about their successes in games, for he rarely missed an important cricket or football match'.[120] In 1927 when Jesus yet again went Head of the River, Watt brought a long life of involvement in Jesus athletics to a contented close, remarking that he had seen Jesus go Head of the River for the last time and could now sing 'Nunc Dimittis'.[121]

The Morgans, like Warre at Eton and Welldon at Harrow and many other headmasters, embodied a new morality and epitomized a new pedagogic ideal. They were fervent and energetic agents of ideological innovation. Like Gramsci's intellectuals, their role was to spread and legitimatize new convictions, to colonize fresh conceptual territories, and win over young minds. Their motives were mixed; their commitment was considerable. They were not alone. For a full understanding of events and to do justice to the complexity of reality, the attitudes and inclinations of the Morgans must be placed in the wider context of late nineteenth-century university change. The discussion will follow Rothblatt rather than Heyck. The focus, appropriately in this context, will be more on the model of the late nineteenth-century don as moral tutor rather than specialist-researcher.[122]

As in the public schools, donnish enthusiasm for sport was in part the product of a curious amalgam of self-interest and altruism. As Rothblatt has argued, traditional donnishness constituted either amiable indifference or cold remoteness.[123] This polarity had lost favour by the 1850s. Irritated by the dominance of the coaching system, the dons now imitated the 'beaks', but Thring rather than Arnold. The collegiate ideal was redefined to lay emphasis on personal influence and character formation.[124] This ensured legitimacy, promoted self-respect and improved professional image. Of course, this is not the whole story. Some casuistic dons, like some 'beaks', were little more than perpetual public schoolboys. Others were calculating realists to whom institutional athletic repute meant institutional prosperity. Yet others were commonsense pragmatists who followed the expedient practices of mid-century public school headmasters. They promoted the river and the playing fields as necessary mechanisms of control. As undergraduates increased in number as a consequence of the growing wealth of Victorian Britain, the associated expansion of the public school system and the consequent university reforms of the mid and late nineteenth-century, the Colleges faced a classic public school problem – sizeable numbers of students in the grip of boredom born of restriction. They did not always resolve it, although utilizing traditional procedures they went to considerable lengths: College lectures, College examinations, compulsory chapel and dinners in hall had a disciplinary purpose and 'a variety of punishments-admonitions, rustication, expulsion, prohibitions and literary impositions – were customarily meted out for violations'.[125] Heitland wrote of the period after 1860, 'to bring young men together and keep them out of mischief (a vastly important matter), was a function not always performed by College Tutors with success.'[126] The successful, however, like Henry Latham of Trinity Hall (and we can add H.A. Morgan), 'unrivalled in the power of controlling full-blooded undergraduates, made it their business to encourage all forms of bodily exercise, above all rowing'.[127] This is a factor of considerable significance, and perhaps more should be made of a concern for control and less of a concern for character. Pragmatism as much as idealism dictated policy and practice.

If there was an element of Benthamite utilitarianism at large, there was also an element of Homeric idealism. The alleged ideal of Thomas Arnold's Rugby – Greek and cricket[128] – was more accurately the ideal of Walter Headlam's Cambridge. Headlam, the most passionate of Hellenists was 'in spirit and temperament nearly a Greek'. The 'oarsmen's strife and vigorous life' of Cambridge pleased him most. 'If I had not been a Grecian,' he is reported to have said, 'I should have been a cricket pro.'[129] Consequently, 'on a sunny day in the summer or early autumn he would devote all books to the father of lies, and become a

Greek in Disraeli's sense of one who excels in all athletic sports, never reads, and speaks no language but his own'.[130] Headlam and others were seduced by the Athenian concept of 'the whole man'. Sport and scholarship were worthy and linked pursuits which gave rise to a nineteenth-century Graeco-Britannic ideal some certainly pursued in fact and More perhaps pursued in fiction. The sanguine, like Richard Livingstone, could be confident that an ancient Athenian would be at ease among 'the well developed in body and mind' at Oxford and Cambridge; the sceptical, like Matthew Arnold, were of the view that such an Athenian would have speedily recognized that he was in the presence of Barbarians.[131]

There was, of course, a further idealism associated with Oxford and Cambridge sport which was more Spartan in concept: corporate, self-denying and stoic. It is hinted at amusingly by W.B. Glover:

Yet every day it is just the same
Though my nose be red and fingers blue,
I visit the river and sink my name
And become one-eighth of eight-oared crew.[132]

It is described with assertive righteousness by R.C. Lehmann in this depiction of the college and university oarsman:

He will have suffered much, he will have rowed many weary miles, have learnt the misery of aching limbs and blistered hands,...he will have laboured under broiling suns, or with snow storms and bitter winds beating against him, he will have voluntarily cut himself off from many pleasant indulgences. But on the other hand his triumphs will have been sweet, he will have trained himself to submit to discipline, to accept discomfort cheerfully, to keep a brave face in adverse circumstances; he will have learnt the necessity of unselfishness and patriotism...[133]

Here is the essence of Victorian and Edwardian upper-class educational purpose: character training through athletic endeavour. It was no less valid at the university than it was in the public school: 'boating was pre-eminently a means of university education...a high moral lesson', wrote a contributor to the *Fortnightly Review* in 1887, quoting with relish as his source no less an authority than an Anglican bishop.[134] He added his own view that 'one of the highest objectives of a university career should be the formation of character', and expressed disgust at the youth without this objective who remained indoors 'addling his brains in the investigation of obscure historical and philological problems'. On a note pleasing to Lacedaemonians, he ended with a hymn of praise to the nature of young Englishmen at the universities who took such a pride in resisting fatigue, who rejoiced at the display, at its highest pitch, of bodily strength and who were intoxicated by swift, effortless movement. It was this muscular morality above all else which the British product of public school and ancient university took to every corner of the empire. It served school teachers, missionaries and colonial administrators well in their efforts to train the child at home in Britain and the 'child-like' native in the colonies.

It was the moral element which transformed the seemingly parochial indulgences of Jesuan undergraduates into a set of ethical actions with a broader political, social and educational purpose. A mere handful of Jesuan men must suffice to illustrate what was typical of many more, and to demonstrate how deeply the games ethic became embedded in professional action. James Robertson, head-master of Haileybury from 1884 to 1890, was typical of numerous schoolmaster exemplars.[135] At Haileybury he made substantial contributions to the school fabric, intellectual life and athletic organization. In conjunction with so many of the Victorian sporting pedagogues, he showed himself to be possessed of a persistent youthfulness, a firm commitment to athletics as a moral instrument and a determination to ensure they had a central role in educational theory and practice. For these reasons the editors of the official valete in the *Haileyburian* of 1890 wrote with satisfaction: 'our progress under six years of wise and liberal government has been immense... all the older games [are] better organised and more vigorously pursued than before.'[136]

While Robertson trained embryonic imperial administrators on the Haileybury playing fields, one Jesuan imperialist, Charles Hose, was making excellent use of his college experience as government resident in Sarawak, Borneo. Hose left Jesus prematurely in 1884 without a degree, for a post under the legendary Charles Brook: 'With my love of outdoor life, of Nature, and of Romance, an opportunity of realizing my ambitions by work in the Adventurous East was one that was sure to prove an irresistible temptation. Thus it happened that when my uncle, Bishop Hose, wrote to my family offering to get me, if possible, a Cadetship on Sarawak, of all places,... my delighted acceptance was conveyed in the single word... Rather.'[137]

Soon after he found himself in charge of the Baram district: 'Raiding and head-hunting were rife, and constant local feuds prevailed. Interference by an intrusive government was not welcomed and was opposed with vigour.'[138] Hose was patient. After ten years, having played himself in as government representative, he felt the time was ripe to call a conference of the tribes. The purpose of the meeting was to bring *Pax Britannica* to Baram. He wrote later in *Natural Man: A record of Borneo:* 'In calling the conference, I felt that in order to suppress fighting and head-hunting, the normal young Bornean's natural outlet, it would be well to replace them by some equally violent, but less boisterous, activity: and I suggest to the tribes a sort of local Henley, the chief feature of which would be an annual race between the war canoes of all the villages. The proposal was taken up eagerly by the people.' The great boat race duly came about. In his own words:

At daybreak the racing-boats set off for the starting-post four miles up-river. Strict orders had been given that no spears or other weapons were to be carried... but as they started the boats were inspected in turn, and in one or two cases were relieved of contraband.... It was a grand neck-and-neck race all through between the two leading boats, and every man rowed it out to the end.[139]

The undertaking was not without its difficulties. Athletic competition for tribesmen, unfamiliar with the obligations to lose well, had its dangers. Victory on this auspicious occasion presented a considerable problem since the winners were a pacific coastal people who were more skilful at making boats than war. Design, not aggression, had brought triumph. Fortunately, good humour prevailed, and on the following morning the various parties dispersed to.their distant villages, taking with them the news 'of the great boat race...how they swore peace and goodwill to all men, and how there now should be peace and prosperity through all the land'.[140] Imperial policy and Jesuan practice had combined to good purpose.

The efforts of Robertson and Hose are dwarfed by those of Cecil Earle Tyndale-Biscoe who, from 1890 to 1947, with extraordinary strength of purpose, honest Christian zeal and incredible personal stamina, took the athletic activities of English public school and ancient university to the Hindu Brahims of Kashmir. He epitomized Kingleyan virtues and sought to strengthen sinew and develop muscle on the river and the playing field in the interests of knight-errantry.[141]

These three men were both actual and symbolic pieces in a mosaic of moral purpose and practice. They represented a clear-cut attitude to individual, social and political behaviour which, in their simple but certain view, games in part both determined and reflected. In their approach to games, they epitomized a motive which encapsulated a great deal more than personal pleasure, private recreation, disciplinary expedience and egocentric aggrandizement. They were part of an ethical endeavour disseminated from the Colleges of both Oxford and Cambridge to places as varied as the squalid slums of London's East End, the spacious acres of Harrow 'footer' fields, the hot and humid hillsides of Ceylon, the high savannah of the South African veld, the tropical rain forests of Equatorial Africa, and the elegant Chieftains' Colleges scattered throughout the Indian sub-continent.

Jesus contributed enthusiastically to this ethical effort. It was at the centre of a concentric world; close to the centre stood the English public schools, half-way to the centre stood the English grammar schools, while at the circumference itself stood Australian, African, Indian and other imperial emulators. The College provided the wider society with moral exemplars, ideologues and diffusionists who, in a catenulate effort at progagation, preached and practised athleticism in Cambridge, Britain and Empire.

In the light of the evidence available it is reasonable to conclude that during the Victorian and Edwardian epochs, Jesus subscribed to the athleticism ideology as completely as did Harrow, Lancing, Loretto, Malborough and Uppingham. As in those schools, indulgence, rationalization, expedience and idealism were the confused, contradictory or complimentary characteristics of the enthusiastic.

Similarly the causes of this enthusiasm were complex. Glorified schoolmasters in the vanguard of fashion, the prevalence of public schoolboys, the College 'blood' as hero, concern with control, restricted leisure, ethical imperatives all determined action. It is equally reasonable to suggest that the 'broadening' role of the liberal education of late nineteenth-century Oxbridge had a physical as much as a cultural connotation. One dramatic consequence was the fact that Jesus played its full part in a movement – the encouragement and diffusion of organized athletic activities[142] – which transformed exercise into ethical endeavour, influenced the educational practices of Empire and Commonwealth and inspired the future recreational habits of the world. The contribution of other Oxbridge Colleges to this world-wide social revolution, and their significance in this regard, has still to be appreciated, investigated and evaluated.[143] Furthermore the political, social, educational and psychological aspects of this phenomenon have not yet received the attention from historians that their influence and impact merits.

Notes

* This paper was originally presented at a seminar at the Center for Studies in Higher Education, University of California (Berkeley), an extract was delivered at the X HISPA World Congress in July, 1983 and a shortened version has appeared in the American *History of Higher Education Annual*, 1984.

1 Hedley Peek, 'Sport Literature and its Critics', *Fortnightly Review* LXII (November), 797.

2 J.A. Mangan, *Athleticism in the Victorian and Edwardian Public School: The Emergence and Consolidation of an Educational Ideology* (hereafter *Athleticism*) (Cambridge, 1981), *passim*. Victorian public school headmasters promoted an enthusiasm for games for a variety of purposes: to bring unruly pupils under control, to ensure the right social image for their school, to advance a philosophy of 'sound living' and to provide distractions from 'unhealthy and unholy' thoughts.

3 It was a dual matrix involving the public schools and the ancient universities.

4 For example, the role of Dr J.E.C. Corrie in the evolution of Jesus athleticism, see below.

5 Francis Duckworth, *From a Pedagogue's Sketch Book* (London, 1912), p. 42.

6 Esme Wingfield-Stratford, *Before The Lamps Went Out* (London, 1945), p. 144.

7 See W. Baker. 'Sport and University Life in England 1879–1914', unpublished paper presented at the Clemson University Conference on Sport and Society (April 1982), p. 6.

8 See Mangan, *Athleticism*, Ch. 5, for a discussion of this point.

9 *Blackwood's Magazine*, Oct. 1866, p. 448.

10 *Contemporary Review*, March 1866, p. 337.

11 T.H. Huxley. 'Universities: Actual and Ideal', *Contemporary Review*, March 1874, p. 665.

12 Mangan, *Athleticism*, p. 123.

13 *Punch*, quoted in Mangan, *Athleticism*, p. 189.

14 Pattison's actual words, of course, were that the 'Colleges were boarding schools in which the elements of the learned languages are taught to youths', and are to be found in his famous *Suggestions on Academic Organisation with Especial Reference to Oxford* (Edinburgh, 1868), p. 35. I suggest the paraphrase is more appropriate. For a benevolent consideration of Pattison's lugubrious personality, see John Sparrow, *Mark Pattison and the Ideal of a University* (Cambridge, 1967), p. 74.

15 John Honey, *Tom Brown's Universe* (London, 1977), pp. 110, 111.

16 Mangan. *Athleticism*, p. 124.
17 A.C. Deane, *Times Remembered* (London, 1931), p. 53.
18 E.F. Benson. King's College, Cambridge, 1887–1892. For an earlier and non-fictional description of the simple, physical pleasures of Cambridge students see C. A. Bristed, *Five Years in an English University* (New York, 1855), pp. 397–8.
19 Charles Tennyson, *Cambridge from Within* (London, 1913), p. 166.
20 G.P. Gooch, 'Victorian Memories IV: Cambridge in the Nineties', *Contemporary Review*, Jan. 1956, p. 27.
21 F.J. Foakes Jackson, 'School and University in England, A Personal Retrospect', *Columbia University Quarterly* XXIII (4 Dec. 1931), 381. (Frederick John Foakes Jackson (1855–1941), undergraduate at Trinity 1876–79, chaplain and lecturer at Jesus College 1882, Dean 1895–1906. afterwards Briggs Graduate Professor of Christian Institutions in the Union Theological Seminary, New York.)
22 Rowland Prothero, *From Whippingham to Westminster* (London. 1938), p. 45.
23 W.E. Heitland, *After Many Years* (Cambridge, 1926), pp. 115ff.
24 A. Vibert Douglas, *The Life of Albert Stanley Eddington* (London, 1956), p. 7.
25 Heitland, op. cit., p. 115.
26 Leonard Woolf, *Sowing* (London, 1961). p. 159.
27 Leslie Stephen, *Sketches by a Don* (Cambridge, 1855), quoted in *Light and Dark Blue*, Oct. 1866, p. 455.
28 Mrs Humphrey Ward, *Robert Elsmere* (London, 1888), p. 53.
29 Walter Leaf, *Some Chapters of Autobiography with a Memoir by Charlotte M. Leaf* (London, 1909), pp. 70–1.
30 F.W. Pethwick Lawrence, *Fate has Been Kind* (London, 1941), pp. 30ff.
31 C.E. Tyndale-Biscoe, *Tyndale Biscoe of Kashmir* (London, 1921), p. 43.
32 T.C. Worsley, *Flannelled Fool* (London, 1967), p. 41.
33 Arnold Lunn, *Come What May* (London, 1940), *passim*.
34 Noel Annan. 'King's College Annual Report' (1961), p.64, quoted in L.P. Wilkinson, *A Century of King's* (Cambridge, 1980), p. 76.
35 Wingfield-Stratford, op. cit., p. 142. However, even in the rarified intellectual atmosphere of King's, the crude excesses of the hearty and the contemptuous ridicule of the intellectual by the muscular was not unknown. See ibid., p. 171.
36 Shane Leslie, *Long Shadows* (London, 1966), pp. 108–9.
37 Shane Leslie, *Film of Memory* (London, 1938), p. 254.
38 See W.H. Leigh, *Augustus Austin Leigh* (London, 1906), p. 64.
39 *Walter Headlam, His Letters and Poems with a Memoir by Cecil Headlam and a Bibliography by L. Howard* (London, 1910). Leigh is celebrated in *Granta*, 22 April 1893, pp. 273–4, and Headlam won an obituary in *The Sporting Times*, 31 Oct. 1908, p. 4.
40 For a consideration of public school magazines see Mangan, *Athleticism*, Appendix IIIb.
41 *Chanticlere*, Easter Term, 1889, pp. 3–4. The first number of *Chanticlere* in 1885 placed priorities in the right order, not merely by devoting much of its space to sport, but also by linking the Master firmly to this enthusiasm. See No. 1 (October), pp. 14–15.
42 *Chanticlere* No.2, Lent Term, 1886, pp. 3ff.
43 *Chanticlere* No.3, Easter Term, 1886, pp. 8–9.
44 *Chanticlere* No.4, October Term, 1886, p. 8.
45 *Eqq* No. 1, Easter Term, 1961, p. 11.
46 *Chanticlere* No. 7, Easter Term, 1887, pp. 25–6.
47 *Chanticlere* No. 11, Lent Term, 1889, pp. 11–12.
48 *Chanticlere*, October Term, 1887, p. 3.
49 *Chanticlere*, October Term, 1892, pp. 32–5.
50 *Chanticlere* No. 13, Michaelmas Term, 1889, pp. 7–9.
51 *Chanticlere* No.28, Michaelmas Term, 1894, p. 118.

52 Personal reminiscences of Dr L. Gardner-Smith, Fellow of Jesus College, on the occasion of the college dinner to celebrate his eightieth birthday.
53 *Chanticlere* No.63, Michaelmas Term, 1913, pp. 26–7.
54 E. Charwood-Smith, 'A Song of Cricket', *Chanticlere* No. 34. Lent Term, 1897, p. 114.
55 For example in *Chanticlere*, October Term, 1893, pp. 28–9.
56 B.H. Stewart, *Reminiscences* (Jesus College Archives) (1945). Some idea of the enthusiasm for sport at Jesus and the extent of the college's impact on Cambridge sport generally may be gained from this statement in the 1890s: 'An account of modern athletics which omits the revival of interest therein, rampant between 1863–4 at Jesus College, Cambridge is quite as imperfect as a book would be, which professed to describe the Oxford religious movement of 57 years ago, yet made no mention of Oriel College.' *Chanticlere* No. 17. Lent Term, 1891, p. 23.
57 Stewart, *Reminiscences*, Introduction.
58 Ibid., p. 1.
59 Ibid., p. 47.
60 Ibid., p. 69.
61 Shane Leslie, *Mark Sykes: His Life and Letters* (London, 1923), pp. 52–3. Sykes (1884–1919) came from a wealthy northern aristocratic lineage. He became a distinguished expert on the Near East and held various influential government posts including Chief Adviser on Near Eastern Policy (1916–18) until his early death.
62 Leslie, *Mark Sykes*, pp. 43–4.
63 Ibid., p. 44.
64 Ibid., p. 53.
65 H.A. Morgan (1830–1912), undergraduate at Jesus in 1849, Tutor in 1864, Master in 1885. E.H. Morgan (1838–96), undergraduate at Jesus in 1858, Fellow in 1864, Tutor in 1882, Senior Tutor in 1885, Dean in 1886. See Lancing Register, Third Edition, 1848–1932 for details of their careers as schoolmasters.
66 For further exemplars, see Mangan, *Athleticism*, Ch. 5.
67 Arthur Gray, *A History of Jesus College* (Cambridge, 1902), p. 23.
68 Ibid., p. 224.
69 Ibid., p. 227.
70 Ibid.
71 In addition, they were abolished for all university and college offices and for all Fellowships except those confined to clerics. By the University Statutes of 1882 the outcome of the Royal Commission into the Universities set up in 1877 all religious tests were abolished, no Fellows were required to be in Orders except the Dean, and all Fellows were free to marry.
72 Gray, op. cit., p. 229.
73 A. Gray and F. Brittain, *A History of Jesus College* (London, 1960), p.166. At the time Corrie became Master in 1849, there were 56 undergraduates and Jesus was eleventh in size among 17 Cambridge colleges. By 1869 numbers had increased to 100 and the College was sixth in size.
74 No less than five Fairbairn brothers rowed for Jesus. They were Australians, and the College boasted at least three more of their countrymen – their cousins George, Charles and Harry Armytage. It was the heyday of Australian oarsmen at Jesus. Steve Fairbairn, in a letter to Iris Osborne Morgan in the mid-1920s, remarked that her father, H.A. Morgan, was very willing to recruit such Australians provided they were gentlemen and would behave themselves (Letter dated 13 Feb. 1935, Iris Osborne Morgan Scrapbook, pp. 37–8). Steve Fairbairn, the most successful of the Fairbairns (1862–1938) was an extraordinary Jesuan symbol of philathletic enthusiasm and allegiance. He rowed in the Cambridge crews of 1882, 1883, 1886 and 1887. After his College days he spent a lengthy period in Australia, but in 1904 he returned to

England and virtually devoted himself full-time to coaching rowing. He became a famous and controversial coach. For some 30 years he coached the Jesus boats, wrote extensively on the art of rowing and popularized the sport all over the world through his correspondence and his books. The title of his autobiography provides some indication of his affection for his Cambridge college: Steve Fairbairn, *Fairbairn of Jesus* (London, 1937). On his own request, his ashes were buried in the Master's Garden. See *Dictionary of National Biography 1931–1940* (London, 1949), p. 267.

75   Fairbairn, op. cit., p. 71.
76   Gray and Brittain, op. cit., p. 17.
77   The records of the Society for the period up to the Great War are lost but those for the period 1917 to 1960 are extant and provide clear and vivid evidence of the 'bloods' arrogance, power and 'physical exuberance'.
78   Gray and Brittain, op. cit., p. 48.
79   Gray, op. cit., p. 228.
80   R.E. Swartwout, *Rhymes of the River and Other Verses* (Cambridge, 1927), p. 39.
81   *Chanticlere* No. 17, Lent Term, 1891, p. 17.
82   *Chanticlere* No. 17, Lent Term, 1891, p. 23.
83   Iris C. Osborne Morgan, *Memoirs of Arthur Henry Morgan* (hereafter *Memoirs*) (London, 1927), p. 146.
84   P.M. Thornton, *Some Things We have Remembered* (London, 1912).
85   *Blackwoods Magazine*, Oct. 1912, pp. 576–7.
86   Charles Hose, *Fifty Years of Romance and Research* (hereafter *Fifty Years*) (London, 1927), p. 21. For a fascinating synopsis of Hose's extraordinary career as imperialist, civil servant, botanist, biologist and scholar, see *Dictionary of National Biography 1922–1930* (London, 1939), pp. 431–3.
87   Osborne Morgan, *Memoirs*, p. 155.
88   Morgan was one of the early members of the famed and seminal Alpine Club. He was elected to the membership in 1863, six years after its foundation.
89   There are several published references to his famous effort. See *Alpine Journal* I, 97ff, and XXXII, 237–8.
90   Osborne Morgan, *Memoirs*, p. 187.
91   R. St. John Parry, *Henry Jackson OM: A Memoir* (Cambridge. 1926), p. 237.
92   *Chanticlere* No. 13, Michaelmas Term, 1889, p. 9.
93   F. Brittain and H.B. Playford, *A History of Jesus Boat Club* (Cambridge, 1962), p. 10.
94   Osborne Morgan, *Memoirs*, p. 210.
95   Ibid., p. 289.
96   Ibid., p. 212.
97   Walter Leaf, op. cit., p. 72. Perhaps this explains in part the paucity of his own intellectual efforts, at least as demonstrated by publication. Middle age did not bring with it a cessation of rowing effort. For years Morgan was a member of 'The Ancient Mariners', a group of Cambridge dons who steadfastly refused to abandon the river and who formed teams which competed with the undergraduates in the annual rowing competitions. For a nostalgic description of 'The Ancient Mariners', see T.F.C. Huddleston, 'The Ancient Mariners', *Cambridge Review*, 18 Jan. 1912, p. 190.
98   Osborne Morgan, *Memoirs*, p. 203.
99   P.M. Thornton, 'The Athletic Revival', *Chanticlere* No. 17, Lent Term, 1891, pp. 20–4. P.M. Thornton (1841–1918) was at Jesus between 1860 and 1865. He was an enthusiastic sportsman. He was the first Secretary of the Inter-University Sports. In late life he inspired the famous boat race in Ghent in 1911 between a Jesus crew and a Belgian crew which Jesus won. For many years he was honorary secretary of Middlesex CCC C.B. Lawes (1843–1911), Jesus 1862–66, was athletics blue 1864 and rowing blue 1865. He became a sculptor.

100 'Miscellaneous Notes and Accounts of Tutors 1863–1878', Co. 64, Catalogue Books, Muniment Room, Jesus College Archives.
101 T.W. Heyck, *The Transformation of Intellectual Life in Victorian England* (London, 1982).
102 Ibid., p. 171.
103 Stewart, op. cit., p. 30.
104 *Granta*, 17 May 1890, p. 334.
105 Ibid.
106 Gray and Brittain, op. cit., p. 171.
107 Cricket Blue 1888–91 (Cambridge won all four matches and Woods topped the Cambridge bowling averages) and rugby blue 1888–91. See H.M. Abrahams and J. Bruce Kerr, *Oxford versus Cambridge: A Record of Inter-University Contests from 1827–1930* (London, 1931), pp. 218–21 and 335–6.
108 Stewart, op. cit., p. 42.
109 F. Brittain, *It's a Don's Life*, (London, Heinemann), p. 184.
110 Ibid. Curiously Venn records that Morgan remained a bachelor all his life.
111 While they obeyed him, they despised him intensely. Evidence for this assertion is to be found in Gray and Brittain, op. cit., *passim*; in Brittain, op. cit., *passim*, but especially p. 184; *in Vanity Fair*, 19 Jan. 1889, p. 49 and in Osborne Morgan's *Memoirs*. Arthur Gray fulminated against him until his death, and provided the reason for his loathing in a letter dated November 1924: 'Only after his death I discovered the dishonesty of the man and his general incapacity which he concealed under a swagger. He left the College hundreds of pounds in debt and providentially for him his accounts were so muddled that nobody could say who had consumed the wine and cigars which he had bought and had somehow vanished. Almost everything he did in College building was wretchedly bad....' (Scrapbook of Iris C. Osborne Morgan).
112 Gray and Brittain, op. cit., p. 185.
113 Osborne Morgan, *Memoirs*, p. 242.
114 *Scrapbook of E.H. Morgan*, Jesus College Archives.
115 *Punch*, 29 July 1893, p. 37.
116 *Granta*, 17 May 1890, p. 334.
117 *Chanticlere*, Lent Term, 1896, p. 2.
118 See Alec Waugh, *The Loom of Youth* (London, 1917), p. 27, for the famous description of A.C. Carey, the fabled Sherborne games master. While Morgan was undoubtedly addicted to physical activities, this addiction may be placed in some sort of perspective by reference to his judicious and conscientious comments on school academic standards of the time in *The Standard*, 19 Nov. 1886, p. 47, which revealed that the man was more than a mere philathlete.
119 Obituary of J.C. Watt, *Chanticlere* (1931).
120 See J.J. Thompson, *Recollections and Reflections* (London, 1936), p.68. Delightful evidence of the longevity of 'Tommy's' enthusiasm for sport is to be found in a charming letter he wrote to an old Jesuan, Edward B. Ford, in February 1925. It provided a detailed review of life at Jesus including matters athletic, and towards the end he wrote 'Find very great difficulty in walking, don't see well and am a bit deaf but still enjoy life, especially when the mean are up. Games provide much pleasure still.' (The author is indebted to the Jesus College archivist Mr E.F. Mills for drawing his attention to this letter.)
121 Hose, *Fifty Years*, p. 26.
122 Heyck, op. cit., pp. 171, 185.
123 For a brilliant exegesis of the Cambridge don of the period, see Sheldon Rothblatt, *The Revolution of the Dons* (Cambridge, 1968), Ch. 6. In his subsequent study of British liberal education, *Tradition and Change in English Liberal Education: An Essay in History and Culture* (London, 1976), Professor Rothblatt widens his focus and with elegance and

sublety discusses the image of the Victorian don at both Oxford and Cambridge. See especially Chapter 11, 'Vicious Poisons Lie Hidden under Sweet Honey'.

124 Rothblatt, *The Revolution of the Dons*, p. 210.
125 Ibid., p. 246.
126 Heitland, op. cit., p. 143.
127 Ibid.
128 Richard Jenkyns, *The Victorians and Ancient Greece* (Oxford, 1980), p. 216.
129 Quoted in Headlam, op. cit., p. 150.
130 Obituary of Walter Headlam, *The Sporting Times*, 21 Oct. 1908, p. 4. For a splendid example of Headlam's 'Grecian' passion for bodily exercise see his ode to health in *The Cambridge Review*, 17 Feb. 1886, p. 220.
131 Jenkyns, op. cit., p. 221.
132 T.R. Glover, *Cambridge Retrospect* (Cambridge, 1943), p. 130.
133 R.C. Lehmann, 'Rowing at Cambridge', *English Illustrated Magazine*, April 1889, p. 153.
134 Frederick I. Pitman, 'Well Rowed Cambridge', *Fortnightly Review* XLII, 5 (1887), 217 and 222.
135 There were many more schoolmasters who exerted a similar influence. Among the most influential were J.E. Mellor (Jesus 1903–1906), J.H. Bruce-Lockhart (Jesus 1908–11). H.B. Playford (Jesus 1919–21), C.A.F. Fiddian-Green (Jesus 1920–23) and J.T. Badham (Jesus 1919–21).
136 *Haileyburian* VIII. 189 (9 April 1890), 466. See also *Harrovian*, 14 Nov. 1903, pp. 109–11 for an enthusiastic appreciation of his work at Haileybury.
137 Charles Hose, *Natural Man: A Record from Borneo* (London, 1926), p. 14.
138 Ibid., p. 152.
139 Ibid.
140 Ibid., p. 155. For a full description of this famous event, which was recounted throughout Cambridge, see 'A Savage Peace Conference' by 'W. McD', in *The Eagle* (the magazine of St John's College. Cambridge) XXI, 70–82.
141 C.E. Tyndale-Biscoe, *Kashmir in Light and Shade* (London, 1922), p. 268.
142 This will be discussed in the author's forthcoming book, *The Games Ethic and Imperialism: Aspects of the Diffusion of an Ideal* (London: Penguin/Viking, 1986) and republished by Cass in 1999.
143 This subject is currently being researched by the author.

Chapter 4

Athleticism in the service of the proletariat

Preparation for the English elementary school and the extension of middle-class manliness

J.A. Mangan and Colm Hickey

In 1888, with the publication of the Report of the Cross Commission,[1] it was clear that the teacher training colleges of England and Wales had been subjected to a thorough examination and had been found wanting. One significant omission from their educational provision was the absence of any conversion to the playing of team games. In the London colleges, the concern of this chapter, the emerging ideology of athleticism[2] had been neglected or ignored, either deliberately as in the case of Westminster in response to widespread Wesleyan opposition to games playing, or financially as in the cases of Borough Road and St Mary's, neither of whom had the space for these games. Even where games playing was established as in the Anglican colleges, it was on an *ad hoc* basis and did not reflect the acceptance of this increasingly influential educational ideology in the public schools and ancient universities. Within a generation, however, athleticism was to dominate college life. For the first time in the academic community, the reasons why, and ways in which this ideological transformation took place, will now be considered. This chapter, in general, will focus on the process of diffusion and, in particular, on the way in which rituals were used to underpin the diffusion process.

What this process amounted to, at one level, was the extension of a model of middle-class masculinity to the late Victorian and Edwardian teacher training college which served the working-class elementary school. As mentioned above, this extension has not been considered before, and moreover this aspect of socialsation into masculinity *as such* has also been overlooked. It adds another layer to various layers of European inculcation into 'proper' period masculinity. Of course, it is difficult, if not impossible, to measure its full impact although it is clear that it had some impact. It is not difficult, however, to record the attempt to promote an image of masculinity in elementary education which owed much

Originally published in *The European Sports History Review*, 2000, 2, pp. 112–139.
http://www.tandf.co.uk/journals

to the image of masculinity energetically promulgated in the middle-class secondary school systems of England, Britain and the Empire.[3]

If European masculinity is to be understood in its full complexity, and the making of European masculinity is to be considered in all its manifestations, then it is certainly time *teacher training colleges and their equivalents* throughout Europe, came into the reckoning. These institutions from the second half of the nineteenth century onwards, through the teachers they trained, had an influence on the gender expectations, attitudes and behaviour of working-class children, if for no other reason than the fact that these children were a captive audience for much of their childhood. A European comparative study of teacher training as an agency of inculcation into masculinity would be a valuable contribution to gender studies.

It was suggested somewhat tardily in the late 1980s that the sociologist and historian of sport could usefully adopt an interdisciplinary approach since it offers the possibility of a comprehensive analytical framework. 'Sociologists frequently complain that historians lack a conceptual framework for their research, whilst historians tend to feel that social theorists require them to compress the diversity of the past into artificially rigid categories and dispense with empirical verification of their theories. In truth both disciplines need each other.'[4]

This advice came rather late in the day. It was a well-meaning if belated recommendation. This interdisciplinary approach, had already been implemented, of course, some considerable time earlier. The 'new historian', utilising concepts from the social sciences, had been about for quite some time in the history of sport, as well as elsewhere in historical studies. Arguably, J.A. Mangan's *Athleticism* led the way as early as 1981. Mangan, trained in social anthropology, sociology and social history, utilised an integrated conceptual framework that allowed an explanation of key ritualistic manifestations of the Victorian and Edwardian public school system.[5] The distinguished cultural historian, Sheldon Rothblatt, has written of Mangan's integrated approach in *Athleticism in the Victorian and Edwardian Public School*, 'A central question of all exceptional historical work now is how to conceive and describe the ways in which new values and new arrangements for living and bringing meaning into life enter into and inform everyday social and institutional arrangements. This Mangan achieved superbly, combining an eye for the apt, even colourful, moment *with conceptual understandings drawn from sociology (the sociological process) and anthropology (the use of ritual and symbol). No one had quite done this before or done it so consistently* [emphasis added] .... The result was a breakthrough in depicting the development of the public schools and their histories down to our time.'[6] Academic perceptiveness, it could be argued, is far more useful as early implementation than eventual realisation. It is also the outcome of the awareness and recognition of source material. Perhaps it should not be over looked therefore that Mangan had published as early as 1971 papers on sociology, sport and ritual which included references to issues involving historical continuity and ritualism. His analysis of the rituals of the public school system, it is suggested, will now permit an explanation of significant aspects of ritual in the late nineteenth and early twentieth-century teacher training system.[7]

Athleticism in the second half of the nineteenth century influenced all middle-class educational institutions.[8] Donald Leinster Mackay has traced athleticism's development in the preparatory schools[9] while Mangan, especially, has discussed its impact in the public schools, grammar schools and the universities of Oxford and Cambridge.[10] By the late 1880s it had become, at the very least, an influential educational movement. When the teacher training colleges were scrutinised by the Cross Commission and it was found that their curriculum did not match up to mainstream middle-class educational philosophies, a new set of institutional educational priorities inspired by the movement were demanded, and implemented by new 'Oxbridge' educated principals who now introduced athleticism into the colleges.

Athleticism was spread among the colleges by downward 'diffusion'. The term is defined by Everett M. Rogers as 'the process by which an innovation is communicated through certain channels over time to members of a social system'.[11] He identifies six main elements of diffusion: innovation, compatibility, complexity, visibility, communication, and a social system.

As made clear above, by the 1880s athleticism was already becoming an established educational ideology in the middle-class schools and the ancient universities. At this time it was new, however, to the colleges. Rogers asserts that, 'it matters little ... whether or not an idea is objectively new as measured by the lapse of time since its discovery or invention ... If an idea seems new to the individual and he uses it then it is an innovation', and so it was in the colleges.[12] Somewhat self-evidently, an innovation, claims Rogers, will be more readily adopted by a group if it is felt to be advantageous and if the innovation is shown to be compatible with the existing values, past experiences and needs of the group. He adds, perhaps equally obviously; that if an innovation is not too complex then there is a much greater chance of successful adoption and that the benevolent visibility of an innovation is important for its widespread adoption. In short, the easier it is for individuals to see the beneficial results of an innovation, the more likely they are to adopt it. Rogers further claims that the essence of any successful diffusion process is the enthusiastic emulation of the ideas of those who have persuaded their neophytes of the value of these ideas. Truistically, successful communication is also a significant factor in the diffusion process: most individuals depend greatly upon a positive evaluation of an innovation clearly conveyed to them by individuals who have previously adopted it.

Finally, an important element in any successful diffusion is the presence of a social system. It allows the promotion of innovation. Within the social system individuals have an important role to play. Rogers identifies two distinct types: 'change agents' and 'opinion leaders'. Change agents introduce change formally within institutions. The men appointed as college principals in the wake of the Cross Commission were undoubtedly change agents *par excellence*. They implemented the values and practices of athleticism in the colleges, not least by the provision of facilities. Opinion leaders influence others within the system in an informal way. They are more cosmopolitan, enjoy higher social status and are more innovative than others with the result that 'they are at the centre of interpersonal communication networks'.[13] Their leadership is earned and maintained by personal competence, social accessibility and institutional conformity. The last decade of the nineteenth century and the first decade of the twentieth century saw a cadre of young, well educated, athletically minded Oxbridge men appointed to posts as junior tutors within the colleges, who ensured, consolidated and accelerated the assimilation of athleticism. They were clearly opinion leaders.

As agents of change, the principals of the London Colleges in the role of influential proselytisers such as P.A. Barnett, H.L. Withers, A. Burrell and F.J. Hendy at Borough Road; G.A. Gent and L.A. Hudson at St Mark's, Canon Cromwell and E. Daniel at St John's, H.B. Workman at Westminster and the Irish triumvirate of W. Byrne, A. Moynihan and E. Sheehy at St Mary's, all sought to advance athleticism within the colleges, but they required the support of opinion leaders. Confident, articulate staff who had been educated in schools and universities where athleticism already prevailed and who could persuade by word *and* deed were necessary. The principals, therefore, purposefully sought and appointed young mostly Oxbridge graduates who exemplified an enthusiasm for the ideology. Earlier in the public school system, this policy of recruiting similar enthusiasts had been adopted, of course, by G.E.L. Cotton at Marlborough for exactly the same purposes.

A particularly good college example is Leigh Smith who was appointed to the staff of Westminster College[14] as a history lecturer in 1905 some two years after the appointment of Herbert Workman who had become principal on the death of J.H. Rigg in 1903. Smith was educated at Kingswood School, Bath, which was mainly for the sons of Wesleyan ministers, and which had as its headmaster, Workman's brother. In 1898 Smith entered Durham University, the 'Oxbridge' of the north, as a classical scholar. In 1901 he obtained a first class honours degree in classics and philosophy. This was followed by a fellowship from 1903 to 1904. He then joined the staff at Harrogate College for a year. Then followed a brief period as a tutor at Hatfield Hall, Durham. At Westminster, Smith's official role was to lecture in classics and English history and to be one of four house tutors. However, his impact was to be significant in other ways! As the college historian, F.C. Pritchard, has observed, 'There was...nothing of the academician about him. He had shown his athletic prowess at school; he had represented his university also at cricket and rugby football; he had represented both Durham County and Lancashire at cricket.'[15]

The college had a lamentable record in competitive sport, and Pritchard is quite explicit about Workman's purpose in appointing Smith: 'the new principal resolved that the college should be preeminent in other directions besides academic study. That was the real reason why Dr Workman was determined to obtain the services of Leigh Smith, a man of 'boundless and contagious enthusiasm'.[16] Westminster, of all the London colleges, had the worst facilities for games, but under Smith's inspirational leadership, as will now be made clear, the students eventually made the most of their limited surroundings. They took to athletics and to the streets, running energetically about the area. Smith had his work cut out. An inter-year athletic sports meeting had been instituted by Workman in February 1906 inspired by the recent presentation of a London Inter-College Challenge Shield by G.B. Clough, a former student (1875–77). Smith organised training programmes for the students in preparation for the Shield competition that the college had entered for the first time two years earlier with disastrous results. It had finished bottom and Workman had ruefully noted in his log book, 'the participation of Westminster College in these competitive sports between the London training colleges for the first time was accompanied with some difficulty in getting the men to join'.[17]

Workman and Smith therefore systematically devised a programme of athletic events designed to ensure that Westminster's record in the Inter-College Shield would improve. Rather than waiting until the summer term to pick a scratch side the students were placed on a year-long athletic treadmill. An athletics meeting was held for the junior students in the autumn term. This meeting resulted in a junior team being selected for the annual seniors versus juniors meeting in the Easter term. The result determined the inter-college team. As Pritchard noted:

> Athletics became in fact what it has been ever since: an all-the-year round interest and not one limited to a mere few weeks. Individuals were encouraged to enter for events in various sports meetings in different parts of London, and experience began to make itself felt as a valuable ally of keenness. Leigh Smith persuaded the Principal (who needed little persuasion) that the holding of the inter-Year Sports at a recognised athletic centre would have a good psychological effect, and they were held at Stamford Bridge...[18]

This new competitive programme was augmented, as mentioned earlier, by regular training sessions inevitably supervised by Smith. They were not without their urban dangers. 'Training runs were organised, mainly taking place in the evenings, through the streets past the walls of the Gas, Light and Coke Company's domain; [and] in other directions, round Vincent Square which did at least provide fewer hazards in the shape of hansom cabs, though excited dogs have always been a problem!' And, records the college historian approvingly, 'it was in all this determined effort Leigh Smith himself who showed in practical fashion what is the keynote of all success: Keenness'.[19]

Workman and Smith thus did all they could to motivate the students. It is not entirely surprising, therefore, that articles urging the students to keep fit appeared with increasing frequency in the college magazine, *The Westminsterian*. Rhetoric reinforced running! As one contributor observed sanctimoniously:

> To keep in training is not a hard matter, if the rule of simplicity and moder-ation in all things be kept well in view. Some people think that to get themselves into training they must make themselves miserable and deny themselves everything they have been used to, and everything they like. There is no greater delusion. Peace of mind is of as great importance as soundness of

mind and limb...if a man gets plenty of sleep, is careful not to smoke too much, eats and drinks just enough good wholesome food to satisfy him, takes two or three short brisk runs each week and plays football once or twice a week he is bound to be in good trim...[20]

In 1908 Westminster *won* the coveted Inter-College Shield. It was, it appears, a worthy corporate effort! The winning team, it was reported in *The Westminsterian*, 'was truly representative of the efforts of the *entire* (emphasis added) College, for not only had the Principal sanctioned increased expenditure, but the kitchen staff had co-operated in the provision of a special diet'.[21]

Unquestionably the most extraordinary illustration of Leigh Smith's serendipitous influence on the students came in the First World War. Lieutenant William Thomas Forshaw of the Manchester Regiment, a student of Westminster between 1908 and 1910, won the Victoria Cross fighting against the Turks. Forshaw held his trench for 41 hours continually throwing bombs at the enemy for the entire period. After the war Forshaw, in a visit to the college and 'in a modest speech told his hearers that it was to Leigh Smith that he owed most, for the correct method of dealing with bombs was to go for the bomb and throw it out; that on the occasion he was holding the trench he remembered Leigh Smith's teaching in rugger: go for the ball! He had gone for the bomb each time one appeared and thrown it out, and in that very act he said, he recalled the practice in putting the shot at Westminster and felt that it was indeed standing him in good stead.'[22] Forshaw's tongue was certainly as smooth as his arm action.

Leigh Smith is clearly both the post-Cross Commission epitome of period middle-class masculinity, and the ideal period opinion leader, while Workman clearly fulfilled the part of institutional change agent. They were an impressive ideological 'double act'. Leigh Smith, for his part, effortlessly fitted into Workman's new post-Cross Commission vision for the college. His public school, university and athletic background ensured that he was a period *persona grata* in the new ideological climate. Unsurprisingly, when he left Westminster in 1914 to take up a post inspecting secondary schools in what was then Ceylon, the governing body was moved to note in its minutes that

> In parting with Mr Leigh Smith the Governing Body desires to put on record its sense of the great service that Mr Smith rendered to the College during the nine years that he fulfilled the post of Tutor in Classics. Not merely in the lecture room but in the life of the students Mr Smith held a place that cannot easily be filled. By his unfailing courtesy, tact and spirit of helpfulness, he won the affection and respect of all. The Governing Body, while congratulating Mr. Smith on his promotion recognises the loss which the College has suffered by his removal.[23]

On the face of it, even this encomium was something of an understatement! Leigh Smith is an outstanding example of one of the successful means by which athleticism was assimilated into an Edwardian London teacher training college.

He participated, he motivated, he organised, he coached – all with considerable success. In his years at the college it won the coveted Inter-College Shield four times. He proved to be the perfect opinion leader; he was also a presentable muscular Christian in the Kingsleyian mould: robust, decent, conscientious. In a word, manly. It is reasonable to suggest that at Westminster he was an influential and inspirational mover in the genesis of a new educational ideal, as well as the personification of period moral masculinity.[24]

Other examples of the transforming opinion leader are easily located. Cecil Rolo Peyton Andrews was educated at Merchant Taylors' School[25] from 1879 to 1888. He was awarded a scholarship to St John's College, Oxford, from where he graduated with a first class in classical moderations and a second class in literae humaniores. On leaving Oxford in 1893 he served the obligatory muscular and other educational apprenticeships. He was first a master at Highgate School.[26] A year later he became Master of the sixth form at Forest School.[27] In 1896 he was appointed to the staff of St John's College, Battersea.[28] An appreciative article about him appeared in the college magazine three years later.

'Mr. Andrews' honours are not confined to the Examination Room. As a boy at Merchant Taylors' he won his colours in the school boat and the 'Fives' Team. He rowed at Oxford for three years in his College Eight and was tried for 'Trials'. Since joining Battersea he has acted as Hon. Treasurer of the Sports Committee and has taken an active interest in the athletic life of the College which he has represented both in tennis and 'Fives'.[29] Here then is yet another ideological inseminator spreading his influence and bringing his college into the educational, *and gender*, mainstream of the period as demanded by the Cross Commission.

Another St John's tutor, H.S. Foster, was appointed as lecturer in classics and history in 1904. He had been educated at Marborough[30] from where he had gained an open exhibition to Merton College, Oxford. At Marlborough he had been an accomplished athlete gaining his colours at rugby and winning the 880 yards in the Public Schools' Championship in record time. At Merton he was Captain of Rugby and President of the Athletics Club. At St John's, the editor of the college magazine observed approvingly soon after his arrival, 'He has already turned out for the College fifteen and we hope to have his advice and guidance in preparation for the Inter-College Sports on May 7th.'[31]

And yet another with impeccable mainstream middle-class manly credentials was Clement Henry Swann. He attended Perse Grammar School, Cambridge, and Christ's College, Cambridge, in 1902–5 and became a member of staff at St Mark's College[32] in the same year. Some time later he wrote an article on cross-country running for the college magazine. It is informative. It began with a quotation from Robert Browning:

Oh our manhood's prime vigour! No spirit feels waste,
Not a muscle is stopped in its playing nor sinew unbraced.
Oh, the wild joys of living! the leaping from rock up to rock,
The strong rending of boughs from fir tree, the cool silver shock
Of the plunge in a pool's living water.[33]

The article continued in the same vein. It was a didactic piece of Edwardian prose celebrating confident *manliness*. 'You have endured a course of training, more or less rigorous, and this is to be the final test of the discipline you have made yourself subject to . . . you are determined to do your best, and what is more, feel a calm confidence in the certain knowledge of a latent power thus to extend yourself, owing to your fit condition.'[34]

G.F. Bartle has offered an almost convincing explanation for the appointment of these young Oxbridge games-playing tutors. Residential teacher training colleges, he has argued uncontroversially, had come in for a great deal of criticism at this time from many educational commentators and observers. One criticism centred on low academic standards. In consequence, the Education Department's regulations now permitted students to take university in place of Teachers' Certificate examinations. This new concession led to a rapid growth in the number of students seeking matriculation, intermediate and even degree qualifications while at college. To provide for the academic demands of these courses, the college committee gradually extended the policy it had adopted in the case of the principal and senior tutor and engaged young Oxford and Cambridge graduates on short-term contracts as junior tutors alongside the ex-students it had employed during the previous twenty years.[35] Bartle sees this change of policy as highly significant arguing that for example it,

> hastened the transformation of Borough Road[36] at Isleworth from a proto-type of the Victorian residential training college into an institution not unlike a Victorian public school, with a new emphasis on examination successes, a prefectorial system and a strong emphasis on games and physical fitness . . . Junior staff were selected almost as much for their athletic prowess as for their academic qualifications and all staff apart from Vice-Principal Barkby, were expected to participate personally in games.[37]

Bartle is walking on quicksand in his claims for a late Victorian public school emphasis on examination success but on all the other points he is on firm ground.[38]

What is clear of Borough Road is that to accommodate the new 'strong emphasis on games', new staff and new premises were urgently sought. The result was both a new site and a new principal, P.A. Barnett, whose arrival was described by a contemporary as the start of a new era.

> The College received a new life and a new milieu. The spirit of the elementary school and the grammar school was replaced by the richer and freer spirit of the university; the drab streets of Southwark were exchanged for the open fields of Isleworth. The new Principal looked a mere boy, but in the skill with which he affected the grand trek, and in the wisdom with which he reformed the system of education at the College, lifting it to a higher level and fitting it better to the tastes and talents of the students – in all this he proved himself a man, and a man of insight and courage.[39]

In the provision of 'open fields' he certainly showed himself 'a man'. Oxbridge staff at the new Borough Road include L.B.T. Chaffey, Christ Church Cathedral School, Oxford, and Christ's College, Cambridge, where in 1894 he represented his college at cricket, tennis and football as well as playing for the university XI at football, A.V. Houghton, Hertford College, Oxford, who presented the college with a Goodwill shield for cross-country running in 1895, and an interesting odd man out, Frank Harry Busbridge Dale. His father was an electrician and the family lived at 38 Connington Road, Shepherds Bush. He was a Foundation Scholar at St Paul's School in 1885, and won an Exhibition to Balliol College, Oxford, in 1889. He had a brilliant academic career at Oxford: Craven Scholar 1891, first class classics moderations 1892, fellow of Merton College 1894, Derby Scholar 1895, MA in 1897. In 1888 he joined the staff at Borough Road. And odd man out though he was – lower middle-class academic *par excellence* – he was a man for all athletic seasons. He had an immediate impact on the college. An editorial in the *B's Hum* (the college magazine) of February 1897 commented 'All Bs are proud of the fact that such a brilliant classical scholar is on the staff of the B.R.C. His work throws him into...intercourse with the Inter-Arts men and he has gained much popularity among them because of the vigorous way in which he is carrying them through their studies.' More to the period point perhaps, the editorial continued, 'He takes a prominent interest in sports and may frequently be seen in the fives courts. Mr Dale is too, an enthusiastic supporter of the football teams, even accompanying the teams when playing away.'[40]

As an influential period opinion leader, keen to make his mark, involvement in games was essential to Dale's masculine image, his professional popularity *and* his career. It is clear that Dale was not an outstanding athlete. There is no evidence in the Balliol College archives of his involvement in college or university teams, but he was nonetheless a period games enthusiast. His encouragement of the college sports teams, it may be quite reasonably suggested, had beneficial long-term educational consequences for himself, the training colleges and the elementary schools. His subsequent career after leaving Borough Road in 1900 prompts this suggestion as he left to become an HM Inspector of Schools, a post he held until 1906 when he became a HM Inspector of Training Colleges. A period as Divisional Schools Inspector followed and, in 1913, he became Chief Inspector for Elementary Schools in England and Wales. Here then was a man of influence in elementary education who subscribed to sport as an integral part of the gender education of working-class boys and who was in a position to ensure his views were taken into account. After 1906, it might be noted in passing, team games *as well as* drill, became part and parcel of formal elementary schooling![41]

An equally important figure in the spread of athleticism into the colleges arrived on the scene in 1900 with the appointment of Allan Ramsey Smith as house tutor at Borough Road. Smith had been educated at Loretto School,[42] a highly influential school in the heyday of athleticism,[43] under the headship of Hely Hutchinson Almond. He had a brilliantly successful career at the school representing it at fives, hockey and rugby and captained the XV. He was also a prefect and editor of the school magazine *The Lorettonian* before, predictably, becoming head boy. From Loretto he went to Trinity College, Oxford, where he was secretary of the athletics club as well as captain of the university XV in the varsity matches of 1897 and 1898, and from 1895 to 1900 he was a Scottish rugby international, captaining the side in 1900. He graduated from Oxford in 1898 with a 3rd class in classical moderations and a second class in literae humaniores, and then spent two years travelling around the world (his father was a wealthy cotton broker in Liverpool) before taking up his post at Borough Road.

Smith's stay at Borough was just over a year, but during that time he made an impressive impact on college life. He played for the 1st XV and was a dominant figure, who contributed substantially to the ethos first introduced by Barnett. After leaving Borough Road in 1901 he was for two years a Junior Inspector of Schools and then, from 1903 to 1908, Inspector of Schools in Liverpool. The governors of Loretto School then appointed him headmaster. They declared that they were satisfied they had 'chosen a man strongly imbued with the teachings of the late Dr Almond, and...whose training and experience preeminently fit him for the Headmastership of Loretto'.[44] Later Frank Stewart, author of a history of the school, almost superfluously, commented that 'Smith was a devotee of Almond and in full sympathy with his educational theories including a determination to train the body as well as the mind'.[45]

It is instructive to consider Smith more closely to obtain a full measure of his commitment to Almondian principles. This commitment was so complete that he would certainly have carried it with him into the English elementary schools which he inspected and advised. It certainly inspired his work with working-class boys outside school hours.

At Loretto Smith faithfully followed in Almond's footsteps, espousing what Almond had described as Lorettonianism.[46] He was a muscular Christian of non-doctrinal inclination concerned with the health of body and soul. His collected school sermons,[47] published the year after he died in 1927, reveal a man who saw life as a series of struggles against temptations and vices of all kinds that could only be rejected through a combination of moral and muscular fitness. He once counselled his Lorettonian boys: 'If you would strengthen your faith, be not ashamed to show admiration for what you know to be right, for moral courage always brings faith with it.' He went on to link physical and moral courage.

We have many opportunities here for showing courage in the face of difficulties, and you are generally quick to appreciate it when it is shown upon the cricket or football field. But this is not always the most difficult kind of courage. If you would strengthen your faith – the shield wherewith ye shall be able to quench all the fiery darts of the wicked – you must learn to appreciate and practise the courage which will not win applause, but which will be greeted with ridicule or resentment.[48]

Sermons that he preached during his headship covered such varied topics as 'The Great Call, Patriotism, Arming for Life's Battles and True Greatness'. All, however, contained the moral imperative that one should walk in the footsteps of

Christ, be prepared for possible criticism, and by drawing strength from Christ's life, rise above it: 'Teach yourself now, as the choosing and chosen followers of Christ, to find in His example a greatness of spirit. Be courageous for His sake where you will gain nothing here.'[49]

It is important for the purposes of this chapter, to appreciate that Smith was a committed supporter of Almond's Lorettonianism for all social classes. He sought a classless acceptance of his views. As Stewart, has observed:

> Smith, among his many qualities was a great humanitarian. His main interest was in people, and especially in boys. But his interest was not limited to the class of boys which fortune had put into his care. When a young man, working as an Inspector of Schools in the Liverpool area, he felt a desire and respon- sibility to spread the principles of Lorettonianism further afield in some practical way. The large mass of the population, he declared, and especially the poor classes, were absolutely ignorant or regardless of the laws of health, and an organised effort should be made to spread the knowledge of these laws. So, in 1908, he and some other Lorettonians in Liverpool had started a Boys' Club there which was run in conjunction with St James' Parish Church and was called the St James' Lorettonian Club.[50]

After the First World War, anxious to spread the Almondian principles of health further, Smith approached the Headmaster of Fettes and together they founded a boy's club in Edinburgh known as the Fettesian–Lorettonian Club which was run on the same lines.[51] Like Dale, he unquestionably exerted an influence on the elementary school and the elementary schoolboy and attempted to shape him in his own 'manly' image.

The evidence then, is clear: public school and university-educated games-playing enthusiasts were deliberately sought by the Principals of Borough Road, St Mark's, St John's and Westminster. The recruitment of these men represented at least an attempt to establish a symbiotic relationship between the world of relative privilege – public school and Oxbridge, and the world of relative poverty – elementary school and pupil-teacherdom. The teacher training college was a con- duit along which middle-class experiences, ideals and values were transmitted. The Oxbridge-educated tutor could bring things to the colleges that they badly lacked – social status, bourgeois idealism, a middle-class muscular morality and a games-playing commitment, whilst the colleges could give the young graduates embarking on an educational career, the one thing that they had no knowledge of, experience of elementary education. Many of the junior tutors used the college as a stepping stone to educational administration, 'and after a brief stay went on to better paid posts and more distinguished careers, elsewhere'.[52] In transit they brought with them contemporary educational ideas, ideals and activities and ensured their acceptance.

How successful were these Oxbridge tutors in promoting athleticism, and a manly, muscular Christianity in the colleges? How quickly did these ideals spread?

How fully were they accepted by staff and students? Answering these questions *in part* will involve an examination of the ways in which ritual was used to advance acceptance. It will also provide an illustration of how an inter-disciplinary approach on the part of cultural historians can throw light on historical change.

The introduction of athleticism into teacher training college life was reinforced by patterns of behaviour that were highly ritualised in nature. Before discussing and analysing the ritualistic life of the students and demonstrating the ways in which ritualism helped promote athleticism's diffusion, it may be helpful to consider the general importance of ritual and symbol to individuals and communities.

As J.A. Mangan has observed, 'To define ritual is not a simple task. Social scientists have many definitions and diverse opinions.'[53] He favours the definition of T. Paterson: 'Rituals are formalised behaviour patterns, methods of communication, verbal and non-verbal, necessary for the establishment of relations among members of a group or between groups.'[54] In his discussion of ritual Mangan sees it as having five main purposes: it serves as a mechanism for the transmission of cultural values through the systematic repetition of actions; it strengthens the accepted value system by the development of a mass reflex action; it acts as a focusing mechanism by creating a frame for experience which assists concentration and minimises distractions; it helps memory by making vivid what was dim and recalling what was forgotten; finally, it controls experience and shapes social reality 'in the sense that by producing powerful emotive responses to relationships it makes these relationships lasting'.[55] In these ways ritual helps develop, promote and reinforce feelings which determine roles and role-playing in society. This fundamental view of ritual, it is argued here, has both relevance and significance to an analysis of the late Victorian and Edwardian London teacher training colleges and their espousal of athleticism as means of inculcating period moral manliness.

B. Bernstein, H.L. Elvin and R.S. Peters for their part, in a complementary consideration, believe that ritual 'generally refers to a relatively rigid pattern of acts specific to a situation which construct a framework of meaning over and beyond specific situational meanings'. For Bernstein, Elvin and Peters 'the symbolic function of ritual is to relate the individual through ritualistic acts to a social order, to heighten respect for that order, to reverify that order within the individual and, in particular, to deepen acceptance of the procedures used to maintain continuity, order and boundary and which control ambivalence towards the social order'.[56] Bernstein and his colleagues also maintain that schools (and by extension here training colleges) operate at two levels, transmitting both an instrumental and expressive culture. The instrumental culture relates to the specific curriculum, whereas the expressive culture is concerned with consensus.[57] This expressive culture utilises consensual and differentiation rituals. Consensual rituals bind a community together. 'They recreate the past in the present and project it into the future … relate the school's values and norms to those held by, or alleged to be held by, certain dominant groups in the non school society … give the school its specific identity as a distinct and separate institution,'[58] and they 'consist of assemblies and ceremonies of various kinds together with the consensual lineaments of dress, the imagery of signs, totems, scrolls and plaques for revivifying of special historical contests and other symbolic features'.[59] Differentiation rituals, on the other hand, 'are concerned to mark off groups within the school from each other, usually in terms of age, sex, relation or social function…[They] deepen local attachment behaviour to, and detachment behaviour from specific groups; they also deepen respect behaviour to those in various positions of authority, and create order in time.'[60] In this latter way, these differentiating rituals can, and do, bond communities and individuals through the creation of stable, ordered, hierarchical frameworks within which to operate.

Mangan has further identified three of the most common types of school ritual activity: rites of passage, rites of deference and rites of intensification. Rites of passage 'assist individuals or groups [to] effect a successful change of status by providing formal and public recognition of the change'; rites of deference stress a pattern of 'subordinate superordinate relationships so as to create social order through regularised social relationships', and rites of intensification 'are a means of strengthening group cohesion primarily in times of stress, but not necessarily so. They also function as regular on-going cohesive processes.'[61]

Mangan, together with Berstein and his colleagues in their respective discussion of ritual in schools, it is suggested, offer useful conceptual tools with which to explore the role of ritual in the London teacher training colleges in their effort to implement both the precepts and practices of athleticism. The last years of the Victorian age and the beginning of the Edwardian age witnessed a burgeoning of ritualised behaviour in the colleges linked to sporting activities and associated dress codes and hierarchical relationships, that served, directly and indirectly, to bind the members together and to promote order and stability.

For reasons that will become apparent later, to reiterate, it should be made absolutely apparent that differentiating rituals are commonly used to establish institutional 'pecking orders' in the interest of community cohesion and control, and this was the case in the colleges. This is made abundantly clear from the following comment by P.B. Ballard, writing of his time as a student at Borough Road during 1883–85. He observed that between

> the Seniors, or second-year men, and the Juniors, or first-year men, was a great gulf fixed. It was the Seniors who fixed it, and they who preserved it. A Junior who met a Senior in the street had to raise his hat, but the Senior was not obliged to return the salute. A clear lack of respect was punished by slippering. The culprit's bedroom was raided at dead of night, and he received an assault upon his person which left him smarting – and thinking.[62]

This was not all. It was 'during the first week of the year that the Seniors made their privileged position most palpably felt. They had a set of hoaxes, some traditional, some spontaneous, which they sprang on the new-comers.'[63] There was, for example, the traditional football hoax. In an early football match between the Seniors and Juniors, the Seniors deliberately fielded a weakened team thus allowing the Juniors to win. Then, with the replay, observed Ballard, 'came the real match, which involved a penalty for the losers (such as providing jam all round for tea), and this time the Juniors were beaten to a frazzle!'[64]

Similar rituals were to be found in all the London colleges although the precise nature of the ritual differed from college to college. They were, however, by no means unique to the metropolitan colleges. A particularly good example is provided by St Paul's, Cheltenham.[65] On their first morning at St Paul's the juniors were woken at 6.30 and told to dress for drill. The drill sergeant was a senior student who took them on a countryside march and slipped away unnoticed leaving them completely lost, and on their second night 'the juniors were subjected to a visit from the "Jury", twelve men chosen from the Senior Year to undertake the management and education of the Juniors. The Jury grotesquely attired, holding candles and whistling a mournful tune marched through the Junior corridors, halted and shouted "Juniors must not be familiar with their Seniors. Juniors beware. This is not a joke!" '[66] Juniors were subsequently christened with nicknames, including demeaning names such as 'Nancy' and 'Soapy'. 'The christening involved the anointing of students with various obnoxious substances.' Furthermore, throughout the year 'the Juniors had to perform various minor acts of abasement, such as snapping their fingers when entering a room. They could be punished for failure to do this or for generalised crimes such as "cheek". Punishment consisted of "cold baths, gauntlets of knotted towels and the like." '[67] The pecking order was thoroughly established.

Similar ritualised behaviour occurred at St Luke's College, Exeter, a Church of England college founded in 1839. F. Fuller, the college historian, has described the first day of the college year. When the new students arrived they were met by a number of leading senior students. The same Drill hoax as at St Paul's followed. The seniors would form 'the whole junior year into a drill squad and march them to Exeter Drill Hall, leaving the poor Juniors to work out their own salvation'.[68] This was to ensure, of course, that they quickly appreciated that there was 'a great distinction between the Senior and Junior years'. Furthermore, the newcomers soon learnt, painfully if necessary, that 'Seniors...had to be addressed by the Juniors with almost awe and reverence'.[69]

From these descriptions of the ways in which new students were received into the various colleges, it is clear that the colleges had elaborate, well-prepared and well-rehearsed rituals which served to ensure the humiliation of juniors. These activities were far more than student high jinks. They had a more profound significance and it is now time to emphasise their fundamental purpose. The actions of the senior students are assertive rites of differentiation and deference, relating 'the individual through ritualistic acts to a social order, to heighten respect for that order...and in particular, to deepen acceptance of the procedures used to maintain continuity, order and boundary'.[70] From the first moment of their arrival these 'freshmen' were made sharply aware of institutional precedent. Juniors were subordinate to seniors, seniors to their elected officers (the 'Jury' at St Paul's and 'the Poets' at Borough Road) who in turn were subordinate to the junior tutors, who were subordinate to the house tutors and so on, in a reflection of the considerable importance attached to hierarchy in Victorian and Edwardian education and society.

Charles More, rather curiously, in his analytically myopic history of St Paul's Training College, Cheltenham, is critical of the transparently obvious comment that such rites 'can be defined as ways of stressing a structured pattern of subordinate/ superordinate relationships...which create social order through regularised social relationships',[71] and thus by extension, of the views, of both Mangan and Bernstein and his colleagues, not to mention the views of the most distinguished of social anthropologists.[72] Since More does not appear to have consulted the work of anthropologists of the calibre of Victor Turner and Mary Douglas, he remains easily confident in his ignorance. More argues that while rites of deference might or might not have a functional role, 'their functionality for an institution depends on whether structured patterns of subordinate/superordinate relationships are the aim of the institution'. The fact that many institutions at the time got on perfectly well without such rites, claims More, bravely without a scrap of supporting evidence, 'shows that they are not functional to social order as such'. Therefore, he concludes that 'given that there was no particular reason in a training college why senior students should lord it over juniors, it seems likely that the St Paul's rites of deference were needless to say actively dysfunctional'.[73] There are, of course, several obvious institutional reasons why seniors should 'lord it' over juniors. They have been mentioned above. They will be discussed further shortly.

More adds somewhat brashly that, whatever *post hoc* reasons anthropologists, in his injudicious words, 'dream up', at St Paul's, deferential rituals had no positive institutional reason for existing![74] More's idiosyncratic argument that not only St Paul's but *many* institutions, crucially unnamed and unlocated by him, got on well without rituals functional to social order, is interesting. Clearly it would be illuminating to obtain an accurate list of Victorian and Edwardian educational institutions *indifferent* to structured patterns of subordinate/superordinate relationships! A new field of scholarship would open up.

More's analysis then leaves a great deal to be desired. His reading is unacceptably limited and his empirical evidence casually omitted. Mangan, in contrast, has the basic virtue in his analysis of the public school of providing ample evidence of the functional *and* dysfunctional purposes of ritual.[75] In his analysis of the teacher training college, unfortunately, the same cannot be said for More. His unsubstantiated assertion that as many institutions got on perfectly well without such rites reveals that they are not functional to social order as such, should not go unchallenged. It is a glib assertion. Evidence from the London colleges alone contradicts his casual and complacent view. There is clear evidence that rites of deference were an integral part of the college ritualisation process. These rites served positive purposes. For this reason, and others, they were endorsed by the college authorities. Among other things, they taught students to *know their place* – a valuable lesson for later schoolroom discipline, a point More overlooks completely. A further salient point that More overlooks is the crucial role that the public school and ancient university personnel had as 'change agents' and 'opinion leaders' in an age much given to the security and stability provided by hierarchical structures. The public schools and ancient universities were replete with deferential rituals. What these institutions also had was cachet. For this reason alone if no other, they were to be imitated by the colleges. There are more compelling purposes served by ritual. They will be considered later.

By the time More wrote dismissively of rites of deference, Mangan, of course, had devoted an important segment of what has become accepted as a seminal work, to the processes of ritual, symbol and myth in the *public school*. He had not extrapolated to the training colleges. He might usefully have done so. His analysis fits them tightly. Any blindness of vision is More's.

There is a further dimension to any consideration of ritual in the colleges. One significant way in which ritualisation for order, security and stability was promoted was by what has been elegantly called the invention of tradition, 'a set of practices, normally governed by overtly or tacitly accepted rules and of a ritual or symbolic nature, which seek to inculcate certain values and norms of behaviour by repetition, which automatically implies continuity with the past'.[76] Three overlapping types of invented tradition have been suggested: 'those establishing or symbolising social cohesion or the membership of groups real or artificial communities; those establishing or legitimising institutions, status or relations of authority; and those whose main purpose was socialisation, the inculcation of beliefs, value systems and conventions and conventions of behaviour'.[77] This list is important for understanding the ways in which the various forms of ritual affected behaviour in the colleges. The invented deferential rites that new students had to endure for example, were clearly meant, among other things, to legitimise an institutional system of student authority. An authority established in this way by students over other students resulted in a student hierarchy which ensured order and discipline within the student body, and thus by extension within the college itself! Such a system, of course, was perfected, initially, in the public schools.[78] One perfectly understandable purpose was that it reduced the burden of control carried by the senior college authorities and made life more tolerable for them!

In the assertion of student authority, the 'Poets' at Borough Road appear to have had a role similar to the public school 'bloods' (successful athletes). Every year 12 of the most prestigious athletic seniors were elected and given the name 'Poets' after the corner of the dormitory that they occupied.[79] Bartle states that one of their functions was 'to maintain college enthusiasm at football and cricket matches, where they acted as cheerleaders' – a practice common in public schools of the time! More particularly, says Bartle, their role was to keep the juniors in their place – a practice equally common in the public schools of the time.[80] The 'Poets' were augmented by college prefects 'who applied college rules and supervised private study and who seem, on the whole, to have collaborated with the 'Poets' in enforcing subordination'.[81] Juniors from their first evening in the college:

> ...were regimented in Nazi-style by Prefects, given orders with shouts, threatening, and epithets, and instructions on their behaviour when in the presence of Prefects, Poets, Seniors in general. They were forced to button their coats,

to wear certain ties, to be practically dumb and certainly without a laugh at the meal table...forbidden to leave till 'their Seniors' had finished. In the Common Room they sat clear of the easy chairs, in their cubicles they listened in silence to chants, threats and fearsome stories of former Juniors who had transgressed the law...they were excluded from privileges and sometimes from teams. And not till they got to know each other and found safety in numbers did they dream of finding their feet, let alone swim against the tide.[82]

The power of the Poets was considerable. Juniors who tried to stand up to them would find themselves 'seized at the dead of night by the Poets and slippered in a particular cubicle along "Poet's Corner" which was used for the purpose'.[83] As Mangan has written of similar punishment rituals in the public schools 'Through a single punishment ritual they defined social position, emphasised the location of power and moulded group behaviour.'[84] Apart from physical beatings the Poets could also order acts of public humiliation for junior students such as sweeping the leaves off the football pitch for displaying insufficient enthusiasm at a college football match. E.J.W. Killick, at Borough Road from 1912 to 1914, has written that the juniors were made 'to sing for the amusement of the Seniors after Saturday tea, which was the occasion for the vociferous rendering of the College song, finishing up with the "war cry" '.[85] Bartle has observed significantly that 'No interference with this practice seems to have come from the House Tutors who had themselves been Prefects and Poets in earlier college generations and probably believed that awkward Juniors deserved putting in their place.'[86] Furthermore, the Poets were clearly sanctioned and supported by the principal. One of his favoured students, Herbert Milnes, was a prominent Poet. In this role he upheld college policy to the satisfaction of Burrell. 'In the B.R.C. Parliament of 1894 he entered with a fancy waistcoat expanded to the utmost, kid gloves, walking-stick, buttonhole, tall hat, and even an eye-glass...His answers to all political questions referring to Fives Courts, Rushers, and Brown Bread Returns were considered very happy and all opponents were silenced.'[87] Burrell's admiration for Milnes' orthodoxy was such that when Allan R. Smith, the Loretto and Oxford-educated house tutor left for a position with the Inspectorate, 'the Committee on Burrell's strong recommendation, immediately appointed Milnes as House Tutor'.[88] Thus deference rituals should not be carelessly dismissed. As the eminent social anthropologist Mary Douglas has reminded us:

if we accept that the social relations of men provide the prototype for logical relations between things, then, whenever this prototype falls into a common pattern there should be something common to be discerned in the system of symbols it uses.... The first logical categories were social categories; the first classes of things were classes of men...It was because men were grouped and thought of themselves in the forms of groups that in their ideas they grouped other things. The centre of the first scheme of nature is not the individual; it is society.[89]

Douglas further refers to the 'rule of distance' in which 'the more the social situation exerts pressure on persons involved in it, the more the demand for conformity tends to be expressed by a demand for physical control'.[90] The sometimes trivial, sometimes terrifying, but always purposeful rites of deference, physical and otherwise, of the Poets and others are crucial to an understanding of the ordered group arrangements of the London colleges.

The views of Victor Turner are also illuminating on this topic. He provides thoughtful explanations of the purpose and value of deference rituals as mechanisms of social order. Turner has written informatively of hierarchy, humility, status elevation and status reversal. In his consideration of rituals of status reversal, he writes of 'the liminality frequently found in cyclical and calendrical ritual usually of a collective kind in which, at certain culturally defined points in the seasonal cycle, groups or categories of persons who habitually occupy low status positions in the social structure are positively enjoined to exercise ritual authority over their superiors; and they, in their turn, must accept with good will their ritual degradation'.[91] The jam hoax at Borough Road is an excellent example of this. By deliberately allowing the junior students to win a preliminary football match, the senior students appeared ridiculous and second best. However, they reasserted their power by subsequently defeating the juniors some weeks later, to the juniors cost in more ways than one. In this way the seniors and their superior status was driven home and reinforced and internal order established and secured. More may find Turner's anthropological analysis unconvincing, 'dreamed up' to use his expression, but it is certainly more convincing and intellectually rigorous than his own explanation of a 'gradual historical process' of emerging stability, security and order due exclusively to rites of intensification, which incidentally, he neither defines, explains, or traces.

In summary, ritualisation in various forms was an integral part of the students' lives, ordering, stabilising and structuring their relationships. It reveals a lack of investigation, contextualisation, comprehension and sensitivity to suggest otherwise. In the college, rites of deference maintained discipline, established order, provided a stable hierarchical security, ensured desirable and desired positions of power and offered the opportunity for the acquisition and display of high status – all functional elements in college, and later, life.

Of course, rites of intensification *were* also powerful phenomena in college life. One was the annual athletics meeting of the colleges held at Stamford Bridge. First inaugurated in 1898 by the Principals of Borough Road, St John's and St Mary's, it soon became *the* major sporting event for all the colleges. This athletic meeting was a pre-eminent rite of intensification. As Mangan has written, such rituals 'bound together the whole group as a moral community'.[92] In this regard, for the public schools, he suggests, the annual Eton versus Harrow match at Lord's was 'a focusing mechanism, mnemonic agent and value filter *par excellence*'.[93] For the colleges the athletic meeting at Stamford Bridge served the same purposes. It is difficult to overstate its importance. T. Adkins, the author of *St John's College History*, and himself a former student of the college, provides clear evidence both of the seriousness with which the students viewed this competition and other athletic activities, and of the new muscular masculine world they now inhabited: '...the Sinjun of today is a vigorous and enthusiastic athlete keeping himself in training for sports of all kinds and scoring successes all round...we see energetic younger brethren hard at it sprinting, leaping, putting the weight and preparing themselves in all sorts of ways to go anywhere and do anything'.[94]

By the end of the first decade of the twentieth century athleticism was firmly entrenched in the London colleges. Its diffusion from private school and privileged university to teacher training college was more or less complete. Diffusion had been promoted, reinforced and consolidated in part by a student lifestyle that was marked by a new and highly ritualised masculine behaviour. Rituals had played a part in establishing in the young students, a masculine, muscular Christian view of the world. It was a view ensured essentially by certain criticisms made by the Cross Commission, by the appointment of middle-class principals sympathetic to these criticisms and to the public school and university games cult that in part produced them, by the recruitment of appropriate young staff from the same background with the same convictions – that there were moral values to be learnt on games fields, that in part 'manliness' was to be achieved there, that in part masculinity was to be learnt there, that in part by way of these things a 'proper' masculinity was to be transmitted via the elementary school to the working-class boy to his advantage, for his betterment and for the harmonious well-being of society.

Athleticism, of course, was a complex educational ideology. It became both a popular and fashionable college ideology for more than educational reasons. It was popular because it offered a distraction, as in the public school, from what was otherwise a sterile and restricted training college classroom curriculum. It was fashionable also because it allowed the college the chance to emulate the upper and middle classes. In a period when the status of the elementary schoolteacher was held in low esteem, the opportunity to mix with, ape and compete against socially more advantaged opponents, was attractive. In a valedictory farewell in the *B's Hum* to A.V. Houghton, a graduate of Hertford College, Oxford, who was a tutor at Borough Road from 1895 to 1898, the writer wrote appreciatively:

> Of his powers in the cricket and football fields we cannot speak too highly, and it must be remembered that it was largely through the instrumentality of Mr. Houghton that our teams have been able to meet (and even vanquish) such redoubtable opponents as Old Etonians or the strong cricket team which Mr. Lacey brought down last year.[95]

The teacher training colleges fully recognised that they needed to improve their social image if they were to flourish, win favour, earn greater respect. So it was due to mixed motives that athleticism arrived, flourished in and spread from the teacher training college. Whatever the reasons behind the diffusion, assimilation and reproduction of athleticism, however, it was responsible for gradually promoting a new masculinity, a masculinity of the games field, in the elementary schools and among the elementary schoolboys of England, Britain and the Empire.[96] This responsibility within the colleges is considered here for the first time. In a consideration of the making of masculinity in Europe, it is argued here in addition that the significance of this chapter goes further. It establishes a precedent. The relationship between gender construction, identification and expectation and the teacher training college and the consequent influence on the working class boy in the elementary school system merits further and fuller consideration *throughout* Europe.

Notes

1   Education featured strongly as an issue in the general election of 1885, which was won by the Conservatives under Lord Salisbury. The Catholic Archbishop, Cardinal Manning, had led a campaign to protect the status of denominational schools and had written to Salisbury seeking his support. When in power Salisbury established a Royal Commission to 'inquire into the working of the Elementary Education Acts, England and Wales'. The chairman was his Home Secretary, R.A. Viscount Cross (1823–1914). The Commission sat for three years before producing a final, but divided Report in 1888. See R.A. Cross, *A Family History* (Eccle Riggs, 1900) *and A Political History* (Eccle Riggs, 1903). Interestingly, in neither memoir does Cross refer to his role on the Commission.
2   For what is generally recognised as the authoritative study of athleticism as an educational ideology, see J.A. Mangan, *Athleticism in the Victorian and Edwardian Public School: The Emergence and Consolidation of an Educational Ideology* (Cambridge, 1981). *Athleticism* was reprinted by Frank Cass (London) in 2000.
3   See J.A. Mangan, *The Games Ethic and Imperialism* (London, 1998).
4   R. Holt, *Sport and the British: A Modern History* (Oxford, 1989), p. 357.
5   See Mangan, *Athleticism*. For a consideration of ritual and symbol in the public school system incorporating an inter-disciplinary approach see especially ch.7.
6   Sheldon Rothblatt, Introduction to the Cass edition of *Athleticism in the Victorian and Edwardian Public School* (London, 2000), p. xix.
7   In fact, J.A. Mangan utilised concepts from the social sciences in a very much earlier study of sport in society. See J.A. Mangan, 'Physical Education as a Ritual Process', in J.A. Mangan (ed.), *Physical Education and Sport Sociological and Cultural Perspectives. An Introductory Reader* (Oxford: Basil Blackwell, 1973), pp. 87–102. Indeed, an earlier paper published in *Research Papers in Physical Education, Carnegie College of Physical Education*, 2, 1 (Jan. 1971), 2–7, dealt with ritual.
8   For evidence of the ideology at 'Oxbridge', see for example, J.A. Mangan, 'Lamentable Barbarians and Pitiful Sheep: Rhetoric of Protest and Pleasure in Late Victorian and Edwardian "Oxbridge" ', *Victorian Studies*, 34, 4 (Summer 1991), 473–90.
9   See Donald Leinster-Mackay, *The Rise of the English Prep School* (London, 1984).
10   See J.A. Mangan, 'Grammar Schools and the Games Ethic in the Victorian and Edwardian Eras', *Albion*, 15, 14 (1984), 313, and see notes 2,7 above.
11   Everett M. Rogers, *Diffusion of Innovations* (London, 1983), p. 5.
12   Ibid., p. 11.
13   Ibid.
14   Westminster College was established in 1851. The impetus for its construction came from the Wesleyan Education Committee who believed that a Training College was vital if Methodism was to spread throughout Britain. A number of sites were examined in London with Westminster being chosen as it was an area containing a large and poor

population. The College was built to accommodate 100 students, male and female, with a satellite practising school of 1,333 pupils. See F.C. Pritchard, *A History of Westminster College 1851–1951* (London, 1951).

15 Pritchard, *A History*, p. 104.

16 Ibid., p. 108.

17 Principal's Log, 7 May 1904, Westminster College Archives A/3/C/1.

18 Pritchard, *A History*, p. 109. Stamford Bridge was built for two brothers, James and William Waddle of the London Athletic Cub by R. and G. Neale of Wandsworth for £2,899 in 1876. The ground was first used on Saturday, 28 April 1877. The ground hosted many Amateur Athletic Association Championships. It became the home of Chelsea Football Club in 1905. For full history, see Colin Benson, *The Bridge: The History of Stamford Bridge* (London, 1987).

19 Pritchard, *A History*, pp. 108–9.

20 *The Westminsterian* (Oct. 1906), 11.

21 Pritchard, *A History*, pp. 109–10.

22 Ibid., p. 111.

23 Minutes of Governing Body of Westminster College, 12 Oct. 1914, p. 46.

24 See Mangan, *The Games Ethic*, p. 173 for a description of Bishop John Coleridge Patteson, a role model for men like Leigh Smith.

25 Cecil Rolo Peyton Andrews (1870–1951) attended Merchant Taylors' School from 1879 to 1888 and St John's College Oxford (1889–93). After a short spell teaching in Highgate School and Forest School in London he became a lecturer at St John's Training College in Battersea. He emigrated to Western Australia and became Principal of a Teacher Training College from 1901 to 1903. He was made head of the Education department of the University of Western Australia in 1903 and a member of the Senate in 1912. He became Pro Vice-Chancellor and retired in 1929. For a history of Merchant Taylors' see F.W.M. Draper, *Four Centuries of Merchant Taylors' Schools* (London, 1962).

26 Andrews was appointed to Highgate school in Sept. 1893, and stayed less than a year leaving in March 1984. See T. Hinde, *Highgate School: A History* (London, 1993).

27 Forest School was founded as a Proprietary School in 1834 and catered for about 200 boys at the time of Andrews' appointment in 1894. For a full history see Guy Deaton, *Schola Sylvestris* (the School, 1972) and G. Wright, *Forest School 1834–1894* (the School, 1994).

28 St John's College was originally founded as a private venture in 1840 by Edward Tufnell and Dr James Kay-Shuttleworth who was the Secretary for the Committee for Council on Education which had been set up in 1839. The College was built according to the principles of the Established Church. By 1842 the cost of maintaining the College was beyond the resources of the two men and the College passed into the hands of the National Society. For a complete history see T. Adkins, *The History of St. John's College Battersea. The Story of a Noble Experiment* (London, 1906).

29 *St. John's Magazine*, 11, 2 (Dec. 1899), 19.

30 Marlborough, of course, played a major role in the evolution of the ideology of Athleticism, see Mangan, *Athleticism, passim*.

31 *St John's Magazine*, 11, 3 (Feb. 1904), 54.

32 St. Mark's College Chelsea was founded by the National Society in 1841. The Society had the official aim of 'promoting the education of the poor in the principles of the Established Church throughout England and Wales'. The first Principal was Derwent Coleridge (1800–83) who was the son of the poet Samuel Taylor Coleridge. The College was located in Chelsea and from the earliest times tried to have a more liberal and relaxed environment than was ever the case at either Borough Road or Westminster. See G.W. Gent, *Memorials of St. Mark's College* (London, 1891).

33 C.H. Swann, 'Cross Country Running', *St. Mark's College Magazine*, 6, Michaelmas Term (1905), 91–3.

34   C.H. Swann, 'Cross Country Running', *St. Mark's College Magazine*, 6, Michaelmas Term (1905), 91.
35   G.F. Bartle, 'Staffing Policy at a Victorian Training College', *Victorian Education*, Occasional Publication no.2 (1976), 16–23.
36   Borough Road College was originally founded by Joseph Lancaster in 1798. The College was run on non-denominational lines (Lancaster was a Quaker) and administered by the British and Foreign School Society. By 1888 it was one of the best and most famous teacher training colleges in the country. For a complete account see G.F. Bartle, *A History of Borough Road College* (Kettering, 1976).
37   Bartle, 'Staffing Policy...', p. 20.
38   See Christopher Hibbert, *No Ordinary Place: Radley College and the Public School System 1847–1997* (London, 1998).
39   P.B. Ballard, *Things I Cannot Forget* (London, 1933), p. 47.
40   *B's Hum*, 8, 67 (Feb., 1897), 1.
41   See J.A. Mangan and Colm Hickey, 'English Elementary Education Revisited and Revised: Drill and Athleticism in Tandem', *European Sports History Review*, Vol.1 (1999), 63–91.
42   Frank Stewart, Loretto *One-Fifty: The Story of Loretto School from 1827 to 1977* (Edinburgh, 1981), p. 159.
43   See Mangan, *Athleticism, passim.*
44   Stewart, *Loretto*, p. 159.
45   Ibid., p. 164.
46   Lorettonianism was 'an elaborate and systematic programme of health education covering food, clothes, physical exercise, sleep, fresh air and cold baths', Mangan, *Athleticism*, p. 54.
47   A.R. Smith, *Loretto School Sermons* (Oxford, 1929), p. 5.
48   Ibid.
49   Ibid., p. 28.
50   Stewart, *Loretto One-Fifty*, pp. 196–8.
51   For a complete history of the club, see Ian Hay, *The Cliff Dwellers* (Edinburgh, 1949).
52   Bartle 'Staffing Policy...', p. 21.
53   Mangan, *Athleticism*, p. 142.
54   T. Paterson, 'Emotive Rituals in Industrial Organisms', *Philosophical Transactions of the Royal Society of London*, 257, Series B (1966), 437.
55   Mangan, *Athleticism*, p. 42.
56   B. Bernstein, H.L. Elvin and R.S. Peters, 'Ritual in Education', *Philosophical Transactions of the Royal Society*, 251, Series B (1966), 429.
57   Ibid.
58   Ibid.
59   Ibid., p. 430.
60   Ibid.
61   Mangan, 'Physical Education as a Ritual Process...', p. 88.
62   Ballard, *Things*, p. 44.
63   Ibid., p. 44.
64   Ibid., p. 46.
65   C. More, *The Training of Teachers, 1847–1947. A History of the Church Colleges at Cheltenham* (London, 1992).
66   Ibid., p. 156.
67   Ibid., p. 157.
68   F. Fuller, *The History of St. Luke's College*, 4 Volumes, Vol. II, 1886–1933 (Exeter, 1970), p. 324.
69   Ibid., p. 323.
70   B. Bernstein *et al.*, 'Ritual in Education...', p. 437.

71 Mangan, 'Physical Education as a Ritual Process...', p. 88.
72 There is no reference to these distinguished authorities in More's bibliography.
73 More, *The Training of Teachers*, p. 158.
74 Ibid.
75 See Mangan, *Athleticism*, Ch.7.
76 E. Hobsbawm, 'Introduction: Inventing Traditions', in E. Hobsbawm and T. Ranger (eds), *The Invention of Tradition* (Cambridge, 1983), p. 1.
77 Ibid., p. 9.
78 See Mangan, *Athleticism*, *passim*.
79 For a discussion of the public school 'blood', see Mangan, *Athleticism*, pp. 171–7.
80 Bartle, *A History*, p. 78.
81 Ibid.
82 'Retrospect by Yeldor', *B's Hum* (1939), 61.
83 Bartle, *A History*, p. 78.
84 Mangan, *Athleticism*, p. 141.
85 Bartle, *A History*, p. 91.
86 Ibid., p. 78.
87 A. Burrell, *Bert Milnes: A Brief Memoir* (Letchworth, 1922), p. 14.
88 Ibid., p. 16.
89 Mary Douglas, *Natural Symbols: Explorations in Cosmology* (London, 1973), pp. 11–12.
90 Ibid., p. 12.
91 Victor Turner, *The Ritual Process* (London, 1969), p. 167.
92 Mangan, *Athleticism*, p. 143.
93 Ibid.
94 T. Adkins, *The History of St John's College Battersea*, p. 240.
95 *B's Hum*, 9, 74 (Jan. 1898), 2.
96 See J.A. Mangan and Colm Hickey, 'A Pioneer of the Proletariat: The Proselytiser Herbert Milnes and the Games Cult in New Zealand', in J.A. Mangan and J. Nauright (eds), *Sport in Australasian Society: Past and Present* (London: Cass, 2000), pp. 31–48.

Part III

Sport and emancipation

Chapter 5

The social construction of Victorian femininity

Emancipation, education and exercise

J.A. Mangan*

Modern sport is, of course, a phenomenon with considerable social, cultural, economic, political, spiritual and aesthetic dimensions. E.J. Hobsbawm has called it one of the most significant of the new social practices of late nineteenth century Europe, then the Dominant Continent.[1] Its significance throughout the world has massively increased in the twentieth. Its integration into the fabric of modern societies constitutes nothing less than a worldwide social revolution – and it has not yet run its course, as the so-called Third World will amply demonstrate in the coming decades.

In the late nineteenth century, Hobsbawm has further suggested, sport played its part in the emancipation of Western middle-class women.[2] This is the theme of this chapter. The essential concern is the social construction of femininity, and the approach is eclectic, embracing the history of ideas, gender, education and society.

To avoid confusion and to ensure comprehension, sport here is used as a generic term covering physical activities intended to improve physical, mental and moral health.[3] At the outset it is important to realize that sport is a cultural artifact which, more often than not, both determines and reflects the dominant values of society.[4] Furthermore, it is replete with rituals and symbols which are, in turn, powerful and elaborate mechanisms of social integration, consolidation and domination. In passing it should not be overlooked that this century has witnessed the creation of the most sustained and extended exercises in the fabrication of athletic ritualistic and symbolic traditions in the history of the world. This is no accident. It reflects the twentieth-century construction of new nations, new identities, new hegemonies and new ideologies.

Among these new international ideologies is modern feminism. In locating its origins and exploring its relationship to modern sport in Western societies (more precisely, for reasons of space, in the United Kingdom and the United States), the intention here is to examine the way in which social change creates and mirrors

Originally published in *The International Journal of the History of Sport*, 1989, 6(1), pp. 1–9.
http://www.tandf.co.uk/journals

those social tensions associated with definitions of gender and its related roles.[5] It is a story of control, of confrontation, assimilation and change. Our starting point is this succinct assertion by Kathleen McCrone:

> Sport is laden with rituals, symbols, and preconceptions that disseminate, affirm and reinforce a plethora of idealized social values, and hence, it often acts as an effective mechanism of social control. In social systems dominated by men, such as that of Victorian England, a useful means of controlling women was a projection of the view that sport was essentially masculine, requiring physical and psychological attitudes and behaviour unnatural to women, and thus it was beyond *their proper sphere* (emphasis added).[6]

To set this inquiry into gender equality, socialization and social change in historical perspective it is necessary to look briefly at the evolution of aspects of modern sport in the United Kingdom in the nineteenth century. In a celebrated article in *Victorian Studies* entitled 'They Taught the World to Play', Charles Tennyson considered the contribution of Britain to the evolution of modern sport.[7] It is an extraordinary fact that in the second half of the nineteenth century this small island off the mainland of Europe, then possessing the largest empire the world has witnessed, as a by-product of industrialization, embourgeoisement, education and wealth gave *inter alia*, soccer, rugby, rowing, track and field, tennis, golf and recreational ski-ing to the modern world, and indirectly inspired other activities like the Olympic Games, American baseball and Australian Rules Football. *The matrix of modern sport is the United Kingdom.* Against this background, and in this context, we examine the early evolution of the modern sportswoman – as a symbol of emancipation.

Relevant to our analysis are the anthropological concept of 'pollution' and the arguments of the social anthropologist Mary Douglas,[8] to whom pollution represents social 'disorder'. Mankind contrives to impose order on events to create stability, regularity, security. Categorization, therefore, is a human necessity. To deny or restructure established categories is to confuse, threaten, repudiate. It causes social tension.

The nineteenth-century Anglo-Saxon world (Britain, its Dominions and the United States) possessed a rigid separation of sex roles – the consequence of a male-controlled classification system. The denial of its validity and attempted replacement resulted in the immediate invocation of, and consequent repudiation of social pollution beliefs[9] in pursuit of the stability of the *status quo* and change to the social system respectively. As a consequence Anglo-Saxon late nineteenth-century society became in this context, a culture, 'at war with itself'.[10]

At the centre of the conflict was the nature of femininity (a contemporary paradigm of innocence) and to quote McCrone again:

> ...since supposition about [woman's] physique were the most powerful factor controlling role and place, and since her exclusion from sport was deeply rooted in Western cultural traditions, physical barriers were among

the last to fall. The invasion by women of the world of sport involved unprecedented physical activity and opportunities for physical liberation. It stood at the junction of transformation process, on the threshold between definitions of male and female and between women of the past and future; and it symbolized the manifest changes affecting not only women by the value orientations of societies as a whole.[11]

Physique became the gender battleground because, as the Rosenbergs have informed us, the roles assigned to women, in society from at least the time of Hippocrates and Aristotle, have attracted biological justification.

In the nineteenth century when 'the intellectual and emotional centrality of Science increased speedily' pseudo-scientific argument was used in 'the rationalization and legitimization of almost every aspect of Victorian life'.[12] More than this, of course, in a time of dramatic, stressful, rapid change – ideological, scientific, technological and cultural – conservative Victorians summoned all the power of custom and religion as well as science in defence of the extant social structure and philosophies. In both, woman had an idealized image and location. Belief in her alleged basic characteristics, nurturance, domesticity, passivity, affection and intuitive morality[13] had its foundations in biological argument, which in turn, supported an edifice of ideological assertion.

In *The Evolution of Sex* published in 1889, for example, Patrick Geddes and J. Arthur Thompson provided a biological basis for social arrangement. They postulated a theory of sexual dimorphism based on cell metabolism: male cells were katabolic, active and energy-dissipating; female cells were anabolic, passive and energy-conserving.[14] The difference was immutable. From biological source came social role – at least for the middle classes. A Victorian concept of *Separate Spheres* was born, with women located in the home and men in the market place.[15] An ideal of womanhood was created (in conjunction with an ideal of the model family):

> Women, it was argued, were eminently suited, because of their innate physical and emotional characteristics, to stay at home and be good wives and mothers, and, by the same argument, were poorly equipped for the productive sphere. This was an integral element of the rhetoric of Social Darwinism incorporating the medical case for women's physical inferiority which was employed to justify 'maternity as the "highest function" of womanhood – essential to the healthy progress of the nation'.[16]

In a famous and dominant metaphor, woman was 'the angel in the house'. Needless to say, the ideal woman, 'passive, gentle, emotional and delicate', had neither the strength nor the inclination to undertake strenuous exercise.[17] The 'stylized formulae' of femininity contained a series of cutting paradoxes: woman's idealization was also the source of her humiliation, her body was her strength and her weakness, her role was the source of apparent domestic power and certain public powerlessness. Patricia Branca has neatly summarized the allotted role of 'the Victorian lady': 'In her role as mistress of the house, in her relationship with domestics, and most importantly in her role as mother, the middle class woman of the nineteenth century defined herself.'[18] However, as Branca states, her historical role transcended the boundaries of the family. She was caught up in the transformation of society and part of the process of modernization. Paradox conjoined with marked changes in society (economic, technological, scientific and demographic), and with philosophical shifts in human aspirations towards self-fulfillment, mobility and independence[19] 'spawned a women's movement that raised questions about women's abilities and constricted place in society and sought a partial redefinition of sex roles',[20] and stimulated the admission of women into spheres previously dominated by men. With the result that, in the words of Sheila Fletcher, 'one of the most vivid images of female emancipation at the turn of the century – one that recurred there in the illustrated journals and lodged itself in the popular mind was that of the New Woman engaging in sport'.[21] The emerging model of the 'New Woman', of course, coexisted with the traditional image of the 'True Woman',[22] yet seldom harmoniously and frequently contentiously. The reactionary Arabella Kenealy, for example, in a splendid surge of romantic retrospection condemned games-playing schoolgirls, calling their newly acquired musculature 'stigmata of abnormal sex-transformation' and labelled their enthusiasm as 'the cult of Mannishness'.[23] The source of this condemnation was a widespread medical suspicion of education for women which hinged on the principle of 'the conservation of energy'.[24] The body contained only a limited and fixed amount of energy. Its expenditure in one part denied another. At puberty, so the argument went, a girl's energy should be reserved for the development of the reproductive organs – the essence of her womanhood. Cerebral effort at this time would produce nervousness, feebleness and even sterility. And worse, she would bear sickly and neurotic children capable only of producing degenerate versions of themselves. In short, racial soundness was not consistent with advanced female schooling: brain and ovary could not develop simultaneously.[25] This theory, promulgated by leading physicians of the period, held sway for years. It had the solid and powerful force of medical orthodoxy behind it. Paradoxically, however, it offered hope for radicals. Medical opinion was on the side of mild exercise as a prophylactic against academic strain. With this as a beginning women educationists established in girls' schools and colleges 'carefully supervised programmes of physical education while playing meticulous attention to the health of their pupils'.[26] Simultaneously 'biological' femininity came under attack from feminist doctors such as Elizabeth Garrett Anderson, with the result, as Paul Atkinson has observed:

> the medical and gymnastic were part and parcel of the same movement in women's education, and were of major significance in the ideological disputes surrounding the foundation of schools and colleges to provide academically sound education for young ladies. Such a movement among educationalists was a self-conscious reponse to medical opposition to the aspirations of feminist pioneers.[27]

In short, the nineteenth-century evolution of women's participation in the sports of Western society was 'firmly grounded in debates over women's capacity to withstand the rigours of intellectual effort'.[28]

Rebuttal of medical mythology, however audacious and determined, was neither speedy nor total. It was greatly retarded by strategic adherence to the principle of 'assimilation' rather than 'accommodation' (to borrow the well known Piagetian terms). In the process of accepting new concepts, Piaget has suggested that through 'assimilation' categories of thought remain the same but are adapted to the new circumstance, but by means of 'accommodation' broader categories of thought are developed in order to incorporate contradictory ones.[29] Feminist reformers did not reject 'the predominant conceptual schemes of Victorian society, they modified them'.[30] Theirs was a confrontation *à plaisance* rather than *à outrance*. Further analytical terms must be added to our historical glossary: 'discretion' and 'insularity'. Women's exercise was carefully monitored, regulated and circumscribed. Feminine demeanour was insisted upon: 'It was imperative...for women players to be in every way "ladylike" in their behaviour both on and off the pitch'.[31] In the telling phrase of Jennifer Hargreaves, they were 'to play like gentlemen and behave like ladies'. 'Separate spheres' were retained on playing fields and in gymnasia. 'Assimilation' not 'accommodation' was the order of the day; discretion was the password![32] Another agreed password was 'insularity'. For the most part, 'women played their sports away from the prying eye of the public...events remained largely cloistered'.[33] Insularity ensured no challenge, posed no threat, suggested compliance to traditional mores.

The result was relatively small progress and smaller controversy. The storm passed leaving the landscape much the same. Both outcomes were the direct products of 'the care taken not to violate behavioural rules, the generally inoffensive type of games played, the undoubted femininity of the players and the fact that for years play was virtually invisible within the protected confines of college or private grounds where it was completely separate from and no challenge to 'men's sport'.[34] In other words, sport served still to reinforce traditional ideas on gender, and continued to contribute substantially to the maintenance of prevailing ideologies about the roles of men and women.[35] At the same time sport did assist the general improvement of the social position of women. Concessions had been made within established sexual boundaries. Shifts in values, image and action had come about. In essence, therefore, there was both change and continuity, advance and retreat, defiance and compliance and 'the biologically determined (female) stereotype co-existed along with the more vigorous model of the sporting woman'.[36]

It was too much to expect that formal education could free women wholly from the constraints of conventional femininity. And, as we have seen, education served in part as a mechanism of conservatism: 'The new schools and colleges in some ways even...helped to produce the very same issues and forms of behaviour which girls had learned from childhood onwards in the family.'[37] Nevertheless, these establishments created 'space' for women, allowed social development, access to new reference groups and ideas and the opportunity to acquire limited knowledge, status and power. In short, they were both agencies of conservation and transformation. Within the new programmes of physical education in school, colleges and universities were illustrations of both dependence and autonomy. Women's games were an instrument of moral education and in this belief the girls' schools were at one with the boys', but their gymnastics were their own: a female tradition, creating a new woman for a new era.[38]

Carol Dyhouse has argued that an 'understanding of the education of girls in the nineteenth century must commence with some study of family life'.[39] The family, she maintains, is 'the primary and most powerful agency of socialization', and in Victorian and Edwardian society, she asserts, its role was especially critical with its extensive power over its young members.

To a considerable extent the family and schooling during the Victorian period were mutually reinforcing agents of socialization creating initially images of conspicuous recreational femininity – period 'accomplishments' (crocodile walks, callisthetics and social dance) forming an ideal preparation for 'conspicuous living'.[40] At the same time, therapeutic exercise was also a feature of an early Victorian affluent life-style. Delicate women required delicate exercise. Robust fitness was vulgar.

As we have already seen, both these Victorian interpretations of upper and middle-class feminine needs can be located in adapted form in the later era of the New Woman. We can discern continuity in change rather than discontinuity. Throughout the nineteenth century upper- and middle-class family and school moved in substantial harmony. The reforming women's schools and colleges *in loco parentis* reproduced the structure and ideologies of the 'perfect' Victorian home. The College Principal was head of the house (mother and father in combination), staff were elder siblings, students younger siblings: 'The theory and practice of familism in the colleges,' states Hargreaves, 'reproduced the structure and morality of the patriarchial bourgeois family and reinforced conventional sexual divisions in society'.[41] At one level she is correct, and at another incorrect. To an extent the colleges, in effect, were 'matriarchal' societies, and these enclaves of women, as we have earlier, offered sanctuary from society, common support for liberalism, common opportunity for experimentation. In consequence, in this institutional extension and adaptation of the family there was theoretical and practical change as well as continuity.

To pull the threads together: the 'incompatibility with reason and reality'[42] of the Victorian ideal of 'True Womanhood', by the twentieth century, produced by way of reaction the idea of the New Woman; it was a product of biological, psychological, sociological, educational and economic confrontation; an elite of upper- and middle-class women resisted theories of disability, disposition and destiny; and physical activity was a focus of subsequent conflict, compromise, controversy and change. This situation was assured by the biological basis ascribed to social constructs of femininity. Progress towards total physical emancipation, however, was partial. Assimilation within prevailing gender definitions rather than accommodation to new concepts was the reality, and women's social inequality continued to be reinforced by theories and practices in sport implying inferiority well into this century.[43] And there is a further point of significance. It was not all a process of successful change and assertion albeit cautiously circumscribed. Change came from pressure applied, but itself applied pressure. In a sometimes bewilderingly transformed world some middle-class women responded positively and some negatively. On the one hand there was the stability of asserted physical release, on the other there was the lethargy of drug and alcohol dependence. Care must be taken to describe reality rather than to re-establish stereotypes. Nevertheless, the involvement of late Victorian upper- and middle-class women in the sports of the new industrialized, urbanized culture, comprised if not 'a significant part of the general movement for female emancipation,'[44] then at least part of that movement. This is a state of affairs insufficiently considered by commentators such as Delamont and Duffin, Branca and Dyhouse.

By the end of the nineteenth century, in the cause of equality a little had been achieved; more was to be eventually attained. To conclude with a quotation from Kathleen McCrone: 'While the circumstances of the Victorian period differed markedly from those at present, then, as now, . . . in counteracting the stereotype of female frailty, sportswomen reflected feminist hopes of diminishing the significance of [social] sex differences, providing women with every opportunity to develop all their powers, and enabling them to gain control over their own lives and bodies'.[45] Arguably, what the First World achieved yesterday the Third World will achieve tomorrow. History has provided a lesson for our times. To adapt a metaphor from Macaulay, the issue is a lava which is still glowing.

Notes

* This is an abbreviated version of a paper presented to the Academic World Congress of the Seoul Olympiad, Seoul, September, 1988.
1 Eric Hobsbawm, 'Mass-Producing Traditions: Europe, 1870–1914', in E. Hobsbawm and T. Ranger (eds), *The Invention of Tradition* (Cambridge: Cambridge University Press, 1983).
2 Hobsbawm, *Invention of Tradition*, p. 299.
3 This is an adapted version of Roberta J. Parks' definition in 'Sport, Gender and Society in a Transatlantic Victorian Perspective' in J.A. Mangan and Roberta J. Park (eds), *From Fair Sex to Feminism: Sport and the Socialization of Women in the Industrial and Post-industrial Eras* (London: Frank Cass, 1987), p. 58.
4 See Park, 'Sport, Gender and Society,' p. 70.
5 Carroll Smith–Rosenberg and Charles Rosenberg, 'The Female Animal: Medical and Biological Views of Women and Their Role in Nineteenth century America,' in Mangan and Park (eds), *Fair Sex to Feminism*, p. 29.
6 Kathleen E. McCrone, 'Play Up! Play Up! And Play the Game! Sport at the Late Victorian Girls' Public Schools,' in Mangan and Park (eds), *Fair Sex to Feminism*, p. 98. Regrettably Professor McCrone's excellent *Sport and the Physical Emancipation of English Women, 1870–1914* (London: Routledge, 1988) appeared after this paper was submitted. It includes extended and additional arguments and evidence associated with this point.
7 Sir Charles Tennyson, 'They Taught the World to Play', *Victorian Studies*, Vol. II, No. 3, March 1959, pp. 211–22.

8 See Sara Delamont and Lorna Duffin (eds.), *The Nineteenth Century Woman: Her Cultural and Physical World* (London: Croom Helm, 1978), pp. 13–16.
 9 Ibid., p. 23.
10 Ibid, p. 24.
11 McCrone, 'Play Up! Play Up! And Play the Game', pp. 97–8.
12 Smith–Rosenberg and Rosenberg, 'The Female Animal', p. 13.
13 Ibid, p. 14.
14 Carol Dyhouse, *Girls Growing Up in Late Victorian and Edwardian England* (London: Routledge & Kegan Paul, 1981), p. 153.
15 Joan H. Burstyn, *Victorian Education and the Ideal of Womanhood* (London: Croom Helm, 1980), p. 19.
16 Jennifer A. Hargreaves, 'Victorian Familism and the Formative Years of Female Sport', in Mangan and Park (eds), *Fair Sex to Feminism*, p. 131.
17 McCrone, 'Play Up! Play Up! And Play the Game', p. 30.
18 Patricia Branca. *Silent Sisterhood: Middle Class Women in the Victorian Home* (London: Croom Helm, 1975), p. 144.
19 Smith–Rosenberg and Rosenberg, 'The Female Animal', p. 30.
20 McCrone, 'Play Up! Play Up! And Play the Game', p. 99.
21 Sheila Fletcher, 'The Making and Breaking of a Female Tradition: Women's Physical Education in England, 1880–1980', in Mangan and Park (eds), *Fair Sex to Feminism*, p. 145.
22 Park, 'Sport, Gender and Society', p. 76.
23 Fletcher, 'The Making and Breaking of a Female Tradition', p. 145.
24 Paul Atkinson, 'The Feminist Physique: Physical Education and the Medicalization of Women's Education', in Mangan and Park (eds), *Fair Sex to Feminism*, pp. 41–4.
25 Smith–Rosenberg and Rosenberg, 'The Female Animal', p. 19.
26 Dyhouse, *Girls Growing Up*, p. 155.
27 Atkinson, 'The Feminist Physique', p. 41.
28 Ibid., p. 53.
29 Burstyn, *Victorian Education*, p. 21.
30 Atkinson, 'The Feminist Physique', p. 54.
31 Hargreaves, 'Victorian Familism', p. 142.
32 McCrone, 'Play Up! Play Up! And Play the Game', p. 105.
33 Park, 'Sport, Gender and Society', pp. 86–7.
34 McCrone, 'Play Up! Play Up! And Play the Game', p. 106.
35 Park, 'Sport, Gender and Society', p. 59.
36 See McCrone, 'Play Up! Play Up! And Play the Game', p. 118.
37 Dyhouse, *Girls Growing Up*, p. 175.
38 Fletcher, 'The Making and Breaking of a Female Tradition', p. 147.
39 Dyhouse, *Girls Growing Up*, p. 3.
40 Hargreaves, 'Victorian Familism', p. 134.
41 Ibid., p. 140.
42 McCrone, 'Play Up! Play Up! And Play the Game', p. 99.
43 Ibid., p. 121.
44 Branca, *Silent Sisterhood*, p. 148.
45 McCrone, 'Play Up! Play Up! And Play the Game', p. 99.

Chapter 6

The 'lady blue'

Sport at the Oxbridge women's colleges from their foundation to 1914

*Kathleen E. McCrone**

The relationship between sport and women's history is extremely important, for its examination reveals how social change both caused and reflected tensions surrounding formal definitions of gender roles, how sport simultaneously modified and limited the female role, and how women's increased involvement in sport, although not a major feminist issue, was integral to the late Victorian movement for female emancipation.

Victorian women's entry into sport was directly related to the campaign for female higher education which began in the 1860s and was one of the most crucial parts of the women's rights movement, even though many reformers of female education were not especially notable as advocates of the general rights of women. The successful establishment of women's colleges at Oxford and Cambridge resulted from the collective efforts of men and women who shared a common interest in broadening women's opportunities and creating educational institutions which emphasized academic achievement. Its significance cannot be exaggerated, for it was a spectacular example of tangible progress towards the day when sound education would be generally accessible to women and a new ideal of female excellence would be accepted.[1]

I

The founders of women's colleges were primarily concerned with establishing and developing the intellectual capacities of women in order to prepare them better for both domestic and professional roles. They believed, in addition, that women had a right to develop their bodies; and through games and exercise, they sought to make students as fit as possible in order to prove that women could endure, without damage, the strain of higher learning.[2] The latter was of critical importance, for the most potent and durable arguments against higher education were that maturing females possessed only a finite amount of energy, that the

Originally published in *The British Journal of Sports History*, 1986, 3(2), pp. 191–215.
http://www.tandf.co.uk/journals

brain and reproductive system could not develop simultaneously and that the hard labour required by university training would produce permanent damage detrimental to future generations.

At issue was the very nature of woman and her physical and mental capacities. From time immemorial women's biology had determined their destiny, in effect imprisoning them in roles derived from their reproductive system. This was particularly true in the nineteenth century when the feminine ideal became practically a holy vocation demanding lifelong sacrifice and submission, and when the authority of science increased dramatically and began to be applied to areas where change inflicted stress on existing social arrangements.

As women started questioning their sex's constricted place in society and so threatening traditional belief structures and male monopolies, members of the scientific and medical communities in a highly emotional and unscientific manner developed an elaborate body of 'scientific' evidence which 'proved' that women's unique physical and emotional characteristics and natural roles were rooted inevitably and irreversibly in the prescriptions of science and that sexual equality could be achieved only at the risk of reproductive damage.[3]

In the 1870s an attack that lasted for years was launched against the university-educated woman by two eminent physicians who were convinced that a tide of feminist reform threatened traditional roles and relationships and ordained gynaecological disaster. Dr Edward Clarke of Harvard University and Dr Henry Maudsley of University College, London, issued polemics, in 1873 and 1874, in which they insisted there was sex in mind as distinctly as in body and that good health and rigorous intellectual activity were incompatible. Both men subscribed to the limited energy theory, the essence of which was that females had a finite amount of vital force. Since the proper development of the organs of reproduction during puberty was energy-intensive, they argued, the diversion of too much energy to the brain through strenuous intellectual activity would sap their vitality and ruin their health, most likely permanently. University education, they asserted, was 'out of harmony with the rhythmical periodicity of the female organisation'. It was bound to endanger the future of humanity by producing coarse, imperfectly developed hermaphrodites, and thus was nothing less than a crime before God and humanity.[4]

Paradoxically, medical opinion was at first relatively unconcerned about the potentially high-energy demands of exercise, perhaps because there was still little exercise to worry about. In fact, in the case of exercise, it not only failed to invoke the constitutional over-strain theory, but actually supported moderate amounts and types as a counterweight to the strain produced by serious study, and so was actually partly responsible for the introduction of sport and physical education at educational institutions for women.

With views on the important conjunction between students' physical and mental health and on the need to protect them from over-strain reforming educators generally agreed. But whereas critics of women's higher education assumed that intellectual effort would deplete physical reserves, supporters suggested that gender differences assumed to be natural were more closely related to conformity to cultural norms than to absolute biological determinants. Since one of the most potent arguments against females receiving a sound education was that they were too weak, new institutions deliberately set out to prove they were not and at the same time to make them stronger. This was at the root of most of the early physical activities within them and it dictated their form.[5]

It was certainly true of the women's university colleges, and explains why they became centres of athletic pioneering as well as intellectual advancement. Their visionary founders usually resisted compromising principles by watering down academic programmes, and instead emphasized physical fitness as an important corollary of academic success. From the start they encouraged students to take excercise and engage in sport; and the response was enthusiastic. By the 1870s, when the first women's colleges were established, sport was becoming an increasingly important feature of university life and, not unnaturally, young women who were subjected to a course of study similar to men's sought to emulate, however imprecisely, other aspects of the male undergraduate experience.[6]

Although its nature was very different, sport, as at men's colleges, eventually played an important socializing role at the women's colleges. For years, however, discretion was the watchword. The rules forbidding the marriage of fellows were not abolished until 1882, and until then there were practically no women in university life except the wives of heads of colleges. While the women's colleges owed their success to the support of a number of distinguished male academics, many university men, undergraduates and dons alike, strongly disapproved of the presence of even a few female students on the grounds that higher education was incompatible with true womanhood and that it threatened clerical and masculine governance of the universities. Furthermore, they had a 'strong sense that admission of women to the privileges of higher learning would be derogatory to the dignity of the learned craft',[7] not to mention of sport. In a sermon preached in 1884 in the chapel of New College, Oxford, in response to Oxford University's decision to admit women to the most of the same examinations as men, John Burgon, the Dean of Chichester, summarized the prejudice women were up against when he called education 'plainly subversive' to women's best interests. 'To their great injury', he predicted, it would lead them to become independent and competitive and to 'imitate the manners, the demeanour, the phraseology of the undergraduate rivals...they will [even] adopt men's games where it is possible'.[8]

However revolutionary their aims and ambitions for women, the first heads of women's university colleges internalized many of the values of their culture and were locked into a rigid mould of respectability.[9] Allegations that overwork would produce infertility, brain damage or mental breakdown and about the inappropriateness of women to the university world put them very much on the defensive. Fully aware that all eyes were upon their students and that any inconvenience and offence created would provoke censure and jeopardize chances of acceptance, they insisted upon discreet, inconspicuous behaviour. Every detail of conduct was closely monitored for years, and exercise, while encouraged, was circumscribed.

II

The story of women's collegiate sport began modestly in 1869 when Emily, Davies' plan to make university education accessible to women resulted in the opening of Hitchin College in Hertfordshire to five young ladies. Permission from Cambridge University having been obtained, they immediately undertook the work prescribed to candidates for honours degrees, under the watchful eye of several professors who generously volunteered their teaching services.[10]

Early in her campaign for educational reform Davies noted the 'importance of physical health to the life of the nation', and lamented that 'women are not healthy…[and show] a want of stamina'.[11] At Hitchin her concern for physical as well as mental development was manifest in encouragement to students to take long country walks, properly chaperoned of course, and to play croquet, fives and a crude form of cricket in the seclusion of the college garden, which they apparently did 'with great laughter and fun, but small skill'.[12] Since none of the students could swim, Miss Davies urged them to patronize the local open-air swimming bath on the one day a week it was open to ladies, and even provided an aquatic role model by taking to the water herself. When they began to play a very mild form of football, however, she quickly forbade in on the grounds that outside knowledge of such an overtly masculine activity would be taken as incontrovertible proof of the unsexing consequences of higher education.[13]

By 1873, when Hitchin College moved to Girton on the outskirts of Cambridge, women had hardly begun to participate in sport. But from the first, despite a lack of facilities, the authorities of the new Girton College considered students' health of such importance that free time for physical recreation was provided each afternoon; and during the next decade the growing number of Girtonians obtained 'exercise and pleasure' from activities such as walking, racquets, fives, croquet, badminton, gymnastics and lawn tennis.[14]

Plans for the first college buildings included a gymnasium; and although the death of the donor delayed its construction, Constance Maynard, who was at Girton from 1871 to 1874 and later founded West field College, London, recalled that 'we seem to have been greatly taken with gymnastics…and…tried to learn from each other vaulting handswing, rope ladder and fencing'.[15] Other students remembered that in 1874 the question of appropriate attire for gymnastics caused friction among Miss Davies, students and members of college, until the liberal view prevailed that students should be allowed to choose their own costume as long as it was worn only for gymnastics and included nothing unfitting and objectionable.[16]

In 1877 a building designated 'the gymnasium', but not fitted out as such and containing a racquets court at one end and fives court at the other, was finally opened. Its multi-purpose use apparently caused problems, for a letter to the *Girton Review* in 1882 complained about the storage of old lumber and broken furniture and the cramped conditions ensuing when racquets was played while gymnastic exercise was being taken. Three months later the *Review* announced the removal of the lumber and the acquisition of new apparatus through the generosity of members of a recently formed gymnastics club, whose disinclination to practise regularly resulted four years later in the termination of the club's existence.[17]

The first game to capture the interest of Girton women was the newly invented lawn tennis. Despite a lack of proper courts, student initiative led, in 1873, to the playing of matches on the 'scanty and rough' lawn outside the dining hall. In this connection an informal club gradually arose, to be followed by a second and formal one in 1878, and the amalgamation of the two in 1883. Gravel courts were also built, and came under the management of a separate club instituted in 1882.[18] Inter-college competition began in 1878 when Girton accepted an informal challenge to a doubles match by the recently founded Newnham College, and won a victory that began a domination that lasted to 1914. From 1882 the inter-collegiate match was an annual fixture of considerable importance in the lives of both colleges, and from 1883 a silver challenge cup, presented anonymously by Charlotte Scott, Girton's first wrangler, was the reward for the doubles champions. Singles competition was added in 1883, and although there was no challenge cup until 1891, those who participated received silver racquet badges, the quest for which greatly 'increased the level of play and keenness'.[19]

The year 1883 also witnessed the inauguration of women's inter-university sports competition when two representatives of Cambridge's Girton and Newnham engaged two from Oxford's Lady Margaret Hall and Somerville in a doubles match on a private court in Essex, safely away from the public eye. Cambridge, with four times as many students to choose from, was victorious, as was to be usual for many years to come. Simultaneously, the oldest challenge trophies in women's inter-university sports competition were introduced when two gentlemen members of the Girton Committee presented silver bowl and gold medal prizes for the first and second champions of the winning side. By 1894, when an Old Girtonian presented a silver challenge cup, the inter-university tennis match had long since become a regular institution. Because they were held on courts belonging to private clubs and individuals, inter-university matches could be watched by past and present students and their friends without the risk of a scandal arising over players making themselves publicly conspicuous. The 1890 match was hosted by the Archbishop of Canterbury at Lambeth Palace in memory of his late daughter, a student at Lady Margaret Hall, while that in 1894 was played before about 200 enthusiastic spectators' at the All England Club, Wimbledon.[20]

Throughout the pre-war period lawn tennis remained a major sport at Girton. Over the years the number of courts, players and contests increased steadily. By the early 1890s, for example, the college had eight courts, four lawn and four gravel. The tennis club, born in 1886 from an amalgamation of the separate grass and gravel court clubs, boasted 63 members out of a college enrolment of approximately 114. A self-governing body with elected officers who took their activities very seriously, it developed elaborate rules for different types of competitions, arranged dates, locations and order of play, provided badges and cups and specified attire.

From the early 1890s as well Girton played outside matches against London University and its women's colleges; spectators travelled to foreign matches to lend moral support; the college team increased in size; and a second team and matches were organized, as were diverse contests within Girton involving individuals, years, tripos and Old Girtonians. Eighty-two of the latter formed in 1882 the Girton College Lawn Tennis Club Honorary Members' Association, and thereby gave substance to the hope of exercise-advocates that an interest in sport developed at college would be carried on afterwards.[21]

Lawn tennis was a sport which even the staunchest male athletic exclusionists had difficulty protesting against college women's participation in, as for years it was played in impeccably feminine style and costume, which meant there was little running, stretching or vigorous movement. Girton's tennis records are totally free of controversy apart from the occasional indication that early players sometimes experienced a struggle between their urge to 'play the game' and retain, unsullied, their femininity. It was such a struggle that moved the college magazine in 1883 to condemn:

> the tendency shewn by some players to consider attitudes and what they are pleased to think 'good style' as of the first importance [which] . . . if allowed to spread will have the most disastrous results on play in general. Quiet style is above all things important, but low hard strokes well to the back of the court and into the corners, and good judgement in waiting for and placing the balls will do more to make a good game and to win a match than any amount of attitudes and so-called 'pretty play'.[22]

Students eventually seem to have concurred, for by the end of the century, as skill became more important to players than appearance, the *Girton Review* forsook expressions like 'quiet style' and 'pretty play' for 'hard returns', 'spirited volleys', 'sharp backhands' and 'deadly overhand serves'.[23]

III

Apparent risks to body and propriety delayed the introduction of hockey but, late in 1890, following a motion by the lawn tennis club that a hockey club be formed, a group of prospective players organized one. With little difficulty they persuaded the college to provide a ground on the site of an asphalt tennis court, towards the preparation of which the tennis club donated £20.

Despite fear that 'the revelation that "those Girton girls had actually taken to hockey"', would create 'a national shudder',[24] the game rapidly developed into the main sporting attraction. Between 1891 and 1895 a miscellany of matches between years, and against Old Girtonians, Newnham and Oxford were arranged. The Newnham contest, which dated from the Easter 1892 term and was played for a cup presented by an Old Newnhamite in 1893, immediately became the major event of the sporting year at both colleges, the one which aroused the greatest excitement and emotion among players and spectators alike. Also exciting, if somewhat less so, was the inter-university match between Oxford and Cambridge, an annual event from 1894 and from 1898 played for a trophy presented by two sisters who had attended Newnham and Somerville. As with tennis, participants in the inter-collegiate and inter-university matches received distinctive silver badges.[25]

Following the narrow victory by Cambridge in the first inter-university match, at the Wimbledon Hockey Club, Mr Punch manifested the contempt in which males often held women's sport. Laughing uproariously at the whole 'hilarious' spectacle, in a parody of 'The Battle of the Baltic' he sarcastically warned that the Cambridge ladies' triumph rendered insignificant any victories in other sports by teams of Oxford men.[26] If he was still laughing 20 years later, however, he did so less openly, for by that time hockey had become established as the premier women's team game in the country. The annual inter-university ladies' match attracted several hundred Old Girls, parents, friends, and college and school staff members and students to a ground in Richmond, and even merited coverage in *The Times*.[27]

In 1895 Girton, along with several other colleges, became a charter member of the All England Women's Hockey Association (AEWHA), and five years later membership of the college team was regularized when Girton (and Newnham) agreed that only residential students were eligible, and so excluded those who had gone down. In due course a second college XI was formed and Old Girtonians organised a Ladies' Hockey Club Honorary Members' Association.

The supremacy of hockey was demonstrated by the *Girton Review*'s devotion of far more space to it than to any other sport or activity, the enlargement of the hockey ground several times and the constant expansion of the list of home and away fixtures.[28] Matches of all sorts were watched and played with great enthusiasm; a militant 'beat Newnham' hockey song was sung to the tune of 'Knocked 'em in the Old Kent Road'; and playing in the college first XI came to be considered one of the greatest honours a Girtonian could acquire. There was one prominent Girtonian, however, who was distinctly unenthusiastic about the game. Constance Jones, who became Mistress in 1903, is reported to have cautioned her charges: 'If you *must* play hockey, do try to hit the ball gently!'[29]

As attitudes to women liberalized, as students' pre-college sports experience increased and as enrolment grew, sporting activities at Girton became increasingly diverse, vigorous and frequent. From the early days, students went for long walks in the Fens. A racquets club, formed in the mid 1870s when a court was fitted out in the new gymnasium, survived for about ten years until the attractions of outdoor sport proved entirely irresistible. Between 1891 and 1902 the college had a golf club and its own nine-hole course. Although Newnham declined an invitation to participate in an inter-college match, within Girton, particularly in the mid-1890s, there was a good deal of interest in competing for a challenge brooch donated by an old student in 1893, a brooch that, until 1900, when past students were prohibited from playing college hockey, was the only trophy limited to students resident in college. Enthusiasm for golf waned around the turn of the century, and the club disbanded in 1902 when a new building was constructed on part of the course.[30] In the realm of aquatic sports, the swimming bath that opened in 1900, thanks to the largesse of old students and friends of the college, immediately went into 'constant use'. Students formed a swimming club the next year, which arranged races and water-polo matches between students in different subjects and years. From 1907 inter-college and inter-university meets were held, the latter involving first Oxford and then London Universities.[31] As for boating, because of Girton's distance from the river the club that students started for recreational purposes in 1906 did not become popular and received no mention in the *Review* after 1907. Although 'not a strenuous thing at all' and involving 'no races or anything competitive',[32] boating was considered potentially dangerous, and for safety's sake the club required members to pass proficiency tests in swimming and rowing.[33]

As far as team sports were concerned, in addition to hockey students played a primitive form of cricket from the Hitchin days, and continued to do so at Girton. Hertha Ayrton, a scientist who assiduously avoided sport while up in the late 1870s, wrote to Barbara Bodichon of her fellow students' cricket playing: 'You have no idea how funny they look; they run shockingly with their heads a mile in front of them...I suppose they will improve in time but at present they send me into fits of laughter'.[34] Girton records indicate that cricket was not taken particularly seriously, but a cricket club was established in 1893, and matches were played 'on a grassy space sheltered from the public eye',[35] in other words the hockey ground and then the golf course. Informal matches against Newnham were held during the long vacation for some years until the first formal contest in 1897 for which a challenge cup was donated by an Old Newnhamite. There were no inter-university matches before 1914 since cricket was played very little at Oxford; but within Girton contests between years, students and lecturers were organized, and in 1907 a professional coach, with 'the highest testimonials' to his character, was engaged.[36]

The game of lacrosse was introduced to Girton by students from St Leonard's School, St. Andrews. A club was formed in 1899 as a result of initiatives taken by the Games Club, but it laboured 'under difficulties as hockey is so much played...that there is little time for those who wish to practise lacrosse'.[37] These difficulties evidently killed it, for in 1913 the *Review* reported on the formation of a new lacrosse club and the start of intra-college matches. Later the same year it made much of a Girton XII's defeat of Newnham for a trophy donated by Girton, and of Girtonians' membership in a combined Cambridge team that beat Oxford for a trophy given by Lady Margaret Hall, before a small crowd at that bastion of male sport – Lords.[38]

Finally, no history of sport at Girton would be complete without mention of the activity which, although not strictly speaking a sport at all, made the greatest contribution to the physical liberation of women. This was bicycling. Like women everywhere during the 1890s, few Girtonians could resist its lure. Promises to parents to do nothing so 'fast' as ride a cycle were quickly forgotten, and students soon found themselves being 'measured for a cycling skirt, with little elastic stirrups sewn into the hem to keep it down to the ankle'.[39] A cycling club, organized in 1894, became instantly popular, and each term so many new cycles were brought up that a storage problem was created, which was not solved until 1910 when a new bicycle shed with space for 160 machines was built.

Until the bicycle's advent, Girton's distance from the centre of Cambridge kept students safely secluded from town and undergraduates, and forced them to travel about in horse-drawn cabs irreverently called 'Girton hearses'. Fearing the effects of the new mobility on, university opinion and students' morals, college authorities at first subjected cycling to strict regulations. Riders had to pass a proficiency test before they could go into town, and they were not allowed to ride on Sundays until 1900 nor around Cambridge until 1903, by which time female cyclists had ceased to be stared at as an extraordinary novelty. The following year students gained permission to ride to lectures after dark, unaccompanied by a don, as long as at least three went together; and by 1906 all restrictions had disappeared.[40]

Sport and physical recreation were so prevalent at Girton by the turn of the century that some observers thought there was an 'all-pervading athletic spirit' in the college which prevented students from 'becoming blue-stockings and bookworms'.[41] Unlike men's colleges such as Jesus, however, Girton never developed an athletocracy or worshipped at the altar of a cult of athleticism. A few students might have become obsessed with games, and some might occasionally have skipped lectures in order to practise or play an important match. But in the eyes of the authorities at least, 'playing the game' never completely lost its therapeutic purpose, and to students and staff alike it was always clearly secondary to the attainment of academic distinction.

While Emily Davies was establishing Girton College, Anne Jemima Clough, the sister of the poet Arthur Hugh Clough, and a group of prominent men and women established a series of lectures and a special examination for women elsewhere in Cambridge in 1869. Unexpectedly large attendance at the lectures created an accommodation problem, and in 1871 Miss Clough was invited to take charge of a house of residence for five students in Regent Street. Thus Newnham College was born.[42]

Although Newnham's founders accepted diluted courses and examinations and lacked the sense of mission that inspired Girtonians, the foundation of Newnham created a new forum for women's higher education. There, from the first, as at Girton, those in charge were concerned about maintaining and improving students' health. Although worried about the possibility of excess and overstrain, the college authorities considered most sports an important contributor to physical, moral and scholastic development, and encouraged students to participate. The afternoon hours were kept free for recreation, and as facilities improved Newnhamites took up games with enthusiasm.

Because of considerations of space, details of the evolution of sport at Newnham will be left to a longer study. For current purposes suffice it to say that sport at Newnham College evolved along lines similar to those at Girton, except that in due course Newnham offered even more variety. Over the years, as a result of student initiative and official promotion, Newnhamites played croquet, fives, tennis, hockey, cricket, lacrosse and netball. They went for country walks, rode horses, did gymnastics, fenced, bicycled, rowed, swam and ice-skated, and a few even took up jiu-jitsu around 1906 after a Japanese man put on a demonstration.

IV

The development of women's sport at Oxford followed a pattern similar to that at Cambridge, although at Oxford there was less variety in activities and more emphasis on boating, and united university clubs in tennis, hockey and lacrosse were eventually established.

The history of women at Oxford began in 1873 with the formation of a committee of women to develop a scheme for women's lectures and examinations. Two years later its lobbying and that of a number of Oxford men resulted in the university's adding to its statute governing the examination of non-members a provision for the examination of women above the age of 18 and the creation of preparatory lectures. Both lectures and examinations were very successful, and in 1878 an Association for the Promotion of the Higher Education of Women in Oxford (AEW) was founded to arrange lectures, engage lecturers and furnish residential accommodation. To the latter end Lady Margaret Hall (LMH) and Somerville opened in 1879.[43]

At Oxford as at Cambridge, the first generations of female students were on sufferance and lived lives far removed from those of male undergraduates to whom they were strange curiosities. Apart from laboratory work, male and female students had little communication until after the First World War. Ruth Butler, who was up just after the turn of the century, recalled, in a fascinating interview in 1981, how the university with its undergraduate activities seemed entirely marvellous and remote to women, and how very separate the existences and experiences of the male and female students were.[44]

Like their Cambridge counterparts, the pioneers of women's education at Oxford had to allay strong prejudices against women, yet maintain high ideals about the nature of female education. Aware that their students were on probation and that any false step might destroy chances of acceptance, they too insisted on discreet, inconspicuous behaviour, while students for their part felt a responsibility to live up to the privileges of study, and so dutifully observed irksome rules framed in deference to opinion in men's colleges that did not even acknowledge their existence.[45]

The first two residences for women opened without fanfare. LMH, which had strong ties with the Church of England, began life in a house in Norham Gardens with a complement of nine students. Its lady principal from 1879 to 1909 was Elizabeth Wordsworth, the daughter of the Bishop of Lincoln, a mild-mannered and conservative woman who did not share Emily Davies' views on women's rights or their need to follow the same academic programmes as men. Miss Wordsworth urged students to cultivate womanliness, which perhaps explains why LMH became known as a kind of finishing school for ladies.[46] But at the same time she seriously promoted the cultivation of intellects; and for health reasons and because of her girlhood experience at a Brighton boarding school where the only exercise provided was dancing and crocodile walks, she encouraged the playing of outdoor games.[47] Practising what she preached, Miss Wordsworth herself took a walk each morning, and in her annual reports made a regular point of commenting on the attention given to physical devëopment, on general and individual health and on the hall's athletic activities.

Although the Norham Gardens house lacked facilities for games, because of the concern of LMH's principal and Council for physical as well as mental growth, two hours were set aside each afternoon for recreation and exercise. This consisted initially of croquet, taking country walks in pairs or groups, skipping in corridors on wet days and playing tennis on a couple of makeshift courts.[48] The first permanent building, which opened in 1882, included a small gymnasium, thanks to the generosity of donors,[49] and on its spacious grounds proper grass and asphalt tennis courts were promptly constructed. For years thereafter tennis was the chief outdoor amusement. A club was formed, trophies were donated, matches against Somerville were played 'amidst much cheering and excitement' and the results of contests at all levels were regarded as important news.

Between 1881 and 1884 the council raised money for and conducted protracted discussions regarding the acquisition of a racquets court.[50] When a suitable site proved unobtainable, in 1885 it approved the diversion of funds to the purchase of a boat and boat house on the River Cherwell, which flowed right past the hall garden. From then on boating loomed large in students' lives. Since few could swim, those wishing to boat were required to obtain the written permission of parents and principal – permission Miss Wordsworth was pleased to give for she regarded early morning swims as conducive to health – and to produce a certificate of proficiency or pass a test of swimming 50 feet. As the number of boats increased through student subscriptions and private and conciliar donations, the qualifying test became more stringent. But despite the 'grim and nerve racking rituals' the test involved, the joy of taking a boat out proved irresistible.[51]

By the turn of the century, when a boat club was belatedly formed under Miss Wordsworth's presidency, most LMHers could swim and many could be found on any day but Sunday happily boating on the Cherwell. They were not allowed on the River Isis, however, for they might have interfered with the relatively much more important boating activities of undergraduates; and there was no question of inter-college competition. Boating at LMH was for fun, not serious exercise, and the complicated club rules and qualifying regulations had more to do with increasing safety than skill.[52]

Paradoxically, the council no sooner approved boating than it banned hockey. In the spring of 1885 Miss Wordsworth conceded that 'perhaps there was too great a preponderance of the out-of-door athletic side of life throughout the term;'[53] but she was exceedingly annoyed that the council, 'feeling the strength of certain objections to the game of hockey, think it desirable that it should be discontinued for the present'.[54] The minutes of the council meeting are bland in the extreme and give no indication of the nature of the 'certain objections' or the controversy that must have ensued during the discussion of the prohibition. There are, however, several possible explanations: a concern that too much game-playing was responsible for LMH's examination results the previous year having been inferior to Somerville's, disapproval of LMHers behaving like undergraduates and, in the full flush of a victory over Somerville, building a bonfire in the hall garden, and, at what was a very early date for young ladies to be playing hockey, the conviction that their doing so was improper. Whatever the reasons, Miss Wordsworth was unconvinced, and her next report acidly blamed the poor health at the hall on the diminution of outdoor games.[55]

The ban lasted until 1893 when the council, responding to the winds of change, finally gave students 'leave to play hockey in a field to be hired for the purpose; the parents' permission to be obtained in each case'.[56] Students immediately formed a hockey club and in short order arranged a variety of inside and outside matches, to the evident satisfaction of the principal who reported in 1894 that 'the good deal of hockey' that was played 'told favourably on [students'] health and spirits'.[57]

The next 20 years saw the number of college XIs increase to three, coaching by male dons at first and then by an expert especially hired for the purpose, graduating students' donation of a cup for inter-house competition, the abandonment of the Somerville ground for home matches when LMH obtained facilities of its own and the formation of an Old LMH Hockey Club, which, despite much enthusiasm, had difficulty getting enough players together for games because of familial and professional demands on their time. During the same period *Fritillary*, the magazine of the Oxford women's halls, commented on occasion about the poor attendance at LMH hockey practices and about the inexcusability of the first team's losing its collective head during matches.[58] Learning to 'play the game' evidently took time.

In addition to tennis and hockey, LMHers eventually participated in a variety of other physical activities, including athletic sports, skating, swimming, lacrosse and, of course, cycling.[59] Permission to cycle occasioned a degree of excitement second only to that over hockey.[60] A cycling club was formed in 1895 by 37 of the hall's 53 students, despite the dangers of scrapes and sprained ankles and the inevitable restrictions on where and when students could ride. Sunday riding was prohibited at first, unless it facilitated attendance at church, as was riding over the Magdalen and Folly Bridges, but LMH women were never prevented from cycling into Oxford. When, at the age of 60, Miss Wordsworth herself took up tricycling, out of a conviction that it would decisively benefit her health, restraints became less stringent than elsewhere. And at LMH, as at all the women's halls, the bicycle had an immediate impact on the relaxation of chaperonage rules.[61]

One sport LMHers were not allowed was cricket. The subject first came up in 1886 when Somerville refused to permit LMH to use its grounds for the purpose, and it arose again in 1901 when students petitioned the LMH Council 'that they might be allowed to play cricket with the High School Games Club or any other Ladies Clubs in Oxford'.[62] The council's negative response was supported by Miss Wordsworth, who regarded the game as entirely too masculine. None of the Oxford women's halls fielded a cricket team before 1914, although St. Hilda's and the Home Students' Society permitted individual women to play with local clubs.

For a number of years the academic demands at LMH were not great, while the interest in sport was. It is doubtful if games ever gave more pleasure than those in the early years. They loomed large in students' lives and conversations, and if play was amateurish by later standards, it was vigorous and enthusiastic.[63] Winifred Knox Peck (1901–03) recalled that:

> Hockey in spring wind or rain or misty autumn sunshine on our admirable ground, our great matches with Cambridge and Somerville, and long, long conversations about them over tea-tables by blazing fires, were the centre of our early terms. When summer came we filled punts and canoes with gay cushions and pushed off from our boathouse on the Cherwell, feeling that Lady Margaret was our world.[64]

Sport was never allowed to dominate life at LMH, however. Elizabeth Wordsworth, for all her promotion of the athletic spirit as an aid to good health, shared her generation's concern about excess and overstrain, and was always careful to guard against athleticism becoming a cult.

> Are we not carrying the reaction in favour of physical culture a little too far? [she asked in 1894] It is no secret among medical men that many of our young women have already fallen victims to the overstrain which an eager nature, acted upon by that *esprit de corps* which is so strong in school and college girls, has often led them to undergo in playing, when a sensible mother would have insisted on their declining to do so. If our young men sometimes sacrifice their health to an over enthusiasm for games that is no reason why our young women should do likewise.[65]

The sporting history of the other Oxford women's societies was largely unexceptional, and will be examined in detail in a longer study.

Somerville Hall, one of the two original foundations and eventually much the largest, was non-denominational as well as less strict and more academic than LMH. Somerville stood for complete intellectual and religious liberty in addition to scholarship and culture. A strong spirit of individualism permeated its atmosphere, and in due course it earned a reputation for cultivating in women a sense of professionalism and the need to fight women's battles.[66]

It was an Old Somervillian, Lilian Faithfull (1883–86), who in 1890 first recommended that special badges be awarded to all those who competed for Oxford and Cambridge in the inter-university tennis match, so they could say, like the undergraduates, that they had received their 'blue'. All four colleges concerned implemented the suggestion the very next year, and thus the 'lady blue' was born.[67]

As at Girton, Newnham and LMH, hockey became Somerville's premier sport in the 1890s. Its only serious rival was boating, which was allowed on the upper Cherwell from 1884, for recreational rather than competitive purposes, at times when undergraduates were unlikely to be encountered. The river proved widely appealing; and before long, despite increasingly exacting swimming tests that initially prevented some of the best athletes from joining, the boat club boasted a large membership and ownership of several craft that were in 'constant use'.[68] The slowness of attitudinal changes and the longstanding necessity women experienced to defer to masculine interests are strikingly revealed in the following contemporary observation, however.

> Athleticism is as strong a point at Somerville as at any of the women's colleges of the present advanced day. But here again great care is taken that the college should not clash with the men's colleges. A Somerville boat would be very much disliked on the river, so, though the college owns five boats, two canoes and a punt, these are kept on the Cherwell... On the lower river these boats never appear; they sometimes go on the upper river for picnics, but that is all.[69]

At St. Hugh's, which was founded in 1886 by Elizabeth Wordsworth for women who could not afford the fees at LMH, although the initial enrolment was only four, students immediately took up tennis and formed a club. Eight years later it placed a representative in the Oxford team selected to meet Cambridge, and in 1903, still with less than half the enrolment of the older halls, St. Hugh's carried off the inter-college trophy.[70]

The fourth women's hall, St. Hilda's, was established in 1893 by Dorothea Beale, the legendary principal of Cheltenham Ladies' College, primarily for Cheltenham students intending to enter the teaching profession. Its original enrolment numbered only seven, and for several years, like St. Hugh's, it remained too small to support more than limited sporting activity. From the start, however, for the good of their health, students were expected to spend time outdoors between lunch and tea walking, playing croquet and tennis and cycling.[71]

Since the River Cherwell flowed past St. Hilda's garden, students soon formed a boat club, which in due course acquired a half-outrigger, a punt, a four and an eight. A man from Salters, the boat hirer, coached the four and must have been amused to see his charges encircling their skirts with elastic bands in order to prevent entanglement in the sliding seats. As for the eight, St. Hilda's was the first women's college to acquire such a craft, but because it was strongly identified with masculine sport, it was used only on a secluded part of the river so as to avoid undesirable attention. St. Hilda's also had a canoe club from 1901 to which instruction was given for a time by a Canadian Rhodes scholar.[72]

What was unique about St. Hilda's sport was the rifle club, the existence of which, at a hall whose students were not particularly sports-oriented, provides an excellent example of the emulation of male models.[73] Formed in October 1909 by 28 of the hall's 44 students, it competed for a fine silver goblet donated by one Alice Andrews, whose largesse stemmed from the unusual conviction that 'If any of our students go to the colonies they might find this art useful'.[74] For the next five years, until the demands of war resulted in an ammunition shortage and the commandeering of the practice site, the club averaged about 20 members a year and held weekly practices at the local rifle range. Several students apparently became first-class shots, although it is not recorded whether their skill was of any use in the colonies![75]

After the opening of the various halls of residence for women at Oxford, there remained students, like the daughters and relatives of dons and women from various parts of Britain and the world, who preferred living in private homes to the communal life of a hall of residence. To these the term Home Students first began to be applied in 1890–91, and in 1898 the council of the AEW officially designated them the Society of Oxford Home Students.

Among the Home Students, small numbers, scattered living quarters, the lack of their own grounds and a variety of ages and nationalities retarded the development of sport. Nevertheless, Home Students established tennis, boat and hockey clubs in the 1890s, and were warmly encouraged to do so by Bertha Johnson, their principal. Mrs Johnson strongly supported activities such as sport that brought the students together as a recognized body and developed among them a corporate identity. Her reports included regular comments on sports: in 1897 she noted proudly that the Home Students' Society had been admitted to inter-college hockey competition for the first time and that two Home Students were members of the Oxford team that played against Cambridge.[76]

At Oxford, unlike Cambridge, students formed united university clubs in tennis (1899), hockey (1901) and lacrosse (1912), to combine the best players from all the women's societies. Members were selected by a committee of experts from the various halls, their numbers were limited, and from among them the sides that represented the university in outside competition were selected. The united clubs brought together women from across the university in a way unusual at the time; and although the numbers involved were not large, they may have contributed to Oxford women's particular sense of 'University'.[77]

V

The Oxbridge women's colleges were far from being all of a piece. There were obvious and subtle differences between them, involving size, endowments, attitudes and social standing, which affected both academic and athletic orientation. While Girton and Newnham each had about 165 students in 1913, Somerville, the largest of the Oxford colleges, had 110 and St. Hilda's, the smallest, only 47.[78] The evidence is overwhelming, however, that large or small, academically oriented or less so, up- or down-market, by 1914 in the majority of colleges students were physically active, and of those who were not, most were involved as spectators. Enthusiasm for games may not have been quite universal, and on occasion may have been more a matter of pressure to keep up with the athletic Joneses than genuine inclination, but there is no doubt that sport played a major socializing role in female collegiate life.

On going up, freshers were vigorously lobbied to join sports clubs, a complicated series of which, at the university, college, hall and old students' level in a plethora of major and minor activities, made regulations about eligibility, behaviour, and dress, levied subscription fees, purchased equipment, hired coaches, awarded an extensive array of cups and colours and arranged practices and matches that involved competitions from the university level down through colleges, halls, years and subjects of study. Photographs and club and team membership lists reveal a remarkable number of familial athletic dynasties and all-rounders. Athletes of distinction were major personages, and the annual tennis and hockey matches between Girton and Newnham and LMH and Somerville riveted the attention of the entire colleges and generated excitement comparable with that inspired by the publication of the honours examination lists, for upon their results college honour was thought to depend.[79] The larger colleges developed extensive sporting facilities in which they took great pride; and 'lady blues' on occasion experienced the thrill of playing for their university before crowds numbering several hundred at sporting meccas such as Wimbledon and Lords.

Sport probably never gave more joy than it did to the first generations of college players to whom it meant freedom and an exhilarating awareness of physicality and the potential significance of body control.[80] Filtered and enhanced by the passage of time, memories of long hours on playing fields, tennis courts and the river, and of the paroxysms of excitement and nervousness that preceded major matches, were among those most cherished. Years later, old student after old student recalled the feeling of bliss that accompanied running at full tilt in relatively comfortable sports costumes, or, as one put it, 'the rightful joy in suppleness of body and in speed of foot'.[81] They recalled too the stiffening of their characters, the welcome relaxation during matches of the formality that normally governed relations between senior and junior students and students and dons, the pride in being chosen for a first team, the thrill of travelling to away matches, the precious friendships formed, the sense of responsibility that accompanied election to a captaincy or sports club executive and the tremendous feeling of achievement invoked by improvement of skills, receipt of colours and the gaining of victory. At times, with Olive Dunlop, one can almost 'smell the damp grass of the old [Girton] hockey ground' where 'the ghosts even of our old, old age will be fluttering…playing once again the game of ball and the game of life'.[82]

Unlike the situation in some of the men's colleges, however, at the women's colleges, while sport developed a vigorous life of its own and many of the rituals of affiliation characteristic of male sport, and while some students were undoubtedly games-mad, athleticism never became a cult, for its dangers were appreciated by principals and mistresses and forestalled early on. The Oxbridge pioneers never forgot that their primary purpose was to demonstrate and develop the capacity of the female mind, or that integral to the ideology they developed to justify their efforts was the encouragement of exercise and sport as a means of improving the health of students to make them better able to tolerate the stresses and strains of higher learning.

Relative to the prolonged and heated debate on the question of degrees for women, the emergence of the female collegiate athlete created remarkably little controversy. There was never any question of the competition between the sexes in the classroom that men found so menacing and women so essential to intellectual respectability being extended to the playing field, despite the conservative prediction in the 1890s that, if women were allowed to become full members of the universities, 'the boat race, which is far more popular...than the progress of Women, would be replaced by a vapid contest at lawn tennis between the Women of Cambridge and the Men of Oxford'.[83] In addition, except for cricket at Girton and Newnham, overtly masculine games were eschewed; and although the female manner of games-playing became more vigorous and skilled with the passage of time, it always occurred in appropriately modest attire and carefully avoided flagrant violations of behavioural rules. Women's sport thus remained so far removed from the male variety as to minimize stress in participants and offer little threat to femininity or masculine exclusivity. Descriptions of players as graceful and ladylike, as well as healthy and athletic, presented a reassuring compromise between images of the old and new woman. In addition, for years women's play was conducted within the sheltered confines of college or private grounds and was thus virtually invisible to the public; and it was always given a degree of legitimacy by its acknowledged value as a curative or preventive of the physical and mental defects supposedly caused by higher learning.

Lest an unduly positive picture be painted, however, it must be recalled that the debate on the physical, psychological and personal effects of higher education continued for years. Despite overwhelming evidence to the contrary, the view endured in some quarters that university studies prejudiced a woman's health and femininity; and in the midst of the debate sport did not entirely escape controversy. This is evident in Lady Margaret and Somerville Halls' bans on hockey and cricket in the mid 1880s and the strict rules everywhere surrounding the use of bicycles. It is evident too, at the individual level, in letters between Violet Cooper of Girton (1906–09) and her fiancé, Cecil Brown, in which she promised not to 'overdo' hockey, and sought to minimize his 'shock' over the news that she was trying to meet the qualifications for boating and intended to wear a 'short' shirt for golf and walking tours.[84]

Even more to the point is the fact that, although women might have been *at* the universities since the 1870s and the women's colleges might have come a long way since their experimental foundation, they were still not really *of* the universities by 1914. Male and female students lived very separate lives, and many Oxbridge men simply ignored women throughout the pre-war period, except when their presence offered inconvenience or became a national issue, such as when the contentious questions of degrees or votes were raised. Certainly, despite the fact that on occasion men coached women's teams and provided funds for the purchase of facilities, equipment and trophies, and men's colleges chivalrously loaned tennis courts and hockey grounds for women's matches,[85] women's sport was usually either assiduously ignored or summarily dismissed, for the simple reason that, like women themselves, it had 'little place in the general life of the universities'.[86] In 1897, in an act more powerfully symbolic than they probably realized, the 'gentlemanly' Cambridge undergraduates hung an effigy of a woman on a bicycle in front of the Senate House in celebration of the Senate's rejection of degrees for women, and by so doing, in one fell swoop condemned the intellectually and physically liberated woman.

The opinion of the Cambridge matron, reported by the *Cambridge Review* in 1913, that a satisfactory Girtonian 'was a nice girl, with rosy cheeks and nice manners, and nicely dressed... [who] you would never have thought knew anything' – presumably about either the classics or cricket – was a reflection of the still conservative attitudes of many members of the university community.[87] The *Review*'s first report on the women's inter-university hockey match that same year, and its congratulations to the Cambridge victors, represented only a slight compromise.[88]

College women may have emulated undergraduates in playing games, in some of the games played, in the organization and operation of sports clubs, in the adoption of the terminology, rituals and symbols of the masculine enterprise and in using sport as a powerful mechanism for the development of *esprit de corps*, traditions and allegiances. But the heart of the matter was that, while men's sport was considered natural, desirable, serious and important, women's continued to be regarded as somewhat unnatural, amusing and frivolous. Moreover, despite notable advances in the status of women, until 1914 the wider world of club, army, education, business, Church, civil service and empire, that sport in general and the earning of a blue in particular opened to university men,[89] remained firmly closed to women, athlete and non-athlete alike. About the only professional use to which a woman could put a college sports career was in obtaining a teaching post at a school where games were emphasized.[90]

VI

Ultimately, however, the significance of women's sport lay not in what university men or even public opinion thought of it but in what it meant to the women themselves. This, in a word, was freedom. To attend a women's college between 1870 and 1914 was to become a member of a small, privileged society of serious-minded, generally hard-working young women, at least some of whom felt part of a stirring campaign. It meant participating in an exhilarating experiment which, despite the restrictions of college life, brought freedom from the often oppressive atmosphere of family, freedom to mix with women of similar background and freedom to be alone on occasion and to look after one's own needs rather than those of others.[91] It brought a plethora of unique new experiences and the opportunity to think, achieve and take genuine physical exercise; and to some at least it brought an awareness of the potential and reality of mental and physical power.[92]

Active feminism played little part in the entrance of university women into the world of sport. Most collegiate sportswomen participated because so doing was fun rather than part of a crusade for the physical rights of the female sex.[93] It did not matter much that propriety had prevented their mothers and grandmothers from 'playing the game' or that they themselves were far from being considered the sporting equals of their male counterparts. Furthermore, while pioneering principals and mistresses may have shared a vision of intellectual and physical liberation, they were rarely militant feminists, and usually held liberal views on certain aspects only of the woman question.[94] Their encouragement of sport certainly helped to make it a respectable activity for young ladies. But, like their counterparts in the public schools, they actually perpetuated the identification of vigorous physical activity with masculinity by continuing to perceive games-playing females as acting in a masculine manner, by insisting that they manifest moderate, feminine behaviour and by accepting the notion that certain sports, ways of playing and costumes were unacceptable.[95] The female collegian was thus compelled to accept limitations on the playing field which had been rejected in the classroom. Her sporting image and activities compromised with and accommodated to middle-class mores without radically challenging them, although they 'revitalized them in ways which allowed some adaptation to the broader social changes occurring at the time'.[96]

Despite their willingness to make accommodations with societal expectations about appropriate female roles and behaviour, however, it was extremely important to the emancipation of women that university educators took up mental and physical aspects simultaneously. The Oxbridge women's colleges were a special domain, a circumscribed social world in which training and development occurred outside traditional spheres. Their enrolment may have been small and the majority of middle-class women may have remained at home in a kind of psychological and physical bondage. But the colleges could not be other than significant instigators of social change and pioneers in the drive towards greater female autonomy, for their establishment was an aggressive act, a deliberate attack on the Victorian mind-set that held the incapacity of women to be perpetual. When college women emulated male academic and athletic models and did so successfully, they converted those models into entities that were less exclusively male. In the process society's expectations about the intellectual and physical abilities of women began to be transformed, as were women's expectations of themselves. Whether they realized it or not, the early games players pioneered a drive towards greater female autonomy and provided extremely valuable role models. Every sphere of university life women penetrated, whether it was the lecture hall, the honours examinations or the sports field, told in favour of opening new spheres of activity and conceding to women rights to personal and public liberty.

The 'lady blue' was thus a major actor in a larger social drama, as important in her own way as the lady wrangler. Her very existence made a significant contribution to eradicating the view that physical weakness was admirable in women, and it epitomized the fundamental feminist principles of self-determination and emancipation.

Notes

* The author is pleased to acknowledge research grants from the Social Sciences and Humanities Research Council of Canada which greatly facilitated work on this project.
1 Joyce Senders Peterson, 'The Reform of Women's Secondary and Higher Education: Institutional Change and Social Values in Mid- and Late-Victorian England', *History of Education Quarterly* X (1979), 61–2.
2 Emily Davies, *Thoughts on Some Questions Relating to Women, 1860–1908* (Cambridge, 1910), pp. 68–9; Eleanor M. Sidgwick, *University Education of Women* (Cambridge, 1897), pp. 8, 31.
3 Pauline Marks, 'Femininity in the Classroom: An Account of Changing Altitudes', in Juliet Mitchell and Ann Oakley (eds), *The Rights and Wrongs of Women* (Harmondsworth, 1976), p. 177; Susan Sleeth Mosedale, 'Science Corrupted: Victorian Biologists Consider "The Woman Question"', *Journal of the History of Biology* XI (1978), 1–2; Carroll Smith-Rosenberg and Charles Rosenberg, 'The Female Animal: Medical and Biological Views of Woman and her Role in 19th Century America', *Journal of American History* LX (1973), 332–3; Janet Sayers, *Biological Politics: Feminist and Anti-Feminist Perspectives* (London, 1982), pp. 1–17.
4 Edward H. Clarke, *Sex in Education* (Boston, 1873); Henry Maudsley, 'Sex in Mind and in Education' *Fortnightly Review* XV n.s. (1874), 466–83. See also Joan Burstyn, *Victorian Education and the Ideal of Womanhood* (London, 1980), pp. 84–96; Deborah Gorham, *The Victorian Girl and the Feminine Ideal* (Bloomington, 1982), pp. 84–97; Carroll Smith-Rosenberg, 'Puberty to Menopause: The Cycle of Femininity in Nineteenth-Century America' in Mary Hartman and Lois W. Banner (eds), *Clio's Consciousness Raised* (New York, 1974), pp. 24–7.
5 Jonathan Gathorne-Hardy, *The Public School Phenomenon, 597–1977* (London, 1977), pp. 271–2.
6 For information on Oxbridge men's sport see J.A. Mangan, '"Oars and the Man": Pleasure and Purpose in Victorian and Edwardian Cambridge', *British Journal of Sports History* I (1984), 245–56; J.A. Mangan, *Athleticism in the Victorian and Edwardian Public School: The Emergence and Consolidation of an Educational Ideology* (Cambridge, 1981), pp. 122–7.
7 Thorstein Veblen, 'The Theory of the Leisure Class' in L.D. Abbott (ed.), *Masterworks of Economics: Digests of Ten Great Classics* (Garden City, NY, 1946), p. 750.
8 John William Burgon, *To Educate Young Women like Young Men, and With Young Men – a Thing Inexpedient and Immodest* (Oxford, c. 1884), p. 23. See also pp. 27–9.
9 Martha Vicinus, '"One Life to Stand Beside Me": Emotional Conflicts in First Generation College Women in England', *Feminist Studies* VIII (1982), 605–7.
10 Rita McWilliams-Tulberg, *Women at Cambridge: A Men's University – Though of a Mixed Type* (London, 1975), pp. 25–35, 40–9, 62–3; Barbara Stephen, *Emily Davies and Girton College* (London, 1927), pp. 202–68. Girton was the only women's college that from the outset encouraged students to keep to the university regulations governing undergraduates. Elsewhere, for a number of years, students had considerable latitude in subjects studied, examinations sat and number of terms spent in residence.

11 Emily Davies, *On Secondary Instruction as Relating to Girls* (London, 1864), pp. 8–9.
12 Louisa Lumsden, *Yellow Leaves* (London, 1933), p. 51; *Girton Review* (Michaelmas Term 1907), 18.
13 Muriel C. Bradbrook, *That Infidel Place: A Short History of Girton College* (London, 1969), p. 43; Catherine B. Firth, *Constance Louisa Maynard* (London, 1949), pp. 113–14; E.E. Constance Jones, *Girton College* (London, 1913), p. 24; Barbara Stephen, *Girton College 1869–1921* (Cambridge, 1933), pp. 224–5.
14 Anonymous, *Life at Girton*, (Girton College Archives, 1882), p. 6.
15 Constance Louisa Maynard, quoted in Firth, *Maynard*, p. 114.
16 Stephen, *Girton College*, pp. 152–3.
17 *Girton Review* (December 1882), 16, (March 1882), 14, (July 1883), 14, (December 1883), 16, (July 1884), 14. By December 1886 the *Review* had ceased to mention the gymnastics club.
18 *Girton College Clubs, etc.* (c.1895), p. 10.
19 *Girton Review* (July 1883), 10. For a number of years students deemed overhand serves unladylike and resisted adopting the style.
20 *The Daisy*, Vol. 5 (1 November 1890), 23; *Fritillary*, No. 3 (December 1894), 45; *Girton College Clubs, etc.*, pp. 11–12; Girton College Tennis Club (GCTC), *Minutes, 1883–1924*, pp. 141–6; *Girton Review* (March 1882), 11–13, (July 1884), 16; Newnham College Club (NCC), *Cambridge Letter* (1884), p. 16, (1887), pp. 12–13; Stephen, *Girton College*, p. 154; Kathleen Waldron, 'Won on the Playing Fields: the Story of Some School and College Challenge Trophies', *Girls Realm* IV (1901–2), 680. Girton dominated the annual tennis matches with Newnham, winning 21 times, 1882–1914, while Cambridge dominated the inter-university matches, defeating Oxford 20 times, 1882–1914.
21 GCTC, *Minutes; Girton Review* (1882–1914); Royal Holloway College, *Letter* (July 1891), p. 13.
22 *Girton Review* (July 1883), 10–11.
23 *Girton Review* (August 1898), 7–9.
24 Kathleen Waldron, 'Hockey for Ladies', *Lady's Realm* III (1898), 399.
25 *Girton College Clubs*, pp. 20–1.
26 'A Cambridge Triumph', *Punch* (24 March 1894), 141. During the early years of hockey competition Newnham had much the best of things in the inter-collegiate matches and Cambridge in the inter-university.
27 *The Times*, 11 March 1913, p. 15.
28 V.E.L. Brown, *The Silver Cord* (Sherborne, Dorset, c. 1954), p. 31. In the Lent Term 1898 the fixture list included the Chiswick, Saffron Waldon, Hitchin and North Hertfordshire, and Wimbledon Ladies' Hockey Clubs, Royal Holloway College, Dartford Physical Training College, Wycombe Abbey School, Harrogate School and Blackheath High School. Between 30 November and 13 December 1907 Girton students played in eight hockey matches involving either their college or university.
29 Bradbrook, *Infidel Place*, p. 103.
30 *Girton Review* (December 1891), 12, (January 1898), 13, (May Term 1901), 21, (Lent Term 1902), 22.
31 *Girton Review* (January 1897), 10, (Easter Term 1906), 7–8, (May Term 1912), 9.
32 Brown, *Silver Cord*, p. 37.
33 *Girton Review* (Easter Term 1906), 8; 'Are Athletics Over-Done in Girls' Colleges and Schools? – A Symposium', *Woman at Home* VI n.s. (1912), 247.
34 Evelyn Sharp, *Hertha Ayrton 1854–1923* (London, 1926), pp. 71–2.
35 Sara A. Burstall, *English High Schools for Girls: Their Aims, Organisation and Management* (London, 1907), p. 64.
36 *Girton Review* (May 1907), 4. See also Brown, *Silver Cord*, p. 25; *Girton Review* (March 1894), 15, (August 1896), 12, (August 1898), 10. In 1896 a Games Club was created when the tennis, hockey, golf and cricket clubs, while retaining their separate

existences, agreed to amalgamate their finances for the sake of efficiency. It is interesting to note that while students usually headed individual sports clubs, staff members occasionally served as president, and not infrequently played.

37 *Wycombe Abbey Gazette* II (March 1902), 25.

38 *Girton Review* (April 1899), 21, (July 1899), 9 (Lent Term 1913), 8, (Michaelmas Term 1913), 9–10; Newnham College (NC), *North Hall Diary* (1913); *Thersites*. No. 30 (7 March 1913), No. 33 (11 November 1913).

39 Bradbrook, *Infidel Place*, pp. 106–7.

40 Bradbrook, *Infidel Place*, p. 155; B. Megson and J. Lindsay, *Girton College: an Informal History* (Cambridge, 1960), pp. 40–1.

41 R.W. Bell, 'Concerning Girton', *Windsor Magazine* VI (1897), 351.

42 Mary Agnes Hamilton, *Newnham: An Informal Biography* (London, 1936), p. 80; McWilliams-Tulberg, *Women at Cambridge*, pp. 59–61; Alice Zimmern, *The Renaissance of Girl's Education in England: A Record of fifty Year's Progress* (London, 1898), p. 50.

43 Vera M. Brittain, *The Women at Oxford: A Fragment of History* (London, 1960), pp. 37–135.

44 Ruth F. Butler and M.H. Prichard (eds), *The Society of Oxford Home Students: Retrospects and Recollections 1879–1921* (Oxford, c. 1930), p. 114; Interview with Ruth F. Butler (OHS 1902–05), Oxford, 14 November 1981.

45 Butler and Prichard (eds), *Society*, p. 42; Muriel S. Burne and Catherine H. Mansfield, *Somerville College 1879–1921* (Oxford, 1922), p. 58; Vera Farnell, *A Somervillian Looks Back* (Oxford, 1948), p. 44; Somerville Students' Association (SSA), *Report* (October 1914), p. 57.

46 Winifred Knox Peck, *A Little Learning: or A Victorian Childhood* (London, 1952), p. 166.

47 Georgina Battiscombe, *Reluctant Pioneer: a Life of Elizabeth Wordsworth* (London 1978), p. 90.

48 Battiscombe, *Reluctant Pioneer*, pp. 88–90; Lady Margaret Hall (LMH), *Council Minutes* (1 November 1879); LMH, *Log Book* (1 November 1879), p. 6.

49 In 1893 the gymnasium was sacrificed to the enlargement of the chapel. LMH, *Lady Principal's Report* (Summer Term 1893).

50 LMH, *Council Minutes* (1 December 1881–March 1885); LMH, *Log Book* (1 December–5 March 1885).

51 Irene M. Martin (LMH 1912–15), Diary c. 1894–1970, Leonard Miller (ed.). Lady Margaret Hall Archives, p. 168.

52 LMH, *Council Minutes* (5 March 1885), (5 March 1903), (30 April 1903); LMH, *Log Book* (5 March 1885), p. 20, (8 March 1900), p. 52. While the London University women's colleges encouraged competitive rowing before 1914, it was not allowed at Oxford until the 1920s. Women's Inter-university racing was inaugurated in 1965, but the general public paid no attention to women and rowing until 1981 when Susan Brown was chosen to cox the Oxford eight in the boat race.

53 LMH, *Report of the Lady Principal* (May Term 1885).

54 LMH, *Council Minutes* (22 October 1885). See also LMH, *Log Book* (22 October 1885), p. 22.

55 Gemma Bailey (ed.), *Lady Margaret Hall: A Short History* (Oxford, 1923), p. 47; Lilian M. Faithfull, *In the House of My Pilgrimage* (London, 1924), p. 62; LMH, *Report of the Lady Principal* (October Term 1885). Elizabeth Wordsworth was preoccupied by the health of her students. Virtually all her reports comment on the general state of health in the hall and on that of individual students. With striking frequency, she remarked on students having to return home because of their own or their mothers' ill health.

56 LMH, *Council Minutes* (16 February 1893). See also LMH, *Log Book* (16 February 1893), p. 32.

57 LMH, *Report of the Lady Principal* (Lent Term 1894).

58 *Brown Book* (1898), 15–16, (1909), p. 29; Fritillary, No. 37 (March 1906), 620–1, No. 42 (December 1907), 710, No. 49 (March 1919), 845; LMH, *Report of the Lady Principal*

(Summer and October Terms 1899); St. Hilda's Hall (SHH), Oxford, *Chronicle of the Old Students' Association* (1906), p. 10.

59 In 1907 a student-run Sports Committee was formed to co-ordinate the activities of the various clubs and approve their rules and regulations.

60 Paul Atkinson, 'Fitness Feminism and Schooling' in Sara Delamont and Lorna Duffin (eds), *The Nineteenth-Century Woman: Her Cultural and Physical World* (London, 1978), p. 123; *Brown Book* (1913), 28; *Fritillary*, No. 11 (June 1897), 194, No. 15 (December 1898), 254–5, No. 44 (June 1908), 748; LMH, *Council Minutes* (11 March 1886), (7 March 1901); LMH, *Report of the Lady Principal* (Lent Term 1886); LMH, *Log Book* (13 May 1886), p. 22.

61 Battiscombe, *Reluctant Pioneer*, p. 155; *Fritillary*, No. 5 (December 1895), 104, No. 7 (March 1896), 127–8, No. 8 (June 1896), 153–4; LMH, *Report of the Lady Principal* (January 1896).

62 LMH, *Log Book* (7 March 1901), p. 56.

63 Barbara Hammond, 'Reminiscences', *Brown Book* (December 1928), 98–9.

64 Peck, *Little Learning*, pp. 157–8.

65 Elizabeth Wordsworth, *First Principles in Women's Education* (Oxford, 1894), p. 12.

66 Byrne and Mansfield, *Somerville College*, p. 12; Helena C. Deneke, *Grace Hadow* (Oxford, 1946), p. 28.

67 SSA, *Report* (September 1890), p. 8, (September 1891), pp. 9–10.

68 In 1898 approximately 40 of Somerville's 76 students belonged to the boat club, and in 1901, 58 out of 82. Most of the boats were gifts to the club from friends of the hall or old students. By 1909 they included five sculling boats, two punts and three canoes. In 1898 the boat, tennis, hockey and gymnastics clubs formed an amalgamated Games Club, to which they turned over their funds.

69 'Ladies' Colleges: Somerville College, Oxford', *Ladies' Field* (31 December 1898), 106–8.

70 SSA, *Report* (October 1903), p. 17.

71 Christine M.E. Burrows, 'History of St. Hilda's College' (unpublished manuscript, St. Hilda's College Archives), Chapter 7.

72 Burrows, 'History of St. Hilda's', Chapter 7; *Fritillary*, No. 53 (June 1911), 939.

73 Most of the men's colleges had rifle corps with the purpose of training future soldiers.

74 *Fritillary*, No. 48 (December 1909), 837, No. 51 (December 1910), 900–1; SSH, *Chronicle* (1910), pp. 19–20.

75 Burrows, 'History of St. Hilda's', Chapter 7; SHH, *Chronicle*, pp. 19–20.

76 Butler and Prichard (eds), *Society*, p. 61; Oxford Home Students (OHS), *Report of the Principal* (October 1895); OHS, *Annual Report* (1895–96), p. 10; OHS, *Report* (Lent Term 1897).

77 See *Fritillary* (June 1899–March 1913); SSA, *Reports* (November 1899), p. 11, (October 1902), p. 17.

78 Approximate comparative college enrolment figures based on college registers and annual reports were as follows:

	1887	1897	1913
Girton	91	105	163
Newnham	112	167	173
Lady Margaret Hall	96	52	72
Somerville	31	76	110
St. Hugh's	9	25	52
St. Hilda's		16	47
Home Students		32	101

79 Evelyn Wills, 'Women's Colleges at Oxford and Cambridge', *Lady's Realm* V (November 1898), 43.
80 Hilda Jackson (Somerville c. 1902), letter, 19 September 1970, Somerville College Archives; Janet Sondheimer, *Castle Adamant in Hampstead: A History of Westfield College 1882–1982* (London, 1983), p. 31.
81 Olive J. Dunlop, *Leaves from a Cambridge Note-Book* (Cambridge, 1907), p. 76. See also Brown, *Silver Cord*, pp. 9–51.
82 Dunlop, *Leaves*, pp. 76–9.
83 Charles Whibley, 'The Encroachment of Women', *Nineteenth Century* XLI (1897), 534.
84 Brown, *Silver Cord*, pp. 41–5.
85 The Oxford University Lawn Tennis Club loaned its courts to its female counterpart in 1901 for the annual match against Cambridge, and Corpus College, Cambridge, allowed the women's inter-varsity hockey match to be played on its ground in 1905. *Fritillary*, No. 24 (December 1901), 386; NCC, *Cambridge Letter* (1905), pp. 59–60.
86 Howard Savage, *Games and Sports in British Schools* (New York, 1926), p. 77.
87 *Cambridge Review* XXXV (1913), 122.
88 *Cambridge Review* XXXIV (1913), 385.
89 Bruce Haley, *The Healthy Body and Victorian Culture* (Cambridge, MA, 1978), p. 120; Savage, *Games and Sports*, pp. 219–31.
90 Kathleen E. McCrone, 'Play Up! Play Up! and Play the Game! Sport at the Late Victorian Girls' Public School', *Journal of British Studies* XXIII (1984), 106–34.
91 Deneke, *Grace Hadow*, p. 27; Peck, *Little Learning*, pp. 155–6; Vicinus, 'One Life' p. 606.
92 Jackson, 'Reminiscences'; Sondheimer, *Castle Adamant*, p. 31.
93 Interview, Butler; Interview with Mrs A.B. White (Newnham 1911–15), Cambridge, 16 November 1984.
94 Battiscombe, *Reluctant Pioneer*, p. 155; Butler and Prichard (eds), *Society*, p. 31; *Young Woman* V (1896–1897), 165.
95 McCrone, 'Play Up', pp. 130–2.
96 Jennifer Hargreaves, 'Playing Like Gentlemen While Behaving Like Ladies: The Social Significance of Physical Activities for Females in Late Nineteenth and Early Twentieth Century Britain', unpublished MA thesis, University of London Institute of Education 1979, pp. 200–1. See also p. 87.

Part IV

Sport and religion

Chapter 7

Sport and the Victorian Sunday

The beginnings of middle-class apostasy

*John Lowerson**

Widespread attention was recently drawn to the strength of apparent clashes between Sabbatarianism and sport by the film, *Chariots of Fire*, with its dramatically enhanced images of Eric Liddell, the Olympic sprinter and Presbyterian missionary, firstly reprimanding a lad for kicking a ball on the Sabbath and subsequently confronting the Prince of Wales and others before an Olympic heat to refute charges of his lack of patriotism with appeals to a higher loyalty. The event never happened in the way the film portrayed it, although Liddell did refuse to compete in Paris on a Sunday in 1924.[1] The appeal of the dramatic incident was to demonstrate both the perseverance of older beliefs in 'outer Britain' and the tensions their observance could produce in the context of a more secular inter-war social climate. In a similar fashion the persistence of the 'Ulster Sunday' still draws attention to the close interdependence of value conflicts and the political problems of the fringes of the United Kingdom.[2] Sabbatarianism has been examined, *en passant*, in a number of studies during the last twenty years, principally by Hugh Macleod in the context of religion in the city, by Peter Bailey and Hugh Cunningham in terms of commercialized entertainments and 'social control' and, more fully, by John Wigley in a more legalistic frame.[3] Rather surprisingly there is no real assessment of it in Owen Chadwick's monumental *Victorian Church*.[4]

It is my intention in this paper to discuss the phenomenon in three main areas: the changes of emphasis towards Sunday rather than Sabbath in some Victorian theology; the chronology of challenge to fundamentalist Sabbatarianism in the development of certain activities, loosely described as 'sports'; and, finally, the stressing of human rather than supernatural criteria as prime models of behaviour, and the place of the conflict within arguments about moral behaviour amongst the late Victorian and Edwardian middle classes, particularly in terms of the entropy of leadership. These are tall orders and I am anxious not to place greater stress than it can bear on the agency of sport as an instrument of change, but in

Originally published in *The British Journal of Sports History*, 1984, 1(2), pp. 202–220.
http://www.tandf.co.uk/journals

terms of its offering pleasure rather than strenuous physical development alone and, in view of its requiring alternative uses of limited committed time for its participants, sport was identified by many contemporaries as both a symptom and a cause of progressive religious decay in English society at the turn of the century. I say 'English' advisedly because, as will become apparent later in this paper, there were significant variations in what is now so often called 'Outer Britain' and in the reaction to the core experience of the United Kingdom. I shall deal here with the debate largely in terms of the middle classes, to invert slightly the focus of so many recent articles on modes of social control designed primarily for the industrial working classes. I hope also to demonstrate that much of the debate by no means concerned as simple an issue as its protagonists made out, either in terms of a specifically secular attack on an unchanging fundamentalism, or of a bit of harmless recreation being restricted by killjoys. One theme that will run through the discussion, with rare exceptions, is the male dimension of many of the issues.

I

The first problem is that of the 'Victorian Sunday' itself. The starkest expression of how it should be spent was probably that given by the Reverend Francis Peake, the secretary of the Lord's Day Observance Society (hereafter LDOS), in his evidence to the House of Lords' Select Committee on Sunday Observance in 1895: 'Public instruction, public worship, the instruction of the young, the visiting of the sick, looking after people who are in trouble and difficulty, showing acts of kindness'.[5] In terms of altruism these were, indeed, are, singularly unobjectionable to many Christians. It was not the Gospel *per se* which was to be questioned in general, although some of the practitioners of anti-sabbatarianism clearly had limited social consciences, but rather the socio-legal context in which Peake's claims were enshrined and the model of divine ordinance for what was often, despite his hopes, a singularly joyless experience. The Evangelical revival, spreading from Anglicanism into Methodism in the later eighteenth century, and fighting both aristocratic indifference and working-class depravity, had forced through the 1780 Lord's Day Observance Act with its ban on Sunday entertainments, but had also imposed a far wider than legal notion of acceptable behaviour for the Sundays of early Victorian society. The description of Arthur Clennam's disillusionment with the English Sunday in Dickens's *Little Dorrit* is well known, although it needs to be reiterated that he had just returned from living on the Continent; the European dimension for criticism was sharply rein-forced by Hippolyte Taine's wondering what dreadful crime had been committed by the English to deserve their being punished with a Sunday whose apparent alternatives of church attendance or illegal drinking he found so singularly unattractive.[6]

The key point was, of course, the desirability of repeated acts of public worship during the day, at least twice where possible. This view provided for a ritualized division of time offering, in the course of a week, a tripartite separation of work, rest and recreation, which allowed for powerful notions of individual and social discipline and furnished considerable expectations of the percolation of good behaviour by strong hierarchical example. Overall, these were bound up with the regulations and sanctions provided by Divine Will as revealed in the creation narrative in Genesis. They also had an historical validity in terms of the tenets of seventeenth-century puritanism (a parallel which their Victorian defenders adverted to and to which I shall return) and a contemporary validity as a moral justification for the introduction of new capitalist work practices. I do not wish to become embroiled here in the cruder claims of the social control lobby, but the value of earned leisure being spent away from the disruptive crowd behaviour (familiar to pre-industrial recreations at both ends of society), as a means of ensuring an efficient work force, has been amply demonstrated by both Bailey and E.P. Thompson as well as Malcolmson.[7]

The Victorian or 'English' Sunday was never, in fact, anywhere near being the total reality that Dickens and Taine would have us believe, except in the most 'respectable' of households; as we shall see, the near-hysterical emphasis on it in the late Victorian period contained powerful elements of nostalgia. Attacks on this Aunt Sally took many forms and disentangling the process into discrete compartments must be for the convenience of the historian alone.

It is necessary, briefly, to examine the tensions within the churches themselves on the issue because the arguments marshalled by the LDOS against sporting activities were by no means universally supported amongst religious groups. A combination of theological uncertainty about the role of Sunday and changing perceptions of the social place of organized religion as well as internecine divisions fuelled by other religious crises meant that the churches could not present a united front. Much Sunday sport, at least amongst the respectable classes, was able to slip into being and habit because many religious leaders half-accepted that the secular reasons advanced for its introduction had some theological justification. This is most true of the Church of England; most dissenting groups kept to a harder line with only a fringe weakening of the Nonconformist Conscience amongst some leaders of individual congregations. The Anglican church faced particular problems – as the national body it claimed comprehensiveness and the period under review saw a repeat of its continued discomfort (and its legendary flexibility) when attempting to contain apparently irreconcilable wings, a fate it has barely escaped at any time since the Elizabethan Settlement with the possible exception of the early eighteenth century.

It was probably inevitable that theologians would turn to the question of Sunday observance in view of the wider currents of historical debate on the Bible which spread after the publication of *Essays and Reviews* in 1860. James Hessey, subsequently archdeacon of Middlesex, gave Oxford's Bampton Lectures in that year, publishing them soon afterwards under the title, *Sunday*, and opened the way for a debate into which sporting activities could slip easily:

> ...the Clergy should, so it seems to me, not frown on those who consider Sunday to be, within certain limits, a day of cheerful relaxation, of family union, of social enjoyment, as well as religious services. There is nothing in Scripture to forbid this, even though Sunday be [which it is not], identical with the Sabbath.[8]

The question of the 'certain limits' was to be crucial; Hessey did not support restrictive legislation nor did he countenance 'continental licence'. There was in his approach a pragmatism which could be exploited by the more liberal: 'men of different labours and pursuits need differences of relaxation'.[9] His prime concern was with the poor but such a sentence offered possibilities of a class dimension of separate and exclusive leisure pursuits, all on Sundays. At its simplest, the lines of argument he opened up ranged along the clash between Old Testament notions of Judaic law and the flexibility offered for human needs by a liberal interpretation of Christ's teachings, related to a new appreciation of the relativity of Sunday practices to different periods of Christianity's historical experience. Extended in secular terms the debate moved easily but without ecclesiastical sanction into articulating polarities between a repressive Judaism and an hedonistic Hellenism such as Matthew Arnold identified in *Culture and Anarchy*, although many of the sports later identified as culprits hardly came within the latter category. The extent to which Evangelicals could feel threatened, even rejected, by this development could be seen later in the shocked reaction to the Reverend Stuart Headlam's claim in 1913 that the London County Council's refusal to sanction Sunday games on its public spaces was tantamount to the creation of an artificial sin.[10] Headlam, an Anglo-Catholic, was a Christian Socialist, the founder of the Guild of St Matthew, and a London County councillor who favoured the accommodation of the recreational needs of the city's workers, whatever the day. His Sunday heresies only increased his natural role as a target for Protestant opposition.

The main thrust of this new thinking was towards a view of Sunday rather than Sabbath, inverting the creation image of rest after a week of toil, expressed strongly in the fourth Commandment, to provide instead the sense of a joyful beginning. This reversal of traditional teachings, at least within post-Reformation churches, was based on an historical analysis of the Bible and the practices of the early Church, but reinforced by a sharp sense of modern social realism. The Reverend Dr Linklater, the Anglican editor of *Sunday Recreation*, a symposium of 1889, pointed out that neither legal enforcement nor moral injunctions to Sabbatarianism had reclaimed any men to godliness since mid-century: 'we have to face the fact that this severe system does not succeed in making our people religious'.[11] His fellow-contributors, asking for a greater emphasis on Joy, still rejected the use of Sunday for totally secular pleasures, especially for the rich, but they recognized the overwhelming needs of the poor for 'recreation', open air and escape. One of them, Archdeacon Hessey, acknowledged the pressure 'to escape from stifling dwellings and low associations, and from the thoughts of business' when he favoured the Sunday use of railways.[12] Another, the Reverend Edgar Smith, vicar of All Saints, Highgate, remarked, 'I would not make it a sin that a young man, wearied with the work of "the city", should take his bicycle, and go for a "spin" on Sunday afternoon'.[13] In effect they were now treading a narrow line towards a destination they could only dimly comprehend but which already provided some alarm.

In 1902 one of these writers, the Reverend W.B. Trevelyan of St Matthew's, Westminster, returned to a similar theme – speaking of the decline of the English Sunday and of its enveloping quiet he could look back almost with nostalgia to the purity of the Evangelical outlook whilst deploring, as an Anglo-Catholic, its essential narrowness. Sunday, for him, was being destroyed by the combined pressures of city living and the irresponsibility of the wealthy as it was absorbed into their growing cult of the 'weekend'. His remedy was to offer a balanced synthesis of modest religious observance and gentle secular activity.[14]

The issue of adaptability to social pressures on religious time was exacerbated within Anglicanism by the identification amongst many fundamentalists of Sunday laxity with the High Church heirs of the Oxford Movement, ritualism marching hand in hand with slackness, if not worse. John Keble, whose Oxford Assize sermon of 1833 conventionally marks the beginnings of the ecclesiastical storm, spent much of the subsequent 30 years as a retiring country clergyman at Hursley in Hampshire where he compounded his Tractarian wickedness in more Protestant eyes by leading out his parishioners to play cricket after evensong on summer Sundays.[15] In fact, so also did the ascribed founder of Muscular Christianity and firm enemy of the Tractarians, Charles Kingsley, the son of an Evangelical clergyman, in a parish elsewhere in the same diocese.[16] For the reformers who followed Hessey, Keble's ministry – quiet and rural with its careful balance between worship and paternally-directed leisure – was a model to set against the noisome city and the individualist pleasure-seeking of the affluent middle classes. For their opponents, it signified the road to damnation; with Sunday sports could only come the paraphernalia of the Mass and Roman Catholicism in which collective spectacle would replace an individual's sense of being chosen for heaven, a strange echo of another contemporary debate expressed in more secular terms, the conflict between the values of spectator and participant sports. This prejudice lingered on; much later, one of the characters in John Cowper Powys's novel, *Wolf Solent*, would be made to observe: '...Bob says that High Church be a religion what lets a person play cricket on Sundays'.[17]

This was oversimplified perhaps, but the yearning for a new secular and religious integration, founded on a roseate past, possibly helped some clergy win back part of the ground lost since 1800, if not expand the Church's hold on the popular mind and weekly habits. Concern for justice to those oppressed by urban working conditions ran aground, however, when faced with a growing middle-class penchant for Sunday play. It would be wise at this point to establish the chronology of this apostasy and some of the limits on the movement.

II

The limits were fairly clear, although frequently questioned; amongst the traditional gentry sports which boomed in the period, hunting, shooting and game fishing, there was a fairly clear embargo on any Sunday activity. When wildfowling, not covered by earlier game legislation, grew in popularity in early Edwardian

England, a number of county councils acquired powers to ban it in their areas on Sundays.[18] The same general inhibition applied to county-level cricket and to emergent mass spectator sports such as association football as well as to almost all athletic events and teamgames. Moral considerations apart, most of these would have been illegal anyway because their growing dependence on gate money would have entailed breaches of the 1780, and subsequent legislation prohibiting paid entertainments. In actuality the legal ban on the paid extended to amateur contests as well. The Amateur Football Association, founded out of a split with professionalism in the Football Association in 1907, still discouraged Sunday play amongst its membership.[19] In 1908 the Essex Football Association took active steps to ban its members participating in the widespread Sunday games in Leyton and Leytonstone.[20] Amateur contests continued notwithstanding, but without the umbrella of respectable organisation. In London, as in the other cities, such workers as could made their way to open spaces for relatively informal football and cricket matches in season. Hackney Marshes, Epping Forest, Hainault, and other common spaces saw growing levels of popular, unstructured takeovers after the 1880s. It was this that prompted the repeated and futile attempts to persuade the London County Council to legitimize *de facto* sporting use of the grounds it controlled. Stuart Headlam's complaint about artificial sins was laughed (nervously) out in 1913 and voted out by 44–39 as well, although the size of the minority indicated a significant shift towards his position. London was not alone in witnessing this debate; in Newcastle-upon-Tyne the Reverend Vibert Jackson drew cries of 'No, no!' when he proposed to a diocesan conference that the churches should actually encourage working men to play football on the Town Moor on Sundays.[21]

Sabbatarianism apart, there was a widespread feeling among traditionalists that the spread of Saturday or mid-week half-day holidays (by no means as universal as has often been claimed) meant that there was no justification for Sunday play. In fact, as the satirical journal, *Truth*, pointed out, significant numbers of paternalist merchant employers who provided sports grounds in the London suburbs for their employees' mid-week use also encouraged Sunday use, presumably to feel that the investment was justified.[22] And here is part of the key issue (which will appear again) – much turned on the question of the privacy of certain sports – of possibilities of concealment and smallness of scale as against visibility.

The culprits identified as the vanguard of secularism by Sabbatarians were the middle classes. The prime charge was that of abnegation of responsibility, a rejection of the necessity of example (at least in religious terms) compounded by the issue as to whether an individual's choice of his path to hell actually interfered with the liberty of another's possibility of salvation – not so much through the risk of being misled as of forcing irreligion by demanding unavoidable paid employment. In his contribution to Linklater's book, the Reverend Edgar Smith, whom we have seen with a liberal stance, had identified a growing crisis in the upper and upper-middle classes:

> The 'rich' and those who are called, not always quite correctly, the leisured classes, are becoming great offenders in this respect and on them rests much

of the responsibility for the prevailing desecration of the Sunday amongst us. I would condemn no one on this day to imprisonment within the four walls of his house, or to see nothing of his neighbours. Friendly intercourse is a real refreshment, and in no wise to be discouraged; but the great afternoon receptions and lawn tennis parties, and dinner parties, are all of this world, and in no sense help to give that rest of mind and body which Sunday should promote according to God's ordinance, in addition to which they necessitate work on the part of others, and afford an example which others are not slow in following.[23]

In this process the publications of the LDOS are invaluable to historians not so much because of their constant reiteration of certain values but because they offer, through the reporting of local networks, a fairly constant evaluation of the progress of Sunday sport and a guide to the more overt points of crisis in the process.

Sunday sport for the middle classes was centred in three main locations: the rivers (especially the Thames) and the sea; the roads; and the specialized grounds of croquet lawns, tennis courts and golf courses. It was the last which provoked the most agonised discussions although the numbers involved were far greater than for the first two, their impact, however, being more seasonally limited. The extent of the process in quantitative terms is largely irrecoverable and it is probable that the actual numbers involved in early years were quite small when related to the total potential constituency. Their importance to the critics lay in their being the tip of an iceberg, not so much of rampant atheism or secularism as of a growing indifference to the extending time demands of late Victorian religious revivals, whether in terms of the expounded Word amongst the more fundamentalist groups or of the sacerdotalism and sacramentalism of the successors of the Tractarians. I shall return to this at the end of this paper but for now shall examine the activities themselves more closely.

III

For those fit enough and with money enough to make the limited journeys and meet the hiring charges, namely, young clerks and upwards, the River Thames in season proved a growing mecca from the 1880s. The more indolent could take passage on steamboats, bypassing Sunday restrictions in their guise as transport, but the adventurous or exhibitionist could row or punt, particularly in the less tidal reaches westwards, for which Maidenhead proved a centre of business and sinfulness. One sharp criticism came early from the Bishop of Oxford in 1884, all the more telling because Dr Mackarness, a former college oar, had a strong reputation as a liberal and friend of the Tractarians and their heirs:

You will see, as you come nearer to London, a scene of Sunday desecration, distressing to those who remembered how the oars which we had plied so busily all week lay untouched on Sunday, however brightly the sun might shine. Now the skiff and the canoe dart in and out among barges laden with revellers, and the steam launch, especially odious at all times to the veteran oarsman, troubles the vexed river with its ceaseless whirl. The idlers cannot omit one day in the week from their quest of pleasure.[24]

The river offered space, exercise and a limited relaxation of sexual *mores* for white-collar workers who still worked sufficiently on Saturdays, despite the Bishop's claims, to make the summer use of the river difficult on that day. Its appeal was enshrined in Jerome's *Three Men in a Boat* of 1889, in his description of Moulsey Lock:

All the inhabitants of Hampton and Moulsey dress themselves in boating costume, and come and mouch round the lock with their dogs, and flirt, and watch the boats, and altogether, what with the caps and jackets of the men, the pretty coloured dresses of the women, the excited dogs, the moving boats, the white sails, the pleasant landscape, and the sparkling water, it is one of the gayest sights I know of near this dull old London town.[25]

What Henley Regatta and the Sunday 'church parades', often of non-attenders, at fashionable resorts could provide for the upper-middle classes, the river offered to the lower – colour as against both the physical drabness of the town and worka-day clerical garb. E.V. Gregory's famous painting of *Boulter's Lock on Sunday Afternoon, 1895* celebrated minor frivolity just as Frith's *Railway Station* did a more serious purpose, a rejoicing in relative harmlessness to be set against ecclesiastical condemnations of the insertion of the thin end of a wedge. Its scale could be daunting; on the first Sunday in August 1900, it was estimated that over 1,000 boats and 70 launches passed through Boulter's.[26] The pressures continued unabated and became more organized – indeed, by the mid-1900s some minor tradesmen's clubs had begun to stage Sunday rowing competitions, although Leander and the other prestigious clubs, with strong contingents of clerical ex-blues, frowned upon them. One very conspicuous addition to this was the Hammersmith Sculling Club for Girls (which some men were allowed to join in order to carry the boats), founded by the Chaucerian scholar, Dr Frederick Furnivall, in 1896, which encouraged rowing along the 14 miles to Richmond and back every Sunday of the season.[27] It proved a rare example of organized female Sabbath-breaking. One minor compromise elsewhere appeared in the boating diary of a Wesleyan architect, J.R. Halkes of Lincoln, who took his motorboat, *Asp*, up Fosse Dyke to the Trent on Sunday 28 July 1907, then went to an evening service at Torksey before returning to the boat where 'a little part singing of hymns was indulged in before reclining for the night'.[28] He was not typical; what mattered on the Thames was the rapid growth of commercial provision for those poorer and less pious than Halkes.

The other English rivers had slightly less appeal for the oarsmen but a growing one for the working-class match fishermen who spread along northern and midland rivers and canals during the same period whilst attracting far less overt criticism. By 1900 many railway companies were prepared to mount special Sunday anglers' trains for any association ready to guarantee 300 passengers.

Another parallel boom, this time for the middle classes, had its greatest effect in the Essex coastal area and on the Solent; small-scale yachting and coastal cruising, usually at a very different level of cost and participation from the expensive and prestigiously structured regatta weeks at Cowes. Here the emphasis was on the limited weekend voyage by a small amateur crew, often from one estuary to another, such as the Crouch to the Blackwater, picking up a train for the return to London and reversing the direction the following weekend. The extent to which the habit became removed from conventional Sunday observance may be gauged from the obituary tribute to one of the pioneers of this trend, George F. Holmes, founder of the Humber Yawl Club in 1883: 'He was deeply religious, and when away on a cruise on Sunday he invariably set off in the dinghy to the nearest Church, whether his crew accompanied him or not.'[29] Generally, yachting attracted little religious attention or execration, perhaps because it was so distinctly individualistic and involved people well away from the public gaze.

The same could not be said of the greatest semi-organized lower middle-class invasion of Sunday, the cycling craze which reached a peak in the mid-1890s. Track-racing on the Sabbath was effectively banned by the Amateur Athletics Association and the National Cyclists' Union, but unofficial 'scorching' as well as general touring were significant in country districts round most large towns. Reactions were usually unfavourable, questioning the validity of the pursuit as recreation:

> One of the moral objections to the Lord's Day, even when so arranged as not to force Sunday work on others, is that, in addition to the neglect of distinctive Sabbath duties, there is a corresponding unfitting for the weekday duties. The cyclist who incurs this double blame does not 'serve God truly all the days of his life'.[30]

Such a defence of the Protestant ethic against the violation of the spirit of the day absorbed into religious argument a pragmatic use of secular criteria.

Cycling was, in fact, one of those sports which caused a singular perplexity for Sabbatarians – where they failed to persuade of the direct immorality of an activity they would fall back on claiming that it should not require the employment of others. It did not, in theory, do this but the growth of peripheral support ranging from repairs through to cream teas did. The scale of the developments could be seen in an LDOS report that, almost a decade after the great boom, one of their observers counted on a Sunday in 1904, 125 motor cars, 125 female and 1,797 male cyclists passing the *Red Deer* at Croydon in a two-hour period.[31] There were occasional hints of punishment; the LDOS reported with exaggerated glee the defeat of English participants in a French Sunday cycle race in 1900, an illustration of their repeated claim that God would contribute to the defeat of transgressors, a logic which could not, however, be applied to those who won.[32] These warnings were made freely available with the publication in 1902 of a Society pamphlet, *To Cyclists – this hill is dangerous.* It seems to have had little effect, although monitoring of the decline went on.

Cycling offered, however, the first real possibilities of some ecclesiastical compromise with Sunday sport in that, unlike dawdling on the river, it fitted in with simple ideals of Christian athleticism and it could be accommodated by the more flexible proponents of the Sunday, as distinct from the Sabbath, and adaption came fairly early. From the mid-1880s the vicar of Ripley, Surrey, provided Sunday afternoon cyclists' services in his church; in 1889 a group of the grateful participants gave him a typewriter and work table, being rewarded with a sermon on the theme, 'So run the race that ye may obtain the prize'.[33] This provision spread after the 1895/6 boom but was often rather scattered. The vicar of Giggleswick, North Yorkshire, placed a notice in his church porch inviting visitors to worship in cycling dress, even if they left before the sermon: 'You do not sin cycling on Sunday, but you do most certainly sin against God and wrong your neighbour if you neglect your clear duty, which is to publicly adore your Saviour, Jesus the Christ'.[34] This compromise was at its strongest around London, the half-bolting of the stable door, a long way from the LDOS's teaching which only allowed Sunday cycling as possible if unavoidable for the purposes Peake had outlined to the Lords, a case for which he had been gently taunted by Lord Tring, a keen tricyclist.[35] Some more adventurous churches took the Devil on at his own game, using bicycles for evangelism as when, at the end of Victoria's reign, 25 Congregationalists formed a 'Cyclists' Gospel Band' to cover north London and Epping Forest with open-air Sunday meetings.[36] But in general the response was unfavourable, particularly amongst the higher clergy. The 'liberal' bishop of Manchester continued to blame the decline of Sunday observance since 1870 'on carelessness and athleticism, and particularly on the invention of the bicycle'.[37]

Although these developments produced trepidation amongst opponents of the 'craze for pleasure' and noise, more worry, as well as direct local conflicts were produced by the greatest boom games of the middle classes – croquet, lawn tennis and golf. These occupied a continuum, both in terms of chronology from the mid-1870s and in visible scales of threat both to straight Sabbatarianism and to the role of organized religion in late Victorian society. In a sense the first two occupied private rather than public space but this provoked fears of a direct threat to children, servants and domestic virtue, rather than to onlookers at large. As activities of those already well-endowed with private recreational space they could, conversely, be contained as half-observed private vices. Lord Amberley drew opprobrium for instructing a friend in croquet one Sunday afternoon in 1860,[38] Prince Albert had brought his Lutheran habit of playing chess on Sunday afternoons with him, but that could be decently veiled.[39] On a more public occasion, the Prince of Wales drew sharp criticism from LDOS when he took a 'special train' to Epsom to attend Lord Roseberry's lawn tennis party on a Sunday in 1881: 'Lawn tennis was played all the afternoon, where it could be partially seen, and crowds of our own people, I fear of all classes, amused themselves standing in Chalk Lane to watch'.[40] In one delicate adjustment to the possibility of containing temptation in private bounds, Osbert Lancaster recalled the problems caused in his Edwardian childhood during visits to his grandfather who allowed home croquet instead of lawn tennis because: 'Whereas the tennis court was visible from the road and the vicar feared that the spectacle of the gentry at play might lead the villagers into sin, the croquet lawn was concealed by a dense shrubbery so that only our salvation was imperilled, and this was a risk which he thought, on the whole, we were justified in taking.'[41]

Golf was on a different level. The LDOS first identified it as a problem in 1891 when it was being played on Epsom Downs despite discouragement from the local club; the culprits were apparently strays from Wimbledon whose Sunday play there had been stopped on the basis of its being a threat to other users of the common.[42] It is difficult to identify the first English club to adopt Sunday play formally. One witness to the Lord's committee of 1895, where middle-class activities were discussed only marginally, said that since golf had been allowed in the Old Deer Park Richmond-on-Thames he now saw:

> that most peculiar of all dress, golf dress; gentlemen are dressed in scarlet, with large bundles of sticks, and then from our Sunday schools...our lads are taken away to go into the park for the purpose of carrying the sticks, or to go after the balls. These lads are called 'caddies', and altogether we are in Richmond degenerating as a town.[43]

Here is a number of indicators to the problem created by Sunday golf – it used labour, removed the young from religious instruction and affected an area's social tone adversely. It was played theoretically on private land, although on a far greater scale than most other recreational land use. Unlikely to attract spectators, it none the less posed problems because many clubs either occupied common land or that with some public access. Few players were as lucky, or as determined, as the eight men, led by Dr James Greig Smith, who created in the early 1890s a private course of 18 holes over the farmland at Woodspring Priory, outside Weston-super-Mare, solely in order to play the game on Sundays, a pleasure forbidden on the links of the clubs to which they already belonged.[44]

Apart from the risk of pollution by example, Sunday golf was resented by some more liberal critics as putting at risk the legitimate recreational ambitions of local workers and their families by blocking access to country walks in the selfish interests of already privileged sections of the middle classes. In this sense, wherever clubs proposed Sunday play even if unaccompanied by employed labour, local groups could use Sabbatarianism to cloak a series of other resentments – the alienation of scarce land resources and the question of neighbourhood social tone not least; golf did not, despite the cachet that eventually attached to playing, inevitably raise the tone of an area for all its inhabitants. The clearest expression of this was usually to be found in resorts where, as John Walton has recently demonstrated, conflicts within and between broadly similar bands of the middle classes could develop sharply,[45] and 'social tone' which might be enhanced for some by Sunday golf, could be interpreted far differently: 'One of the chief reasons given for that terrible decline of Hastings and St Leonards as a residential place is that Sunday is so ill-observed there.'[46] Sunday play at the seaside had two main justifications, the need of overtired businessmen and professional men working from Monday morning to Saturday afternoon for whom Sunday was the only full day when play was available, and the drive to maintain levels of local economic development in an inter-resort rivalry where clients would go elsewhere if thwarted, taking their money with them.

Most cases aroused considerable local controversy; the work done on this is so far minimal but some illustrations can be given. When the club in Seaford, Sussex, struggling towards a very modest prosperity, proposed Sunday play in March 1894 a debate began which lasted till the year's end. For it, the club advanced the arguments I have already outlined. Against it, the town's leading developer claimed '. . . a man who would play golf on a Sunday would not be very particular whether he paid his debts or not'.[47] The resort's Congregational minister, quite prepared to countenance Sunday bathing for health, drew the line at golf – it had few virtues, would open the way to football on the Sabbath and bring in the 'continental' or 'southern Irish' Sunday. Other arguments included the need to protect access to footpaths across the beautiful downland the golfers had alienated which was the town's greatest asset. But above all, golf would bring rowdiness. In this sense the debate was no longer between sport and religion but between two notions of almost strictly secular development in which appeals to the fourth Commandment appeared largely as buttresses to, rather than bases for, other considerations.

Sunday golf won in Seaford but the battle, monitored by LDOS, waged across much of England and Wales. The Reverend the Earl of Chichester, Vicar of Yarmouth, who protested vigorously against it locally in 1903, was one of many.[48] Greater success attended the Ecclesiastical Commissioners when they refused to renew Llandudno's golfing lease in 1906 unless the lessee forbade Sunday play, despite protests that the embargo would cost the town £20,000 a year and despite the club's offer to stop all its employment of girl caddies as a condition for going ahead.[49] Where local authorities controlled the greens, as at Cheltenham or Cleethorpes, the golfers were saved from the 'discredit of Sunday desecration' after a struggle.[50] Leeds was debarred by its Corporation lease although by 1911 it had fought it through after a long debate in a secret general meeting.[51] When Sunday golf was played at Walton-on-the-Hill in 1905 the LDOS regarded a local caddies' strike on that day as a sign of divine disapproval: 'The disregard of God's laws which is shown by Sunday golfers may be expected to develop an equally lawless spirit in those whom they teach and encourage to profit by their bad examples.'[52]

In at least one case, the new resort of Bexhill, the handling of the issue revealed the layers of perplexity by which the proponents of Sunday play were able to appear as moral as well as secular benefactors. The local club had adopted Sunday play early in the 1900s but without caddies. In February 1910 it decided to employ them, but only if over 14 years of age and on a 'voluntary basis'. The rector, Archdeacon Churton, opposed this on the grounds of 'deterioration of character', making a wider point of the 'dead-end' nature of caddying as a job, although he refused to be drawn into any specific condemnation of Sunday recreations.[53] In this he was supported by an exotic local resident, Oscar Browning, the reforming fellow of King's College, Cambridge, who said the caddies needed a day of church and Sunday schools. An anonymous local rejoindered: '. . . it's all very well for Prof. Browning to sit in his easy chair on Sunday after lunch and think how lovely it is to go to church, but please remember he isn't half-starved and he isn't dependent on a round of golf for a meal'.[54] It was this argument which won the day when combined with some other acute observations that, since the caddies were rarely worshippers, they were probably better employed in working rather than loafing. Thereafter the issue was quietly dropped in favour of the club.

In fact, golf is the only activity where some modest quantifiable assessment of the trend is possible. Virtually no English clubs, even where they practised it, advertised Sunday play in a 1906 directory.[55] The inhibitions seem to have loosened in that, by 1913, 436 of the 1,024 English courses advertised Sunday games but only just under half of those allowed caddies. By comparison, only 18 of the 83 Welsh clubs opened on Sundays and these were in the anglicized south and the northern coastal resorts catering for Liverpool and Manchester. Scotland, frequently lauded by LDOS as the repository of Calvinist purity, despite some unkind reminders that Calvin and his early followers played bowls on Sundays, had only 11 clubs offering Sunday sport as against almost 400 which did not. Of those prepared to open, Kirriemuir advertised that 'Sunday play is allowed but no one plays'. Perhaps worth a detailed local study was the Dumbarton club which allowed Sunday play but whose honorary secretary was the local minister.[56]

IV

Sabbatarian conflicts were by no means exclusively English – Stephen Hardy has noted a similar pattern in his recent major study of nineteenth-century Boston, Massachusetts.[57] Faced with these developments, the responses of the English churches were uneven; having made huge efforts to overcome the deficiencies revealed in the 1851 census of religious worship they were alarmed to find what they regarded as the core of their laity beginning to drop away. In fact it was probably the more peripheral groups that did this initially but most denominations, with the exception of the most predestinarian sects, were predisposed to believe in the possible redemption of all the population, however firm the contrary evidence. Where decline occurred, most obviously in various nonconformist bodies in the early 1900s, it has been suggested that it was not so much net membership which was affected as a decline in the number of 'twicers' and an increase in the practice of occasional attendance.[58]

The LDOS and its sympathisers still saw this as little short of apocalyptic – the introduction of the continental Sunday, even of carnival, the weakening of the moral hold which prevented the working classes both from cutting loose and from being exploited by the commercially unscrupulous. The almost hysterical expression of these views reveal official Christian hegemony as being very frail indeed, with a very powerful notion of fallen man likely to give way only too easily to a repeat of 'Archbishop Laud's ill-omened attempts to rival the Roman church in its appeal for popular favour'.[59] The unlikely possibility of a revival of James I's *Book of Sports*, not only legalizing but also enforcing some Sunday recreations, was a repeated nightmare for many Sabbatarians, yet few supporters of LDOS were prepared to go so far as to demand an effective alternative – the legal prohibition of Sunday middle-class sports. Such a mixture of views was to be found widely in dissent, only occasionally challenged in some of the more progressive fringes of Congregationalism, such as the partial concessions allowed by the Seaford minister already described. At the Congregational Union's annual assembly in 1910, Professor H.T. Andrews of New College asked that 'the Church must restate the grounds on which its demand for Sunday observance was based, but it would be a national catastrophe if all restraints were removed and Sunday became a kind of Bank Holiday recurring every week'.[60] The vague motion the assembly passed in his support reinforcing 'the wisdom of guarding the sacred day from encroachments, perilous to the country's religious life' satisfied no one. The Wesleyans kept on the whole to a much harder line opposing Scouting and Territorial Army training on Sundays.[61]

The most confused response came from the national church. The issue had been raised at the Reading Church Congress in 1883 and in 1887 the Lambeth Conference of Anglican bishops issued some rather vague guidelines urging a return to worship.[62] It surfaced at various diocesan meetings during the 1890s but the peak came in 1905 when seven diocesan conferences debated the problems. The most widely reported was Oxford's, partly because it included the parts of the Thames and many of the western London suburbs where middle-class sport was most overt.[63] This prompted the much-quoted *Daily Telegraph* survey, with its suggestions of widespread apostasy, in September and October 1905.[64] In Hackney the 'gentry' played golf at Chingford, whilst youths played football on the marshes and the Jewish middle classes just enjoyed themselves.[65] In Penge, 'this suburban town has always shown a marked tendency towards the progressive idea as to how Sunday should be spent'.[66] Oddly enough, a survey as comprehensive as the only slightly earlier one made by Charles Booth made virtually no mention of the trend.[67] The Church moved slowly towards an official reluctant compromise with the secular, based largely on assumptions of its innocence, although fulminations about national and imperial decline continued both in convocations and correspondence columns.[68]

It is worth asking 'What was being lost?' At one level the nostalgic image of a former peace and crowded churches which had never really existed had a strong hold. Having lost most of the working classes as regulars the clergy had become frightened of losing what moral imperatives remained through example. Eternal damnation and contemporary national decline seemed to march hand in hand, not least since the Prime Minister. Balfour, was a fashionable Sunday golfer. Despite frequent demands that the LDOS should oppose him at the polls it refused, pragmatically holding that a non-golfing candidate might exhibit even worse faults.[69] For others, such as Canon F. Meyrick, the Evangelical rector of Blickling in the Lincoln diocese, there were ominous historical parallels comparable with other contemporary images of English decline: The cry for *circenses* was an indication of a degraded Roman population, and they were not a means of lifting it from its degradation', and 'The theatres were full during the orgies of the French Revolution'.[70]

Sunday golf hardly went this far but we must ask why it proved so popular for its participants. At one level the justification of release from urban stress was as applicable here as at any other time. But it is necessary to go further and to assess the attractions of playing at a time which could invite social obloquy in some areas. Firstly, it was essentially a male activity, with only very secondary female participation even on the river or cycling. Religious worship was becoming what it has emphatically remained, a participant female pursuit, limited to mornings, strongest outside the summer months with many males appearing only as very occasional conformists.

It would be unwise, however, to assume that this secularization arose, except in a few cases, from any systematic rejection of Christian claims through intellectual processes. The causes of the drift were probably social rather than theological. In developing seaside resorts and the new suburbs the churches often had less cohesion and appeal than the tennis and golf clubs. It has been suggested that emotional needs for status recognition and stability could now be more readily found in the locker rooms of sporting associations than in the pews, and these offered stronger reinforcements for increasingly secular notions of social leadership, consumption rather than moral example as a lead.[71] In strictly operational terms it was easier to maintain club membership for normal life and fall back on the churches for crises and rites of passage. Churches with unrestricted access to pews offered less protection for social differentiation and even the mild social messages to be found in suburban sermons, let alone the more disturbing parts of the Gospels, could raise uncomfortable questions left unmentioned in clubs with stricter criteria of membership. In his study of London, Olsen has pointed to an 1890s' observation that suburban home life had replaced religious practice as the focus of worship with 'rewards of peace and contentment'.[72] Later observers than Olsen's source claimed that middle-class sports were an additional threat to this with the earlier moral inhibitions imposed by servants and children as the bulwarks of respectability being increasingly ignored.[73] This raises some interesting speculations, incapable of adequate pursuit in this paper, that for many men domestic life saw the same intermittent attendance as the churches. The number of semi-humorous works by 'golfing widows' and others in the Edwardian press masked a growing concern about the apparent stability of some families, although it could be rejoindered that these absences actually increased stability in some cases.[74] One frequently suggested compromise – church in the morning, sport in the afternoon – must have raised problems about the role of some heads of families which have yet to be investigated. Perhaps here one should enter a mild *caveat*; in numerical terms, just staying at home rather than either praying or playing may have appealed to the majority of men, and Olsen's source was probably justified.

Beyond these there are the possibilities of rather more deterministic explanations. Sunday observance had fitted the disciplinary needs of an emergent industrial capitalism. In a service sector coming to play a major role in the national economy it was less necessary, perhaps not even desirable, and a gradual relaxation could be permitted. The critics' oft-reiterated claims that Sunday play was the product only of idle West-enders who sought seven instead of six days of indulgence may be discounted generally but they do reinforce the judgement that organized religious participation was coming to be seen as only one amongst a range of leisure choices available to the more socially privileged with limited non-work time.

V

Conventionally, we should say that the processes under way by 1914 accelerated with the war until by the time of peace, Sabbatarianism was dead. In fact, the battle for London's green spaces was fought all over again, eventually with more success for the liberals.[75] This paper is too short to allow an adequate discussion of this and so little work has yet been done on the post-1918 British churches that a full assessment cannot yet be made. But it is probably reasonable to assume that England saw a very rapid decline of the influence of local Sabbatarian opinion. It was in the outer parts of the kingdom that resistance lingered.

It would be instructive here to examine one such case that demonstrates the complexity of motives underlying the defence of the Sunday peace. It is discussed briefly in Kenneth O. Morgan's major study of modern Wales but he sees it exclusively in terms of the chapels' resorting to violence in a departure from the best traditions of a passive nonconformity.[76] My own view is that he understates the complexity of the issues. In October 1927, after a meeting called by the churches and chapels of the town, and with tacit support from the corporation, a crowd disrupted Sunday play on the Aberdeyfi golf course, by using a Welsh mountain ram, herds of cattle and standing six inches from the golfers so that swings were impossible. There were elements in it suggestive of a Compton Mackenzie novel or an Ealing film, not least the interventions of a local landscape artist, Miss Buddug Pugh, given to shouting nationalist slogans in Welsh. Fifteen people were bound over but the golf club dropped attempts to recover damages in the interests of peace. The Welsh Sabbath was the occasion of the protest but it was closely intertwined with a thirty-year-old dispute about common rights and a feeling that the English were destroying Welsh integrity in their lust for play and profit. The club had an embarrassing debt it hoped to reduce with Sunday green fees, an English Lord Justice as a prominent member and a committee dominated by English settlers. It is perhaps instructive that some of the verbal responses from these outsiders appeared in letters to the Liverpool rather than local Welsh press.[77]

By the time of the Aberdeyfi protest 82 English golf clubs, mostly in Cornwall and Yorkshire, 35 Welsh and 213 Scottish ones still forbade Sunday play.[78] Twelve years later, on the brink of another war, the English figure had dropped to 27, the Welsh to 23 whilst the Scottish had risen to 225 – not because of any religious revival but because the new clubs founded in those years largely followed the national norm and did not represent the secular interlopers that could be seen in Wales.[79]

In terms of the overall process since 1880 the LDOS was perhaps not too far wrong when it held that, in England at least, middle-class apostasy and organized, but non-commercial, sport have been major but neglected factors in explaining the steady decline in religious attendance from the 50 per cent or so of 1851 to the ten percent of today. In the 'post-Christian' world chronicled by Gilbert and others, religion rather than sport is now the peripheral activity.[80]

Notes

*   I am grateful to the British Academy and the Twenty-Seven Foundation for the generous research grants which have made it possible to work on the scattered materials incorporated in this paper. The theme will eventually be incorporated in a discussion of national entropy in my book, *Sport and the English Middle Classes, 1880–1914*. An earlier version was read to the British Society for Sports History and I wish to record my thanks for the many helpful suggestions made there. My greatest debt is to Dr Norman Vance of the University of Sussex for casting such a helpful and critical eye over my earlier draft.

1 Sally Magnusson, *The Flying Scotsman* (London, 1981), p. 40ff.
2 Norman Vance, 'Is faith dangerous? An Irish question', *Theology* (Nov. 1978), p. 409ff.
3 See, for instance, B. Harrison, 'Religion and recreation in nineteenth-century England', *Past and Present* 38 (1967), p. 98ff.; W.S.F. Pickering, 'The Secularised Sabbath' in M. Hill (ed.), *A Sociological Yearbook of Religion in Britain* 7 (1972), p. 33ff.; J. Wigley, *The Rise and Fall of the Victorian Sunday* (London, 1980), *passim*.
4 Owen Chadwick, *The Victorian Church* (London, 1966–70).
5 Select Committee of the House of Lords on the Lord's Day Act, Parliamentary Papers 1895 (HL 178), q. 1708.
6 Cf. H. Taine, *Notes on England, 1860–70* (London, 1957 trans.), pp. 10 and 12.
7 Cf. E.P. Thompson, 'Time, Work-discipline and Industrial Capitalism', *Past and Present* 38 (1967), *passim*; B. Harrison, loc. cit., Peter Bailey, *Leisure and Class in Victorian England* (London, 1978), *passim*; R.W. Malcolmson, *Popular Recreations in English Society, 1700–1850* (Cambridge, 1973), *passim*.
8 J.A. Hessey, *Sunday, its Origin, History and Present Obligation* (London, 1860), p. 333.
9 Ibid., p. 321.
10 *The Times* (9 July 1913 and 22 July 1914); L[ord's] D[ay] O[bservance] S[ociety], O[ccasional] P[paper] (Oct. 1914).
11 R. Linklater, *Sunday and Recreation; A Symposium* (London, 1889), p. 8.
12 Ibid., p. 43.
13 Ibid., p. 81.

14 W.B. Trevelyan, *Sunday* (London, 1902), p. 1.
15 Linklater, op. cit., pp. 80–81, 196.
16 LDOS, *OP* (Oct. 1876).
17 J.C. Powys, *Wolf Solent* (London, 1929, 1964 ed.), p. 77.
18 S. Duncan and G. Thorne, *The Complete Wildfowler* (London, 1911), p. 55.
19 Amateur Football Association, *Annual* (1907/8 *et subs., passim*).
20 *Truth* (16 Sept. 1908); LDOS, *OP* (Oct. 1908).
21 *Times* (19 Oct. 1910).
22 *Truth* (5 Oct. 1910).
23 Linklater, op. cit., pp. 76–7.
24 LDOS, *OP* (Feb. 1884).
25 J.K. Jerome, *Three Men in a Boat* (London, 1889, 1957 ed.), p. 56.
26 R.T. Rivington, *Punting, its History and Techniques* (Oxford, 1982), p. 45.
27 Frederick James Furnivall, *A Volume of Personal Record* (Oxford, 1911), pp. 2 and 77ff.
28 Lincolnshire Records Office, Diary of J.R. Halkes of Lincoln.
29 Hull Central Library, Humber Yawl Club, *Yearbook* (Hull, 1940), p. 4.
30 LDOS, *OP* (Dec. 1900).
31 LDOS, *OP* (Oct. 1904).
32 LDOS, *OP* (Dec. 1900).
33 *Hull and East Riding Athlete* (4 Dec. 1889).
34 *Daily Telegraph* (11 Oct. 1905).
35 Lord's Committee, q. 1732.
36 Charles Booth, *Life and Labour of the People in London*, 3rd series, *'Religious influences'*, Vol. 7: 'Summary' (London, 1902), pp. 167–8.
37 LDOS, *OP* (Oct. 1902).
38 H. Mcleod. *Class and Religion in the Late Victorian City* (London, 1974), pp. 261–2, n.37.
39 Trevelvan, op. cit., p. 268ff.
40 LDOS, *OP* (Nov. 1881).
41 O. Lancaster. *All Done From Memory* (London, 1953), p. 152.
42 LDOS, *OP* (Jan. 1891).
43 Lords' Committee, q. 2588.
44 James Greig Smith, *Woodspring* (Bristol, 1898); I am grateful to Trevor Hearl for this reference, *passim*.
45 J.K. Walton, *The English Seaside Resort: A Social History 1750–1914* (Leicester, 1983), p. 187ff.
46 *Daily Telegraph* (4 Oct. 1905).
47 *Seaford and Newhaven Gazette* (10 March 1894).
48 LDOS, *OP* (April 1903).
49 *Truth* (15 Feb. 1906); LDOS, *OP* (April 1906).
50 LDOS, *OP* (April 1904, July 1904).
51 Leeds Golf Club, *Minutes* (January 1910) – I am particularly grateful for permission from the secretary to use this material.
52 LDOS, *OP* (July 1905).
53 *Bexhill-on-Sea Observer* (19 Feb. 1910).
54 Ibid. (26 Feb. 1910).
55 *Nisbet's Golf Yearbook* (1906).
56 *Golfer's Handbook* (1913).
57 Stephen Hardy, *How Boston Played; Sport, Recreation and Community, 1865–1915* (Boston, 1982), pp. 58–60.
58 A.D. Gilbert, *The Making of Post-Christian Britain* (London, 1980), p. 95.
59 LDOS, *OP* (July 1906) and *Annual Report* (July 1906).
60 *Times* (13 May 1910).

61 *Times* (21 July 1910).
62 Trevelyan, op. cit., pp. 298–9.
63 *Times* (28 April, 29 June, 13, 20, 26 Oct., 9 Nov. 1905); *Church Times* (29 Sept. 1905).
64 *Daily Telegraph* (29 Sept. and 3, 4, 5, 6, 7, 9, 11, 12, 13 Oct. 1905).
65 *Daily Telegraph* (6 Oct. 1905).
66 *Daily Telegraph* (10 Oct. 1905).
67 See note 36 above, *passim*.
68 For example. *Times* (14 May 1914).
69 LDOS, *OP* (April 1906).
70 F. Meyrick, *Sunday Observance* (London, 1902), p. 116.
71 Pickering, loc. cit.; J. Kent, 'The Role of Religion in the Cultural Structure of the Late Victorian City', *Transactions of the Royal Historical Society* 5th series, Vol. 23 (1973).
72 D. Olsen, *The Growth of Victorian London* (London, 1979), p. 209.
73 H. Mcleod, 'Class, Community and Religion' in M. Hill (ed.),*A Sociological Yearbook of Religion in Britain*, 6 (1973), pp. 31 and 61.
74 For example. Sir Hugh Seton-Karr, 'Golf and Matrimony', *Golf Monthly* (Dec. 1912).
75 H. Snell, *The Case for Sunday Games, Against Sabbatarian Prejudice* (London, 1923).
76 K.O. Morgan, *Wales, 1880–1980* (Oxford. 1982), p. 201.
77 *South Wales News* (18 and 24 Oct. 1927; *Cambrian News* (7, 14, 21, 28 Oct., 11, 18, 25 Nov. 1927).
78 *Golfer's Handbook* (1927).
79 *Golfer's Handbook* (1939).
80 Gilbert, op. cit., *passim*.

Chapter 8

To pray or to play?
The YMCA question in the United Kingdom and the United States, 1850–1900

*William J. Baker**

The founders of the Young Men's Christian Association were a narrowly focused evangelical group of young men. They were business-men – laity, not clergy. Driven by Protestant piety, not playfulness, for the better part of half a century YMCA leaders vigorously debated whether or not they should encourage 'mere amusement', physical exercise, and competitive athletics. Until well into the twentieth century, Britons and North Americans arrived at different answers to the question. Especially in the United States, the YMCA lent institutional support to earlier, more theoretical muscular Christian preachments. In becoming a kind of priesthood of believers in the gospel of muscular Christianity, the Y solved the perennial problem of all ideological movements: the need to translate prophetic inspiration into organized form and ritual.[1]

Enthused but not amused

Like so much of modern sport, the YMCA began in England, in response to the urbanization that accompanied the massive commercial and technological surge that we have come to know as the Industrial Revolution. In the beginning was no building and no programme, only a few young men gathered for mutual support. Founded in London in 1844, the Y was one of many evangelical alliances, associations, institutes, self-improvement societies, and city missions catering to the moral and religious needs of young men recently arrived in the city.[2] The prime mover, George Williams, was the son of a Somerset farmer. After an apprenticeship with a local draper, at age twenty he went to London and found a job as a clerk in a retail cloth shop. London threw him into severe culture shock. Having been reared on a simple chapel diet of daily prayers, Bible classes, temperance meetings and exhortations to sexual purity, he found the City an ungodly, intimidating place. In contrast to the small, quiet village of his West Country youth, London was populous and noisy, brimming with variety and options.

Originally published in *The International Journal of the History of Sport*, 1994, 11(1), 42–62. http://www.tandf.co.uk/journals

For Williams, those attractions amounted to 'intemperance and dissolute living', temptations to be resisted. Taking refuge in the upstairs room provided by his employer, he soon began meeting regularly with other young clerks and apprentices who shared similar provincial, religious backgrounds. They found mutual support in prayer, Bible study and discussions. Encouraged by their boss, George Hitchcock, they distributed gospel tracts in the vicinity of the firm, and for a while called themselves the Drapers' Evangelical Association.

For three years they functioned without formal organization, but in early June 1844 a dozen or so members of the group convened officially to designate themselves the Young Men's Christian Association. Their purpose, in the words of some minutes of the meeting, was to arouse converted men 'to a sense of their obligation and responsibility as Christians in diffusing religious knowledge to those around them either through the medium of prayer meetings or any other meetings they think proper'.[3] From the outset, the purpose of the YMCA was clear and firm, the methods flexible.

Too flexible for some. Most self-improvement societies of that day set up their own little libraries ('reading rooms') and sponsored lectures to propagate their views, but several members of the Y adamantly opposed those 'secular' measures. One, William Edwyn Shipton, railed for years against any dilution of the Y's central function as a centre of Bible study, prayer, and missionary work. Deeply suspicious of education, Shipton exhorted London Y leaders to 'confine themselves entirely to those religious agencies which were peculiarly the work of the Association'. The YMCA, he insisted, should 'seek to do first of all, last of all, and entirely, SPIRITUAL WORK' until all those sinners 'now scattered up and down this naughty world' were brought into the fold. George Hitchcock agreed. Believing that one should pray before sitting down to read a book (for Divine guidance through erroneous parts), he wanted 'as few secular things as possible' in the first YMCA buildings he helped furnish.[4]

If libraries and lectures were suspect to some early Y leaders, 'mere amusements' were anathema to all. In November 1845 the first annual report of the London YMCA beckoned young men 'to the library of useful knowledge, rather than to cards and billiards, the cigar divan and concert-room, the theatre, and the seducting and polluting retreat'. The Y, after all, existed to keep young men off the 'broad path' of city pleasures that led to destruction. To bring those worldly games and recreational activities into the YMCA parlour would risk ruin, or so the founders believed. Confronted with a proposal for a chess room in the Leamington branch of the YMCA, W.E. Skipton in 1862 had the last word in this opening round of debate: 'I do not think it is part of the Association's work to provide any man with amusements.'[5]

This negative attitude, common among the English founders of the YMCA, derived in part from a native puritan tradition that included John Bunyan and seventeenth-century Dissent, John Wesley and eighteenth-century Methodism, and Hannah More and early-nineteenth century Evangelicalism – all fearful that frivolous pleasures as well as the carnal allurements of Vanity Fair would damn the soul.[6] More immediate inspiration came from abroad. English Congregationalists, Presbyterians, Methodists, and Evangelical Anglicans (the prime sources of YMCA enthusiasm) all responded warmly to the intensely personal, evangelistic and moralistic message of American revivalist Charles G. Finney. They devoured his *Lectures to Professing Christians* (1837) and *Lectures on Revivals of Religion* (1840); in 1849–50, and again in 1858–60, they eagerly welcomed his evangelistic crusades to the British Isles.[7]

Charles G. Finney was their kind of man, speaking their kind of message. From their lower-middle rungs on the pecking order of British society, they applauded his condemnation of 'parties of pleasure, balls, novel-reading, and other methods of wasting time'. Christians should happily claim the title of 'a peculiar people', Finney assured them, 'and thus pour contempt on the fashions of the ungodly in which they are dancing their way to hell'.[8] According to George William's biographer, the secret of Williams' 'certainty of belief' and 'absorbing passion for souls and for the work that wins souls' lay in Finney's emphasis on prayer, conversion and holy living.[9] Finney's teachings were certainly one of the keys to the London YMCA's niggardly attitudes towards amusements.

In search of familiar moorings among the fleshpots, religious young men from the boonies were attracted, not deterred, by strict YMCA standards. By the time of the Great Exhibition of 1851, seven branches of the Y thrived in London and fourteen more were spread around the United Kingdom. Several American and Canadian visitors to the Great Exhibition took the opportunity to examine the Y at first-hand. Duly impressed, they returned home determined – as an editor of a Boston Congregationalist magazine put it – 'to transplant it hither'. In November 1851 the first YMCA in North America was founded in Montreal; just a month later, Boston seized the honour of being first in the United States. In the early summer of 1852 a YMCA was organized in New York City for 'the improvement of the spiritual, mental and social condition of young men', and 'to promote evangelical religion among the young men of this city and its vicinity.' By 1856 no fewer than fifty-six YMCAs could be found in North American cities ranging from Halifax, Nova Scotia, and Savannah, Georgia, on the east coast to San Francisco and Stockton, California.[10]

As local branches proliferated they were everywhere the same in evangelical intent but everywhere different in emphasis and clientele. In Louisville, Kentucky, for example, diverse interests converged towards the creation of a YMCA in 1853. Protestant ministers wanted evangelistic assistance in winning the city's 'irreligious element' to Christianity; local businessmen welcomed the Y's emphasis on discipline and hard work as antidotes to the spirit of indolence that seemed to threaten the economic life of the city; Louisville's German Protestant community sought institutional support for the moral and intellectual improvement of young German immigrants.[11]

Then as now, the YMCA offered something for everybody. In addition to Bible classes, prayer groups and evangelistic services, most Ys provided reading rooms, public lectures and debating societies. Before they bought their own buildings and converted them into sleeping quarters for homeless or lonely young men, local branches posted lists of respectable boarding houses beside lists of employment opportunities. They also assisted charitable organizations, especially in poor relief and the more occasional flood relief. Further diversifying in a way that the YMCA in England never did, American branches linked up with colleges and universities. The great day of the YMCA student movement lay in the post-Civil War era, but campus organizations appeared in 1858 at the universities of Michigan and Virginia.[12]

An English visitor to the United States saw these innovations as evidence of the 'peculiar practicalness of endeavour' that characterized the American YMCA on the eve of the Civil War. Americans were developing 'more of the secular element than in England', thought Thomas H. Gladstone, a patron of the London YMCA.[13] Had he inquired more closely, Gladstone would have even found a more secular, practical attitude towards 'fashionable amusements'. As a new YMCA organ of opinion, the *Young Men's Magazine*, put it in 1857, amusements like card-playing, dancing and novel-reading were best confined to one's juvenile years and the privacy of the home, but these amusements were useful – and therefore reluctantly to be accepted – if they restored the mind and body for work. Otherwise, they were a waste of time, 'and time wasted is a plunge downward,' added the editor as he manoeuvred back onto a familiar puritan track.[14]

Scarcely was the 'amusement question' settled prior to the Civil War. In 1867, at the 12th annual North American YMCA convention, a Methodist clergyman threatened to withdraw his church from Y sponsorship 'if a resolution favoring amusements were adopted.' Reportedly, the threat was 'received with anything but favor', but no pro-amusements resolution was adopted. As late as 1875 the editors of a national YMCA journal, *The Watchman*, reminded their readers that the purpose of the Association was 'not the providing of even rational, or elevating amusements.'[15]

Lords of the gym

Sociable amusement was one thing; a physical activity programme would be something else for the YMCA to sponsor. In the 1850s a number of voices insisted that a physical dimension be added to the YMCA's moral, spiritual, and intellectual emphases.[16] The loudest, most reasonable arguments came from Brooklyn, New York, where muscular Christian apologist Henry Ward Beecher pastored Plymouth Church. 'There ought to be gymnastic grounds and good bowling alleys, in connection with reading rooms' in every YMCA in order 'to give to the young men of our cities the means of physical vigor and health, separate from temptations and vice,' declared Beecher. Yet he saved his finest nudge for a gathering of Boston YMCA friends in 1857. Impishly observing that the Boston Y regularly sponsored two 'amusements', lectures and social teas, he lauded starchy-stiff Bostonians for being ahead of New York and Philadelphia in these matters. But he wanted more: health-giving activities, physical exercise that put 'muscle on a man'.

Why shouldn't the YMCA promote boating, running, quoiting and javelin throwing? All would be 'advantageous and innocent in practice,' promised Beecher.[17]

In 1860 the leaders of more than 200 American and Canadian YMCAs, representing some 25,000 members, gathered in New Orleans for their seventh annual convention. They unanimously agreed on 'the importance and necessity of a place of rational and innocent amusement and recreation for young men, especially in large cities and towns', and resolved that each local branch of the YMCA should build a gymnasium with all due haste. Unfortunately, that resolution fell victim to the guns that opened fire on Fort Summer. During the Civil War, as the YMCA helped provide food, shelter, clothing and spiritual counsel for the combatants, the gymnasium question got momentarily put aside.[18]

At the end of the war (1865), most YMCAs were located in church basements or in some downtown rented building. Not a single one had a gymnasium. By 1890, however, about 400 YMCA gyms dotted the North American landscape, half of them with hired supervisors of physical activity. This phenomenal growth of buildings and professionally trained physical directors transformed the YMCA into the institution that we know today.[19]

The New York City YMCA led the way. Its 'secretary' (director), Robert R. McBurney, a Protestant immigrant from Northern Ireland, barely waited for the smoke to clear from the Civil War battlefields before he launched a fund-raising campaign for the construction of a magnificent building on Twenty-third Street at Fourth Avenue. He especially wanted a gym. Knowing that to be a novel, controversial idea, he directed a committee to prepare a 'scientific' survey of the moral and physical dangers facing young men in the city in order to make apparent the need for physical fitness. In 1866 he manoeuvred a change in the constitution of the New York YMCA, making it the first Association in the world to specify 'physical' as one of its fundamental goals of self-improvement.[20]

In the autumn of 1869 new YMCA buildings, with gyms, opened in Washington and San Francisco. Finally, in December of the same year, the New York building officially opened to much fanfare as 'the only one planned, erected, and equipped' for physical activity. It was certainly the largest and finest-built of the three. Whereas Washington's 'magnificent building' was completed for $200,000 and San Francisco's (with a bowling alley as well as a gym) for $57,000, New York's four-storey stone edifice cost $487,000. For years it reigned as the model for YMCA architecture. Yet by today's standards the gym was a mere exercise room, small and poorly equipped. Seventy feet long and fifty feet wide, it was cluttered with a wooden horse, parallel bars, a springboard and ladders at various angles from the walls. Flying rings, pulleys, a trapeze and a punching bag hung suspended from the ceiling. Lumpy mats covered portions of the floor reserved for wrestling and tumbling.[21]

New Yorkers apparently loved it. Despite a silly warm-up drill in which participants lined up, marched around the room and stopped at designated painted circles on the floor (a kind of musical chairs without music or chairs), the gym was regularly filled to overflowing. According to McBurney's annual report of 1870, only the Y's bowling alleys rivalled the gym in popularity. By 1876 gym attendance averaged 300 men daily; all 879 'dressing boxes' (lockers) were rented, and more were needed.[22]

Meanwhile, enthusiasm for the gym grew slowly but surely throughout North America. In 1872 the Boston Association purchased a large old building, the Tremont Gymnasium on Eliot Street, that had long been used as a commercial, fee-paying place of exercise for urban 'gentlemen of the ledger'. In the following year, the oldest YMCA on the continent, Montreal, completed the construction of fine new quarters. A spacious, well-equipped gymnasium set Montreal at the head of a Canadian gymnasium mania that would take off in the 1880s.[23]

Unique circumstance caused the Chicago YMCA to lag behind in the race to facilitate 'physical work'. In brief, that circumstance was the heavy presence of revivalist Dwight L. Moody. From a rural village in western Massachusetts, Moody first made his way to Boston where he worked as a boot and shoe salesman, joined the YMCA, and underwent a religious conversion. He moved to Chicago in 1856, in quest of economic opportunity, and virtually became a charter member of the Chicago Association at its birth in 1858. Moody energetically plunged into the evangelical work of the downtown Y. He led noontime prayer meetings, distributed gospel tracts on the streets and bluntly accosted street-people and church-people alike with the question, 'Are you a Christian?'[24]

In 1860 he abandoned his work as a leather-goods salesman to devote himself entirely to religious work. For the next decade he worked in and for the YMCA. As an agent of the Association, he ministered to the wounded and dying during the Civil War. For four years, 1866–70, he served as president of the Chicago Association's board of directors. From wealthy businessmen like copper magnate William E. Dodge, banker J.P. Morgan, meat packer J.F. Armour and industrialist Cyrus H. McCormick he raised money for the construction of three YMCA buildings (the first two were destroyed by fire).

Appropriately, through the YMCA Moody met the man who would be singularly instrumental in his evangelistic ministry. In 1870, at an international Y convention in Indianapolis, the ability and sincerity of song-leader Ira D. Sankey convinced Moody to invite him to Chicago. They worked well together and in 1873 departed for a successful two-year gospel crusade in Britain. Returning home, they renewed the revival fires stirred earlier by Charles G. Finney throughout North America. Yet Moody remained a life-long friend of the YMCA and on several occasions raised funds for specific branches. To the end of his days he claimed that the YMCA did 'more, under God, in developing me for Christian work than any other agency'.[25]

He left the Chicago YMCA structurally and ideologically committed to evangelism, not to 'physical work'. Moody and Robert McBurney once engaged in a public debate over the best means of appealing to young men. McBurney wanted a gym; Moody wanted more Bible classes, sermons and edifying lectures. He got his way. As one visitor recalled, the 'principal feature' of the YMCA building was a huge lecture hall filled to capacity each Sunday for a sermon by Moody. None of the funds he raised ever went into the building of a gymnasium.[26]

The first general secretary of the Chicago YMCA, A.T. Hemmingway, was a man after Moody's heart: warmly supportive of evangelistic activities, cool to demands for programmes of physical exercise. 'Such work', recalled a Chicagoan years later, 'was known as worldly activities'.[27] Under great pressure from his members, however, Hemmingway appointed a committee to study the feasibility of going the gym route. Finally, in 1879 a second-floor room formerly used for prayer meetings was converted into a gymnasium. By then, Moody himself was recommending 'a gymnasium, classes, medical lectures, social receptions, music and all unobjectionable agencies' rather than 'simply evangelistic meetings' in the YMCA.[28] But his change of mind came too late to erase the shabbiness of the Chicago gym. An old-timer later sadly remembered it as 'a large, dirty, smoky walled room with a few parallel bars, rings attached to ropes fastened to the ceiling, and a few pairs of dirty boxing gloves. That was all.'[29]

While Chicago dragged its feet, other Associations dashed ahead in the building or renting of gyms, and in the hiring of 'physical directors' to supervise their use. In supervision, as in gym construction, the New York YMCA led the way. Shortly after opening their new gym in 1869, they hired William E. Wood as the first full-time YMCA physical director. An English immigrant, Wood owned and operated several commercial gyms in New York before casting his lot with the YMCA. Although he reportedly functioned 'without relation to the Y.M.C.A. [religious] purpose', the earnest, gentlemanly and physically fit Wood aptly demonstrated the newly emergent image of YMCA manliness.[30]

One of his major concerns was gym safety. In the early years, circus performers, weightlifters and pugilists found Y gyms cheaper and sometimes better-equipped than athletic clubs as places to keep fit between professional engagements. Their flamboyant antics invited imitation.[31] The Boston YMCA was especially vulnerable to mishap because a large troupe of circus performers wintered in the area, filling the Tremont Gymnasium with circus acrobats, tumblers and trapeze artists practising their stunts. In the Tremont's very first year as a YMCA site, a young man killed himself trying to perform a double forward somersault off a springboard. Shortly thereafter the board of directors hired a circus rope walker to supervise the gymnasium, reasoning that a circus man could best curtail circus exploits. He lasted just two years only to have YMCA religious purposes bow to pragmatism once again in the selection of his successor, an acrobat and tumbler.[32]

In 1876 the Boston YMCA did an about-face with the appointment of a devout Baptist, Robert J. Roberts, as gymnasium superintendent. A wood-turner and mechanic by trade, the twenty-seven-year-old Roberts had achieved some local fame as a rower, swimmer, gymnast and weightlifter. In 1864 he joined the Tremont Gymnasium (eight years before the YMCA took it over) and often went across the street to work out with heavy weights at a private gymnasium run by Dr George B. Windship. Only five feet five inches tall with a forty-three inch chest and a thirty-two inch waist, Roberts proudly lifted 2,200 pounds with a yoke, raised a 120-pound dumbbell over his head with either hand, and dead lifted 550 pounds from the floor with one finger.[33]

Still, when he coined the term 'body building', he meant something other than the efforts of a bulky weightlifter. For popular YMCA use, he recommended light, simple apparatus as a compromise between the 'fancy gymnastics' of the circus variety and the 'heavy work' espoused by Dr Windship. Pioneering in the use of dumbbells, indoor running tracks, medicine balls and physical examinations, Roberts urged 'safe, easy, short, beneficial and pleasing' exercises for purposes of health and agility. In 1881 he appeared on the programme of the YMCA international convention in Cleveland, Ohio, in full gym uniform, demonstrating his dumbbell drill. That was the first time the convention had ever made a place on its programme for the gymnasium question, and YMCA men mark it as the turning point in the Y's larger interest in physical development. In the same year of President Chester A. Arthur's death by assassination, the YMCA witnessed a birth of gymnasium excitement.[34]

Prior to his address and demonstration, Roberts offered 'a fervent and simple prayer', a gesture not lost on his audience. For several years YMCA leaders had anxiously feared that the gymnasium was secularizing the Association rather than the Association Christianizing the gym. Roberts' work, coupled with his regular column in *The Watchman*, allayed those fears. He presented himself as a Christian who directed physical activities, not a physical director who happened to be a Christian (or worse still, non-Christian). As the Boston YMCA secretary happily observed, Roberts was 'a Christian worker' who stationed himself 'on the floor and mat of the gymnasium primarily to promote the coming of young men into the Christian life.'[35]

Before young men could be won to Christianity, however, they had to be enticed into the YMCA itself – and for some YMCA men that was reason enough to build, equip and supervise gymnasiums. In one case, a gymnasium apparently saved an Association from extinction. The Dayton, Ohio, Association began in 1858 only to collapse at the onset of the Civil War. Resurrected in 1870, its membership list declined so badly that it could scarcely pay the bills. Finally, the secretary identified the problem: that there was no incentive for a young man to buy a membership if he was not interested in religion or reading. With only fifty members in 1885, he announced plans for a gymnasium and immediately received membership pledges of $10 each from 300 young men.[36] Practical and idealistic motives blended freely in the YMCA's baptism of the gymnasium.[37]

Yet one should not dismiss the gym mania as a mere means to an institutional end. Granted, in 1888 most YMCA men agreed with Luther Gulick, who reminded them that the gymnasium should always be a means to the end 'of leading men to Christ,' but then everything was a means to that end for evangelicals.[38] By the mid-1880s YMCA leaders were affirming, not merely accepting, the gym, and for principled as well as opportunistic reasons. At the annual international convention of 1887, in San Franciso, policy-makers bowed to Lord Gym as 'an integral part' of the Association's fourfold purpose: 'Physically, the gymnasium should be a distinct department of our work; morally, it should be conducted on the purest principles of the Association; intellectually, it should be made educational; spiritually, it should be a place where active and associate members meet and where Christian influence prevails.'[39]

Doing good with games

By 1886, some 1,066 YMCA local branches in North America had 101 gymnasiums but only thirty-five physical directors.[40] Likely as not, those thirty-five were all trained in some variation of the 'hands on' method perfected by Robert J. Roberts, who reportedly recruited and trained twenty to thirty instructors at the Tremont Gymnasium in Boston. Probably not one of them had a college degree, much less special religious or professional training. In this regard, they were little different from the first YMCA secretaries.

Beginning in the mid-1880s, secretaries and physical directors embarked on a process of professionalization akin to the route taken by lawyers, doctors, clergymen and university professors in the late nineteenth century: theoretical study and supervised practical application in professional schools founded specifically for the task.[41] Compared to these other professions, of course, the YMCA functioned humbly. Aspiring secretaries first found training in summer institutes at Lake Geneva, Wisconsin. Then in 1885 an ambitious pastor of a Congregational church in Springfield, Massachusetts, opened a new School for Christian Workers. The original intent was to train YMCA secretaries, Sunday School superintendents, and pastors' assistants, but the Association focus quickly became dominant.[42] In 1890 the name was changed to the International Young Men's Christian Association Training School, in part to distinguish it from a similar new school in Chicago. Later the Springfield school would take on yet another name, Springfield College, and become known for its emphasis on physical education and social work.[43]

Instruction in physical education began in 1887 as a two-year course combining philosophical foundations and practical techniques. To teach the latter, Robert J. Roberts moved – with dumbbells in hand – from Boston to Springfield. For the more theoretical pedagogy, twenty-one-year-old Luther Halsey Gulick joined the staff. Born of missionary parents in Honolulu, Gulick attended Oberlin preparatory school in Ohio and the Sargent School of Physical Training in Cambridge, Massachusetts; just a year before he accepted the Springfield job, he began medical school at New York University. Concerned primarily with hygiene and exercise for the prevention of disease, he completed his medical degree in 1889 eager to explore 'the relation of good bodies to good morals'.[44]

He did more than that. To the service of the YMCA (or as he put it, to Christ) he committed the most reflective, best-read and widest-ranging mind in the entire history of the Association. During his thirteen-year tenure at Springfield, he taught philosophy, psychology and history of physical training; physiology, hygiene and anthropometry (scientific measurements), plus gymnastics and athletics. Students came into his classes with serious plans as future gym directors; they left with a 'recreative' imperative added to their 'educative' schemes. Most of all,

Gulick sealed the place of the gymnasium with a solid rationale and opened up YMCA thought to yet another era by insisting on the potential benefits of athletic competition.

Unfortunately, the issue of athletics brought him into conflict with his Springfield colleague, R.J. Roberts. As Elmer Johnson observes, the two men were vastly different in temperament and style. Gulick was quick-witted, imaginative and experimental; Roberts was methodical, conservative and predictable.[45] Yet they also thought differently, especially about the way the YMCA should relate to the competitive sports that were sweeping the country in the 1880s. Roberts forbade any competitive activities in his Boston gym and refused to teach advanced recreational courses at Springfield. He advised young men *'never* to enter competitive sports'. At the least, they should refrain until age twenty-two, and then only under the care of a doctor and athletic trainer – and without the blessing of the YMCA. The 'spirit of competition' should be altogether removed from Y-sponsored activities, argued Roberts. Only if young men learned to exercise for purposes of health rather than 'for the sake of competition' would they 'live the longer to do better work for God and humanity'.[46]

Similarly enthusiastic for health, God's work and service to humanity, Gulick differed sharply on the place of competition in the grand scheme of things. He was sixteen years younger than Roberts[47] and came of age with competitive rowing, baseball, football, lawn tennis and a host of lesser sports. A contemporary recalled him as a baseball pitcher with 'a swift underhand ball',[48] but in truth Gulick did not distinguish himself as an athlete. Unlike Roberts, he observed better than he performed, and in the late 1880s he observed that YMCAs all over North America were purchasing or renting nearby open land for baseball and football games, track meets, bicycle races, tennis matches and horseshoe games. The official historian of the YMCA exaggerated in his suggestion that Gulick 'found the Y.M.C.A. doing calisthenics and left it on the basketball court and playing field', but not by much.[49] Gulick found the YMCA timidly stepping onto the playing field, uncertain of its right to be there; from the podium and with the pen, he removed the doubts.

Gulick's effectiveness can best be gauged in the changing character of *The Watchman* and its successor, the *Young Men's Era*. For several years after its first edition in 1874, *The Watchman* carried scattered, infrequent references to gymnasium issues and even fewer to competitive sports. Early in the year 1889, a 'Physical Department' section appeared but with mere brief reports from around the nation taking up less than half a column of a three-column page. In October 1889, however, Gulick became editor of the Physical Department section and immediately enlarged it to an entire page. Announcements and scores of games stood jowl to jowl beside reflective essays such as 'Athletics in Paul's Writings', by Hartford Theological Seminary professor C.S. Beardsley.[50] The *Young Men's Era* succeeded *The Watchman* in 1890; by the end of 1892 the Physical Department section averaged three to four pages each issue. The issue of 18 December 1892 devoted seven full pages to gymnastics and sports.

Notices of games and scores ranged from hand ball to pentathlons, but commentary focused primarily on baseball, football and basketball. For YMCA leaders, baseball was something of a disputed territory. Many agreed with the general secretary of the Cleveland, Ohio, Association who thought it 'worthy of being called our "national game"' because it was 'clean, healthful, invigorating and recreative, both to the player and the spectator'. Others refused to endorse baseball as a YMCA-sponsored game because of its 'pernicious habits, such as Sabbath playing, betting, drinking and the like', as the Y state secretary of Ohio put it.[51] More subtly, some thought baseball failed to contribute to the well-rounded development of lungs, muscles and total health that was the hallmark of the Y's physical ideology. Worst of all, baseball was the one team sport that had gone professional, disqualifying it as a game that YMCA leaders could encourage unreservedly. 'Professionalism aims at money and even sacrifices health and morals to obtain it', the *Young Men's Era* reminded its readers – for whom health and morals were paramount.[52]

Billy Sunday's story confirmed the YMCA's ambivalence toward baseball.[53] A 'rube' from the fields of Iowa, Sunday signed as an outfielder with the Chicago White Stockings in 1883. For five years he wielded a weak bat but displayed good speed and daring on the bases for the White Stockings, then moved on for three more years with Pittsburgh and Philadelphia. As Sunday himself often told it, one evening in 1887 he and five baseball mates staggered out of a saloon to encounter a noisy brass band making its way down the street to the headquarters of the local Rescue Mission. Sunday followed the band, heard the Gospel preached and was 'saved' on the spot. In the classic style of the evangelically converted, he turned his back on alcohol, swearing, gambling and the theatre. Refusing to play any more Sunday baseball, on Sundays he gave inspirational messages to boys at the YMCA in whatever city the team happened to be.

Finally, nudged by a pious wife, Billy Sunday hung up his baseball gear in exchange for a YMCA secretaryship. He took quite a hefty cut in salary that year. As he followed the revivalist trail blazed by Dwight L. Moody, he kept audiences on the edge of their seats with his athletic antics. According to one observer, Sunday underwent 'gruelling exertions' racing back and forth across the podium like a 'restless gymnast'. Sliding safely home seems to have been his favourite means of illustrating salvation. His favourite homily – 'You can't measure manhood with a tape line around the biceps' – was taken right out of the YMCA gym. Warnings about sin and destruction often came in the form of yarns from his hell-raising days in major league baseball.[54]

By contrast, football was a highly respectable campus sport whose tacit professionalism was hidden from view.[55] In the 1880s the American version of football was adapted from British rugby, creating a much rougher, more dangerous game.[56] Yet football appealed to YMCA leaders because of its potential for 'all around' physical development. Legs and arms, lungs and loins – all were exercised 'in the writhing and twisting and pushing of the rush line', insisted one contributor to the *Young Men's Era*. Unlike baseball, football demanded constant motion and innovation rather than long periods of inactivity punctuated by repetitious moves. Best of all for aspiring middle-class YMCA men, football rewarded hard work: grittiness more than natural talent.[57]

Strange (or even impossible) as it might now seem, innumerable Associations sponsored football teams in the late nineteenth century. Before equipment, coaching and insurance became prohibitively expensive, YMCA squads competed against teams from other Y branches, athletic clubs, colleges, prep schools and seminaries. Leaders endlessly debated the 'brutishness' of the game, but a sure sign of the YMCA's acceptance of football appeared in the autumn of 1890, when the Springfield Training School first fielded a team.

A former football and baseball star at Yale, Amos Alonzo Stagg, created and captained the Springfield team. At the outset, Stagg faced the formidable task of finding eleven decent players from a student body that numbered fewer than fifty. He succeeded brilliantly. In its first season, Springfield won five of eight games, finishing with a splendid performance in a 16–10 loss to the national champions, Yale, in Madison Square Garden. Facing a much tougher schedule the next year, Springfield still won five, lost eight and tied one. Again led by the quick, stocky Stagg, the 1891 squad averaged a mere 151 pounds; they stood less than five feet, eight inches on the average, earning them the nickname of the 'Stubby Christians'.[58]

More than Luther Gulick's essays, Amos Alonzo Stagg's athletic exploits and coaching skills momentarily sealed the YMCA's connection to the gridiron. From Springfield, Stagg went directly to the new University of Chicago as athletic director and head football and baseball coach, and from that prominent perch he frequently preached the gospel of games and good sportsmanship.[59] As he explained shortly after arriving at Chicago, years earlier he had gone to Yale intending to become a Presbyterian minister, but had changed his vocational course as he came to see that his opportunities 'for doing spiritual good' were better in athletics and student work than in a pastorate. Thus he 'deliberately concluded' that he 'would be going away from rather than into the vineyard by being ordained'.[60]

Another YMCA worker in the vineyard of the Lord, James B. Naismith, arrived at Springfield on a route remarkably similar to Alonzo Stagg's. Like Stagg, he grew up in a Presbyterian home (in Ontario, Canada) that was strong on moral precepts; like Stagg, he went off to college (McGill University in Montreal) confidently feeling 'called' to study for the Christian ministry. Naismith, too, was a notable athlete, anchoring the front line of McGill's rugby football team even though 'it was not thought proper for a "theolog" to engage in that sort of activity'.[61]

During his undergraduate years, Naismith regularly worked out at the Montreal YMCA, near the McGill campus, and continued to do so during his three years of theological studies at a Presbyterian seminary in Montreal. In conversation with the Montreal YMCA secretary, he began airing the possibility 'that there might be other effective ways of doing good besides preaching'.[62] Although he finished his programme of theological study and in 1890 was licensed for the ministry, the prospect of a career that would combine religion and athletics sent him to Springfield to prepare for YMCA work.

At Springfield he distinguished himself in the classroom as well as on the football field. Most importantly, he invented basketball – one of the few modern games without ancient roots. In response to Luther Gulick's suggestion that some sort of indoor team competition was needed to fill out the sports calendar between football and baseball seasons, Naismith drew up thirteen simple rules to govern a game that featured the tossing of a soccer ball into peach baskets suspended from the balcony railing at each end of the gym. The first game of basketball was played in December 1891; from Springfield it spread quickly throughout North America, and around the world, by means of YMCA literature and Springfield-trained personnel.[63]

The attractiveness of basketball brought an end to the YMCA argument over competitive sports. As American colleges and high schools took to the game, Luther Gulick observed that Y-sponsored athletics held far more promise than gymnastics because athletics were 'more interesting to the average man.'[64] While Gulick served as the first head of an Athletic League formed in 1895 to control Association competition, he and his colleagues repeatedly reminded themselves that they were promoting physical and spiritual health, not 'mere sport as such'.[65] Sport, they insisted, was a means to moral ends.

Yielding to the flesh

One of those ends was the reassertion of manliness, which seems to have been a constant need in nineteenth-century America. Despite all the blood and bluster of the Civil War, the American male's 'fear of feminization' did not abate. If anything, during the last quarter of the century it intensified among young men who had been too young to fight for the blue or grey. By the 1880s and 1890s, they could only wonder anxiously if they would have displayed the bravery of their fathers, uncles and older brothers. Moreover, the rise of corporate government, big business and the bureaucratic workplace robbed middle-class men of the outlets for creative individuality and self-assertion that their fathers had enjoyed. Little wonder that Teddy Roosevelt's vision of 'the strenuous life' and heavyweight champion John L. Sullivan's emergence as America's first national sports hero coincided with the YMCA's commitment to competitive athletics. American masculinity was at stake, or so it seemed.[66]

By definition, the Young *Women's* Christian Association lacked the need to encourage sport as a means of building Christian manliness. Like the YMCA, the YWCA originated as a group of prayerful youths eager to avoid the evils of the big city. In the 1850s several women's organizations sprang up in London and New York; the first to call itself a Young Women's Christian Association appeared in Boston in 1866. Assuming the importance of prayer, Bible study and Christian witness, the first YWCA concerned itself with decent housing for women, then with job training. At the Y a young woman could obtain instructions to become a seamstress, stenographer, bookkeeper, typist, or telegraph and telephone operator. Physical culture was never a prominent part of the YWCA programme. The first class in calisthenics was held in the Boston Y in 1877; the first YWCA gym appeared seven years later, also in Boston. Still, by 1893 only nine gyms could be found in the fifty-two city YWCAs scattered throughout North America. Sport figured marginally in the late nineteenth-century YWCA because it occupied no central place in the definition of womanhood.[67]

For quite different reasons, the British YMCA also took half-heartedly to sport. Not one of the founders of the YMCA went to a British 'public school', where sports were becoming the rage in the middle years of the nineteenth century. George Williams, George Hitchcock, W.E. Shipton and their friends were all pious businessmen, not athletes. As youths, they had no opportunity to play organized games; as serious, money-making, God-fearing adults, they had no inclination to watch the many rowing, cricket, rugby and soccer matches that their less earnest contemporaries enjoyed. Their conservative views dominated London's central YMCA committee and from London they exerted influence throughout the Kingdom. In 1871, for example, they informed a Dover group that the new Dover YMCA should stick to the basics of prayer meetings, Bible study, and evangelistic activities. Recreative literature and programme of physical exercise 'should not be looked for in connection with the arrangements for the Young Men's Christian Association'.[68]

As one might expect, the great English popularizer of muscular Christianity, Thomas Hughes, abhorred the YMCA's 'narrow groove' of spiritual, religious emphases that failed to touch the English working class. Yet Hughes curiously supplied ammunition for the anti-sports brigade. In 1873, just sixteen years after the publication of *Tom Brown's Schooldays*, he admitted to a reluctance in talking about athletic games because 'these things are made too much of nowadays, until the training and competitions for them outrun all rational bounds'. Apparently the athletic enthusiasm in the wake of the founding of the Football Association (1863) and the Rugby Football Union (1871) knocked him off his kilter. Hughes pined for 'a revival of the muscular Christianity of twenty-five years ago', which probably meant more Christianity and less muscularity. Athleticism was still 'a good thing if kept in its place', he concluded in 1880, 'but it has come to be very much over-praised and over-valued amongst us'.[69]

London Y leaders certainly had good reason to fear that sport would be overvalued in branches beyond their control. In populous Manchester, a new YMCA building opened in 1876 with a well-equipped gymnasium that attracted 600 new members within the first year. In addition to gym work, the Manchester Y sponsored cricket, swimming and walking clubs for 'vigorous, recreative exercises' to complement religious activities. The Liverpool YMCA made similar moves with similar results. In 1882 they renovated a large private gym, hired a gymnastics director and sponsored numerous indoor and outdoor athletic events.[70]

Americans lauded these measures as 'sensible', 'wise' and 'useful'; older London leaders saw them as potential first steps down the slippery slopes to perdition, leading the YMCA astray from its original religious purposes.[71] This suspicion (if not outright hostility) towards physical culture caused a kind of roller coaster existence for the Central London YMCA. Exeter Hall, long a centre of evangelical, reformist crusades, in the late-1870s was saved from being turned into a music hall by an energetic fund-raising drive led by George Williams. Finally the YMCA took over the lease, renovated the building and opened it in April 1881 with a double gymnasium in the basement. Seven years later the gym was moved to a nearby building, but when its lease expired in 1894, the governing committee decided not to renew it. American YMCA leaders, by now having come to terms with athleticism, were simply appalled. They believed, as one put it in a report to a physical education journal, 'that a portion of the [London] Committee do not and never have looked with favor upon the physical department, and tolerated it only as a necessary evil, or as a kind of sop to public opinion in general and young men in particular'.[72]

London at least had a sop. To the west of the City, a branch of the YMCA in the town of Reading had not even that. Founded in 1846 under the auspices of the Church of England and at the hand of a prosperous seed merchant, Martin Hope Sutton, the Reading Y operated by strict evangelical principles: all religious piety, no fun and games. At the opening of a new building in 1897, George Williams reminded them that the sole purpose of the YMCA was to enable a young man 'to go into his counting house or workshop' strengthened by Bible classes, prayer and testimonial sessions and missionary endeavours. The Reading Y closed its doors in 1903, partly because of its unwillingness to offer the kind of recreational and physical activities that appealed to youths.[73]

Even the most pietistic gestures sometimes got wrapped in modern sporting garb. The gods of sport took revenge on George Williams, it seems. When Williams died in 1905, several commemorative speeches and gospel hymns rattled off the walls of a YMCA gymnasium in Weston-super-Mare; on the next Saturday, the Preston YMCA soccer team wore black armbands in his honour.[74]

Old soldiers lumbered on to the end. The last surviving member of the original group that met at Hitchcock's drapery shop in 1844, William Creese, wrote to a friend in 1909 that he was utterly saddened by developments in the YMCA. Billiards, bagatelles, card games and ping-pong tables, not to mention cricket, football and cycling clubs – what was the world coming to? What was the YMCA becoming? 'It was born of the spirit', lamented Creese, 'and now it appears to be yielding to the flesh'.[75]

Notes

* I am grateful to the Lilly Foundation for a research grant that made possible this essay as part of a larger study of religion and sport.
1 Historian Bernard A. Weisberger identifies 'the perennial problem of religious movements' in this manner: 'What is conceived in ecstasy must be reduced to form,

doctrine, ritual and organization in order to perpetuate itself. The tension between organization and inspiration – between priest and prophet – lasts throughout the life of a religion', *They Gathered at the River: The Story of the Great Revivalists and their Impact upon Religion in America* (Boston: Little, Brown and Company, 1958), pp. 129–30.

2 Much of the following is taken from Clyde Binfield, *George Williams and the Y.M.C.A.: A Study in Victorian Social Attitudes* (London: Heinemann, 1973).

3 Ibid., p. 120.

4 Ibid., pp. 185, 273–4, 277.

5 Ibid., pp. 276, 298. For other references to the amusement question in the early years of the YMCA in England, see pp. 162–3, 300–1, 567; cf. Doreen M. Rosman, *Evangelicals and Culture* (London: Croom Helm, 1984), p. 3, for Sydney Smith's *bon mot* against 'these gloomy people' who 'hate pleasure and amusements'.

6 For the contours of what radical journalist William Cobbett called 'the puritanical school' (*Cobbett's Annual Register*, 20–27 Feb. 1802) in early nineteenth-century England, see Thomas Walter Laqueur, *Religion and Respectability: Sunday Schools and Working Class Culture, 1780–1850* (New Haven: Yale University Press, 1976); Brian Harrison, *Peaceable Kingdom: Stability and Change in Modern Britain* (Oxford: Clarendon Press, 1982); Ford K. Brown, *Fathers of the Victorians: The Age of Wilberforce* (Cambridge: Cambridge University Press, 1961); K.S. Inglis, *Churches and the Working Classes in Victorian England* (London: Routledge and Kegan Paul, 1963); Rosman, *Evangelicals and Culture*.

7 On Finney's impact, see Binfield, *George Williams*, pp. 17–21, 210–12, and J.E. Hodder Williams, *The Life of Sir George Williams, Founder of the Young Men's Christian Association* (New York: Association Press, 1906), pp. 30–6.

8 Williams, *Life*, p. 35.

9 Ibid., p. 32.

10 Charles Howard Hopkins, *History of the Y.M.C.A. in North America* (New York: Association Press, 1951), pp. 18, 23–4; Cleveland E. Dodge, '*Y.M.C.A.*': A Century at *New York* (1852–1952) (New York: Newcomen Society, 1953), pp. 9–11.

11 Lawrence W. Fielding and Clark F. Wood, 'The Social Control of Indolence and Irreligion: Louisville's First YMCA Movement, 1853–1871,' *The Filson Club History Quarterly* 58 (April, 1984), 219–36.

12 See Hopkins, *History of the Y.M.C.A.*, pp. 25–32, 34–9.

13 *Young Men's Magazine* 1 (May 1857), 25.

14 *Young Men's Magazine* 1 (August 1857), 148–51; (October 1857), 255. The editors of this magazine were less tolerant of 'the fascinating seductions of the theatre, the casino, the gin-palace, and the gambling-saloon' (June 1857), 78.

15 Owen E. Peuce (ed.), *The Hundred-Year Book: A Synoptic Review of Association History* (New York: Association Press, 1944), n. p., 1867 items; *The Watchman* 2 (Nov. 1875), 4.

16 Elmer L. Johnson, *The History of YMCA Physical Education* (Chicago: Association Press, 1979), pp. 22–5; cf. Hopkins, *History of the Y.M.C.A.*, pp. 32–4 and *Hundred-Year Book*, n. p., 1856 and 1857 items.

17 *Young Men's Magazine* 1 (July, 1857), 137.

18 For 'The Y.M.C.A.'s and the Civil War', see Hopkins, *History of the Y.M.C.A.*, pp. 84–98.

19 See Mayer N. Zald, *Organizational Change: The Political Economy of the YMCA* (Chicago: University of Chicago Press, 1970), pp. 28–38.

20 Richard C. Morse, *My Life with Young Men* (New York: Association Press, 1918), p. 67; Dodge, '*Y.M.C.A.*', p. 19.

21 Johnson, *YMCA Physical Education*, pp. 31–4; Morse, *Life with Young Men*, p. 67; J. Gardner Smith, 'History of Physical Training in New York City and Vicinity in the Young Men's Christian Associations', *American Physical Education Review* 4 (1899), 303–8.

22 Smith, 'Physical Training in New York City', 304; *Hundred-Year Book*, n. p., 1870 item; *The Watchman*, 2 (March, 1876), 6; Johnson, *YMCA Physical Education*, p. 38.

23 See L.L. Doggett, *History of the Boston YMCA* (Boston: privately published by the YMCA, 1901), and William B. Whiteside, *The Boston Y.M.C.A. and Community Need: A Century's Evolution, 1851–1951* (New York: Association Press, 1951); I.E. Brown, *Young Men's Christian Association Buildings* (Chicago: W.W. Vanarsdale, 1885); M.G. Ross, *The YMCA in Canada: The Chronicle of a Century* (Toronto: Ryerson Press, 1951).

24 Amid the massive bibliography on Moody and his evangelical tactics, probably the most balanced critique is James F. Findlay, Jr's *Dwight L. Moody: American Evangelist 1837–1899* (Chicago: University of Chicago Press, 1969).

25 Morse, *Life with Young Men*, 74; Richard C. Morse, *History of the North American Young Men's Christian Associations* (New York: Association Press, 1913), pp. 122–4. For Sankey's point of view, see Ira D. Sankey, *My Life and the Story of the Gospel Hymns* (New York: Bigelow and Main, 1906).

26 *Hundred-Year Book*, n. p., 1866 item; Morse, *Life with Young Men*, p. 66.

27 P.W. Coke (ed.), 'Some Significant Gleanings from the History of the Young Mens' Christian Association of Chicago' (1940), Chicago Historical Society, YMCA Collection, Box 7, Folder 4.

28 Hopkins, *History of the Y.M.C.A.*, p. 188; on Hemmingway, see Johnson, *YMCA Physical Education*, p. 36.

29 John R. Patterson, 'Recollections of Early Days of the Chicago Y.M.C.A.' (1940). Chicago Historical Society, YMCA Collection, Box 7, Folder 4.

30 G.F. Thompson, 'History of Physical Work in the YMCA', *Association Seminar* 12 (May, 1904), 307; Hopkins, *History of the Y.M.C.A.*, p. 247. See William E. Wood, *Manual of Physical Exercises* (New York: Harper and Brothers, 1867).

31 In some cases, people were simply mesmerized by the circus crowd. Circus apparatus should be avoided 'as you would a trick mule', warned one gym director. 'When they come in the 'actors' begin to 'act', the others watch them because they cannot imitate, and all real beneficial work is at an end', Thomas C. Diggs, 'Some Gymnasium Don'ts', *Young Men's Era* 17 (5 Feb. 1891), 90.

32 Johnson, *YMCA Physical Education*, pp. 34–5; Doggett, *Boston YMCA*, p. 50.

33 D.D. Brink, *The Body Builder* (New York: Association Press, 1916), p. 10; 'Short Stories About Physical Directors: Robert J. Roberts', *Young Men's Era* 19 (25 May 1893), 663–64; cf. Luther H. Gulick, 'Robert J. Roberts and His Work', in R.J. Roberts (ed.), *Home Dumb Bell Drill* (Springfield, Mass.: Springfield College pamphlet, 1894).

34 Johnson, *YMCA Physical Education*, pp. 39–41; Hopkins, *History of the Y.M.C.A.*, pp. 249–50; Morse, *Life with Young Men*, p. 264; cf. Morse, *History*, pp. 167–9.

35 Morse, *Life with Young Men*, pp. 263–4.

36 Zeld, *Organizational Change*, p. 44.

37 See Lawrence W. Fielding and Clark F. Wood, 'From Religious Outreach to Social Entertainment: The Louisville YMCA's First Gymnasium, 1876–1880', *The Filson Club History Quarterly* 60 (April, 1986), 239–56.

38 *Young Men's Christian Association Monthly Bulletin* 6 (Bangor, Maine), June, 1888.

39 *Hundred-Year Book*, p. 53.

40 Owen E. Pence, *The Y.M.C.A. and Social Need: A Study in Institutional Adaptation* (New York: Association Press, 1939), pp. 47, 75.

41 For that larger 'culture of professionalism', see Robert Wiebe, *The Search for Order, 1877–1920* (New York: Hill and Wang, 1967); Paul Boyer, *Urban Masses and Moral Order in America, 1820–1920* (Cambridge, MA: Harvard University Press, 1978); Burton Bledstein, *The Culture of Professionalism: The Middle Class and the Development of Higher Education in America* (New York: W.W. Norton, 1976); Barbara Ehrenreich, *Fear of Falling: The Inner Life of the Middle Class* (New York: Harper Collins, 1989).

42 Dwight L. Moody and Robert McBurney were on the first board of trustees: *Hundred-Year Book*, n.p., 1995 item.

43 For the early history of Springfield College, see Leonard L. Doggett, *A Man and a School* (New York: Association Press, 1943).

44 Hopkins, *History of the Y.M.C.A.*, pp. 251–3; Morse, *Life with Young Men*, p. 265.

45 Johnson, *YMCA Physical Education*, pp. 57–8.

46 For Roberts' views on competitive sports, see his 'Hints to Competitive Workers', *Young Men's Era* 17 (5 Feb. 1891), 90; 'The Boston Gymnasium', ibid. 18 (11 Feb. 1892), 182–3; 'Value of Simple Work', ibid. 18 (24 March 1892), 373; 'Competitive Athletic Work', ibid. 18 (2 June 1892), 693–4; 'Boxing in Association Gymnasiums', ibid. 19 (21 Dec. 1893), 1425.

47 Roberts was born in 1849, Gulick in 1865.

48 Hopkins, *History of the Y.M.C.A.*, p. 253.

49 Ibid., p. 246.

50 *The Watchman* 15 (3 Oct. 1889).

51 *Young Men's Era* 7 (8 Oct. 1891), 633. For more on the baseball question, see William J. Baker, 'Disputed Diamonds: The YMCA Debate over Baseball in the Late 19th Century'. *Journal of Sport History* 19 (Winter 1992), 257–62.

52 L.B. Smith, 'Baseball', *Young Men's Era* 18 (2 June, 1892), 692; O.E. Ryther, 'Athletics', ibid. (16 June, 1892), 758–9; ibid. (22 Sept. 1892), 1204. J. Gardiner Smith, 'The Athletic Problem in the Young Men's Christian Association', *Physical Education* 1 (April, 1892), 33–5, connected specialization and prize-winning as the beginnings of professionalism.

53 For the following, see William T. Ellis, *'Billy' Sunday: The Man and His Message* (Philadelphia: John C. Winston, 1914), pp. 24, 31–4, 38, 40–4, 46–7; and McLaughlin, *Billy Sunday*, 7.

54 Ellis, *'Billy' Sunday*, pp. 70, 75, 77, 138–9.

55 See Ronald A. Smith, *Sports and Freedom: The Rise of Big-Time College Athletics* (New York: Oxford University Press, 1988), pp. 165–74.

56 See William J. Baker, *Sports in the Western World* (Urbana: University of Illinois Press, 1988), pp. 127–31.

57 Paul C. Phillips, 'Rugby Football', *Young Men's Era* 17 (8 Oct. 1891), 632; cf. Luther H. Gulick, 'Foot-Ball Debate', *The Triangle* 1 (15 Dec. 1891), 131–3.

58 'Foot Ball at the Association Training School, Springfield, Mass.', *The Triangle* 1 (Feb. 1891), 6–8; 'Foot Ball', *The Triangle* 1 (Dec. 1891), 125–31; Hopkins, *History of the YMCA*, p. 259.

59 Gulick, 'Foot-Ball Debate'; 'Athletics at Chicago University', *Young Men's Era* 18 (10 Nov. 1896), 1431. Numerous invitations for Stagg to speak at churches, colleges and clubs are in the A.A. Stagg Papers (Box 109, Folder 2) in the Department of Special Collections at the Joseph Regenstein Library, University of Chicago; for manuscript examples of Stagg's addresses, see Box 109, Folders 3 and 7; for a proud YMCA report on Stagg's sermonic efforts, see 'Stagg at Rochester', *Young Men's Era* 18 (10 March 1892), 310.

60 'Physical Department', *Young Men's Era* 18 (20 Oct. 1892), 1332.

61 James B. Naismith, *Basketball: Its Origin and Development* (New York: Association Press. 1941), p. 22. On Naismith, see Bernice Larson Webb, *The Basketball Man: James Naismith*, (Lawrence: University Press of Kansas, 1973), and John Dewar, 'The Life and Professional Contributions of James Naismith' (Unpublished Ed.D. dissertation, Florida State University, 1965).

62 Naismith, *Basketball*, p. 23.

63 See Johnson, *YMCA Physical Education*, pp. 86–97; for the geographical diffusion of basketball, see Naismith, *Basketball*, pp. 100–60.

64 Johnson, *YMCA Physical Education*, p. 78; cf. Lawrence W. Fielding and Brenda G. Pitts, 'The Battle Over Athletic Priorities in the Lousiville YMCA 1892–1912', *Canadian Journal of History of Sport* 20 (Dec. 1989), 64–89.

65 Ibid., 80; J. Gardner Smith, 'Physical Training in New York City', 303–8; Bangor YMCA *Monthly Bulletin* 12 (Nov. 1893), 1.
66 See Steven A. Riess, 'Sport and the Redefinition of American Middle-Class Masculinity', *International Journal of the History of Sport* 8 (May, 1991), 5–27, especially pp. 16–17; E. Anthony Rotundo, 'Body and Soul: Changing Ideals of American Middle Class Manhood, 1770–1920', *Journal of Social History* 16 (Fall 1983), 23–38.
67 Mary S. Sims, *The Natural History of a Social Institution – the Young Women's Christian Association* (New York: The Womans Press, 1936), pp. 33, 40, 42.
68 Binfield, *George Williams*, p. 289.
69 Thomas Hughes, *Memoir of a Brother* (Boston: James R. Osgood, 1873), p. 18; *The Manliness of Christ* (Boston: Houghton, Osgood and Company, 1880), pp. 2–5, 20–1.
70 *The Watchman* 4 (1 April 1878), 1; 'The Liverpool Gymnasium', *The Watchman* 17 (7 May 1891), 298. For similar patterns of recreational and athletic expansion in Cambridge, Chelmsford and Ipswich, see Binfield, *George Williams*, pp. 291, 306.
71 *The Watchman* 5 (15 Oct. 1879), 1; (3 Jan. 1889), 1.
72 Bienfield, *George Williams*, p. 305; 'British Notes', *Physical Education* 3 (July 1894), 86.
73 Stephen Yeo, *Religion and Voluntary Organisations in Crisis* (London: Croom Helm, 1976), pp. 204–5.
74 Bienfield, *George Williams*, pp. 297, 379.
75 Ibid., p. 299.

Part V

Sport and recreation

Chapter 9

Culture, class and respectability

Racing and the English middle classes in the nineteenth century

Mike Huggins

For some years the working classes and sport in the nineteenth century have been a central focus for sports historians, but recently middle-class involvement has become an increasingly important area of research.[1] Some middle-class sports were characterized by the code of amateurism as embodied in public school teams, and emphasized notions of fair play. Alongside this code came the social exclusiveness of a whole range of new middle-class suburban recreations, ranging from golf to gymnastics, cruising to croquet. A second group of sports, including football, cricket and rugby, show clear evidence of middle-class organization and spectatorship, and some participation, even though predominantly played and watched by working men. Despite a clear antagonism to aspects of professionalism, such sports were still generally portrayed as respectable. But other sports had only limited middle-class support. Most sports involving animals, such as bull baiting, cock-fighting, or dog-fighting, had already fallen into this less 'respectable' category by the early Victorian period.

Historians have tended to categorize horse-racing as similarly less 'respectable' and as having very limited appeal for the middle classes, although the attraction to some upper and lower class groups was conceded. John Lowerson interpreted the standard text on racing, Wray Vamplew's *The Turf* (1976), as firmly stressing that the growth of racing was 'virtually without middle class support'.[2] Likewise Richard Holt echoed conventional wisdom in seeing racing as a sport 'that remained very exclusive in social terms but also had a huge popular following' and accepted that 'the bulk of middle class opinion...tended to frown upon the sport'.[3] Hugh Cunningham, using notions of leisure cultures, saw horse-racing as predominantly an aspect of urban popular working-class culture and explicitly contrasted it with the 'respectable credentials' of sports in middle-class urban culture.[4]

Initial more detailed forays into the world of racing tended to lend some limited support to such views. In a study of the survival of the Teesside courses, the key points emphasized were the contribution of the upper classes to sustaining the

Originally published in *The International Journal of the History of Sport*, 1994, 11(1), pp. 19–41. http://www.tandf.co.uk/journals

races and the importance of the races both as an unofficial holiday for working men and as the basis of betting.[5] The historical and traditional role of the upper classes is certainly of key importance in racing's history, a point well worth stressing. Working-class attendance at meetings and involvement in betting were equally a central part of popular culture.

But my more recent work leads me to suggest that the invisibility of the middle classes and the lack of respectability of racing were more apparent than real. The following article is drawn from a broader study of the social and economic history of nineteenth-century flat racing. It begins by analysing the middle-class opposition to racing, then goes on to look at a variety of ways in which some groups amongst the middle classes could be involved in racing, as attenders, shareholders, organizers and managers, owners or bettors. Finally, the discussion links racing to the broader debate about culture, class and respectability.

I

The description and analysis of social class has often suffered from a lack of definition.[6] In working on the topic, therefore, I have where possible provided occupational examples whilst drawing heavily on John Lowerson's discussion of the subject.[7]

As we shall see, racing was a focus for competition between two contrasting middle-class value systems. It was located on a major frontier of socio-cultural change, where there were struggles over the 'right' use of time, territory and income. The story of racing is in part an interplay between the attempts by reformers to close meetings and control betting, and the adaptable vitality of a cross-class cultural form.

So what was the nature of the middle-class resistance to racing? Opposition was particularly against the betting and gaming, drinking and prostitution associated with the sport. It was not, therefore, new in the nineteenth century. Some religious groups in late Hanoverian England detested racing as one of 'the devil's entertainments',[8] although the 1813 York August meeting was 'fashionably and genteely attended' *inter alia* by at least ten named clergy.[9] Thereafter the Anglican revival and growth of Nonconformism led to a stiffening of opposition.[10]

In the 1830s a range of leisure activities came under attack, linked to processes of urbanization and industrialization. For racing, this had some effect on entries for meetings in the industrial north. Whilst *numbers* of meetings showed little change, many courses suffered major drops in quality and popularity, although few actually closed down. By 1838 Hargrove's *New Guide to York* stated that 'the races at York have fallen off exceedingly within the last few years and are at present miserably attended'. Preston races came to an end after the meeting of 1833. Derby closed in 1835, although revived later, at a point when *Sporting Magazine* felt that many country meetings were 'on their last legs'.[11]

To ascribe the courses' struggles of the 1830s largely to the efforts of anti-race groups, however, is true only indirectly. Much of this arose out of the challenge to the economic power, political control and social prestige of the gentry by emerging middle-class urban elites. The gentry had used certain county towns as social centres, but were withdrawing by the late 1820s. Entering horses at local meetings had been part of that activity and patronage. The 1830 election and 1832 Reform Act were a watershed as some towns attempted to cast off gentry support. Where there was a political balance both Whig and Tory gentry had supported the races by contributing subscriptions and entries. A political defeat could lead to withdrawal, as at Preston following the defeat of the Derby candidate in 1830.[12] At Lancaster attacks on the races by dissenting ministers and Anglican clergy went alongside a refusal by the Liberal town council to support races supported by the Tory Lord Hamilton.

Even after mid-century the expansion of middle-class recreation and greater economic security failed to diminish some of the earlier fears. With the growth of a cheap regional and local press aimed in the main at a middle-class, 'respectable' urban audience, a wider number of arguments against horse-racing's associations were given full rein.

Some urban dwellers, with no association with or love of horses, simply saw racing as irrelevant. Some industrialists, merchants or other employers opposed the races on economic grounds. Industrialists lost money because large-scale absenteeism forced the closure of works, and time which should have been spent on production was lost. The Manchester Whit races caused absenteeism throughout that week, not just Whit Monday, and employers generally were powerless to enforce sanctions in the face of resistance.[13] It was also argued that much of the money spent on the races was not spent in the area but left in the pockets of bookmakers and others, thus taking money out of circulation. There was increased criminal activity, including passing of counterfeit money, pickpocketing and other thefts.

A more paternalistic argument accepted that there need be no interference with the betting of the rich, who could well afford it. But working-class betting was a personal vice, a moral weakness, which could have tragic results, poverty and destitution for the gambler and his dependants. There was possibly also the rarely spoken further fear that this would increase demands for social relief. Some of the middle classes saw profit as legitimate only if based on thrift, hard work and skill.[14]

There was a particularly potent mixture of fear and disapproval attached to the behaviour so often to be found on or *en route* to the courses; and to the equally visible blocking of urban streets by large numbers of working-class betting men and bookmakers, often using foul language and failing to display the appropriate level of deference. Racing generated large crowds, associating in dangerous ways. The Dean of Chester saw the races in 1870 as attracting 'like an army of locusts' some of the 'vilest and most degraded' of characters.[15] Racing could therefore be seen as a territorial threat to the social order. Such objections to the races could most particularly be found amongst church and chapel goers, of whatever class. They were also prevalent amongst some urban business and professional groups.

Economic and social objections often emerged publicly as moral and religious arguments, continuing the 'rational recreation' debate of the 1830s and 1840s.[16]

A fundamental shortcoming of such views was their lack of understanding of racing. Few, if any, objectors actually visited the races or associated with those who did.

What forms did anti-race activity take? Preaching against the activities going on at meetings can be found throughout the century and throughout England in both Nonconformist and Church of England places of worship. In 1865, for example, the Dean of Carlisle preached one of a number of anti-race sermons which saw racing as 'a kind of pleasure which seemed to be unmitigatedly evil'.[17] Such preaching was almost always entirely to the converted, in chapel, church or hall, and was singularly ineffective, as was the less common preaching and tract distribution at courses.[18]

A common approach was therefore to organize distractions from the races. Rail excursions came early, and Sunday school organizations were prominent amongst these, keeping children away. Indeed, the first recorded arrangement for a privately organized excursion train thus far traced was when about 150 members of the Bennett Street Sunday School visited Liverpool during the Manchester Race week of May 1831, through the good offices of the Manchester borough reeve.[19]

More local counter-attractions came in various forms. Many were collectively organized by anti-race and temperence groups. At Newcastle, after the move to Gosforth Park in 1881, the Town Moor was used for temperence meetings offering such rational recreations as foot races, bicycle matches, assaults at arms, football matches and other sports, and a fair. In Middlesbrough and Stockton, as in many other places, a joint Sunday School Union was set up to offer activities 'as an antidote to the attractions provided by the races'.[20] Prominent local industrialists lent facilities and support.[21]

By the end of the nineteenth century the number of such privately organized alternatives had almost ceased, owing to funding difficulties. Private rail excursions had to be underwritten and sometimes lost money. The Galas were also costly. At Stockton the gala organized by the Sunday School Union 'resulted in a heavy loss' and it was discontinued after the mid-1880s.[22] But it was also becoming clear that the policy of offering children alternatives to the races was ineffective. Race weeks had become unofficial holidays in many towns and trips were now commercial enterprises organized by rail companies primarily for adults.

Another way of attempting to combat the betting associated with race meetings was by restricting betting information. A number of liberal Nonconformist newspapers gave little or no coverage to racing, and indeed, by giving column inches to those who opposed the races, appeared to act as a key agent of indoctrination. The *Northern Echo*, for example, printed in Darlington and dominated by the Pease family of Quaker industrialists, set its typeface firmly against racing results and reports from the 1870s, and like other regional papers gave strong support in the 1890s to the Anti-Gambling League.

Libraries in a number of towns blacked out racing results before putting papers on display either at the instigation of local councillors or because of the attitude of the chief librarian.[23] Indeed, libraries in the United Kingdom discussed the question of blacking out betting news, betting quotations and racing results on more than one occasion, and in 1893 a vote showed them to be equally divided on the subject.[24]

Middle-class anti-race activity also had some limited success after mid-century in closing down courses. Occasionally control over land at long-standing meetings fell into the hands of anti-racing owners, who terminated the lease as at Malton, Durham or the Manchester Kersall Moor and Castle Irwell sites.[25] At Bradford, popular but poor quality races were held until 1877, when the corporation became owners of the freehold and closed them down, alleging course drunkenness and disorder.

There was much more chance of anti-race groups succeeding where a new meeting was setting up in an urban area without a strong racing tradition. At Halifax a new enclosed course was set out in 1878, at a cost of nearly £40,000, but strong opposition was led by a Congregationalist pastor, the vicar of Halifax and local councillors including the mayor. Here strength of opposition was such that workmen were not able to absent themselves from work with impunity. To attend the races was to run the risk of job loss. By 1884 the meeting had such poor attendance it was forced to fold. At Leeds the racecourse company's attempt to develop a new enclosed course foundered because of 'great opposition' from Leeds magistrates, Nonconformist and Church of England parsons.[26]

The National Anti-Gambling League was formed in 1889 from a coalition of Nonconformist churches and led the opposition. The twice yearly *Bulletin* documented its activities – public meetings, lectures and sermons. It also lobbied Watch Committees and politicians, and its actions were supported by the more liberal, Nonconformist press. The League's supporters brought out a number of books and other publications to stimulate discussion from the early 1890s.[27] They also initiated a number of prosecutions, attempting to force an end to racecourse betting, starting with one against Messrs Trail at Northampton racecourse in 1894, and further unsuccessful actions in 1895.

In 1897 another Anti-Gambling League-sponsored prosecution initially gained a ruling that betting enclosures were in fact 'places' within the meaning of the 1853 Betting House Act, and therefore open to prosecution, although this was overturned by a majority verdict in the Court of Appeal. Thereafter the League began to concentrate more on off-course working-class gambling.[28]

II

The key question, however, is how widespread such hostility to racing and betting actually was during the nineteenth century. It is more illuminating to look at the successful opposition to anti-racing views seen in the majority of traditional racing towns than those expressed in the columns of the liberal Nonconformist sections of the press. Although the numbers of racecourses open varied through time, there were major elements of continuity about the existence of most courses, and very few closed simply because of opposition. Whilst few new courses opened up, this was mainly because setting up costs were prohibitive and, with only limited numbers of possible entries, approval of the Jockey Club and a good date were critical. It was thus an extremely high risk venture. In looking at a range of examples, a number of clear strategies for survival emerge, as do the major advocates of racing.

One important battle was fought inside the predominantly middle-class local authorities who controlled a significant range of executive functions. They varied in their attitude to the races, and financial support was erratic. It could be withdrawn, as at Preston in 1832, when pressure, albeit temporary, was exerted by the evangelical element.[29] But at many meetings the corporation gave strong support to the local race committees on a fairly continuous basis.

Doncaster and York are good examples. The Doncaster town council controlled the moor and saw the meeting as benefiting the town. Up until 1860 the minutes of the General Purpose Committee document their decisions.[30] After 1860 the Corporation formed a special Race Committee to govern decisions. Doncaster Corporation contributed financially. Four hundred pounds in the 1830s had increased to £1,000 by the 1840s, and reached £1,200 by 1864.[31] There was a well-known anti-racing group on the town council, who wanted funding and support withdrawn, but they were always well outvoted. The 1850s saw a number of such 'periodical fierce racing rows in their council chamber which have become part and parcel of their turf history' described by the Druid as the 'anti-bigotry conflict'.[32] In 1867, and again in 1875, the editor of the *Doncaster Reporter* tried to bring an end to the widespread illegal bookmaking on the course carried out on land let by the Corporation, but with little success, and no significant Corporation support.

At York the corporation held the Knavesmire course on behalf of the Micklegate ward freemen, leasing the grandstand, and leaving the actual organization to a Race Commitee. But they retained other links through the period. Early in the century they made annual subscriptions to the races.[33] Later in the century the Watch Committee reports show the policing was organized by the city, and the Race Committee always contained councillors or aldermen.

Corporation support could also be found at many smaller meetings. The Corporation cups found early in the century at a number of northern meetings were often funded from corporation revenues. These however become fewer by mid-century. At Newcastle, the Herbage Committee which controlled the Town Moor gained revenue from tents and stands, whose position they controlled. At Morpeth land was leased from the corporation. When in 1875 a new stand's foundation stone was laid by the Mayor on behalf of the Morpeth Grand Stand Co. Ltd., he could claim that 'it had been decided by a majority of the inhabitants that a race meeting should be held'.[34]

Opposition to anti-racing views could also be expressed through active local popular resistance, although the actual mechanisms remain unclear. In the vast majority of northern towns with a single long-standing annual meeting, the races were the 'nearest approach' to a 'real holiday' of the year.[35] They benefited the towns economically and were generally supported. A Doncaster solicitor who organized an 1828 public meeting against the races and gambling there was met with a number of speeches opposing him and a pelting on the way home.[36] In 1850 a public meeting to oppose the races was organized by clergymen, a Unitarian minister, industrialists, Chartists and other 'respectable parties',[37] but the meeting was rowdily broken up, and the organizers pelted. At Ripon an attempt to have the races discontinued in 1845 'met with the most determined opposition from the bulk of the inhabitants, who have risen en masse'.[38] At Lancaster, when in 1840 the Liberal council passed a motion to abolish the races, they were voted out of office as a result.[39]

The press also provided an arena for the debate. The early nineteenth-century press generally gave racing its support, especially in those counties such as the North Riding, the East Riding and Lancashire where the sport had deep roots. The cheaper local press of the later period was split. At Doncaster the *Gazette* was strongly pro-racing, whilst the *Reporter*, with a much smaller circulation, was strongly opposed. The same pattern can be found elsewhere. But attempts to attack betting by refusing to print racing results were ineffective. As the popularity of betting spread, the vast majority of newspaper editors found themselves engaged in a circulation war in which anyone failing to give race results saw a loss of circulation, and the practice was soon discontinued. When the Middlesbrough Watch Committee asked the editor of the *York Herald* to stop placing racing result telegrams in his Middlesbrough office window, to reduce the crowds, the response stated the paper's concern to 'maintain our position in Middlesbrough by not giving our local contemporary such a palpable advantage as it would have if we discontinued'.[40] The Watch Committee accepted the view.

The anti-race group tried to categorize racing as lacking respectability. But a whole range of evidence can be brought forward to show that those of the middle classes involved in racing suffered no diminution in general respectability. Perhaps one example initially makes the point. As a young man in the early nineteenth century, James Bake went through an apprenticeship as a saddler, setting up in business himself subsequently. Alongside his business he had an interest in betting and was responsible for bringing the news of the St Leger winner to Manchester on relays of horses each September. He disposed of the business to become the landlord of the Post House Hotel, a Manchester betting centre, and was therefore the key figure in Manchester's growing prominence as the northern betting market centre. He retired with a 'competency' in 1849, still associated with list house betting whilst representing first Oxford and then Cheetham wards as a Manchester councillor in the 1850s. He was a key member of the Manchester Race Committee when elected alderman in 1865 and died wealthy.[41] Racing and respectability went hand in hand.

This point cannot be too heavily stressed. There were middle-class groups who strongly opposed the races. But there were many others who gave active support, through attendance, contribution to funds, share ownership, organization, office holding, racehorse ownership, or by betting. Such activity reflected tensions in middle-class society, encompassing inter-generational gentrification at its higher levels and cultural accommodation. Association with racing was by no means a bar to success in local government. As we have seen, many JPs and councillors voted for its continuance.

To what extent did the middle classes actually attend meetings? Whilst impossible to quantify, since the social composition of crowds in terms of age, sex and status is an important but notoriously difficult area of research, there is a great deal of evidence to demonstrate their attendance. General descriptions of open meetings in the first half of the century regularly refer to all 'classes' attending. Even when attendances were down nationally in 1832, the absence of 'the numerous class of the middling order of interested individuals' at Doncaster was commented on with some surprise, whilst at Epsom although fewer 'of rank' attended, and the 'neighbouring peasantry disappeared', the 'middle classes, who always put the best face on things…increased in numbers' and were 'most agreeably sober'.[42]

Data provided by the long newspaper lists of attenders in the grandstands, when matched with local directories, more explicitly show middle-class attenders, especially at the smaller meetings. Epsom, Newmarket, Ascot, Liverpool, Doncaster and York press lists were dominated by the aristocracy, so middle-class attenders were omitted for reasons of space.

The lists of attenders, like resort visitors' lists, reflect views about status. So middle-class attenders may have gained status from their association with the gentry and aristocracy, as well as excitement from the races themselves. Only occasionally, as at Stockton in 1875, were councillors noticeably absent, though twenty-nine landowners could be identified, and a further fifteen, including a doctor, solicitor, printer, farmers and shopkeepers clearly came from the Stockton area.[43] More typical was an 1882 Durham list containing eight JPs and councillors, two solicitors, the clerk to the Brandon Local board, a coal owner and alderman, a veterinary surgeon, a grocer, together with landowners from the surrounding area, and others described as Durham 'private residents'.[44]

Further evidence is provided by the reports of prosecutions, accidents etc. occurring on or around racecourses. This shows clearly the unsurprising fact that open meetings were an occasion for local holidays and were cross-class in their attendance, with strong female and child presence, perhaps insufficiently stressed by historians. Races were also a magnet for middle-class visitors from further away. At the 1875 Beverley races, for example, a Hull chimney-sweep's wife died when a cart containing them, their children and their man-servant overturned on the way home from the races, whilst a Hull manufacturer was charged with assaulting a woman in one of the drinking booths.[45]

Powerful evidence of middle-class attendance is also supplied by the anti-race writers themselves. The crusading Liverpool journalist Hugh Shimmin, totally against the 'vicious practices' and 'questionable pursuits' of racing, still accepted that 'crowds of people from every class' attended Aintree in the 1850s.[46] The picture which emerges from such descriptions is of a section of the Victorian middle class who worked hard and played hard, playing one role at work and another quite different one in their leisure. Shimmin describes 'more respectable people...merchants who on the Exchange and at home pass for gentlemen' engaged in 'indecorous and unbecoming' dalliance in a notorious brothel-keeper's booth, and 'members of parliament, magistrates, aldermen, town councillors, merchants, brokers, publicans, businessmen of every grade, and many men of questionable character' betting in the ring. He contrasts that with their work on county sessions, their speeches at public meetings on the need to purify and regenerate society, their support for missions, religious and benevolent associations, or their political ambitions.[47] Manchester exhibits similar examples. A series of articles in *The Free Lance* paints an unregenerate middle class, bent on pleasure, and describes the Manchester grandstand as 'graced, or otherwise, by a great many who regard themselves as the aristocracy from a monetary and cottonian point of view'.[48] Clearly these were the 'respectable' middle classes.

A final piece of additional evidence is provided by the large number of racing pictures which show crowds at meetings. These tend to be of Classic or other major events, so tend to have a much larger group from the upper classes. Nevertheless they reflect right through the century the points made above.

What of another group of attenders, the top trainers, jockeys and race officials? Race officials had to be literate, numerate, men of probity with good organizational skills. Thomas Sotheran, the York clerk of the course in the 1820s, was a bookseller and stationer. Joseph Lockwood, the clerk and judge at Doncaster (1803–31), was elected an alderman in 1821. Of those race officials whose original occupations can be identified, almost all had solid, respectable middle-class backgrounds, often being from the professions. Several were originally teachers, including one of the most successful clerks in the north after mid-century, Thomas Craggs, who was reputed to have left £40,000 on his death.[49] Only Edward Elliott, the Manchester commercial traveller, or Thomas Dawson and Miles I 'Anson, sons of trainers, may have been at all borderline, and the latter two were employing servants by 1881. Some top trainers and jockeys likewise had high incomes and were servant owing. They too can be seen as middle class.

The composition of Race Committees, whose chief responsibility was raising sufficient 'added money' to ensure good entries, was also predominantly middle class. In the early nineteenth century there were sometimes two committees, one upper and one middle class, with different functions. At Liverpool, for example, in 1838 there was 'the one from the nobility and gentry of the vicinity who are to arrange the stakes, the periods at which the meetings are to take place and the general routine of the sport; and the other to consist of residents who will collect money, tolls, rents, and all the necessary material'.[50] At York the local Race Committee organized the appointment of a committee of County noblemen and gentlemen 'to communicate from time to time with the present Racing Committee and to set on foot an annual county subscription' and to help 'the ancient capital of this great county...to boast an August meeting equal to its former importance and celebrity'.[51]

Membership of local Race Committees was always dominated by middle-class groups. As early as 1791, the original twenty proprietors of the Preston Grandstand included a majority which can be identified from contemporary directories as local merchants, manufacturers or in commercial occupations, and the first race committee was formed predominantly from these groups.[52] Certain occupations, such as brewers, inn and hotel keepers, wine and spirit merchants, lawyers and solicitors, Tory newspaper publishers and surgeons occur extremely frequently on membership lists across the north. At York the 1864 committee included two brewers, two hoteliers, and an architect, solicitor, newspaper publisher and proprietor of a livery stables. If anything, status of the major committees was rising in the late nineteenth century. The York 1885 committee included four JPs, one of whom was the major wine and spirit merchant and alderman, James Melrose, a key figure in promoting the races. Another was Joseph Terry, the confectionary manufacturer. Four others were private residents.[53]

Subscription lists provide further evidence of middle-class support for racing. The *Racing Calendar* lists of races often show money for events 'added' by local magnates and the local MPs. But the significant number of Tradesmen's and Innkeepers' plates and cups hint that contributions also came from further down the social scale. A number of subscription lists survive and confirm this view. A 1824 list from the small North Riding market town of Richmond was compiled by the mayor, for the purpose of 'encouraging the races'.[54] It shows £25 12s 6d was collected on a circuit round the town from 37 named individuals, whilst 71 others refused, a useful assessment of the town's degree of *active* commitment. Three of the eleven aldermen and six of the twenty-four councillors contributed. Eleven of the twenty-three inns and taverns contributed either a guinea or 10/6d in order to be allowed a booth. Other individuals contributing included a surveyor of taxes, three grocers, two linen and woollen drapers, a malster, wine and spirit merchant, a timber yard agent and an esquire, almost all giving 2/6d. At Preston, although innkeepers were expected to contribute as a condition of getting a booth, 'the butchers and some of the shopkeepers' were also expected to contribute.[55]

Some subscriptions clearly had a pay-off for the givers. Visitors put a great deal of money into circulation, paying excessive prices for accommodation, food and services. At Chester in 1844 the brewers and malsters who contributed £36 would almost certainly expect to see a return. The eight bakers who contributed £5 2s might well have done. But what of the three booksellers, the six builders and carpenters, or the brush manufacturer? Overall the 250 tradesmen subscribers included a significant number for whom any payoff was unlikely.[56] At Durham in 1859, over 300 subscribers gave to the fund, including a significant proportion of the shopocracy.

The occupational background of grandstand and race company share-holders provides another insight into the social patterns of overt race support. Using the returns made by registered companies to the registrar, an examination was made of a range of northern shareholder lists.[57] Shares were clearly not aimed at the working man, since costs of single shares were usually £5, and Carlisle and Leeds both valued their shares at £10.

The surviving joint stock limited companies shareholder lists proved to be extremely varied. Carlisle Race Stand Company, set up in 1873 with a share capital of £1,730, and seventy-eight shareholders, was perhaps the most dominated by the gentry group, with its twenty-three gentlemen and eight esquires, plus five farmers and three yeomen, a butler, a major, a land agent and four widows. Many of this group lived outside Carlisle. A second group was much more Carlisle based, and included professionals, manufacturers, builders and contractors, and the wholesale and retail group, plus seven clerks. The drink trade was poorly represented, although a wine merchant and two innkeepers bought shares.

Some companies had fewer shareholders. The nine shareholders of the Ripon Grandstand Company were all local and included a bank manager, brewer, dentist, draper, farmer, surgeon, tallow chandler and two retired men. Manchester Racecourse Company, set up in 1868, fluctuated around twenty shareholders. In 1869 it included six gentlemen and three merchants, two civil engineers, a manufacturer, coal proprietor, importer, victualler, two salesmen and a law clerk, as well as a racecourse judge and starter. The thirty-six shareholders of the 1959 Stockton Grandstand Co. Ltd. were dominated by the local merchant and manufacturing group, and the professions.

On Tyneside the 1864 Newcastle Grand Stand Company share capital was much more widely spread, including twelve agents, an architect, two auctioneers, three bankers, a boot-maker, thirty brewers and inn-keepers, five brokers, two builders, a butcher, a cattle salesman, a chandler, a chemist, three coach proprietors, three coal owners, two concert hall proprietors, a confectioner, four drapers, a dentist, five esquires, a fishmonger, three gentlemen, two hairdressers, a horse dealer, a hotel keeper, eight manufacturers, an iron master, seventeen merchants, a law student, miller, newspaper proprietor, pawnbroker, two plumbers, a postmaster, provision merchant, two shipowners, five solicitors, a shipowner, two surgeons, a theatre lessee, three wine merchants, two wives, and two vets.

The Morpeth Grandstand company had by 1884 forty-six shareholders, dominated by the drink trade, butchers, farmers and gentry, but other shareholders included a soda water manufacturer, an accountant, printer, solicitor, timber merchant, agent, and two smiths. A miner and gardener each owned £25 worth of shares.

Generally, therefore, the majority of the shareholders were middle class. The drink trade everywhere except Manchester played a major role, as was to be expected, especially in initially buying shares in the new enclosed grounds. At Leeds, for example, the ill-fated Leeds Racecourse Company was dominated by three innkeepers and a maltster. The only member of the aristocracy come across, Lord Zetland, owned shares at Stockton. Individuals described as gentlemen and esquires certainly owned shares, but their holdings were relatively small. The eighteen shareholders of Scarborough Grandstand and Racecourse Company in 1874 included four farmers, a brewer and brewer's agent, two solicitors, an accountant, a widow, one deceased, and seven described only as 'esquires'. But the latter actually included a Nottingham bookmaker, a Malton ex-trainer and race-course official, and two other trainers. In Yorkshire at least, the terms gentlemen and esquire had very loose usage, and this can only inflate middle-class share ownership.

Why did they put money into racing? Such purchase was not necessarily to be seen as a money-making gesture. At some racecourses, shares were to be redeemed as soon as possible, after which profits were to be applied to the benefit of the races. Thomas Craggs, the secretary of the Stockton company, wrote in 1878 telling the registrar that 'the share-holders who took shares for the good of the races have had their shares redeemed and paid off with the exception of very few'. At almost all courses interest on shares had not to exceed five per cent, with anything in excess going to further the objects of the meeting. Like the late eighteenth- and early nineteenth-century subscribers to grandstands at York, Beverley, Richmond and elsewhere, subscribers to many companies did get free admission to the stand. Share purchase can thus be seen as a commitment to and a gesture of support for the races, as well as an investment.

What did directors of limited companies gain? As with the capitalization of football and cricket, the love of the sport, the hope of influence or social prestige, were at least as important as financial return for many, although there was often a higher proportion of gentry in the directorate than in shareholders generally. At Newcastle, the 1864 directorate included two 'gentlemen', along with two coal-owners, three manufacturers, an ironmaster, solicitor, baker and wine merchant. Better interest rates than 5 per cent could have been obtained elsewhere, but many of Newcastle's leading citizens had family and property links with county society and this may be the case here. Only more detailed local studies will provide the answer. Being on the directorate was an unpaid task, involving significant work. The chairman at the final winding up of the Durham meeting, Alderman A.O. Smith, a local solicitor, claimed that directors 'had filled, without favour or reward, and with a positive loss to themselves, functions that in other companies were invariably discharged by salaried officials'.[58]

Being on directorates or Race Committees was an opportunity for exercising patronage. It was another middle-class opportunity to sponsor, through their support and organizational skill, activities which that particular group approved. In many ways it paralleled the unpaid voluntary work associated with Mechanics Institutes, temperance societies, Sunday school associations and the like. Not all the urban middle class espoused the rhetorical claims of the bourgeois culture of 'art exhibitions, museums and civic buildings' and concern with 'higher things'.[59] The sporting world was also run by the middle classes. Football, with its professionalism, working-class fanatical spectatorship, and play to win philosophy, was organized and run by a very similar group to that which ran racing.[60]

The extent to which the middle classes owned racehorses is a question fraught with difficulty, since neither the *Stud Book* nor the *Racing Calendar* give more than names, some of whom are assumed. But titled and gentry owners are readily identifiable, and a very substantial second group proved to be racing insiders.

Even in the early nineteenth century some of the 'legs', the early bookmakers, were both well known and successful in the classic races. Although held in low status by the aristocracy, their wealthy lifestyle and employment of servants must number them amongst the middle classes. Examples included John Gully, ex-pugilist, and later Pontefract MP and coal-owner, Ridsdale, Crockford, the Blands, or the money-lender Padwick. They stayed at the same hotels as the aristocracy, and many, like Gully or Ridsdale, aped the gentry patterns of lifestyle and consumption. Later in the nineteenth century it was a common practice for wealthier bookmakers, property owning and servant employing, to own and run horses. John Jackson, owner of Fairfield Hall and stud near York, the 'Leviathan of the North', and worth over £40,000 on his death in 1869, was an early 1860s example.[61] John Devereux, the Stockton bookmaker, was running horses all over the north in the early 1880s. Joe Pickersgill of Leeds, ex-butcher's boy, registered his colours in 1881 and was worth £746,459 on his death. Another Leeds bookmaker, George Drake, built his own stables at Middleham.[62]

What might be termed the rural middle classes often owned horses. Trainers, who I have described elsewhere as 'marginal men', since they were both servants of owners and yet wealthy servant employers themselves, were often extremely successful.[63] Chifney, Day, Dawson, Scott, I'Anson and other trainers achieved classic successes and wealth. Some of the wealthier jockeys were also owners. The ex-stableboy John Hutchinson won the St Leger as early as 1791; another, the high-betting Jack Hammond, won the 1884 Derby. The other group which tended to be successful were wealthier tenant farmers. Alice Hawthorn, bred and owned by the North Riding farmer John Plummer, won 52 of her 71 races in the 1840s.

Local owners can sometimes be identified, when press references show them running at local meetings, or in the writings of those with racing interests. A number of urban owners were brewers or licensed victuallers. The landlord of the George and Dragon Inn, Catterick Bridge, won the St Leger in 1819, and a Masham wine and spirit merchant won in 1843. In Stockton Mr McCann, of the Station Hotel, Thornaby, was a 'popular local sportsman' and owner in 1883.[64] William Allison, in his memories of childhood near Thirsk, could recall a number of local owners there in the 1870s. They included not only the local squire, but also Sammy Cass, a Liberal brewer, William Rhodes, brewer and 'back-bone of the local Conservative party', and his father's solicitor partner, who ran horses under an assumed name.[65] At Durham, William Ainsley entered his horses alongside printing the racecards.

Industrialists, merchants and manufacturers who were on the way up in status often bought property and turned to racing, as a way of gaining respect and status. Early century examples abound. Thomas Houldsworth, a Manchester cotton manufacture, ran horses from 1804, bought Sherwood Hall, Notts, and became an MP in 1818.[66] The 'railway king', James Hudson, ex-linen draper, owned horses and officiated as steward at northern meetings after buying Newby and Londesbrough Parks.[67] Mr G. Foster, well known in the Newcastle iron trade, won the Northumberland Plate in 1857, 1858 and 1859. R.C. Naylor, a Liverpool banker, High Sheriff of Chester in 1856, and the purchaser of Hooton Hall, won the Derby in 1863. In the second half of the nineteenth century a number of wealthy Scottish owners entered racing successfully, including the Glasgow brewer Frederick Gretton, owner of the best horse in England, Isonomy, in the late 1870s. The Scottish ironmaster James Merry, son of an itinerant pedlar, had seven Classic successes. The iron-founder millionaire George Baird reputedly wasted his fortune on 'horse racing, prize fighting, and harlotry'.[68] Later again, the friendship of the Prince of Wales was almost a guarantee of social success. His racing friends included the Tottenham Court Road furniture magnate Sir John Maple, who had three Classic successes in the 1890s; Lucien and Maurice de Hirsh, the Austro-Jewish railway contractors, who had racing success in the 1880s and 1890s, or the Joels, sons of an East End Landlord, who made a fortune out of the South African diamond fields before beginning racing in 1900. By the end of the century, in the north at least, many owners were described as either 'men making a business of the sport' or 'commercial men with local associations who find the turf a pleasant recreation after the cares of business'.[69] The excitements and uncertainties of ownership, association with the famous and infamous, had their own rewards. And there was always the possibility of winning. The cups and plates, pictures and photographs, still in the possession of some racing families today, handed down as heirlooms, indicate that ownership was more than a mere 'business'. There was clear pride in racing success. The will of the Newcastle chemist, druggist and alderman Antony Nichol, for example, left £60,000 estate and made explicit provision for his wife to inherit his racing cups from Stockton and York, and for his daughter to have them on his wife's death.

To what extent were middle-class punters involved in on- and off-course betting? Research has tended to focus on the working classes. But there was certainly middle-class betting both on and off course from the early nineteenth century. On-course betting was such an accepted part of course life that there is very little evidence about bettors. The three times mayor of Richmond, Michael Brunton, was laying the odds at country meetings all over the north in the 1820s, and by the end of the century a 'reformed' bookmaker was describing many of his customers as having 'made money in trade or business', citing a draper, grocer, solicitor, chemist and market gardener as examples.[70] There are isolated references to a wide variety of middle-class occupational groups in court cases, usually where they got involved with welshers, throughout the period.

By the 1830s, off-course betting was increasing and an early form was the sweeps, which could be found across the north of England, often run by publicans, and widely advertised in the press, at prices between one and five pounds a ticket, well beyond the means of working men. In 1841 James Bake, the Manchester publican, was offering two £5 St Leger sweeps, two horses each, with a first prize of £270, a second of £40 and a third of £15. He was also offering £2 and £1 sweeps to less wealthy customers and advertising in the press, not only locally but further afield.[71] By early April 1845 Paul Ashley, a prominent Sheffield sweep organizer, had already filled one £5 Derby sweep and was onto his fifth £1 sweep.[72] Sweeps were illegal but ignored by local magistrates, this fact and the pricing indicating their widespread support.

There was, however, sufficient opposition to force the government to encourage the Postmaster General to prosecute newspapers containing adverts, and by December 1848 London prosecutions were being reported.[73] These, however, had little effect outside London. In Hartle-pool surviving printers' material contains a significant number of tickets for various sweeps over the period 1850–56 covering the Classics, the Cesarewitch and Cambridgeshire stakes, mostly between £150 and £500 members, at between 1/- and 2/6d each, with 5 per cent held back for the organizer.[74] Such lower stakes reveal target marketing lower down the wealth structure.

But there were also increasing numbers of places in larger towns where racing lists were being exhibited and bets taken on future races. Sylvanus claimed in 1850 that in York, a town 'thoroughly imbued with the genuine spirit of racing', there were 'many retail shops that would give odds on horses' and druggists, publicans and yeomen-traders who would back them.[75] His contemporary, Thomas Holtby, the ex-coachman of the London and Edinburgh mail, was operating the 'Ebor Betting Office', informing his friends that 'his lists are now open on all the forthcoming events for the ensuing year…Tattersall's odds laid…commissions promptly executed on receipt of cash'.[76] Such 'list houses' took ready money bets, but in 1853 governmental anxieties over their use in London by servants, apprentices and working men led to legislation. Such legislation had little effect, and this suggests that most magistrates were prepared to turn a blind eye. Zealous magistrates and officious policemen were rare. An 1869 Manchester prosecution illustrates the point. Aaron Worsely had first been prosecuted in 1859, but 'having seen betting carried on by other people, and thinking that the act had become either a dead letter or the practice was winked on by the authorities', he had reopened his shop.[77] List houses were illegal and prosecuted ones were generally in working-class areas. It may be they continued to be used by the middle classes. But there were other options which were less risky.

One was credit betting. In Manchester the Post Office Hotel was its equivalent to Tattersalls, with entry likewise by subscription but a distinct absence of gentry and aristocratic members except prior to the local races. Its Manchester odds were being published nationally by the 1830s. One anti-gambling covert visitor described both bookmakers and backers found there as 'self-made men', including employers as well as clerks and other employees.[78] By the 1870s credit bookmakers were abandoning the notion of using betting rooms and were using office premises as well as betting on course in Tattersall's ring, almost certainly catering for wealthier upper- and middle-class patrons. Unfortunately, as betting historians concede, there is little evidence of their clientele.[79] A punter could only bet with such a bookmaker once credit was established, and this could present difficulties.

Alternatively, ready money postal bets could be sent abroad. There was a flourishing bookmaker colony in France, well used by middle-class punters. Even the public schools were affected. William Allison, at school in Rugby, was betting with the inaptly named though reliable George Crook at Boulogne in 1870, whilst by 1901 the master of Harrow saw the increase in betting among his pupils as due to parents who encouraged it, sweepstakes and circulars from foreign betting houses.[80]

Anti-gambling magistrates were common enough to put some list bookmakers on the street where they had more chance of avoiding the police, who generally left them alone. But there was no wish on the part of many magistrates to deal firmly with illegal betting unless there was strong public pressure to do so. Some recognized that legislation had a class base. As one pro-racing Middlesbrough councillor said in 1880, 'if they were going to stop betting they should stop it not only among the working men but in the clubs and the higher grades of society'.[81] Significantly, even here in a non-racing town, with its early history dominated by Quakers, the Watch Committee voted eleven to nine not to deal more stringently with persons betting. Councillor Weighell, a racehorse owner himself, paid tribute to the street bookmakers as 'honourable men who paid 20/- to the pound' whilst another councillor, one of the largest employers in the area, said that many of the bettors were amongst his 'very best and most respected workmen'.[82] Attitudes on the middle-class bench here, as elsewhere, therefore show very mixed attitudes to betting. The extent to which fines varied, depending upon which magistrate was sitting, shows this clearly.

III

Overall, the evidence seems to indicate that racing had a solid basis of support amongst certain middle-class groups. It reflected tensions in middle-class society which have perhaps been underestimated. For many of the urban middle class giving their support, there was some self-interest involved, through the commercial gains brought by the races, inter-generational gentrification, or cultural accommodation. But there seems no reason to doubt that many found the excitement of the course, or of betting, a worthwhile experience. Involvement with racing seems to have been no obstacle to success for the many MPs, councillors, aldermen and JPs found at the meetings, or to those lending racing their support in the other ways outlined above. Certain occupational groups, such as the brewers, or doctors and lawyers were, however, certainly more likely to be involved, partly because it was in their financial or social interest so to do.

The anti-racing group, with its bourgeois vision of civilization and moral improvement, was composed of a group of churchmen and dissenters, and their manufacturer, industrialist and shopkeeper supporters. Suspicious of the moral tempations of the emerging leisure world, often liberal in their politics, some were trying to construct a new religious identity. Others saw themselves as economically disadvantaged by the races. The key question is whether this group was actually as typical as it has sometimes appeared to be. A study of racing suggests that there was another 'middle-class' lifestyle, perhaps more unregenerate, or more bent on pleasure. Some individuals may have even been members of both at different times, like William Wilberforce, who prior to his conversion was a regular attender at York races in the 1780s.

Most people may not have strong views on racing. But there was certainly a firm base of public support for its continuance. Even the *Middlesbrough Weekly*

News, a mouthpiece for the anti-racing group, regretfully admitted: 'it is no use discussing the question as to whether the races exert a bad or a beneficial influence on society in the face of the fact that by far the greater portion of society appears not only to countenance but to support them'.[83] A study of support for horse-racing suggests that our picture of middle-class leisure may have in the past been too one-sided, and there may well be a need for more recognition of cultural complexity or diversity and more subtle definitions in any discussion of nineteenth-century social class which attempts to relate it to culture. The 1845 revival of the races at Derby shows this clearly, at a time when the conventional chronology of leisure sees popular recreations as under severe pressure from middle-class evangelicanism and industrial capitalism. At Derby a clear majority of the town council voted for their reintroduction. The pro-racing group, led by the Mayor, William Mousley, a wealthy solicitor and pewholder in the parish church, was composed of professional men, manufacturers, tradesmen and shopkeepers. It was opposed by a similarly mixed propertied and prosperous evangelistic group, indistinguishable in terms of occupation, property and social standing. As Delves has pointed out, here any consensus was both relative and finite, and there were real differences of social identity.[84]

A study of racing therefore links clearly to wider debates about culture and class. Although R.J. Morris felt able to identify an independent, middle-class respectable culture in Victorian Leeds,[85] more recent work has offered only a measured and subtlely qualified view.[86] Whilst earlier emphasis tended to be on such determining factors of middle-classness as utilitarianism or evangelicanism, or work in local government and politics, the increased awareness of cultural complexity and the tensions of cultural aspiration have links to racing and other leisure activities. Manchester, at the industrial heart of Lancashire, had a middle class with a 'complex and contradictory matrix of values, practices and institutions'.[87] Racing culture easily fitted into this, and it becomes unsurprising that it was also the key northern centre of racing and betting, with clear evidence of middle-class involvement with no loss of respectability except in the eyes of a minority anti-racing group. Respectability may have been both complex and contested, and anti-racing pressure could usually only be exercised on those in certain positions, as with the Rev King, who was pressured into resigning his living after his horse won the 1874 St Leger. There was clearly a much larger middle-class group who were more materialistic, hedonistic and secular in their approach, to whom racing brought financial and cultural benefits. In this context, the values and symbols of respectability were redefined.

As we have seen, indulgence in what may have seemed less respectable pleasures was no necessary bar to success in life and business. Racing could be pleasure, profit or purposeful speculation, and for some groups within the middle classes it was a means to possible social mobility. Both the support for racing, and the vociferous opposition to it shows that at times any possible middle-class consensus and hegemony was very limited. Such insights cannot be ignored in attempts to link middle-classness with respectability.[88]

Notes

1 J. Lowerson, *Sport and the English Middle Classes 1870–1914* (Manchester, 1993).
2 Ibid., p. 5. See W. Vamplew, *The Turf* (London, 1976), pp. 133–4.
3 R. Holt, *Sport and the British: A Modern History* (Oxford, 1989), p. 181.
4 H. Cunningham, 'Leisure and Culture', in F.L.M. Thompson, (ed.) *The Cambridge Social History of Britain 1750–1950; Vol II; People and their Environment* (London, 1990), Ch. 6, pp. 305–9.
5 M. Huggins, 'The Growth of the Enclosed Courses on Teesside 1850–1902', *British Journal of Sports History* 3, 2 (1986), 158–72.
6 See for example N. McCord's critical review article 'Adding a Touch of Class', *History* 70, 230 (Oct. 1985), pp. 411 ff.
7 J. Lowerson, *Sport and the English Middle Classes 1850–1914* (Manchester, 1993), Ch. 1 *passim*. Where census data have been available, I have have used Alan Armstrong's methodology based on the Registrar general's occupational classification, and have used the term to refer to those in Social classes I and II not clearly belonging to the landowning gentry and aristocracy, and used employment of servants as an alternative definer. See W.A. Armstrong, 'The Use of Information about Occupation, part I. A Basis for Social Stratification', in E.A. Wrigley (ed.), *Nineteenth Century Society* (London, 1972), pp. 198–225.
8 R. Holt, *Sport and the British* (Oxford, 1989), p. 33.
9 *York Herald*, 26 Aug. 1813.
10 See J. Raven, 'The Abolition of the English State lotteries', *Historical Journal* 34, 2 (1991), p. 376. In lists of attenders after mid-century I have not so far come across any example of clergy attendance at meetings. There were however several clergy who bred and owned racehorses.
11 J.F. Blakeborough, *Northern Turf History* II (London, 1949), p. 153.
12 In 1832 in Carlisle the Lowther family and their connections withdrew their subscriptions to the races 'as a matter of course after the hostile feeling shown towards them by so many of the people of Carlisle' at the election. See *Westmorland Gazette*, 3 Sept. 1832.
13 See M. Huggins, 'The Growth of the Enclosed Courses on Teesside', for an extended discussion of this in the Stockton and Redcar context.
14 The Liverpool *Porcupine* saw the Manchester Cotton Exchange as another form of gambling; e.g. *Porcupine*, 17 May 1862.
15 R.M. Bevan, *The Roodee; 450 years of Racing in Chester* (Northwich, 1989), p. 30.
16 For some Bolton examples of this see R. Poole, *Popular Leisure and the Music Hall in 19th Century Bolton* (Lancaster, 1982), Ch. 3.
17 *Newcastle Daily Journal*, 31 May 1865. For a Chester example see *Baily's Magazine* 28 (June 1876), p. 421.
18 On his way from the Doncaster races in 1853, Dickens commented on 'the Itinerant personage in black ... telling him from the vantage ground of a legibly printed placard on a pole that for all these things the Lord will bring him to judgement', C. Dickens, *Reprinted Pieces and The Lazy Tour of Two Idle Apprentices* (London, 1925), p. 401.
19 R.H.G. Thompson, *The Liverpool and Manchester Railway* (London, 1980), p. 195.
20 *Middlesbrough Weekly News*, 25 Aug. 1865.
21 In 1880, for example, the ironmaster Charles Bolkow held a gala for the United Free Methodists; the primitive methodists had a gala in a local farmer's field, the industrialist T.H. Richardson entertained the Newport Road Baptist School; and the owners of Blair's works entertained St Andrew's Presbyterian scholars. See *North-Eastern Daily Gazette*, 19 Aug. 1880.
22 *South Durham and Cleveland Mercury*, 20 Aug. 1892.
23 For example, a Sheffield magistrate associated with the local Social Question League was instrumental in persuading the city council to have all newspapers taken by

Sheffield Free Library censored. See T. Mason, *Association Football and English Society 1863–1915* (Brighton, 1980), p. 197.

24 *North East Daily Gazette*, 8 Sept. 1893.

25 At Malton the Rev. Best-Northcliffe had the wold enclosed, and at Durham the university Senate refused to renew the lease. A letter from P. Fitzgerald, MA, JP addressed to the Manchester Racing Association giving his reasons for refusing to renew the lease in 1868 is held at Salford Library. See also C. Ramsden, *Farewell Manchester* (London, 1966), pp. 16–17.

26 *Yorkshire Post*, 24 Feb. 1883.

27 For example, S.Churchill, *Betting and Gambling* (London, 1894); W.H. Norris, *A Hint to the Clergy and Other Anti-gambling Crusaders* (London, 1894); J.M. Hogg, *Betting and Gambling* (Edinburgh, 1904).

28 See Vamplew, *The Turf*, pp. 209–10.

29 P.J. Gooderson, 'The Social and Economic History of Lancaster 1780–1914' (PhD thesis, University of Lancaster), p. 144.

30 It is clear that in the details of the arrangements they were relatively deferential to the opinion of the stewards. For an example concerned with the appointment of officials, see Doncaster Record Office, AB 2/2/5/1 Minutes of the General Purposes Committee 10 Dec. 1852.

31 By 1887 the corporation was making a profit of approximately £10,000 after stakes and expenses were paid, and 'at least six times as much' was left 'sticking to the pockets' of the inhabitants, *Baily's Magazine* 57 (Oct. 1887), p. 130.

32 See *Sporting Magazine* (June 1853), p. 450. See also Nov. 1856, p. 352; Dec. 1856, p. 387ff.

33 For example, York Archive Office YCC Chamberlains's Accounts, 11 Aug. 1826.

34 *Morpeth Herald*, 21 Aug. 1875.

35 'Holiday Times', *Household Words* (1853), p. 329.

36 Minutes of Evidence taken before the House of Lords Select Committee on Gambling; evidence of Robert Baxter, 12 March 1844, Q 1019ff.

37 *Doncaster Gazette*, 7 Sept. 1850.

38 *Yorkshire Gazette*, 5 April 1845.

39 R. Hale, 'The Demise of Horse Racing in Lancaster and Preston' (dissertation, Lancaster University, 1991), p. 28.

40 Minutes of Middlesbrough Watch Committee, 7 Oct. 1890.

41 J.T. Slugg, *Reminiscences of Manchester Fifty Years Ago* (Manchester, 1881), p. 112; E.A. Axon, *The Annals of Manchester* (Manchester, 1886), p. 372.

42 *Sporting Magazine* V (Second series 1832), pp. 153, 490.

43 *North-Eastern Daily Gazette*, 18 Aug. 1875.

44 *Durham Chronicle*, 21 July 1882.

45 *Beverley Guardian*, 19 June 1875; 26 June 1875.

46 J.K. Walton and A. Wilcox (eds), *Low Life and Moral Improvement in Mid-Victorian England; Liverpool through the Journalism of Hugh Shimmin* (Leicester, 1991), pp. 72–3.

47 Ibid., pp.75–6, 79.

48 *The Free Lance*, 15 June 1867. See also ibid., 9 Feb. 1867.

49 *Middlesbrough Daily Exchange*, 28 Dec. 1885; 29 Jan. 1886.

50 *Sporting Magazine* (Aug. 1838), p. 368.

51 York Racing Museum, Minutes of York Racing Committee, 5 Oct. 1843.

52 Lancashire Record Office, Preston; DDX 103/4 Fulwood Race Minutes 1790–1829.

53 York Racing Museum, Minutes of York Racing Committee, 30 Dec. 1864; 16 May 1885.

54 North Yorkshire Record Office. DC/RMB Richmond Racing Papers.

55 Lancashire Record Office, DDX 103/4 Minutes of the race committee, 9 July 1829.

56 R.M. Bevan, *The Roodee: 450 Years of Racing in Chester* (Northwich, 1979), p. 47.

57 See Carlisle Race Stand company PRO BT 31/1946/8150; Ripon Grandstand Company PRO BT31/1971/8372; Manchester Racecourse Company PRO

BT31/1385/3874; Newcastle Grand Stand Company PRO BT31/996/1533c; Morpeth Grandstand Company PRO BT31/2133/9791; Leeds Racecourse Company PRO BT31/3118/17929; Scar borough Grandstand and Racecourse Company PRO BT31/1394/3940.
58 *Durham County Advertiser*, 8 June 1888.
59 S.J.D. Green, Review Article: 'In Search of Bourgeois Civilisation: Institutions and Ideals in 19th Century Britain', *Northern History* XXVIII (1992), p. 232.
60 See T. Mason, *Association Football and English Society 1863–1915*, pp. 37ff.
61 For obit. see *Newcastle Daily Chronicle*, 28 Jan. 1869.
62 J. Fairfax-Blakeborough, *The Analysis of the Turf* (London, 1927), pp. 262–3.
63 See M.J. Huggins, *Kings of the Moor; North Yorkshire Racehorse Trainers 1760–1900* (Teesside, 1991), p. 46.
64 *Cleveland News*, 18 Aug. 1883.
65 W. Allison, *My Kingdom for a Horse* (London, 1919), pp. 37–9.
66 R.W. Proctor, *Memorials of Manchester Streets* (Manchester, 1874), p. 83.
67 R.S. Lambert, *The Railway King; a Study of Geo. Hudson and the Business Morals of his Time* (London, 1934), p.218.
68 For details of these and others see R. Mortimer, R. Onslow and P. Willett, *Biographical Encyclopaedia of British Flat Racing* (London, 1979).
69 R. Ord, 'Horseracing in the North of England', *Badminton Magazine* XIX (1902), p. 172.
70 *Sporting Magazine* 125 (1854), p. 140. A Bookmaker 'The Deluded Sportsman', in B.S. Rowntree (ed.), *Betting and Gambling; A National Evil* (London, 1905), p. 92.
71 For example, *York Herald*, 7 July 1841.
72 *Yorkshireman*, 6 March 1845; 12 April 1845.
73 'The Racing season of 1848', *Sporting Magazine* (Dec. 1848), p. 383.
74 Robert Wood Collection, Gray Art Gallery, Hartlepool. See also *Newcastle Weekly Chronicle*, 6 Aug. 1864, 'The Next Great Monster Draw on the St Leger has 5000 shares now at 5/- each, with a first prize of £500'.
75 Sylvanus, *The Bye-Lanes and Downs of England* (1850), pp. 1–20.
76 *York Herald*, 13 Dec. 1851.
77 *Manchester Courier*, 19 May 1869.
78 *Free Lance*, 25 May 1868.
79 M. Clapson, *A Bit of A Flutter. Popular Gambling and English Society* c.*1823–1961* (Manchester, 1991), p. 28 summarizes the position. Clapson's treatment of the earlier nineteenth century is cursory in the extreme.
80 Allison, *My Kingdom for a Horse*, p. 22. Rowntree (ed.), *Betting and Gambling*, appendix.
81 *Cleveland News*, 1 May 1880.
82 Ibid.
83 *Middlesbrough Weekly News*, 17 Aug. 1866.
84 A. Delves, 'Popular Recreation and Social Conflict in Derby 1800–1850', in E. Yeo and S. Yeo (eds), *Popular Culture and Class Conflict 1590–1914* (Brighton, 1981), p. 110.
85 R.J. Morris, 'Middle-class Culture 1700–1914', in D. Fraser (ed.), *A History of Modern Leeds* (Manchester, 1980); R.J. Morris, *Class, Sect and Party, the Making of the British Middle Class; Leeds 1820–1850* (Manchester, 1990).
86 For example, P. Joyce, 'In Pursuit of Class: Recent Studies in the History of Work and Class', *History Workshop Journal* 25 (1988); *Visions of the People: Conceptions of the Social Order in England Before 1914* (Cambridge, 1990).
87 A.J. Kidd, 'Introduction; The Middle Class in Nineteenth Century Manchester', in A.J. Kidd and K.W. Roberts (eds), *City, Class and Culture; Studies of Cultural Production and Social Policy in Victorian Manchester* (Manchester, 1985), p. 17.
88 M. Huggins, *Flat Racing and British Society 1790–1914* (London, 2000) takes this argument further.

Chapter 10

Of pride and prejudice
The amateur question in English nineteenth-century rowing

Eric Halladay

Some years ago, Peter Bailey advanced the view that during the second half of the nineteenth century, just as sporting activities in England were becoming more organized, working-class participants began to find that they were being excluded from taking part by the rules and regulations of the new clubs and associations.[1] He quotes Walter Besant's comment in 1887 to the effect that the middle classes had perceived 'that their amusements – also, which seems the last straw, their vices – can be enjoyed by the base mechanical sort, insomuch that, if this kind of thing goes on, there must in the end follow an effacement of all classes'. Bailey concludes that 'in such circumstances the middle classes stood steady to defend the line of their own gentility with a judicious mixture of discrimination and neglect'.[2]

While recognizing that cricket was an honourable exception to this develop-ment and that association football was in the process of being abandoned to the working classes, Bailey illustrated his thesis by reference to athletics. The Amateur Athletic Club, formed in 1866, deliberately distanced itself from the active pro-fessionalism of the day. In the process it also managed to exclude anyone who earned his living as 'a mechanic, artisan or labourer' and this mechanics clause led to much unease. Matters came to a head in 1879 when the Northern Athletics Association was formed with a constitution that embraced all but the profes-sionals. This northern threat highlighted the general nervousness over the mechanics clause and, threatened with a boycott of its championships, the AAC promptly dissolved itself. It was replaced the next year by the Amateur Athletics Association and all athletes except professionals were welcomed irrespective of class or social status.[3]

Bailey's example certainly illustrates all the prejudices of the age. He points out the fierce arguments used against professionalism and the attendant alarm over gambling and its organizers, the tavern keepers. It allows him to show how, in the minds of some, professionalism was often confused with the working classes on the grounds that manual labour gave a man an advantage physically over other

Originally published in *The International Journal of the History of Sport*, 1987, 4(1), pp. 39–55.
http://www.tandf.co.uk/journals

kinds of opponents. Nevertheless, in the example he particularly stresses, the significant fact is the loss of control by the founding fathers of the AAC to the extent that by 1879 the bottom line for amateur competition was drawn far lower in the social scale than had been the original intention. Here, at least, discrimination, except against professionals, did not work and athletics in this country was established on generously wide foundations.

Bailey might more profitably have examined another sport, rowing. When the Amateur Rowing Association was formed in 1882, similar arguments were used as in athletics and it adopted a mechanics clause exactly like that of the AAC. It looked like a successful attempt to bar what *The Times* called 'the outsiders, artisans, mechanics, and such like troublesome persons'.[4] At the same time there was an equally nervous reaction to such discrimination, sufficiently strong to lead in 1890 to the setting up of the National Amateur Rowing Association which embraced all oarsmen except professionals. But while the AAC collapsed at the first real hint of opposition, the ARA thrived, to the extent that until 1956 there were in this country two governing bodies.

II

Superficially there seems to be considerable similarity in the origins of the AAC and the ARA and it would seem that the only area of investigation ought to be why the ARA survived when the markedly similar AAC collapsed. In practice, however, the story of the Amateur Rowing Association's beginnings arc important since it was itself the product of compromise, one in which a far harsher and narrowly élitist code was, almost at the last moment, forced to accept considerable modification.

In the earlier part of the century, the issue of amateurism did not exist. W.B. Woodgate, an Oxford blue of the early 1860s, recalled that 'the old theory of an amateur was that he was a gentleman, and that the two were simply convertible terms'. Such a man, he went on, 'might make rowing his sport, so long as he did not actually make it his ostensible means of livelihood'.[5] Amateurs of this kind were active on all the major rivers, but especially on the metropolitan Thames where they were organized into exclusive and expensive subscription rooms, mainly to indulge in sculling races. In their approach they hardly differed from the professional watermen of the day whom they greatly admired and from whom they learned a great deal.[6] Among these amateurs fouling was considered normal and proper and they rarely competed unless money was involved. In 1839 a sculler from one of the best known subscription rooms, Leander, argued that he could not 'row a gentleman of the Dolphin Club for "nothing at all"', protesting that 'public interest in the river as well as the spirit of rowing would soon cease if all contests were for honour only'.[7]

Although Woodgate saw these amateurs as an easily identifiable group, he did not claim any particular merit for them as oarsmen. At least as far as sculling was concerned, the professionals still were objects of praise and envy. An aspiring blue in Henry Kingsley's novel, *Ravenshoe*, set in the period of the Crimean War, wished he could row like a waterman. His discouraging friend thought that, given six or seven years, he might do so, 'at least...as well as some of the second-rate ones'.[8] But, while their skills might be admired, some were beginning to question their methods, particularly their emphasis on fouling and the large sums involved in wagers and betting. As early as 1841, *The Times* observed of one professional sculling match that 'if a waterman's wager be the best method of ascertaining which is the better man, and the work of yesterday be taken as an example of it, then the sooner such a system be abolished the better'.[9]

Similar anxieties had already begun to be expressed at Oxford and Cambridge and these were in the end to prove decisive. As long ago as the 1820s, voices had been raised in objection to some of the Oxford colleges using watermen in their crews and feelings had been strong enough temporarily to halt the nascent bumping races.[10] Charles Merivale, a member of Cambridge's first Boat Race crew of 1829, felt compelled to write to his mother 'to caution you not to believe an advertisement which is to be seen in some of the papers about the match being for £500. It is not an exaggeration even, but a lie'.[11] Ten years later, C.J. Selwyn, brother of another member of that same Cambridge crew and himself a Boat Race umpire, publicly stated that 'watermen's ways are not our ways, or watermen's notions our notions', being even more explicit the next year. 'The principles which we always maintained were: first that gentlemen should steer, second (which follows from the first) that fouling should be abolished; and last, not least, that victory should be its own reward.'[12]

It seems clear that Selwyn's use of the word gentleman carried a different meaning from that of the subscription rooms and that he was condemning their approach to rowing as much as he was that of the professionals. Selwyn's plea was soon to be reinforced by others. The reluctance of Cambridge in particular to abandon the assistance of watermen for training the Boat Race crews forced T.S. Egan, former Cambridge cox and coach, to offer his services to Oxford in 1852. He justified his temporary apostacy in *Bell's Life*, of which he was the editor. He set out his view that 'eight-oar rowing necessarily declines from its high perfection in the hands of watermen'. He felt that what was threatened was

> that entire uniformity and machine-like regularity of performance, from which the practised eye looks at once in a university crew and which is the glory and delight of an oarsman...We ought to be able to point to our match crews and challenge the world to produce anything so uniform in motion, so polished in form, at once so speedy and so graceful, as one of those picked eights of the gentle blood of England.[13]

Egan's belief that it was possible with a group of university undergraduates to produce the perfect crew had earlier been reinforced by A.T.W. Shadwell, his friend and great rival both as cox and coach. In his conclusion to what is the first rowing manual in 1846, Shadwell stressed the qualities of character needed to be a good oarsman. Fundamental was good discipline, 'its seven-fold aegis'. He went on to emphasize that

> discipline involves in itself the notion of principles, and these, when carried into practice, enter into men's ways of thinking and feeling, and give a decided bias to their conduct as rowing men. Thus, like any constitutional maxims, they are much more than written laws; they are not letter, but spirit; and become the hereditary guides of every successive set of men in the boat-club, a wholesome pervading system of tradition and a standard which each man endeavours to act up to. Discipline, in truth, has an immense moral effect, and that an enduring one.[14]

The relaxed and uncomplicated views of the likes of Woodgate warn against exaggerating such earnest sentiments. Yet, Leslie Stephen felt that the preaching of Charles Kingsley, Thomas Hughes and others fell upon ground well prepared to receive it.[15] This seems to have been particularly so among the university and college oarsmen, and it is worth stressing that the genesis of that cult of athleticism that was so to dominate the late Victorian public schools and universities may well be found among those active on the Cam and Isis during the 1840s and 1850s. Certainly the rowing connection between its most obvious protagonists was a strong one. Leslie Stephen himself, while a junior fellow of Trinity Hall, took great pleasure in coaching the college boats, and Noel Annan has claimed that it was he rather than Charles Kingsley who deserves to be called the founder of muscular Christianity.[16] He was a close friend of Thomas Hughes, preaching the sermon at the funeral of one of the younger Hughes brothers who died as the result of an athletic injury.[17] Another of the brothers, George, twice stroked the Oxford crew as well as being in the university cricket XI. His cox had been Shadwell whose brother had in turn rowed in the rival Cambridge boat steered by Egan. Much of the action of Thomas Hughes's less well known novel, *Tom Brown at Oxford* (1860) centres on the fortunes of the college boat. Charles Kingsley himself often took his relaxation on the river, occasionally startling his undergraduate audience while he was Regius Professor of History by cutting short his lectures to go sculling on the Cam.[18]

What was emerging at the two universities was a powerful and coherent view about rowing that was in time to embrace most other undergraduate games. But, perhaps because rowing has always demanded the subordination of the individual to the whole, impressionable young oarsmen were particularly susceptible to the altitudes and approach of such as Selwyn, Egan, Shadwell and Stephen, even before they had heard the more mature gospel of Kingsley, Hughes and F.D. Maurice. The result was to push an already sympathetic audience towards the view that university rowing was *sui generis*, something that was out of the ordinary and that could only be practised well by a relatively small and privileged group. Bearing in mind that Egan and Shadwell, together with their disciples, went on coaching on the Isis and Cam for as long as they were able, several, generations of student oarsmen were to come under their influence.[19] There was therefore real pressure to preserve what was becoming a quarantined existence the virtues of which would be paraded twice a year before the general public at the Boat Race and at Henley Royal Regatta.

The problem was that this self-confident and patrician approach to rowing occurred at the moment, from mid-century onwards, when time for leisure activities was growing among all sections of society and this was reflected in the rowing world by a considerable increase in the number of low-cost clubs.[20] On the Thames they threatened and eventually replaced the subscription rooms where the relaxed approach to the sport was already vulnerable in the new climate of opinion. It was inevitable that a number of these new clubs would wish to measure themselves against the standards set by the universities and colleges. Their aspirations would be judged by their ability on the water at the only place where they could meet the student crews on equal terms, namely at Henley. But over and above the standards of rowing were the unwritten rules that governed conduct and behaviour, the importance of which had been the heart of the message of Selwyn, Shadwell and Egan.

The least problem was caused by the few rowing schools, particularly Eton under the influence of the formidable Dr Edmond Warre.[21] The colleges and schools informed and reinforced each other annually as pupils moved to the universities and former oarsmen returned as schoolmasters. Unlike the schools, where there could be no question of their amateur status, the clubs had no rules to guide them. Laws governing the conduct of races had existed since 1849, although regattas adopted them only on a voluntary basis. But in any case, they made no attempt to define what amateurism was and, even as late as 1872, a meeting of some of the leading clubs at Putney to revise the original rules dealt only with fouling.[22] The universities and colleges had no need to widen their horizons by welcoming others into the fold. They had their own complex calendar of racing which insulated them from the outside world except when they raced at Henley. It began to look therefore as if the stewards of that regatta, almost all of them old university men, were becoming the guardians of the unwritten law. They exercised their judgement in 1871 by refusing to accept the entry of Henley Rowing Club on the grounds that they were not 'gentlemen amateurs' even though the crew was acceptable at other regattas.[23] Nevertheless they shied away from the responsibility of actually saying what kind of person such an amateur actually was.

The fact of the matter was that most of those clubs aspiring to join the élite group knew as a matter of instinct what sort of person the stewards were referring to. If they could include former university oars in their crews – which meant being good enough to attract them – then they would certainly possess all the criteria needed. Leander, the only subscription room to survive, found that, by introducing a university qualification, it made membership particularly attractive to undergraduates on whom it began to draw to man its best Henley crews.[24] London Rowing Club (1856) had from the start tried to combine a wider membership with some degree of social exclusiveness.[25] Thames Rowing Club (1860), however, arrived by accident. Originally founded to give pleasure boating to the clerks and salesmen of the large city drapery warehouses and such-like institutions, it had by the 1870s almost completely changed its nature and composition. W.H. Eyre, an early member, recalled at the turn of the century that 'there are very few (if any) "rag-trade" men in the Club now. The social status (conventionally speaking) is, I suppose higher....'. He was partly responsible since, against the wishes of the club's authorities, he formed a four that won at Henley in 1870, the first of many such victories. It was Thames RC's growing reputation for hard competitive rowing that transformed the club and began as a result to attract former university oarsmen. The infusion of men with different aims gradually inhibited those for whom the club had originally been formed. But its becoming one of the strongest clubs in the country was not the result of any conscious decision on the part of the club's executive; in fact just the opposite.[26]

Whether by accident or design, there had emerged on the Thames by the 1870s a group of clubs characterized by their proficiency in rowing and by their links with the two universities whose values they had come to share. They were considered eminently acceptable at Henley where no voice was ever raised against their competing. The situation in the provinces, however, was less clear. The *1862 British Rowing Almanack* listed clubs under three headings: gentlemen's, tradesmen's and watermen's. No club outside the Thames was to be found in the first group other than Oxford and Cambridge.[27] During the next few years a significant number of provincial clubs were to join the list but the criteria of selection were far from obvious.

One club that did aspire to élite status was the Royal Chester RC (1838), not simply because it had won at Henley in the 1850s but because it had its origin in Chester Regatta which, the year before the club's foundation, had excluded manual workers from competing. This early example of discrimination remains odd, being so out of tune with the way other regattas conducted themselves.[28] But a far more likely representative club is that at Agecroft on the river Irwell. Founded in 1861, it had unpretentious origins; but by 1874 it was behaving in a very different way. Part of the change may well have had something to do with a university connection, in particular the fact that two Cambridge blues, the brothers James and John Close, lived in the neighbourhood. Possibly through their influence, crews from the Cambridge colleges, the Thames and the Tyne raced at the club's regatta in 1874. So too did one from the Bolton and Ringley Rowing Club but it was promptly disqualified after winning its event. The Agecroft secretary justified the decision to the local newspaper, claiming that the Bolton oarsmen were artisans. The Bolton club's measured and dignified reply raised what was to become the crucial issue:

> If any gentleman would kindly give us a true definition of what an amateur is, we should feel greatly obliged, as we have always been under the impression that if a person did anything for pleasure and not for money, that person was an amateur, but if he should do anything for money, or in any shape for his living, he loses his title to an amateur.[29]

III

The problem with the Bolton Club's demand was that there was no authoritative body to provide an answer. The nearest to it came the stewards at Henley, a small and self-perpetuating body representative only of the universities and the élite group of metropolitan clubs. But they had never given any indication that they wished to don the kind of mantle worn by the likes of the Marylebone Cricket Club or the Royal and Ancient Golf Club. Nor was there yet any compelling reason to make them think otherwise. They had, as in 1871, disqualified competitors and hoped that future entries for the regatta would understand the message. But their main concern was the affairs of one regatta, held annually in July. For the moment they were content to leave matters that way, although immediate events were soon to place them in an equivocal position.

If a governing body was to be found, it was probable that the initiative would have to be taken elsewhere. The representatives of the two universities, although likely to be influential, were too transient in their membership to be able to assume responsibility. The most obvious candidate therefore to make the opening gambit would be one of the larger metropolitan clubs but only if circumstances existed to move them in that direction. By the late 1870s one of them, London RC, was sufficiently concerned by its own particular experiences to be prepared to make a move. It did so in the larger context of increasing organization and systematization over a wide range of games – football, rugby, and athletics among others.[30] It was London RC's involvement in two matters, its organizing of the Metropolitan Regatta and its experience of rowing overseas, that pushed London RC into a position of prominence.

The Metropolitan Regatta had been founded in 1866 but the original hope that it might provide an alternative focus to Henley had not been fulfilled, largely, according to Woodgate, because it never succeeded in attracting the university element.[31] But it was an important regatta at Putney and provided a venue for many of the smaller Thames-based crews that were unlikely to compete at Henley. From its earliest days, London RC had assumed the major responsibility for its organization and had provided most of the funding. Perhaps because of the financial burden assumed by London, the club's authorities became increasingly sensitive to the varied and changing practices of the smaller clubs and they were aware that they were constantly compromising their own high standards. It was a totally unacceptable situation that in microcosm revealed much about the conduct of rowing throughout the country.[32]

The other area that caused London RC concern was that of foreign competition, all the more so since the club had early on taken the initiative to encourage it. In 1860 it had proposed an international regatta at Putney and had been disappointed that this had proved impossible to arrange.[33] But it had entertained a number of American and German challenge-matches on the Thames during the 1870s and had been among the first clubs from this country to race abroad. On the whole the latter had not been happy experiences. At the 1867 Paris

Exhibition regatta, London RC had objected to a Canadian four on the grounds that they were not proper amateurs but shipwrights and woodcutters. Subsequent events confirmed the London oarmen's alarms since the same Canadian crew rowed a four of Tyne watermen for the professional championship of the world in 1870 and 1871.[34] In 1876 London RC were one of three British crews invited to compete at the centennial regatta at Philadelphia. Fouled by their American opponents and obtaining neither redress nor sympathy, the London four withdrew from the regatta amid much recrimination. *The Times* reported sourly on the affair, commenting that in America 'amateur was an elastic term and included coal-whippers, glass-blowers, hewers of wood and drawers of water'.[35] It was this disturbing experience of events both at home and abroad that prompted London RC, under the chairmanship of one of its best-known oarsmen, Francis Playford, to organize a meeting of the leading clubs at Putney on 10 April 1878.[36]

Together they produced the first definition of an amateur, and it was in every sense a predictable document, the logical conclusion to those attitudes that stemmed from Selwyn, Shadwell and Egan. Basically it consisted of two sets of propositions. The first, positive in its terms, defined the kind of man who might be called a gentleman amateur. He must be

> an officer of Her Majesty's Army, or Navy, or Civil Service, a member of the Liberal Professions, or of the Universities or Public Schools, or of any established boat or rowing club not containing mechanics or professionals.

It concluded with a series of negative propositions to the effect that an amateur

> must not have competed in any competition for either a stake, or money, or entrance-fee, or with or against a professional for any prize; nor ever taught, pursued, or assisted in the pursuit of athletic exercises of any kind as a means of livelihood, nor have ever been employed in or about boats, or in manual labour; nor be a mechanic, artisan or labourer.[37]

The timing of this initiative seemed to be totally justified three months later when four North American crews competed at Henley. Two of them were amateurs according to the Putney rules and excited no comment apart from Columbia College's becoming the first overseas crew to win a Henley trophy. But one of the American scullers, G.W. Lee, was beaten in the final of the Diamonds by only the narrowest of margins, and suspicions at the time about his pedigree were confirmed when he later became a professional.[38] As controversial was the Shoe-wae-cac-mette four from the United States who not only turned out to be lumberjacks but, according to *Bell's Life*, did not receive 'the plaudits bestowed on them with becoming modesty which is generally inseparable from true merit'.[39]

The cumulative repercussions of the Paris regatta, that at Philadelphia and now the events at the 1878 Henley were to be profound. The question of foreign crews rowing at this country's premier regatta was to smoulder on until after the turn of the century, but the immediate reaction of the stewards was to demand that overseas entries be received early to allow some attempt at checking their credentials. In addition such entries had to be 'accompanied by a declaration made before a Notary Public with regard to the profession of each member of the crew'.[40] But of more immediate concern, any attempt by the Henley stewards to test the validity of foreign competitors demanded that they themselves clarified their own position on the amateur question.

The Putney definition represented no more than the opinions of those who had drawn it up, although it reflected in large measure the views of many of those belonging to the élite group.[41] Nevertheless, it had not met with universal acceptance. R.C. Lehmann, writing several years later, recalled that there was a significant gap between the positive and negative propositions into which a number of oarsmen fell and who accordingly were uncertain of their amateur status.[42] The Henley stewards seem to have been conscious of such objections and accordingly phrased their own definition totally in the negative by making clear exactly who they thought were not amateurs. The Henley rules, produced just before the 1879 regatta, declared that

> no person shall be considered an amateur oarsman or sculler –
>
> 1   Who has ever competed in any open competition for a stake, money, or entrance fee.
> 2   Who has ever competed with or against a professional for any prize.
> 3   Who has ever taught, pursued, or assisted in the practice of athletic exercises of any kind as a means of gaining a livelihood.
> 4   Who has been employed in or about boats for money or wages.
> 5   Who is or has been, by trade or employment for wages, a mechanic, artisan or labourer.[43]

The exact arguments behind these Henley rules must be a matter of surmise. The stewards were representative of the major clubs and the universities and as such might have been expected to come to very similar conclusions to those of the Putney meeting. But instead, although keeping a manual labour clause, they refused to accept a definition that was too socially exclusive. The 1879 rules encouraged a far wider group of men to row at Henley than if they had simply endorsed the Putney definition. It seems likely that what governed this decision was the wish to ease the entry problems of foreign crews since social conditions elsewhere were unlikely exactly to mirror those in Britain. But, in making their decision, the Henley stewards managed to produce a remarkably liberal document and one which administered a salutary check to the pretensions of that relatively narrow group that had found its inspiration at the universities of 40 years earlier.

IV

By the end of 1879 there existed side by side two definitions of an amateur but neither had the force of law. The Henley stewards had managed to manoeuvre themselves into the paradoxical situation where they were trying to enforce internationally rules that applied in Britain for only three days of the year over a limited stretch of the Thames. But they gave no indication that they were prepared to go any further and assume the additional responsibility of becoming a national governing body. They were nevertheless to exercise a hidden influence that was to be important but which, through lack of evidence, can only be assumed.

The two definitions were not mutually exclusive but the fact that one was more generous than the other meant that pressure was growing for some form of solution. If Woodgate is to be believed, insinuations were made to the Metropolitan Rowing Association that it should widen its powers and assume the guise of a governing body. Set up in 1879 on the inevitable initiative of London RC, the association had the simple object of forming, when needed, representative crews to race internationally. It drew its support from the same clubs that had produced the 1878 rules, with the addition of Dublin University, and as such it might have been expected to take the conservative and élitist line. But other clubs, mainly Thames-based, seemed prepared to take that risk, perhaps confident that the authorities at Henley would prove a moderating influence.[44]

The association therefore set itself up under the new name of the Amateur Rowing Association in April 1882. Its headquarters were at London RC and the *ex officio* members were Oxford and Cambridge, London RC, Thames RC, Leander, Kingston RC and Dublin University. In addition to its role in selecting crews to race foreign challengers, it set itself the object of maintaining the standard of amateur rowing throughout the country.[45] As a purely voluntary body, it moved at first with infinite caution to the extent that the *British Rowing Almanack* did not even notice its existence until 1885 and then only following its decision on the amateur issue.[46]

The ARA published its draft definition on 1 July 1884, following a meeting at Henley during regatta week. It is difficult to avoid the conclusion that there must have been consultation with the stewards. That the ARA rules differed only marginally from those produced at Henley in 1879 underlined how crucial was the decision that the definition for national use should be basically the same as that which was being imposed on foreign crews. If the ARA had opted for a version of the 1878 rules, which by instinct might have been the case, the credibility of both institutions would have been seriously weakened.

The ARA's draft was circulated for comments. The minor changes to the Henley rules contained the over-harsh addition in the manual labour clause of the words 'and anyone engaged in menial duty'. But most controversy surrounded the new sixth clause to the effect that nobody could be an amateur who 'was a member of a boat or rowing club containing anyone liable to disqualification under the above rules'.[47] In replying, the clubs and regattas, particularly those in the West Country and the Midlands, revealed customs and practices that would have meant the disqualification of a large number of oarsmen. They asked for time to reconsider their future, and this the ARA granted by dropping the new clause for a year. It was never to be restored. But *The Field*, reflecting the tougher line of some of the élite group, took a less generous view, suggesting that, without the threat of the new clause, provincial behaviour would remain unpredictable. Its anger revealed a sense of betrayal and it had no doubt that the blame was to be borne by the Henley stewards 'to whose legislation exception can be justly taken more often than not'.[48]

In fact the ARA had behaved in making its first important decision with sound political sense. It had allied itself with the stewards at Henley and was in the process of cementing what was to become a powerful entente.[49] At the same time it had avoided what might well have been a provincial revolt that would have destroyed the new association at the outset. A degree of expediency and tolerance was needed if it were to exert any real authority. By 1888, 24 regattas had affiliated while others, though claiming to conform, had generous interpretations of the amateur rule.[50] The ARA had been cautioned that this would happen. In commenting on the draft rules, the secretary of Tewkesbury regatta bluntly warned that certain customs and practices might 'shock the delicate feelings of the lavender-gloved amateur; but if rowing is to be encouraged, we must not be too thin-skinned'.[51]

Irregularities and deception there were, such as calling a house-painter an artist, and they would take some years to end.[52] But by the 1890s, the ARA was responding with vigour and many of its meetings seem to have been concerned with issuing warnings about the status of particular individuals.[53] But there were a few clubs for whom concealing the nature of their membership was impossible since most of it was drawn from those groups against whom the manual labour clause was specifically aimed. To have contemplated affiliation to the ARA would have been tantamount to abolition. Such discrimination caused concern to a number of oarsmen who might have been expected to side with the élite. Among them were two Cambridge blues, Sidney Swann and C.J. Bristowe, but towering above them in personality was the formidable figure of Dr F.J. Furnivall. A scholar, philanthropist and former oarsman at Trinity Hall, he had when younger been a close friend of Charles Kingsley and Thomas Hughes.[54] He had admired many of their ideals but set them in a far wider context than many of his contemporaries. He founded his own sculling club, encouraged women to row, and delighted in the company of the less privileged whom he attracted to its premises at Hammersmith.[55]

The manual labour clause and the plight of the debarred oarsmen was just the kind of issue to arouse Furnivall's indignant enthusiasm. He diverted his anger mainly at the universities, isolating what he took to be sad misinterpretations of the ideals that had helped to shape his own life. 'We feel,' he wrote, 'that for a University to send its earnest intellectual men into an East-end or other settlement to live with and help working-men in their studies and sports, while it sends its rowing-men into the A.R.A. to say to these working-men, "You're labourers; your work renders you unfit to associate and row with us", is a facing-both-ways, an inconsistency and contradiction which loyal sons of the University ought to avoid.'[56]

It was such sincere but angry sentiments that led in September 1890 to the setting up of the National Amateur Rowing Association since

> a large body of amateurs in the true sense of the term – men who row for the love of the sport and not for gain – had no definite status or organisation because they did not belong to the A.R.A. on the one hand or the 'Tradesmen' – a professional class – on the other.[57]

One of its first decisions was to approach the ARA to discuss the amateur issue and a meeting between five representatives of each side was held at Oxford in April 1891.[58] The NARA case seems to have been unexpectedly deferential given the mood in which the association had been founded. One of its delegates, F.F. Vincent of the Falcon Club at Oxford, wrote a letter since he could not be present. He did not want the ARA to abolish the manual labour clause since 'I am open-minded enough to understand and appreciate the object of some such classes being barred; the condition of athletics and football form arguments which only those who are wilfully blind cannot see.' What Vincent wanted was for the ARA to modify its rules so that it did 'not exclude men who are only disqual-ified by reason of their having rowed with or against the mechanic classes'. He concluded by saying that what the NARA wanted was a two-tier system – 'I want the N.A.R.A. to represent the people and the A.R.A. the aristocracy. Let the men of the A.R.A. help in the larger association, but at the same time keep their own inner circle free, as it always has been, from any suspicion of taint'.[59] Such an unexpected case, however, was apparently undermined by the somewhat bullish and undiplomatic behaviour of Dr Furnivall, and the ARA firmly rejected the proposal.[60]

The fact was that the NARA was as yet a relatively weak institution and if further progress was to be made, it would have to depend on its sympathizers within the larger body. Two ARA clubs at Burton-on-Trent, for example, tried to persuade the authorities to allow the local Trent RC, most of whose members were working men, to row in the local regatta.[61] The journal *Truth* stated that 'the phrase "menial duty" is one that disgraces any sporting rule. Briefly the case for the reformers is that the rule is arbitrary and unfair, and introduces unnecessary social distinction'.[62] This comment followed *The Field's* description of W.P. Wetherell, captain of Marlow RC and incidentally an Old Etonian, as a malcontent and a traitor for asking the ARA even to contemplate reopening the amateur issue.[63]

That the manual labour clause was becoming a matter of public debate prompted the ARA in the autumn of 1893 to appoint a subcommittee to recon-sider the issue. Its report, published in April 1894, recommended no change but there was an important minority opinion by the ARA secretary, R.C. Lehmann. He argued in favour of ending the disputed clause on two grounds. The first was that rowing, he believed, was as much about skill as muscular power and he doubted whether the working man had any built-in advantage. Secondly, he felt that a significant number of working-class oarsmen who enjoyed the sport for pleasure ought in all justice to be brought under the ARA's authority. He cited in particular those East End clubs connected to school and university missions (all of them to join the NARA) and the manner in which the rule bewildered many provincial clubs and regattas.[64] Lehmann's radical initiative did not please the hard-liners in the ARA. *The Field* commented that

> we can appreciate the spirit of chivalry to the working classes which apparently prompts him to take what may be termed a wider view of the amateur question, but it is a moral duty to be just before being generous. Justice to the amateur competitor in a muscular exercise demands that his opponents, like himself, should have developed their skill and anatomy alike by labouring for love and not for money.[65]

In fact Lehmann did have a minor but important victory in that he had managed to have inserted into the majority report, adopted that August, an exact definition of a professional. The ARA agreed that the word must be taken 'in the primary and literal sense' which meant that it applied only to those who made their living by some form of rowing.[66] In fact what the ARA had done was to concede in effect the demands made by the NARA delegates at the 1891 meeting so that there were now three clearly defined classes of oarsmen: amateurs according to the strict ARA definition, what Lehmann called non-amateurs who are not professionals, and finally the professionals themselves.[67] The NARA would not have been happy with Lehmann's description of most of their oarsmen as non-amateurs but at least the first two groups could now row together for pleasure or against each other in private matches.

V

The conclusion of the debate resulted in an unparalleled situation in British sporting history and one which was to continue until the ARA modified its rules in 1937 and finally absorbed the NARA in 1956. Selwyn, Egan and Shadwell had unashamedly encouraged an élitist approach which in the course of time meant that the concept of the amateur became identified in the minds of some with a small, privileged clique, drawing its inspiration from the two universities. Over the years this was to be reinforced by their undoubted skill on the water, exemplified by Britain's taking all the gold medals at the 1908 Olympic regatta. Many of these oarsmen saw themselves both socially and athletically as a special and separate set. Few of them would have disagreed with *The Times* in April 1880 when it recommended the exclusion of the working class since 'the status of the rest seems better assured and more clear from any doubt which might attach to it and the prizes are more certain to fall into the right hands'.[68] Such sentiments were to linger on and even a small provincial club on the Tyne could, in 1928, see the only remedy for falling numbers to be an approach 'to suitable public schools, varsities, rugby clubs and military garrisons'.[69]

As an example of the Bailey thesis, it could hardly be bettered. But it is only part of the truth. The ARA had in the end drawn the line far lower on the social scale than might have been expected. By opting in July 1884 for a modified version of the 1879 Henley rules, it had effectively prevented rowing in this country becoming the preserve of a narrowly based praetorian guard. Instead, by rejecting the particular interests of its own kind, it had assured a reasonably wide base of support both in the provinces and internationally. It was sad that it could not follow the sentiments of the captain of Marlow RC in 1893 when he argued that 'the spirit of the age in all questions of sport...is rather to weld all classes together by the community of their interests than to create or uphold invidious distinctions'.[70] But for the ARA to have gone that far and to have embraced the NARA oarsmen would have alienated those powerful groups, however insensitive they might be, whose skills the association wished to encourage.

But in any case, it is far from clear at that time and before 1914 that the NARA wanted any further advance. In 1891, the NARA delegation was asking for a modicum of recognition and in essence obtained what it wanted in 1894. As an organization, it could now pursue its own unpretentious path with some degree of confidence as well as some assurance that, in the provinces at least, ARA oarsmen and regattas would often extend a tolerant and helping hand.[71] Apart from Dr Furnivall's explosions of indignation, there seem to be few signs at the time of militant agitation against this state of affairs.

Whatever the practices of the two associations may have been, they were both ironically enough the heirs of Selwyn, Egan and Shadwell. The amateur ethic was central to all that they both did and the NARA was sensitive enough to its importance not to appoint a paid secretary in 1895.[72] Throughout the whole debate, whether it be the extreme views of *The Field*, the rhetoric of Dr Furnivall, or the measured tones of R.C. Lehmann, none doubted the amateur ideal. Perhaps because it had been such a controversial issue, its meaning in terms of attitude and behaviour was so finely honed that rowing today remains almost unique in British sporting tradition in the honour that is paid to it.

Notes

1 Peter Bailey, *Leisure and Class in Victorian England: Rational Recreation and the Contest for Control 1830–1885* (London, 1978) *passim* but especially chapters 4 and 6.
2 Ibid., p. 105.
3 Ibid., pp. 131–6 and 139–40.
4 *The Times*, 26 April 1880.
5 W.B. Woodgate, *Boating* (London, 1888), p. 192.
6 One such was the Thames Subscription Room which was not a rowing club but existed 'to aid poor watermen and to encourage and foster rowing generally'. *British Rowing Almanack 1862* (hereafter *Almanack*), p. 108.
7 W.J. Macmichael, *The Oxford and Cambridge Boat Races* (Cambridge, 1870), pp. 76–9.
8 Henry Kingsley, *Ravenshoe* (London, 1894 edition), p. 55.
9 *The Times*, 9 June 1841.

10 W.E. Sherwood, *Oxford Rowing* (Oxford, 1900), p. 11.
11 G.C. Drinkwater and T.R.B. Sanders, *The University Boat Race: Official Centenary History 1829–1929* (London, 1929), p. 11.
12 Ibid., p. 161.
13 Ibid., pp. 162–3.
14 A.T.W. Shadwell, *Principles of Rowing* (London, 1846) p. 25. Originally published anonymously but now accepted as Shadwell's work. See F. Britain, *Oar, Scull and Rudder: A Bibliography of Rowing* (London, 1930), p. 1.
15 Leslie Stephen, 'Athletic Sports and University Studies', *Fraser's Magazine*, II New Series (1870), 694.
16 Noel Annan, *Leslie Stephen* (London, 1951), p. 29.
17 Ibid., pp. 38–9.
18 S. Rothblatt, *The Revolution of the Dons: Cambridge and Society in Victorian England* (London, 1968), p. 171.
19 Egan and Shadwell both died in 1893.
20 On the question of increased leisure time see Bailey, op. cit., pp. 57–63 and 80–91.
21 Edmond Wane gained a double first at Oxford and became a Fellow of All Souls. He rowed in the 1857 and 1858 Boat Races. Returning to Eton as a master, he was the first important rowing coach at the school. He subsequently became Head master and then Provost of Eton. See *passim* C.R.L. Fletcher, *Life of Edmond Warre* (London, 1922) and G.C. Bourne, *Memoirs of an Eton Wet-Bob of the Seventies* (London, 1933). Of the 713 rowing blues awarded at both universities between 1829 and 1929, 281 came from Eton, just over 40 per cent.
22 *Almanack* 1982, p. 42.
23 Woodgate, op. cit., p. 193.
24 R.D. Burnell and H.R.N. Rickett, *A Short History of Leander Club* (Henley, 1968), p. 17.
25 Charles Dimont *From Strength to Strength 1856–1981: Portrait of London Rowing Club* (London, 1981), p. 7.
26 W.H. Eyre, 'Thames Rowing Club' in R.C. Lehmann (ed.), *The Complete Oarsmen* (London, 1908), pp. 179–205. I am also indebted for further information to Geoffrey Page, former captain of Thames RC and rowing correspondent of *The Daily Telegraph*.
27 *Almanack 1862*, pp. 108–9.
28 Hylton Cleaver, *A History of Rowing* (London, 1957), p. 64.
29 W.A. Locan, *The Agecroft Story: The First Hundred Years of the Agecroft Rowing Club 1861–1960* (Salford, 1960), p. 22.
30 The Football Association was founded in 1863, the Rugby Football Union in 1871 and the Northern Union (Rugby League) in 1895.
31 Woodgate, op. cit., pp. 42–3.
32 *The Field*, 17 July 1886.
33 Dimont, op. cit., p. 10.
34 One cause of London's defeat in 1867 was that the Canadians from St John's New Brunswick rowed in a four without a cox. The races with the Tyne crew were also in a coxwainless boat and it was during the second that James Renforth, the Tyne stroke, collapsed and almost immediately died.
35 *The Times*, 13 Sept. 1876.
36 In addition to London, there were representatives from Thames RC, Leander, Kingston RC and the two universities. Woodgate, op. cit., pp. 193–4.
37 Lehmann, op. cit., pp. 248–9.
38 R.D. Burnell, *Henley Regatta: A History* (London, 1957), p. 103.
39 Christopher Dodd, *Henley Royal Regatta* (London, 1981), p. 71.
40 Burnell, op. cit., p. 103.
41 *The Field*, 10 May 1885.
42 Lehmann, op. cit., p. 249.

43 Ibid., pp. 249–50.
44 Woodgate, op. cit., pp. 193–6.
45 Lehmann, op. cit., p. 251.
46 Unfortunately the early minute and letter books of the Amateur Rowing Association are missing. They can to some extent be reconstructed from the pages of *The Field* and the *British Rowing Almanack* after 1885.
47 Cleaver, op. cit., p. 127.
48 *The Field*, 10 May 1885.
49 The relations have always been close to the extent that the ARA has never asked Henley to affiliate.
50 *The Field*, 13 Oct. 1888.
51 Ibid., 11 July 1885.
52 Ibid., 13 Oct. 1888 and Anonymous, *Frederick James Furnivall A Volume of Personal Record* (hereinafter *Furnivall*) (London, 1911), p. 155.
53 For example, at its meeting on 25 May 1895, the ARA allowed the booking clerk at Henley station to row as an amateur but not an assistant to an ironmonger, a paid tailor or an apprentice to a printer (*The Field*, 29 May 1895).
54 *Furnivall*, op. cit., p. 159.
55 Ibid., p. lxxx.
56 Ibid., p. lxxix.
57 National Amateur Rowing Association Minute Books, kept at ARA Head-quarters, Hammersmith, 9 July 1891.
58 Ibid., 29 April 1891.
59 Cleaver, op. cit., pp. 138–9.
60 *Furnivall*, op. cit., p. 156.
61 *Truth*, 21 Dec. 1893.
62 *Truth*, 9 Dec. 1893.
63 *The Field*, 11 Nov. 1893 and 25 Nov. 1893.
64 Ibid., 5 May 1894. Lehmann, a man of independent means, just missed his blue at Cambridge but became a coach of considerable merit. A radical liberal, he opposed the Boer War and was a Liberal MP from 1906 to 1910. He was secretary to the ARA from 1893 to 1901.
65 Ibid., 5 May 1894.
66 *Almanack 1895*, p. 170.
67 Lehmann, op. cit., pp. 253–4.
68 *The Times*, 26 April 1880.
69 Tyne Amateur Rowing Club Minute Books, kept at Tyne ARC, Newburn, Newcastle, 27 Nov. 1928.
70 *The Field*, 11 Nov. 1893.
71 Ibid., 30 May 1896.
72 National Amateur Rowing Association Minute Books, 23 Nov. 1895.

Part VI

Sport, war and diplomacy

Chapter 11

'No business of ours'?
The Foreign Office and the Olympic Games, 1896–1914

Martin Polley

> The future does not belong to the present diplomats, who make the world so
> difficult to live in, but to coming men out of the present youth who understand
> the old wisdom in the words 'To live and let live' and 'Mens sana in corpore
> sano.'[1]

This claim from J. Sigfrid Edström, President of the International Olympic
Committee from 1942 to 1952, summarizes one of the ideologies that has historically underpinned the modern Olympic movement. A consistent theme in
defence of the Games has been the good effect that sport is supposed to have on
relations between countries, an idea that has at its base an idealistic vision of
international affairs. For historians belonging to the generations that have
witnessed the Cold War being played out in Olympic stadiums, such rhetoric can
seem incredibly naïve; and MacAloon's explanation of his motives for studying de
Coubertin still rings true: 'I felt compelled to understand how on earth someone
came to the extraordinary idea that a group of people running around in short
pants every four years had something to do with international understanding and
world peace.'[2] MacAloon leads us to a crucial point: how have Olympic apologists
attempted practically to link their ideals to the world of diplomacy?

A case study of the British experience before the First World War is instructive
in this context. In this early period of modern Olympic history, we can see the
development of a relationship between British promoters of the Olympic
movement (formalized into the British Olympic Association (BOA) in 1905), and
the British government, largely through the Foreign Office. In the dialogue that
developed between these two agencies before the First World War, we can see the
problems inherent in the idealistic view of international relations summed up by
Edström, problems that have never fully been resolved. The Olympians
attempted to convince the government that the Olympic Games could benefit
the UK's diplomacy by helping to maintain her international position and

Originally published in *The International Journal of the History of Sport*, 1996, 13(2), pp. 96–113.
http://www.tandf.co.uk/journals

influence, and by allowing British sportsmen and women to meet with their foreign counterparts in sporting contests. Accordingly, they argued that the government should assist the Olympic Games in any appropriate way, such as helping with publicity, waiving visa restrictions, providing facilities for Olympic representatives abroad, and granting financial aid. The Foreign Office, however, as the leading governmental department involved in this debate, was never fully convinced; and the permanent officials concerned developed their own view of the Olympic Games throughout this period. On certain occasions, they recognized that the Olympic Games offered potential for promoting British interests, and assisted accordingly. However, the risks of involvement were gradually recognized. The Foreign Office was unable to commit itself structurally and permanently to supporting cultural links with countries that might be out of favour; and the idea of linking the government to emotive and controversial sporting events was never an attractive one.

The experience of the Foreign Office in dealing with the Olympic Games in this period has been largely overlooked by historians of sport and diplomacy in favour of the interwar period, when pragmatic intervention in various high profile sporting events was forthcoming from successive governments.[3] Such intervention developed in direct response to the more structured intervention being practised by the governments of Italy, the USSR and Germany. However, this concentration on the interwar period obscures the fact that British governments had been involved with international sport since before the First World War. By studying the relationship between sport and diplomacy at this early stage, we can achieve a greater perspective on its subsequent history. It can help us to see why governments got involved, what they perceived as being at stake, how these perceptions related to the sporting administrators' perceptions, and what methods of intervention were used. Throughout, there is an element of uncertainty in the Foreign Office's discourse on the Olympic Games: how should this department, recently reorganized and involved on a daily basis in ever more complicated issues in Europe and the Far East,[4] treat the Olympic Games?

A study of this period also helps us to see how the BOA worked during its early years: it certainly helps to demythologize the BOA's claims about its apolitical past, as in the assertion from a 1987 pamphlet that it has 'cherished and defended its independence, and rejected all political interference in its affairs'.[5] Before 1914, the BOA and its officers frequently courted political involvement, and used a variety of arguments to try and have the government work with them. The Olympic movement was then in its infancy. The IOC had been formed only in 1894; and the British Olympic Association was not formed until 24 May 1905, when William Grenfell MP (later 1st Baron Desborough of Taplow, the BOA's Chairman until 1913) chaired a meeting at the House of Commons to bring together those interested in the Olympics.[6] Bearing in mind the enormity of the administrative and logistical tasks faced by the BOA in its first years, notably the organization of the 1908 London Olympic Games, it is not surprising that governmental assistance was solicited. Moreover, there was clearly a perceived community of interests between the men who administered the BOA and the governments of the period. The social and political character of the movement was defined by its amateur and patriotic ideals, and from the beginning it was controlled by an elite of aristocratic and bourgeois sportsmen who often also held positions of power in wider state structures, such as parliament, colonial administration, and the Church of England. Thanks to these structural aspects of the administration of the UK's Olympic efforts, it is unsurprising that the BOA's discourse was dominated by a mixture of Olympic idealism and national promotion. This discourse relied upon the nation and its forms of government for its existence and its identity, but also tried to work above and beyond them by promoting a sporting internationalism. As a result, the BOA approached the government for help, but failed to appreciate the complexities of diplomacy that constrained the government's desire or ability to provide permanent assistance. It is the working out of these two discourses before the First World War that we can now study.

The 1908 Olympic Games are the most obvious starting point for this study: as London hosted them, the Liberal Government had no option but to be involved at some level, and they were the first of the official series to be held after the formation of the BOA in 1905. However, there are earlier examples of diplomatic interest. The British Minister to Athens, Egerton, kept the Foreign Office informed about the planning of the 1896 Olympics,[7] and even wrote a report on 'the Olympian Games' on the closing day: 'nothing could have been better managed, the Greeks appearing in the best possible light as competitors, spectators, organisers and hosts, and it is certain that these games [*sic*] will become an institution and be more attended by foreigners in future than they have been on this present occasion'.[8]

The praise and prophecy are interesting; but so is Egerton's apparent ignorance of the planned moveable nature of the Olympic Games, as he assumed that Athens was to be their permanent home. While this first brush with the Olympics by a British diplomat was nothing more than observational, it is significant that he felt it necessary to report the events to his department. The Foreign Office maintained an interest in the 1900 Paris Exhibition, to which the second Olympic Games were appended, but there is no surviving evidence of any actual involvement in the sporting events, described by Guttmann as 'a disaster'.[9] Similarly, there is no record of official interest in the sports at St Louis in 1904.

However, by the time of the 1906 Intercalated Games in Athens, British, involvement was on a new footing, due to the foundation of the BOA. Governmental involvement also increased. In February 1906, the Greek Envoy to London, D.G. Metaxas, invited the Foreign Secretary, Sir Edward Grey, to send an official representative to Athens for the Games.[10] The lack of official awareness about the Olympic Games is obvious from the Foreign Office minutes on what response should be sent. An official in the Eastern Department had no objection to the idea, but was ignorant of what such a representative should actually do: 'We have never had such an invitation before. The nearest thing to it was an

Archaeological Congress at Athens last March…It is not clear whether [the representative] is to take part in the Games or merely sit as a spectator in the front row.' He suggested that both the Board of Education and Sir Francis Elliot, the British Minister to Athens, should be consulted for advice, and added, 'The last time these Games were held I believe some English Athletes [*sic*] attended but we had nothing to do with it officially.'[11] Elliot duly suggested that the Government should use 'one or two competitors of good standing' as representatives.[12] He drew attention to Lord Desborough, Chairman of the BOA and a member of the British épée team. On being sounded out in a private letter by Sir Charles Hardinge, the Permanent Under-Secretary,[13] Desborough expressed his honour at taking on such a role, and added a rider to his official status: 'I am told that there will be some wild Epée fighters, Roumanians, Bulgarians & others, so I hope I shall be given a public funeral if anything goes wrong.'[14] He was duly appointed as first representative, with R.C. Bosanquet, the Director of the British School at Athens, as second representative.[15]

This incident is a crucial one in the development of the relationship between the BOA and the government. Despite the lack of any precedent, and the unofficial status of the Olympic Games, the relevant political departments, the Permanent Under-Secretary, the Board of Education, and the relevant overseas post all worked to please the Greek organizers. The emphasis on the need for the representatives to be 'of good social standing'[16] suggests the priorities of all the officials concerned at a time when the growth of professional sport was threatening the preserves of amateurism. This was obvious: and with the BOA boasting so many aristocrats, the choice was not problematic. The crucial point, however, is that the British government sent an official representative to the Intercalated Games at Athens. In view of later events, it is significant that the request for such a representative came from the Greek government, and was therefore difficult to refuse, and not from the BOA itself. As in 1896, the British Minister in Athens kept the Foreign Office informed of the progress of the Games.[17] So, in the immediate run up to the 1908 London Olympic Games, a precedent of the government helping the Olympic Games was set.

The keynote that, in this context, links the Intercalated Games of Athens to the next full Olympics, and that sets the tone for much of the subsequent debate about governmental involvement, can be found in Elliot's own report from Athens. His comments summarized the feelings of some of the Olympic apologists that the government was not doing enough to help British performances at the Games. It is an argument that has still satisfactorily to be settled, but it is significant that it was expressed in official diplomatic correspondence: 'The number of British competitors was relatively small, no Government assistance having been given, as was the case with most other countries, notably America, whose athletes were numerous and successful.'[18]

He did not specify the numbers or the positions. In all, the British team consisted of 52 competitors (5 per cent of the total). Britons won eight events, came second in 11, and third in six (10 per cent, 14 per cent, and 8 per cent of the total positions in each category). This performance placed the British in fourth place, behind France, the United States and Greece.[19] This did not meet the standards assumed by the BOA. Although this was the first real team effort for the British at the Olympics, and despite the youth of the BOA as an organizational body, the myth was immediately established that the British were under-achieving. This was expressed most forcibly in the writings of Theodore Cook, a member of the BOA, the non-participating captain of the fencing team at Athens, and a *Daily Telegraph* staff writer. His privately published *The Cruise of the Branwen*,[20] which combines Olympic history with a plea for funding for the 1908 Olympic Games, contains much evidence of this assumption. It is worth dwelling on, as it helps us to see the Olympic apologists' discourse at this turning point in its history.

Cook argued that the historical circumstances that had led to the emergence of so many sports in the UK gave the country a natural superiority in sport. In his view, this background set the UK and the white dominions apart when it came to international competition:

> In considering the record of the various nations, it must be remembered that the English-speaking races have hitherto enjoyed one preponderant and vital advantage, which is that athletic traditions are in our blood, and athletic framework is constantly being bred into the best of our boys.[21]

He feared that this advantage was being eroded by public apathy and governmental indifference, themes to which Cook frequently returned. In appealing for funds in the preface, he pointed out that the BOA 'is left without any official assistance of any sort or kind':

> In order ... to fulfil the expectations of an excellence sufficiently high to form a permanent and universal standard ... [against teams] ... who are assisted by subsidies and the formal recognition of their Governments, we have to depend entirely upon private munificence and upon the generous support of individual citizens.[22]

He drew attention to the positive impact that the Olympics were having on 'international goodwill, ... the peace, and the mutual understanding of the peoples of the world',[23] a theme he developed in the revised edition:

> Of all the influences now at work to stay the cruel hand of war, who shall say that any single one is more potent in its effects than that increase of international athleticism which is the most significant factor in the intercourse of modern nations?[24]

Accordingly, he called for governmental assistance for the 1908 Olympics. Without it, he claimed, the organisation would suffer; and it would be 'something like a national disgrace if we did not come up to the high standard of efficiency expected of us by the rest of the athletic world'.[25] To this end, he listed a number of desirable organisational goals for the London Olympics, including the appointment of a Foreign Office attaché to each visiting team 'to direct and organise all the necessary social obligations and pleasures of which Greek courtesy and hospitality have set a standard that it will always be difficult to equal.'[26]

Even allowing for the bombastic tone of some of his claims, this represents a good summary of the Olympic proselytisers' contemporary discourse on what the Olympics could do for the country, and what the government should accordingly do for the Olympics. In return for public investment, patronage, and organisational assistance, the sporting events would help to secure peace and maintain diplomatic relationships; while in the long run, such aid would help British athletes to regain the supremacy that the historical head-start had given them. These points were made with increasing frequency over the following years, as the Olympians attempted to influence the government; the government, unsurprisingly, developed its own discourse on the Olympics that was less idealistic. By 1914, it was clear to both agencies that they had very different agendas.

The relationship between government and the BOA developed during the planning and execution of the 1908 Olympics. At Athens in 1906, Desborough had agreed that London would host the next Games when Rome pulled out due to Italy's economic crisis.[27] Desborough was acting here only in his capacity as Chairman of the BOA, and not as the British Government's representative, although Elliot informed the Foreign Office of the development.[28] The Games were added to the Franco-British Exhibition of Science, Arts, and Industry that was already scheduled to take place at Shepherd's Bush in 1908. This removed much of the logistical burden from the BOA, and allowed them to concentrate on co-ordinating the sports: for example, rules for all the events were codified; and a judging system was established, complete with an international appeals committee.[29]

The connection with the Franco-British Exhibition gave the Olympics a particular diplomatic resonance due to the UK's developing relationship with France following the Anglo-French Entente of 8 April 1904. Given the Liberal Government's eagerness to strengthen its links with France in the face of growing German hostility, the Exhibition received support as an example of co-operation between the two countries: in January 1907, the Foreign Office informed the Duke of Argyll, the Honorary President of the Exhibition, that the Government 'cordially approved' of the event.[30] Accordingly, the Olympics were given some assistance without prompting from the BOA, although Cook's earlier appeals for funding and attachés were not met. In July 1908, for example, the Foreign Office supported the importation of French small arms for the shooting competition;[31] and in the same month, the Foreign Office dealt sympathetically with a request from the Norwegian Minister to London asking permission for six army officers competing in the Games to wear uniform during their stay in London.[32] Overall, the administrative nature of the involvement suggests that the Games were perceived as marginal but potentially useful in maintaining friendly links with

France and other countries. However, two small incidents show that there was some official discussion over the government's role in the Olympics. These discussions demonstrate a developing awareness of the potential problems that the sports could cause through their emotive and patriotic nature. It is here that we see the first real divergence from the BOA's optimistic discourse.

The first incident concerned the French Olympic rowing team. On 15 April 1908, Sir Francis Bertie, the British Ambassador to Paris, sent Grey copies of two letters he had received from the *Fédération Française des Sociétés d'Aviron* (FFSA), which claimed that the French were being treated unfairly by the Amateur Rowing Association (ARA). Allegedly, the ARA had told the FFSA to register their team by 1 June while other countries had been given an extra month. Bertie had suggested to the FFSA that the French Embassy in London should take the matter up, and simply passed the information on to the Foreign Office.[33] The officials dealing with it were confused by the ARA's stance, but seemed certain that it was not their problem; but Gerald Spicer's minute showed up the ambivalence of the official response: 'We certainly cannot interfere. The Amateur Rowing Association have no doubt excellent reasons for their decision. Lord Desborough is, I believe, the moving spirit, and he might like to know that this appeal has been made to Sir F. Bertie.'[34] The Foreign Office's Legal Adviser, Sir William Davidson, duly wrote a private letter to Desborough, sending copies of the correspondence from Paris. He assured Desborough that 'it is no business of ours', but asked that Bertie be told the reason for the discrepancy.[35] Although there is no result on file, this incident is significant for two reasons. First, it shows a British diplomat and the Foreign Office involving themselves in a potentially embarrassing sporting matter without the prior knowledge or the prompting of the BOA. The French complaint had to be investigated, and the Foreign Office took it upon itself to facilitate this. Second, the language and style of the involvement are worthy of note. The officials concerned seemed quite sure that it was not a Foreign Office or Embassy matter: but having established that, decided to use the covert technique of the private personal letter to defuse a potentially damaging situation, with Davidson offering to act as a discreet go-between for Desborough and Bertie. This private and semi-official mode of intervention was to be frequently used in years to come.

The second discussion of note shows that some officials were already aware that the unpredictable nature of sport, and the emotions it could invoke, made it an unfavourable area for official involvement. The Foreign Office began to realize that cheating, bad refereeing, and unsatisfactory performances all caused unpleasant atmospheres, and began to develop the view that no British government should jeopardize its relations with other countries for the sake of sport. On 20 July 1908, Bertie informed the Foreign Office that the French Government had granted the French Olympic team F50,000. Although this information was not overtly linked with any BOA requests for funding, the idea of a subsidy was not missed by the officials who dealt with the information from Paris. Samuel Cockerell – a young clerk in the Commercial Department who was not hostile to sport, having been

an athletics and rowing Blue at Cambridge[36] – drew immediate attention to the
unpleasant aspects of the Olympics: 'Up to the present it can hardly be said that
the Sports have led to any strengthening of the friendly relations; some of the
French performers are more likely to go home disgusted than pleased. e.g.
Mr Schille [*sic*] the cyclist.'[37]

The reference was to Maurice Schilles, whose victory in the 1,000 metre sprint
was declared void because the time limit had been exceeded. The judges' decision
not to re-run the race, which was in line with regulations against crawling, was
perceived by the French as being linked to the misfortune of the two Britons in
the race, both of whom had suffered punctures.[38] This single example of the contested refereeing that has become synonymous with the 1908 Olympics typifies
the way in which national prestige and chauvinism were becoming tied up with
sporting events: in the words of one sporting journalist of the time, who claimed
that the idea behind the Olympics was 'a fine but impracticable one', the Games
were 'exciting the passions of race rivalry' and thus 'retarding rather than advancing' international amity.[39] This tiny incident shows that some officials at the
Foreign Office were already aware of this in 1908. From that time on, it would be
very difficult for the Olympic apologists to convince the Foreign Office of their
optimistic views on international relations; and many later requests for assistance
were met with an official hostility based on a critical reading of the 1908
Olympics. The good publicity gained was overshadowed in the official view by the
emotive aspects of the sports. The administrative side of the Foreign Office's
involvement in the 1908 Olympics is also worthy of note. Virtually all the
correspondence was dealt with by the Treaty and Commercial departments, not
by the relevant political desks: the discussion of the Norwegian officers was the
exception. Olympic matters were perceived as specialised concerns that did not
merit deliberation by the officials dealing with the countries concerned on a daily
basis. However, the very fact that the Foreign Office allowed itself to get involved
was a significant development from the precedents of 1896 and 1906. It
responded pragmatically to potential problems, thereby setting new precedents:
but its officials learnt through this process that international sport was not
necessarily the key to world peace that some of its apologists claimed.

The experience of 1908 also had an impact upon the Olympic apologists'
discourse. Although the British team won the most medals in London, with 56
golds to the 23 of the second-placed USA,[40] there was some dissatisfaction over
the victory. Home advantage was clearly a factor, as was the relative team sizes:
the British fielded 839[41] to the USA's 160: 424 per cent more competitors but only
143 per cent more gold medals. Some press coverage criticized the lack of success
in athletics, where the British won only eight golds: the *Athletic News* called this a
'deplorable experience', blaming it on the lack of funding for training facilities,
and prophesying that in 1912, 'there will be little done for the glory of Old
England in the way of providing the cost of training; and once more the Yankees
will triumph'.[42] Cook developed the theme of insufficient funding on behalf of

the BOA in the official report:

> in England...we have never been able to count upon any financial contri-
> bution from the public funds through the channels of official administration
> nor have we been able to avail ourselves of the patronage of the Government
> in raising money, by any officially-sponsored scheme, for these objects.[43]

The Franco-British Exhibition, gate money, and a public appeal launched by
the *Daily Mail* had all helped to raise the necessary money:[44] but the bitterness felt
towards the government for failing to fund the Olympics was obvious. Despite the
British successes, and the small amount of government assistance, it was this lack
of full state commitment that was to dominate Cook's discussions with the
government in the years running up to the First World War.

Following the experience of 1908, governmental involvement in the Stockholm
Olympics of 1912 was minimal. Its main involvement came in advising the organizers on the status of British dominions in the competition. The discussion was
initiated in October 1911 by Count Wrangel, the Swedish Envoy to London, and
it involved the Foreign Office, the India Office, the War Office, and the British
Legation in Stockholm. The solution was little more than a formalisation of current practice, whereby the dominions could represent themselves, while Ireland
counted as part of the British entry.[45] The Foreign Office was also involved in
waiving import duties on publicity materials being sent to the colonies from
Sweden,[46] and, more significantly, in encouraging army officers to participate in
the equestrian events. In November 1910, the War Office asked the Foreign
Office for guidance on this, as it did not usually allow serving officers to participate in public competitions.[47] The Foreign Office's discussion clearly demonstrated an appreciation of the potential value of the Olympics for promoting
good relations, despite the lessons of 1908. Spicer's comments encapsulate this
attitude: he compared the Olympics favourably to other competitions, 'from
which the factor of personal gain is seldom or never absent', and stressed that
participation by the officers could be beneficial:

> The games [*sic*] are held every fourth year in the various capitals in turn. On the
> last occasion, 1908, they took place here. The Swedes then not only competed
> in a large number of events but sent over a splendid team of gymnasts who car-
> ried all before them. If we stand aloof in 1912 it will create a bad impression.[48]

The usage of 'we' here is interesting: it is unclear whether Spicer means the government or the country. Also significant is his appreciation of the idea that involvement in sport could create favourable impressions between countries, although it is
worth qualifying this by highlighting the social standing of the competitors involved:
serving officers in an amateur sport could presumably be trusted to behave themselves in an approved manner. This thinking clearly tied in with the ideas behind the

Swedish introduction of equestrian events: in the words of Count Clarence von Rosen, who proposed the sport in 1906, 'the various Governments...would feel much more interest in the Games, were the cavalry officers of different countries to compete with each other.'[49] A British team of four officers duly competed at Stockholm, against teams from Belgium, Chile, Denmark, France, Germany, Norway, Russia, Sweden, and the USA, although it won no medals.[50]

This small amount of involvement was, as before, pragmatic: there was no structured intervention, and no subsidy or official patronage of the BOA. The government simply responded to situations as they arose. Spicer's recognition that impressions at the Olympic Games mattered shows how quickly some officials were getting used to this new phenomenon; and his memory of the Swedish gymnasts from 1908 suggests an interest in the events beyond his official remit. However, there were still gaps in the officials' knowledge. Spicer's assertion in the same minute that the Olympics took place only in capital cities demonstrated an ignorance both of Olympic conventions and of the 1904 St Louis Olympics. A more significant oversight in this context was the way in which another official, Gerald Villiers, dealt with another matter. In September 1911, the Swedish Minister to London sent the Foreign Office ten copies of the Olympic programme and regulations for distribution to the relevant bodies in the UK.[51] Villiers called up the 1906 papers for precedent, and decided to send the programmes to the Board of Education: 'possibly there is a British Olympic Committee: but I don't know how to find out'.[52] At this distance, it is impossible to reconstruct his ignorance of the BOA, and of the seemingly more obvious 1908 precedent; but the fact remains that an official with eight years' experience[53] managed to overlook the BOA; and that none of his superiors or colleagues corrected the error or suggested alternatives. It is salutary to bear such omissions in mind: ignorance was still part of the government's discourse on the Olympics.

Just after the Stockholm Olympics, at which the British team won only ten gold medals, and slipped to third place behind Sweden and the USA,[54] the BOA renewed its criticisms of the government for failing to involve itself fully in the Olympic Games. The official report on 1912, written by Cook, Desborough, and Laffan, directly attacked the public and the government for their lack of interest. The Swedish Government's financial support was cited to show that the Games had a more solid foundation than was the case in a country where the Government held almost entirely aloof from the movement, as happened in 1908';[55] and went so far as to call for the UK to withdraw from the Olympic movement if improvements could not be made:

> while it deprecates any mere passion for records or results as such, the [British Olympic] Council would suggest that this country should cease to be represented at future Olympic Games unless that representation is worthy not merely of the athletes themselves but of the nation in whose name they will compete.[56]

The reasons for the relative decline of the British medals tally from London to Stockholm were varied: the decline in the size of the team by 66 per cent

(839 to 283) while the total number of competitors rose by 25 per cent (2,035 to 2,547) obviously played a part.[57] However, the general reaction of the BOA was to attack the public and the state for failing to appreciate their vision of the significance of the Olympic Games.

While some of the ideas expressed in this report were familiar, the notion that the UK should withdraw from the Olympics if it could not compete properly represents a new theme in the BOA's discourse. This radical suggestion shows how strongly the Olympians felt about the links between the nation and the athletes performing in its name. It was picked up again in *Aims and Objects of the Olympic Games Fund*, an undated fund-raising pamphlet published between the 1912 Olympics and the outbreak of the First World War, during the preparation for the abortive 1916 Berlin Olympics. This pamphlet referred to the 'striking descent'[58] of the British performance from London to Stockholm, and called for the British to 'take the whole thing more seriously',[59] as the nation's prestige was at stake. Alongside familiar calls for government funding and the suggestion that a united British Empire team would be more successful, the pamphlet approvingly quoted an article from *The Times* of 27 July 1912 on the notion of withdrawal:

> We may question if the Olympic Games are good either in their influence on the spirit of sportsmanship or in their effect on international relations of a larger kind. We may regret that the Games were ever instituted. But, if we withdrew from them now, we should inevitably be regarded as having done so in petulance and under the mortification of defeat.[60]

It was in this mood that the BOA conducted its final pre-war dealings with the government.

The preparations for the 1916 Olympic Games were advancing when the war started. The Foreign Office's stance on the prospect of an international sporting event taking place in Berlin became increasingly hesitant as 1914 progressed: the officials realised that a war with Germany, quite apart from presenting logistical problems to the organizers, would preclude the friendly co-operation that was a prerequisite of the Olympic Games. This can be seen at its clearest in the debate between the Foreign Office, the Army Council, and the BOA over the question of British army officers competing in the modern pentathlon at Berlin. This military event, consisting of riding, fencing, shooting, swimming, and running, had been instituted at Stockholm in 1912, with three Britons competing. Early in 1914, the BOA approached the Army Council about the team for 1916. The Army Council was unsure about allowing its officers to compete, as 'no advantage would accrue to the Army',[61] and asked the Foreign Office for advice. The Foreign Office, clearly aware of the diplomatic implications, concurred. Robert Vansittart of the Western Department saw 'no particular reason for supporting the request of the [British Olympic] Association, and some reason for agreeing with the inclination of the Army Council',[62] while his colleague Ronald Sperling overstated the lessons of 1908 in his comment that 'these games [*sic*] usually lead to much international ill-feeling.'[63] However, the matter – significantly being dealt with by the relevant political department – was deemed important enough to refer to Sir Edward Goschen, the British Ambassador to Berlin,[64] who advised that non-participation might offend the Germans, and that the Army Council should wait and see what other countries were doing.[65] The officials involved were clearly reluctant to condone a sports meeting between British and German officers at such a time, a stance which compares interestingly with the Foreign Office's eagerness to encourage British officers to compete at Stockholm just two years earlier. This provides an excellent example of the government's policy towards sport being constrained by prevailing diplomatic conditions. The Foreign Office and the War Office could not afford the luxury of Olympic idealism when faced with German hostility, and could not allow sport to enter their consideration of high diplomacy.

It was just after this incident that the two discourses on the Olympics finally came into conflict. As has been seen, the BOA had frequently criticized the government in public for failing to involve itself in planning and funding, but had not yet directly confronted any department of state; while the Foreign Office and other departments had simply carried on from 1908 with an undefined policy of pragmatic intervention in response to certain situations. In May 1914, however, Theodore Cook – by now the editor of *The Field* – forced the Foreign Office to face up more directly to its attitude towards the Olympics. On 15 May 1914, he wrote to Grey asking for an interview to discuss the 1916 Olympics.[66] An interview with the Head of the Western Department (which dealt with Germany) was offered,[67] although no record of the meeting exists on the file. Contact was evidently made, as Cook wrote a private letter to Robert Vansittart on 2 June which clearly built upon an interview. This letter, marked 'Private' by Cook, set out the problems that faced British participation in the Olympic Games, and asked for some solutions from the government in time for the IOC's Congress in Paris, due to start on 12 June. Cook claimed that the government should become more directly involved in the Olympics through two key areas: financial assistance; and the provision of diplomatic facilities. He justified such a call on the grounds that 'the whole questions raised by the Olympic movement . . . have now assumed in other countries an importance entirely disproportionate to that which they hold among ourselves', and claimed that the Foreign Office's attitude towards the Berlin Olympics would be read by many Germans as an indication of British attitudes towards Germany. The projected Berlin Olympics, he argued, had been raised out of the level of a mere sporting occurrence into an event of international political significance in which any misunderstanding might produce incalculable consequences upon the general cordiality which should exist between the two countries.

He also observed that most other governments were involved in their nations' preparations for the Olympics; and that the UK had 'permanently identified itself' with the Olympics by London's hosting of the 1908 Games.[68] Enclosed with the letter was a self-congratulatory historical 'Short Memorandum of the Olympic Movement', which noted that the 1908 Olympics had been the only Games to date at which the government of the host nation had failed to award decorations to competitors and officials.[69] His condemnation of the British government's attitude was made even more explicitly in another enclosure, 'The Olympic Games – Recommendations'. Here he called for the Foreign Office to provide diplomatic facilities for the British representatives at the forthcoming Paris Congress and in Berlin for the Olympics, to send official representatives to Berlin, and to ensure that Baron de Coubertin be awarded a KCMG.[70]

The Foreign Office's response to this rather audacious approach was circumspect. Vansittart sent Cook a private reply telling him that it was not a Foreign Office concern. He secured a memorandum from Edward Parkes of the Librarian's Department, which backed up his claims that the Foreign Office was under no obligation to get so involved: however, the credibility of this memorandum, which concentrated on 1906, is dented by its claim on the 1908 Olympics that 'there is no correspondence in the archives relative to the meeting'.[71] Vansittart was clearly unimpressed by Cook's arguments – 'My own impression is that Mr. Cook is taking these *démarches par acquit de consciences*' – and urged upon Sir Eyre Crowe, the Permanent Under-Secretary, 'No action, unless and until Mr. Cook recurs to the attack.'[72] In reply, Crowe forcefully expressed his desire for the Foreign Office to stay out of the Olympic Games unless it was absolutely necessary. His minute is worth quoting in full for the attitudes it articulates, and for its very existence as a statement on the Olympics by the Foreign Office's highest ranking permanent official:

> I do not think we ought to be rushed in a matter of this kind. There is much diversity of opinion even in this country about these games [*sic*]. Many sensible people consider them to be pure advertisement of professional sportsmen. If the govt is to take them up officially, it must be after a deliberate decision. It is not a Foreign Office question at all, and cannot be decided by Sir E. Grey.[73]

This statement was perfectly clear: the Foreign Office felt that there were insufficient grounds for the government to become directly involved with the Olympic Games.

The experience of war influenced Cook's Olympism. Many of his writings for *The Field*, collected together in book form, were fiercely anti-German, with the war played out in sporting metaphors: in 1915, for example, he optimistically claimed that 'the "British team" is certainly on its way to Berlin; but in a very different sense from what was contemplated even so lately as in June last'.[74] He resigned from the IOC in 1916.[75] After the war, he was more reflective, as in a letter of May 1919 to Desborough (who had lost two sons on the Western Front) in which he criticised the forthcoming 1920 Olympics:

> If there were no other reason against the proposal that Swedes and Jugo-Slovacs [*sic*] and all the rest should meet Italians and other people on friendly terms, the argument of the terrible losses we have suffered would in itself be sufficient... I do not see how we can contemplate international competition in any sport for some years to come.[76]

The war clearly killed off the idealism of one of the leading British Olympians, and in the post-war period political differences at the Olympics became more overt, seen most obviously in the non-participation of Germany and the other defeated nations until 1928.

For the Foreign Office, the war deferred the need for Crowe's 'deliberate decision', and in 1919 the Foreign Office found itself embroiled in the Olympics without a clear policy, when an official accepted the invitation to send a British team to Antwerp,[77] a situation that led to the government having to support the British team against its better judgement: Crowe even went so far as to call the Olympics 'an international farce'.[78] The subsequent history of Foreign Office involvement in the Olympics, at least until a more structured approach appeared after the Second World War, was characterized by this lack of a policy decision in 1914, allowing a piecemeal continuation of the pragmatic responses that had been present as early as 1906. The failure fully to address the question left the Foreign Office unprepared for the overt politicisation of sport that was to emerge in inter-war Europe. As a result, such crucial matters as the possible boycott of Berlin in 1936, and the intervention in the debate on the projected 1940 Olympics, were lacking any real sense of overview. There was no clear direction: only a general belief that the Olympics were not a government concern, which was frequently dispensed with pragmatically.

In recent years, the popular debate on political involvement in the Olympics has generally been presented from an angle sympathetic to the neutrality of sport. Such crises as Cold War disputes, and the campaign against Apartheid fought through cricket, rugby, and athletics have been presented as somehow corrupting the free nature of sport, and of threatening its independence. This view is evident in the BOA's own contemporary discourse on politics, as seen in a quotation given earlier: that the BOA had 'cherished and defended its independence, and rejected all political interference in its affairs'.[79] However, a study of the BOA's relationship with the government before the First World War helps to shed new light on the whole notion of political involvement. Far from being a period in which governmental activity was resisted, as in the debate on the 1980 Moscow Olympics, it was a time when governmental assistance was actively courted by the BOA. As a new organization containing many influential figures active in the political arena, needing funds and recognition, and perceiving that there was a community of interests between its work and that of the government, it would have been unnatural for the BOA not to have initiated such a courtship. Moreover, the nature of the involvement has always been open to contestation: while the BOA wanted money, patronage, and support, the government naturally developed the view that involvement could mean pressure and influence for diplomatic ends. Now, at a time when critical readings of the links between sport and politics are crucial to our understanding of contemporary sport, the early years of the historical relationship between the government and the BOA must be acknowledged and analysed.

Notes

1 J. Sigfrid Edström, 'Foreword', in Ernest A. Bland (ed.). *Olympic Story* (London, 1948), p. vi.
2 John J. MacAloon, *This Great Symbol: Pierre de Coubertin and the Origins of the Modern Olympic Games* (Chicago, 1981), pp. xi–xii.
3 See Peter Beck, 'England v Germany, 1938', *History Today*, 32, 1982, pp. 29–34; Stephen Jones, 'State Intervention in Sport and Leisure in Britain between the Wars', *Journal of Contemporary History*, 22, 1987, pp. 163–83; Stephen Jones, *Sport, Politics and the Working Class: organised labour and sport in interwar Britain* (Manchester, 1988), chapter 7; Martin Polley, 'Olympic Diplomacy: the British Government and the projected 1940 Olympic Games', *International Journal of the History of Sport*, 9, 1992, pp. 169–87; Brian Stoddart, 'Sport, Cultural Politics and International Relations: England versus Germany, 1935', in Norbert Müller and Joachim Rühl (eds), *Olympic Scientific Congress 1984 Official Report: Sport History* (Niedernhausen, 1985), pp. 385–412.
4 See Ray Jones, *The Nineteenth-Century Foreign Office: an administrative history* (London, 1971); Zara Steiner, *The Foreign Office and Foreign Policy 1898–1914* (Cambridge, 1969); Zara Steiner, 'The Foreign Office under Sir Edward Grey, 1905–1914', in Francis Hinsley (ed.), *British Foreign Policy under Sir Edward Grey* (Cambridge, 1977), pp. 22–69.
5 BOA, *The British Olympic Association and the Olympic Games* (London, 1987), p. 11.
6 Theodore Andrea Cook, *The Olympic Games* (London, 1908), p. 145.
7 Athens despatches 14 and 19, 14 and 28 January 1896. Public Record Office (PRO), FO 32/677.
8 Athens despatch 58, 14 April 1896. Ibid.
9 Allen Guttmann, *The Olympics: A History of the Modern Games* (Chicago, 1992), p. 22.
10 D.G. Metaxas to Sir Edward Grey, 2 Feb. 1906. PRO, FO 371/81, 4072.
11 Minute, 6 Feb. 1906. Ibid.
12 Athens despatch 43, 5 March 1906. Ibid., 8633.
13 There is no copy of this letter on the Foreign Office file. The relevant minutes read 'Perhaps Sir C. Hardinge wd write to him [Desborough] privately in the first instance.' (Eldon Gorst, undated minute), followed by Hardinge's undated minute 'Written Mar. 14.' Ibid.
14 Lord Desborough to Charles Hardinge, 15 March 1906. Ibid., 9252.
15 Eldon Gorst to R. Bosanquet, and Eldon Gorst to Lord Desborough, 22 March 1906. Ibid, 9547. See also 10087, 10333, 10611, and 11681.
16 Sir Francis Elliot to Sir Edward Grey, 14 March 1906. Ibid., 9547.
17 Athens despatch 65, 3 May 1906. Ibid., 15926.
18 Ibid.
19 Compiled from figures in Wallechinsky, *Olympics*, p. xiii and xv, and BOA, *The British Olympic Association*, pp. 32–3.
20 Theodore Cook, *The Cruise of the Branwen* (London, 1908).
21 Ibid., p. 91.
22 Ibid., p. ix.
23 Ibid., p. xii.
24 Cook, *The Olympic Games*, p. xvii.
25 Cook, *Cruise*, p. 16.
26 Ibid. p. 100.
27 John Rodda, 'London 1908', in Lord Killanin and John Rodda (eds), *The Olympic Games* (London, 1979), p. 56.
28 Athens despatch 65, 3 May 1906. PRO, FO 371/81, 15926.
29 Theodore Cook, *The Fourth Olympiad, being the Official Report of the Olympic Games of 1908* (London, 1909). Lord Desborough's personal scrapbook on the 1908 Olympics,

consisting of a wide range of press cuttings from 1906 onwards as well as correspondence from various National Olympic Committees, is an excellent source for this period. Hertfordshire County Record Office (HCRO), D/ERv F25.

30 Foreign Office to Duke of Argyll, 19 January 1907. PRO, FO 368/99, 2505.
31 PRO, FO 368/181, 22457, 22912, 23592.
32 PRO, FO 371/491, 23488, 24976.
33 Sir Francis Bertie to Sir Edward Grey, 15 April 1908. PRO, FO 369/142, 13114.
34 Undated minute. Ibid.
35 Sir William Davidson to Lord Desborough, 24 April 1908. Ibid.
36 Ray Jones, op. cit., p. 169.
37 Undated minute. PRO, FO 368/181, 25297.
38 See Wallechinsky, *Olympics*, p. 221.
39 *The Sportsman*, 29 July 1908, p. 7. For American reactions, see Thomas R. Burlford, *American Hatred and British Folly* (London, 1911), and George Matthews, 'The Controversial Olympic Games of 1908 as Viewed by the *New York Times* and the *Times* of London', *Journal of Sports History*, 7, 1980, pp. 40–53. For the BOA's immediate response, see British Olympic Association, *The Olympic Games of 1908 in London – A Reply to Certain Criticisms* (London, 1908).
40 Wallechinsky, *Olympics*, p. xv.
41 This figure includes the 'winter' events of football, rugby, lacrosse, hockey, boxing, and skating: Theodore Cook, *The Fourth Olympiad* (London, 1909), p. 656. The BOA's 1987 pamphlet claims only 676: BOA, *The British Olympic Association*, p. 33.
42 'The Moral of the Olympiad', *Athletic News*, 27 July 1908, p. 5.
43 Cook, *The Fourth Olympiad*, p. 388.
44 For the accounts, see ibid., p. 394.
45 PRO, FO 371/1226, 43156, 45057, 49142, 50029. Although the BOA welcomed this development, the official report included a table entitled 'Events in which Olympic medals were won by the British Empire outside the UK'. British Olympic Council, *Official Report of the Olympic Games of 1912 in Stockholm* (London, 1912), p. 29.
46 PRO, FO 371/1226, 48090.
47 Sir Arthur Nicolson to Eyre Crowe, 10 Nov. 1910. PRO, FO 371/989, 41086.
48 Undated minute. Ibid.
49 Quoted in Erik Bergvall (ed.), *The Official Report of the Olympic Games of Stockholm 1912* (translated by Edward Adams-Ray) (Stockholm, 1913), p. 564.
50 See ibid., p. 565, and Wallechinsky, *Olympics*, pp. 239–63.
51 Baron de Akerhielm to Sir Edward Grey, 26 Sept. 1911. PRO, FO 371/1226, 37804.
52 Minute, 30 Sept. 1911. Ibid.
53 Ray Jones, *Foreign Office*, p. 186.
54 Wallechinsky, *Olympics*, p. xv.
55 British Olympic Council, *Official Report*, p. 22.
56 Ibid., p. 27.
57 BOA, *The British Olympic Association*, p. 33; Wallechinsky, *Olympics*, p. xiii.
58 British Olympic Council, *Aims and Objects of the Olympic Games Fund* (London, undated), p. 3.
59 Ibid., p. 37.
60 Quoted in ibid., p. 7.
61 War Office to Foreign Office, 10 March 1914. PRO FO 371/1988, 10799.
62 Minute, 11 March 1914. Ibid.
63 Undated minute. Ibid.
64 Sir Edward Grey to Sir Edward Goschen, 16 March 1914. Ibid.
65 Sir Edward Goschen to Sir Edward Grey, 17 April 1914. Ibid., 17138.
66 Theodore Cook to Sir Edward Grey, 15 May 1914. Ibid., 22388.
67 Sir Eyre Crowe to Theodore Cook, 21 May 1914. Ibid.

68 Theodore Cook to Robert Vansittart, 2 June 1914. PRO, FO 371/2186, 24954.
69 Theodore Cook, 'Short Memorandum of the Olympic Movement', in ibid.
70 Theodore Cook, 'Olympic Games – Recommendations'. Ibid.
71 Edward Parkes, memorandum, 6 June 1914. Ibid.
72 Robert Vansittart to Sir Eyre Crowe, 8 June 1914. Ibid.
73 Undated minute. Ibid.
74 Theodore Cook (ed.), 'Public Work and Public Duty', in *Kaiser, Krupp and Kultur* (London, 1915), p. 45.
75 John Rodda, 'Berlin (Cancelled) 1916', in Killanin and Rodda (eds), *Olympic Games*, p. 73.
76 Sir Theodore Cook to Lord Desborough, 21 May 1919. HCRO, D/ERv C807/1.
77 PRO, FO 371/3647.
78 Minute, 10 May 1920. PRO, FO 371/3647, 196763.
79 BOA, *The British Olympic Association*, p. 11.

Chapter 12

Sportsmen and the deadly game

Derek Birley

> The river of death has brimmed his banks,
> And England's far, and honour a name;
> But the voice of a schoolboy rallies the ranks:
> 'Play up! play up! and play the game!'
>
> H.J. Newbolt, 'Vitaï Lampada'

Sir Henry Newbolt's 'Vitaï Lampada' was written in 1898 as Kitchener was crushing the Khalifa at Omdurman and calling the French bluff at Fashoda. Four years later Rudyard Kipling challenged Newbolt's assumption that ball games were a suitable preparation for the heroic defence of Empire. England, he believed, had not learned the lesson of the Boer War. The nation's honour had been saved, but only after much humiliation and by 'a remnant' of the lower orders. The pampered élite who had led so abysmally had afterwards returned to their pastimes, content to while away the hours watching 'the flannelled fools at the wicket or the muddied oafs at the goals'. What would they do, Kipling asked, when the real test came and they had to confront Germany:

> Will ye pitch some white pavilion and hastily even the odds
> With nets and hoops and mallets, with rackets and balls and rods?[1]

This essay attempts to answer that question.

I

Kipling was not alone in regarding the confrontation with Germany as inevitable. The First World War was the outcome of ancient power-struggles that could only be resolved by war. The assassination of Archduke Franz Ferdinand at Sarajevo

Originally published in *The British Journal of Sports History*, 1986, 3(3), pp. 288–310. http://www.tandf.co.uk/journals

in June 1914 expressed the determination of the Pan-Slavonic movement to resist Austro-Hungarian imperialism. The Austrians had to teach the perpetrators a lesson. In turn Russia had to protect the Slavs against the common enemy. It also had to defend its new protégé, Turkey, against Austria's ally, Germany. France was Germany's historic enemy in the West. And Britain was the partner of France and Russia.

Britain also had emotional and selfish reasons for fighting Germany. The rise of German naval power had provoked popular demand for more battleships – 'We want eight and we won't wait' was the slogan – and the Kaiser's support for the Boers had been bitterly resented. Many commercial and industrial interests also saw war against Germany as a way of eliminating competition. Even the rising Labour Party, though generally pacifist, had its belligerents, such as the strongly anti-German Robert Blatchford.

Nevertheless the war came as a surprise. No-one planned it. The immediate causes were, it seemed, accidental. 'Statesmen miscalculated', as A.J.P. Taylor put it. 'They used the instruments of craft and threat which had proved effective on previous occasions. This time things went wrong.'[2] Russia mobilized as a precautionary measure, Germany declared war on Russia, and, according to its long-standing strategy of defeating the western enemy first in the event of war, on France. There seemed at first no reason for Britain to become involved. 'To hell with Servia!' was the verdict of the popular magazine *John Bull*. But when Germany demanded free passage through Belgium Britain could not stand aloof.

For the public the surprise was all the greater because the news broke over the August Bank Holiday Weekend. Despite the shock, the declaration of war was a popular decision. Thousands gathered in Trafalgar Square and Whitehall, singing patriotic songs, waving flags and cheering. Sportsmen were among the first to cheer and to rush to join the colours. Their eagerness was sharpened by the general belief that the war would not last more than a few weeks.

II

Misconceptions about how long the war would last helped to widen the gulf between the governing bodies of amateur and professional sport. Hockey, lacrosse, rugby union, golf and lawn tennis immediately suspended their competitions, assuming that the war would be but a brief interruption. The governing bodies of sports into which professionalism had penetrated – racing, soccer, rugby league, even cricket – which also believed the emergency would soon be over, saw it as their duty to conduct business as usual.

The strange mixture of chivalric attitudes and modern realities was illustrated by the impact of the war on the Davis Cup. Norman Brookes, the Australian Wimbledon champion, and A.F. Wilding, of Cambridge University and New Zealand, were playing the German pair, O. Froitzheim and O. Kreuzer, in Pittsburgh before a strongly pro-German crowd. Froitzheim and Kreuzer had said they would abandon the game at once if war was declared. The president of the Pittsburgh Club, anxious to safeguard the match, cut off the telephones and kept out the press, suppressing the news until the game was over. The Germans left at once, but the delay proved disastrous: a British warship intercepted their boat and landed them at Gibraltar whence they were sent to England and interned.[3] Commander Hillyard, Secretary of the All-England Club, was highly surprised when shortly afterwards he received a letter from Froitzheim seeking help in securing his release on the grounds that it was unsporting to prevent him fighting for his country. Hillyard afterwards recalled:

> In those days, before our eyes were opened to the sort of antagonists we were up against, there was not that intense bitterness against Germany that afterwards developed...I had no particular animosity against the Hun, that came later...So I answered in a half chaffing way that, in the first place, he entirely over-rated what influence I possessed; and in the second, if I had any, I should certainly use it to keep him well-guarded until peace was declared, on the grounds that lawn tennis players of his class were so exceedingly rare that we couldn't afford to lose one, not even a German![4]

Hillyard's pleasantries reflected the common view that the war would be over by Christmas. For thinking otherwise, Kitchener, Secretary of State for War, was considered a Jeremiah. Popular opinion decreed that a decisive sea-battle would quickly settle the matter. This may have been correct, but the German navy remained circumspectly in port and declined to put it to the test.

The naval stalemate was frustrating, but not lethal. On land it was a different story. No-one had bargained for the deadly efficiency of modern armaments. Trench warfare and barbed wire became the backdrop to prolonged and wholesale slaughter. By October 1914, the British Expeditionary Force, under the nondescript leadership of Sir John French at Mons and Ypres, had lost a tenth of its members. Naval intervention in 1915 – a diversionary assault in the Dardanelles – not only failed to break the deadlock on the Western front, but added another land-based stalemate, Gallipoli, to that of Flanders.

The Continental Powers Britain faced had substantial conscripted armies. With the declaration of war came a fervent, patriotic response in Britain to the call for volunteers. 'Your Country Needs You!' declared the posters, under Kitchener's portrait with its heavy moustache and pointing finger. Half a million men joined up in the first month; a hundred thousand followed each month for the next year and a half. They were Kiplingesque heroes. Any ideas of romantic glory soon gave way to resignation. Tommy Atkins dug in. When he marched, he sang songs about Charlie Chaplin. Chaplin was much criticized by superior folk for shirking in America, but for the troops he epitomized the little man, like themselves, standing up for their rights.

After three unsuccessful battles, Sir John French was complaining of the shortage not of manpower but munitions. The volunteers were too numerous to be properly absorbed and trained, and arming them was even further beyond the competence of the authorities. The newspapers, in which Alfred Harmsworth, Lord Northcliffe, was the chorus-leader, were shrill in their criticism of the 'shells scandal'. Kitchener's old-fashioned outlook and the Liberal government's *laissez-faire* approach were equally to blame. Public opinion demanded action. Yet the government, under Asquith – 'unshakeable as a rock, and, like a rock, incapable of movement'[5] – stayed faithful to the pre-war principles of free enterprise in manufacture and gentlemanly compartmentalization in government.

The likely effects of a glut of manpower and a shortage of shells were not immediately apparent to enthusiastic armchair patriots. The Earl of Lonsdale, for example, saw it as his duty to out-do Kitchener and the rest in recruiting volunteers. The war was a new sporting occasion that tickled his jaded palate. The Kaiser's bust remained on his piano, even if Germany was now an opponent to be knocked out. He demonstrated his patriotism in neo-feudal fashion with a personal recruitment campaign, issuing thousands of gaudy posters which asked:

> Are you a man
> or
> Are you a mouse?
> Are you a man who will forever be handed down to posterity as a Gallant
>   Patriot?
> or
> Are you to be handed down to posterity as a rotter and a coward?[6]

Many deplored this crude intervention. The more sensitive remonstrated on principle: it was 'easy to recline in an armchair after a seven-course dinner and urge your dependants to fight' complained one outraged critic. The War Office objected on pragmatic grounds: 'Stop repeat stop collecting recruits,' they telegraphed. The recruits poured in nevertheless and Lonsdale cared nothing for the plans of the War Office. For one thing his old rival, Lord Stanley, soon to be Earl of Derby, was Director of Recruiting.[7] Lonsdale was temporarily diverted by an assignment dear to his heart, touring the remount depôts to report on the plight of the horses which was giving rise to serious concern. But at the battle of the Somme, the great bloodbath of 1916, the Lonsdale Battalion moved into action singing, to the tune of 'John Peel':

> D'ye ken Lord Lonsdale, that sportsman true?
> D'ye ken his charger of chestnut hue?
> D'ye ken that battalion of Cumberland blue
> Who will march to Berlin in the morning?

Most marched to their death. Of 28 officers and 800 men, only three officers and 280 men survived.

III

'With astonishing virtuosity', commented A.J.P. Taylor, 'the British Army grew from 200,000 to five million men and kept its antiquated class-structure inviolate.'[8] As he pointed out, the writers who emerged from the war, and whose imprint was put on later conceptions, were almost all officers. The memorials of the rank-and-file were in their songs, often derived from music-hall successes, to which they put their own words. The lasting image of the private soldier, viewed with affectionate contempt, was 'Ol' Bill', a cartoon character created by Bruce Bairnsfather – himself an officer. Bill's utterance of late 1915, in a shell-hole with mud and water up to his waist, 'Well, if you knows of a better 'ole, go to it!' became the most famous catchphrase of the war, and was regarded as the distillation of the fighting spirit of Britain's first mass army.

This plebian sang-froid was seen as a response to nobler, officer-class ideals. Newbolt's philosophy was being re-interpreted by the young officers whose fate it was to put it into practice. Rupert Brooke's pre-sacrificial offering in 1914 was

> If I should die, think only this of me:
> That there's some corner of a foreign field
> That is forever England.[9]

Julian Grenfell's, the following year, was

> And he is dead who will not fight
> And who dies fighting has increase.[10]

Brooke had played cricket and football at Rugby. Grenfell, a fine allround athlete at Eton, rowed and boxed for his Oxford college. Both lost their lives in 1915.

The schools' sorrow, as their finest products made the supreme sacrifice, was offset by pride. A grieving master, in 1915, offered this consolation to one dead boy,

> Aye, Marlborough knows you played the game,
> Dying you set the gem on her.

And he recalled

> The merry games we played together
> The old squash court, the shine, the rai…

Another victim was told,

> And now you've played a grimmer game;
> Old England called – you heard and came
> To shot and shell, to fire and flame.

A third invoked this tribute:

> Cricket and Hockey, Rackets, Fives –
> Aye, you were the master of them all....
> And now you've played your noblest game
> And now you've won your grandest Blue.[11]

For the Edwardian public schools leadership and sporting prowess were synonymous. Perhaps the rugger men best exemplified how readily the assumed connection was translated into death-and-glory leadership on the battlefield. Nine days after war was declared a Rugby Football Union circular urged all players to join up. National, county and club games were cancelled for the duration. The archetypal hero was Edgar Mobbs of Bedford Modern School, Northampton and England. Thirty-two when war broke out, he was refused a commission. Undaunted, by 14 September 1914 he had raised his own company of 250 sportsmen for the Northamptonshire Regiment. Beginning as a sergeant, by April 1916 Mobbs was in command of his own battalion. He was renowned for his method of leading an attack – booting a rugger ball into No-Man's land and following it up.

Edgar Mobbs was wounded twice and awarded the DSO before losing his life at Zillebeke on 29 July 1917.[12] He was one of 26 English rugby internationals killed in the war. No fewer than nine of the Scotland XV who took the field against Ireland in 1913 died in France, while eight Irish internationals fell in the British cause.

Less spectacularly, but with equal social significance, the rugger men's female equivalents were winning their spurs. Few members of the All-England Women's Hockey Association had been associated with the suffragist cause. In September, 1914, they had suspended county, territorial and international matches, but – no doubt believing the war would not last long – had urged clubs to keep together and carry out fixtures if they could. By 1915, *The Hockey Field*, reduced to four pages a month, was asking 'all able-bodied women who are not engaged in war work of real importance to consider whether they are willing to take up work on the land for the duration of the war'. Women's contribution to the war effort, increasingly needed and valued, helped earn them political recognition once it was over.

IV

In contrast with these intimations of the future there were powerful reminders of the past. The Earl of Lonsdale's brand of armchair warriorship represented an earlier tradition than that of Newbolt. Hunting men were, of course, among the first to volunteer – witness Siegfried Sassoon's George Sherston and his friends.[13] The squire class suffered heavy losses. But because of the age, sex and social structure of the sport, in which farmers were becoming increasingly important, its adherents were convinced that it should carry on despite the war. Lonsdale was in no doubt as to his duty. When, in 1915, the Cottesmore, short of money, fodder for the horses and meat for the hounds, swallowed its pride and misgivings and asked Lonsdale to return as Master, he put his heart and soul into it. To critics he responded, 'What on earth are officers home from the front going to do with their time if there is no hunting for them?'[14]

This spirit – that of the Napoleonic wars – was also invoked by aristocratic supporters of the Turf when puritanical patriots suggested that the Jockey Club should abandon racing for the duration. Patriotism apart, race-meetings diverted railway services from vital war functions. At the very outbreak of war there had been no meetings for three weeks, because of transport problems. Meetings had been held at Haydock Park and Gatwick in the autumn but rail problems, the billeting of troops on racecourses, and, to some extent, local disapproval had led to cancellations at Kempton, Stockton, Hurst Park, York, Derby, Ayr and Newbury. Steeplechasing that winter was also affected by the departure of men and horses to the front.

The Jockey Club saw its duty clearly. Racing had to continue, it was argued in October 1914, not for 'those who go racing for amusement' but rather for the sake of the industry which sustained British bloodstock breeding. As well as 400 jockeys and apprentices there were thousands of stablemen and racecourse employees – gatemen, groundsmen, caterers. Some had enlisted on the understanding that jobs would be kept open for them. Racing ought to continue 'where local conditions will permit and where the feeling of the locality is not adverse to the meeting being held'.[15]

The middle-class public was not convinced. Tempting the lower orders from their work was bad enough in peace-time: now it was insupportable. Nor did every aristocrat share the Jockey Club's view. Early in 1915, a prominent member, the Duke of Portland, withdrew his horses from Epsom and Ascot because he believed it wrong to hold meetings associated with peace-time luxury and pleasure. Ascot was a particular bone of contention, a symbol to both sides. On 14 February, *The Times* racing correspondent assured readers that there was no truth in the rumours that the meeting was to be cancelled: 'Lord Churchill is already beginning the customary preparation'. However, on 4 March, a leading article announced:

> We are convinced that any attempt to hold the great popular racing festivals, such as Epsom, and, above all, Ascot, will make a deplorably bad impression upon our neighbours and lead to misconception in the country. We should like to see them abandoned altogether for this year. The Ascot meeting falls on a date when the war may be at its climax. Can it be seemly to hold it when millions of men, including great numbers of our own people, will be at death-grips?

The Tory MP, Henry Cust, a former editor of the *Pall Mall Gazette*, wrote to express his agreement:

> When many thousands of men have given their lives for their country, and while many more tens of thousands are following their high example,

and will be dying and suffering while the crowds cheer and lunch at Epsom, it is merely monstrous to celebrate the Great National Festival and Ascot etc with all their gay traditions and associations.

Lord Dunraven's comment was withering:

Ascot is a glorified garden-party with racing thrown in. It can be bracketed with Court Balls and functions of that character, and as these are postponed during the war there seems no reason why Ascot should be retained.

A retired colonel of artillery, Henry Knollys, asked whether in 1915 it was 'unreasonable to hope that . . . the upper classes of men and women will forbear from assembling in their tens of thousands . . . at Ascot, peacocking in their plumes and prattling their puerilities . . . .?' The vicar of Sunningdale provided a local view:

The Fourth Berkshire Regiment is expected to go to the Front. If racing takes place at Ascot, everyone will be spending money or making money or rushing about. But for months our interests have been much more wholesome. Golf and football have been nearly discarded . . . Why should we be thrown back into just the same rush for excitement and money as we had last year?

A second leader summing up the mounting opposition quoted a peer who asked whether it was decent 'to persevere in our two great yearly "bean-feasts" against a background of awful tragedy amid a vale of tears?', and the nervous philosopher, Frederick Harrison, doubted the wisdom or safety of gathering crowds when there might be Zeppelins overhead.

Against these arguments and sentiments the Jockey Club's supporters advanced the claims of history and morale. The fifth Earl of Rosebery, typically, while professing to wish to remain 'remote from controversy', appealed to precedent. 'Once before our country has been engaged in a "life and death" struggle at least as strenuous and desperate as this.' The Ascot Gold Cup had been run eight days before Wellington met Napoleon at Quatre Bras. 'Our ancestors', Rosebery averred, 'were no less chivalrous and humane than ourselves.' The Hon Frederick Lambton asked why racing was singled out for censure, pointing out that there were 34 theatrical advertisements in that day's *Times*. His brother-in-law, Sir Hedworth Meux, a non-combatant Admiral, observing that 'The best horses in the world and the prettiest women are to be seen on the Royal Heath', thought it too soon to talk of cancellation, since the war might be over before the summer. Less tendentiously and more relevantly, others argued that soldiers enjoyed a day at the races. *The Times*' racing correspondent reported on the significant amount of khaki at Gatwick. Lord Hamilton of Dalzell recalled the delight of the troops in the Boer War when the C-in-C had sent a signal announcing that the King's horse Diamond Jubilee had won the Derby. Most cogently of all, a wounded officer told the 'amiable and generally non-warlike faddists' to 'curse if you must' at the betting, drink, bookies, jockeys and trainers 'but please don't put the curses in our mouths'.

The Jockey Club meeting on 16 March 1915 was stormy. But after the recriminations, a compromise was announced. Ascot should be held but the social side should be curtailed – no Royal Enclosure, luncheon tents or special trains. The Ascot Stewards agreed to most of this, but decided to keep the Royal Enclosure with increased charges and to devote the proceeds to charity. As late as the beginning of May preparations for the June meeting continued.

With the casualty lists growing ever more enormous and public opinion thoroughly aroused, the Cabinet still did not rule against Ascot, though the Postmaster General informed the Jockey Club that to conserve manpower telegraphic facilities would be withdrawn. What finally impelled the government to action was further controversy about the effect on the railways. The Railway Executive, though ruling out cheap excursions, promised the Jockey Club to put on special trains if they could. As the protests increased *The Times* put out a third condemnatory leader:

> It is the business of the country to see that the movements of its fighting men are not inconvenienced or obstructed by the rush of race-course crowds...Racing still presents its saddening contrasts to the patriotism of those who have devoted themselves to the service of the country.

Parliamentary questions grew in volume and on 19 May 1915, the President of the Board of Trade at last intervened, asking the Jockey Club to suspend racing so as not to congest the railways. The Jockey Club was not finished yet, and offered a compromise: reluctantly to abandon Ascot, provided that in order to protect the bloodstock industry a few other race-meetings could be held. This was agreed – five additional meetings to be held at Newmarket and two at Newbury, another racing town – an arrangement which dismayed course authorities elsewhere, and saddened devotees of Ascot and Epsom, for it made Newmarket more important than ever. On 15 June 1915, the seven races attracted no fewer than 214 runners. The Turf became more exclusive than ever because only the best horses could hope to win and so justify being kept in training. Racecourse authorities on the suspended list were the worst affected, since they had to continue to meet overheads. Among the reported sacrifices was that of the Epsom authorities who sold most of their impressive collection of wines and spirits to help make ends meet.[16]

V

The controversy over racing was to flare up again several times, but the Turf escaped serious damage. Boxing also did well. The amateur side closed down completely, except in the Services, but the professionals, thanks to American neutrality and the protection of such as the Earl of Lonsdale, prospered. Jimmy Wilde, the tiny genius of the Welsh pit-heads and fairgrounds, first became world champion in 1916. This selective treatment was particularly irritating to many cricket enthusiasts, for, like soccer, their game was then in cold storage.

Contrary to what might have been expected by believers in cricket mythology, the county cricket season had not been immediately abandoned when war was declared. There were, of course, some instant volunteers. Mr A. Sharp of Leicestershire did not even wait for his second innings on that fateful Bank Holiday week-end before leaving to join his regiment. But the game against Northamptonshire continued, and for a few weeks, with odd exceptions, so did the whole programme. This greatly displeased W.G. Grace. On 27 August 1914, he wrote a strong letter to *The Sportsman* calling on eligible cricketers to enlist. A few days later the remaining fixtures were abandoned.

For some ageing and impecunious amateur cricketers volunteering for the Army was no great sacrifice. Archie Maclaren and Gilbert Jessop, both in their forties, were commissioned and took part in a successful recruiting campaign. C.B. Fry, a different sort of patriot, had been running the training ship *Mercury* since 1908. His friend, the Indian prince, Rantjitsinhji, demonstrated his intense loyalty to Crown and Empire by financial support and, before wounding himself in a shooting accident, by personal service. F.S. Jackson, who had seen active service in the Boer War, raised and commanded the 2nd/4th West Yorkshire Regiment.

The administration of MCC devolved upon the elderly Lord Harris, a veteran of the Boer War, P.F. Warner, combining the roles of secretary and staff captain at the War Office, and the President, Lord Hawke. Hawke had reached his mid-fifties without achieving recognition outside cricket. As President of Yorkshire CC, in war as in peace, Hawke remained dedicated to raising the moral tone of the professionals. At the beginning of the war, the county had informed all staff that they were required to serve the cause; patriotic involvement 'was made a strict condition of their continued employment'.[17] Little is known about how most professional cricketers actually spent the war: generally, only the names of those who made the supreme sacrifice are recorded in the annals. The examplar was Colin Blythe, of Kent and England, whose Test career was cut short by willing service and a noble death. Less inspiring was poor Frederick Percy Hardy, a Somerset player of moderate ability, who, as *Wisden* recorded, was 'found dead on the floor of a lavatory at King's Cross Station (GNR) on 9 March, 1916. His throat was cut and a blood-stained knife was by his side'. Private Hardy was known to have been deeply troubled at the thought of returning to the trenches and to have taken drink just before his suicide.

VI

The soccer authorities were less easily convinced than their cricketing counter-parts that the national cause would be best served by abandoning their programme. They had been criticised, in August 1914, for their decision to carry on with League fixtures but, for a while, in the atmosphere of a general expectation of an early victory, the criticism died down. By October, however, with the BEF in trouble, a clamour mounted in Press and Parliament for an end to it. *The Times*

which had urged all sportsmen to volunteer – 'All Varsity men, old Public School
Boys, men who are hardened to the soldier's life by the strenuous pursuit of sport,
should enlist at once' – was the natural vehicle for stern condemnation of the
professionals. On 7 November 1914, a letter to the editor, Geoffrey Dawson, from
the historian A.F. Pollard summed it up:

> Some of us who are debarred from enlisting by age or other disqualification
> feel shy of urging on others a duty to which we are not ourselves liable. But
> we now feel no compunction in saying what we think of causes which act as
> deterrents to duty; and we view with indignation and alarm the persistence
> of Association Football Clubs in doing their best for the enemy.
>
> We must, of course, discriminate. Football is an excellent thing, even in time
> of war. Armies and navies can only be maintained as long as the community
> fulfils its function of producing means for their support; and healthy recreation
> is essential for efficient production. A man may be doing his duty in other fields
> than the front. But there is no excuse for diverting from the front thousands of
> athletes in order to feast the eyes of inactive spectators who are either unfit to
> fight or unfit to be fought for…

The FA was embarrassed but also indignant. Many soccer players had been
among the first to join up. The FA itself had asked the clubs 'to place their grounds
at the disposal of the War Office on days other than match days, for use as Drill
grounds', and to permit well-known public men to address players and spectators
to urge them to join up. The clubs had responded well. Public volunteering by
prominent footballers was encouraged, and the crowds were invited to serve with
their favourites. A typical poster, under the somewhat infelicitous heading 'Do you
want to be a Chelsea Die-Hard?', went on to recommend:

> If so,
> join the 17th Battalion
> Middlesex Regiment,
> 'The Old Die-Hards',
> And follow the lead given
> by your favourite Football Players.[18]

The FA, on 28 November 1914, managed to get an article printed in *The Times*
putting forward its point of view, and claiming that 100,000 recruits had already
joined by way of football clubs. It was fighting a losing battle. A few days earlier a
headline in *The Times* had read 'One recruit at Arsenal match'. Another report told
of an emotional appeal by Colonel Burn MP, who had lost his own son in the first
few weeks of the war, which had fallen on deaf ears. The middle-class public was not
to be gainsaid. Why should soccer clubs behave this way? Professionalism seemed the
obvious answer. A correspondent to *The Times* on 25 November spoke for many.

> British sports and British games have done our race a service which other
> nations have emulated too late and freely acknowledge on the field to-day.

Except, however, in this one solitary instance of professional football, they have long since fallen into their proper places as a pastime and a training, not a business or a trade.

The question was becoming academic, because of falling attendances. While MPs debated punitive measures (such as charging double fare for civilian football supporters on the railway or a swingeing entertainments tax) the public decided the issue for themselves. Were it not for the contracts signed with the players which lasted to the end of April 1915, the Football League, because of dwindling gates, by late 1914 would readily have ended the programme. However low the attendances, the League had to collect some money if it was to pay players' wages.

In the fervour of war the debate turned essentially on the degree of patriotism evinced by the various classes. Soccer's defenders argued that the declining crowds were themselves evidence of the game's basic soundness. Where else had the crowds gone but to the front? So, too, the players, for nearly half the 5,000 professionals were already at the front. Most of the rest were married. Were there not single men in other sports still hanging back? If racecourses, golf-links, theatres, music-halls, picture palaces and the like would close then a group of London soccer clubs offered to close their grounds.

The *Athletic News*, a Manchester publication that had risen to prominence along with professional football, took strong exception to the class bias of the pressure to end the Football League programme:

> The whole agitation is nothing less than an attempt by the classes to stop the recreation on one day a week of the masses... What do they care for the poor man's sport? The poor are giving their lives for this country in thousands... There are those who could bear arms, but have to stay at home and work for the Army's requirements and the country's needs. These should, according to a small clique of virulent snobs, be deprived of the one distraction they have had for over thirty years.[19]

There was more to the agitation against League Football than class. Much of the indignation was moral. It stemmed from and was directed at all social classes indiscriminately. Sandwich boards which once had carried religious messages to the sporting crowds now asked them, 'Are you forgetting that there is a war on?' Frederick Charrington, who gave up a brewing fortune to fight for temperance and Christianity, was a particular enemy of war-time sport. The Rev. Spencer H. Elliott denounced gambling in a war-time pamphlet:

> The war found us with forty thousand bookmakers in our country with an annual turnover of at least eighty millions. The law did not touch them. Football coupons flooded the country, offering odds that were utterly unfair, and working men, women, lads, and even girls emptied their pockets into those of anonymous scoundrels.[20]

In 1915, as the death-toll mounted, patriotic opinion hardened. Even private recreation was suspect. Hard tennis courts were widely suspected by the nervously patriotic to be gun emplacements prepared for German invaders. The Oval authorities agreed to put up practice nets for the members of Surrey CCC but expected them to be little used, for those who took a net might be jeered at 'by the men on tram-cars'.[21] Only a few inter-Service and charity games were played. The metropolitan daily press no longer published accounts of League football matches, providing readers with scores only. Attendances at matches continued to fall; more and more players joined up; railway travel became difficult. By April 1915, with players' contracts due for renewal, the League had had enough. Announcing its decision to cancel the following year's programme, the hope was expressed 'that every eligible young man will find in the service of the nation a higher call than in playing football'.[22]

The last big game, the Football Association Cup Final, was played at Old Trafford, 24 April 1915. When Sheffield United beat Chelsea a columnist of the *Sheffield Daily Telegraph* declared that it was a disgrace to the City. Though 2,000 fans met the Sheffield team at the station, there was no civic reception. Lord Derby had spoken for the nation when he told the players, after presenting them with the cup: 'You have played with one another and against one another for the Cup; play with one another for England now'.[23]

Yet soccer did not altogether close down. The enthusiasm and determination of individuals meant that many clubs kept going. There were charity matches, friendlies, also regional competitions, with players on leave from the Services or munition-work turning out for their nearest club. What became abundantly clear, even to the critics, was that soccer was the soldiers' game. In the autumn of 1915, the men of the First Battalion the 18th London Regiment went into battle at Loos with a football at their feet.

The other professional football game, Rugby League, provides a similar if sadder story. The authorities were caught on the wrong foot by the sudden declaration of war. The British tourists returning from Australia after the bruising battle known as Rorke's Drift found the heroes' welcome they expected overshadowed by events. Having, like the Football League, contracts to honour, the Northern Union decided to carry on. As with soccer, there was pressure to stop at once. The Secretary of the Northern Union stated that 'saving King and Country is more important than winning medals on the football field'. The Union's Management Committee, however, were inclined to believe that the game was a valuable aid to morale, both for servicemen on leave and munition-workers.

Like soccer's, Rugby League's crowds began to dwindle as the casualty lists lengthened. As gambling, not surprisingly, was encouraged by the war, those professional sports, like racing and boxing, in which betting played a part, continued, while football and cricket were suspended. Professional athletics is a good example. 'Pedestrianism', as it was called, flourished while the parent football clubs which sponsored many meetings were forced to close down. Pontypridd alone among the major pedestrian centres ceased operations. The leading British sprinter, Willie Applegarth, for his first professional engagement in November 1914, against the Australian Jack Donaldson, was sponsored for £300 by Broughton Rangers RFC.

Applegarth never appeared at Powderhall, the main centre for professional athletics, basically because the promoters refused to pay him appearance money. Powderhall thrived despite Applegarth's absence, with weekly pedestrian and dog-racing meetings. At the New Year Gala, 1915, more than 23,000 spectators attended despite heavy rain and sleet. Donaldson was the star attraction. When he and Applegarth met again on 10 April at Salford RFC's ground, the small crowd that turned up presumably reflected the hostility the Northern Union Clubs were attracting. Nevertheless, later that year, the Victoria Grounds, Newcastle, drew a record gate for their annual Christmas £100 handicap.

The Northern Union had no hope of continuing after the spring of 1915. The 1914–15 season petered out dismally, ending on a sour note. The Challenge Cup Final, before a modest crowd, almost did not take place. The St Helen's players went on strike just before the kick-off for more money. In June 1915, announcing that there would be no more rugby for the duration, the Management Committee indicated that the clubs could not afford to pay the players. The game continued semi-officially with local competitions. The Yorkshire clubs decided to pay their players half a crown (12½ p) 'tea-money' and the Lancashire clubs followed suit. No-one would have bet heavily on Rugby League surviving the war. Runcorn, one of the founder members went out of existence, while Oldham, Broughton Rangers and Wigan, had to sell their grandstands. Only representative matches, played for charity, kept the flickering hope for the game's future alive.

VII

In 1914, the belief that the war would be of short duration had been a delusion common to Germans as well as British. The German Olympic Committee, for instance, had seen no reason to withdraw its application to hold the 1916 Games in Berlin. But when Baron Pierre de Coubertin, the President of the International Olympic Committee, even at the eleventh hour, refused to consider alternatives to Germany, like neutral America or Scandinavia, this was seen as evidence of Coubertin's irrational pursuit of starry-eyed ideals. He was 'deceiving himself and seeking to salvage the fragments of his work', wrote one of his relations. The British saw evidence of something more sinister. Theodore Cooke, a British delegate to the International Olympic Committee, resigned when Coubertin objected to a motion designed to expel the Germans from various committees.[24]

A new urgency vitalised the British war effort. In 1915, Kitchener's conservatism regarding armaments had been circumvented by the creation of a Ministry of Munitions under Lloyd George. The minister's approach – which owed nothing to public schools – offered industry a potent mixture of cash, cajolery and compulsion. The implications, not only for the conduct of the war but for the nature of post-war industry and society were to prove profound. In its lifetime, the new ministry disbursed two thousand million pounds sterling and set up 218 large and 20,000 small factories. Its basic method – offering manufacturers production costs while allowing them 'a reasonable profit' – was inflationary. It bred a contingent of war profiteers, many of them afterwards grateful political supporters of Lloyd George. But it worked.

This unprecedented government intervention was highly significant in British industrial affairs generally. Incentives and controls were introduced. The main instrument of control was the Defence of the Realm Act[25] which operated through materials requisitioning. It also attempted, less successfully, to interfere in the control of the movement of labour. Strikes and threat of strikes, however, obliged Lloyd George to turn from compulsion to persuasion. The trade unions were offered higher wages, in return for the job being done, a shorter standard week and plenty of overtime. These wartime measures, first introduced in munitions factories, subsequently spread throughout industry generally.

By the end of 1915 there was some prospect of weapons supply matching demand. Press attention had meanwhile turned from the munitions scandal to that of the shirkers, allegedly 650,000 strong, who were avoiding war service. A sharp debate preceded the historic decision to introduce conscription for single men.[26] That old values were not entirely lost was demonstrated by the behind-the-scenes debate concerning racehorse breeding. Colonel Hall-Walker had decided to give up his stud at Tully in Ireland and his training stables at Russley Park. He offered the government his bloodstock for nothing if they would buy both establishments. The justification for such overt government involvement in trade was the importance of bloodstock for the Army. Hall-Walker's offer, as he described it, 'met with some difficulties in departmental etiquette'. On the eve of the projected sale, the Ministry of Agriculture won the prize. The establishments cost £47,625 and £18,000 respectively. But the price was less important than the principle. Private breeders, whose importance to the national economy had been impressed upon the government in the earlier debate about the continuance of horse-racing in wartime, naturally were wary about subsidized competition and sceptical about the government's ability to run a stud. Nevertheless, the *Bloodstock Breeders Review*, January 1916, took a charitable and optimistic line:

> We feel sure that if the stud is skilfully managed with a single eye to the purpose it has to serve, is not hampered by restrictions of the red tape order to which governments are partial, and is generously endowed with funds, it has a great and beneficial future.

It was announced that the Earl of Lonsdale, not hitherto famous in racing circles, was to lease the stables and the yearlings. This doubtless reassured those fearful of bureaucracy.

While the Germans and the French fought the bloody battle of Verdun in the spring of 1916, the Jockey Club negotiated an extended programme of racing for the summer. Meetings were promised at Gatwick, Lingfield and Windsor in addition to those at Newmarket and Newbury. Although the north, where most of the munitions factories were, was excluded, and despite an entertainments tax, the deal was considered pretty favourable.

The Nationalist Easter rising in Dublin stirred the government to patriotic reaction. Among the leaders of the Irish Volunteers who seized the General Post Office were many Gaelic footballers. The Nationalist leader, Redmond, hoping to gain credit towards Home Rule, had offered the services of the Volunteers to Britain. Kitchener, though accepting the Ulster Volunteers, had rejected the southerners' overtures. The Easter rising seemed a flash in the pan. Irish rebel plans to secure German backing through the former British Consul in Berlin, Sir Roger Casement, miscarried. The rebellion was put down. Except in Ireland, universal conscription was now introduced. Prime Minister Asquith shirked negotiating Home Rule as the price of peace on Britain's vulnerable western flank. Lloyd George took on the task. The protracted negotiations meant that he could not visit Russia with Kitchener as had been planned. Kitchener's ship, *HMS Hampshire*, was sunk and Lloyd George succeeded as Secretary of State for War. Things were at a low ebb: the Dardanelles expedition had been abandoned in January; at the end of May the Battle of Jutland destroyed the belief that the British Navy could win the war in one swift, decisive action. Three days after Lloyd George took office came the disaster of the Somme. By November 1916, the British Army had lost 420,000 men and the Allied Expeditionary Force had practically ceased to exist. The Somme was the final disenchantment for many who had begun the war with romantic ideals.[27]

A major cause of the heavy casualties at the Somme was General Sir Douglas Haig's persistence in sending wave after wave of infantry to try to clear a way for the cavalry. Many thousands of horses were kept in France waiting for action that never materialized, and throughout the war 'hunting was officially recognised by the Government as being of paramount importance in maintaining the horse supply'.[28] The racing interests' attempts to command similar support met with varying success. At the last moment the 1916 summer programme was restricted to Newmarket, a serious setback both for the Jockey Club and the racing industry.

The bookmakers displayed characteristic ingenuity during these hard times, encouraged by the public seeking to use their services wherever and whenever it could. Powderhall did well both in pedestrianism and dog-racing. It was noticeable during 1916 that pedestrian meetings generally drew exceptional numbers of both spectators and competitors, especially from the North of England, which had been deprived of its racing, soccer and Rugby League.[29] Boxing was another sport that in 1916 attracted crowds and bookmakers wherever it was held. Jimmy Wilde against Tancy Lee and Joe Symonds; Ted 'Kid' Lewis against the American Jack Britton; Johnny Basham against Johnny Summers; Freddy Welsh against the Americans Ad Walgast and Benny Leonard were some of the fights that were talking points of the war years.[30]

When Lloyd George had become Prime Minister in December 1916, his recon-structed War Cabinet was supposed to exercise greater control over the generals and admirals. That it failed to do so was largely because the service ministers, excluded from the Cabinet, out of resentment tended to support the brasshats, encouraging them to become even more independent-minded and defiant than ever. Thus it was the home front ministries – shipping, labour, national service and food – that came under tighter control.

The hunting fraternity was finding life increasingly difficult, Fodder was hard to come by, as was food for the hounds. During the winter packs were drastically reduced in size (by an average of some 40 per cent), while for the rest of the war hunting was generally limited in scope. Many packs were rescued by women Masters. At the Atherstone, Mrs Inge (Mrs Oakfield of Sassoon's *Memoirs*) was a natural choice to follow in her father's and her late husband's footsteps. A brilliant horsewoman, she was the only person who could handle Captain Harry Townshend, a Hunt Secretary of the Old-School, exercising 'semi-benevolent tyranny'. He regarded Mrs Inge as 'a splendid little woman'. Money was usually not a major problem. Although 'many hunting people suffered from increased income tax and rise in prices', subscriptions were readily paid and 'in some favoured countries money was forthcoming from those who had done well finan-cially during the war period'. These included farmers as well as industrialists. Fields were generally smaller, but in some areas were very well sustained by 'farm-ers, veterans of either sex and children', while the 'able-bodied element was almost entirely supplied by officers or yeomanry troopers on leave'.[31]

The increased prominence of farmers presented social problems in some areas. Non-hunting farmers were a bigger nuisance than ever, not only in their patriotic concentration on cereal crops, but in declining to take down wire on the grounds of shortage of labour. Labour was generally a problem: hunt servants had joined up in great numbers, as had game-keepers, and it was hard to find able-bodied veterans willing to turn out at night to stop up earths. Shortage of petrol limited the use of motor vans to visit outlying districts, and hunting specials were a thing of the past. Worst of all, though, was the shortage of food. Many more hounds had to be put down as the war went on. Horses either did not get enough forage or had to put up with inferior hay and oats.

In February 1917, the German U-Boats having resumed unrestricted attacks on shipping, the Jockey Club was told that racing must end altogether after the first spring meeting at Newmarket. There were still some two thousand horses in training and though the actual amount of fodder needed to support them was not critical, the principle – of not risking men's lives in order to feed race-horses – was. Even so, powerful voices were raised against the government's decision. The Thoroughbred Breeders' Association, led by Lord D'Abernon, pointed out that already the price of yearlings had dropped by 60 per cent, and the total income of the industry by between seven and eight million pounds sterling. The end of racing would be the last straw. Leading Jockey Club members – Lords Jersey, Durham, Crewe and Rosebery and not least, Lord Derby the War Minister – rallied to the call. Outside supporters ranged from Lord Curzon, a member of the War Cabinet, to Horatio Bottomley, demagogue, fund-raiser, horse-owner and editor of *John Bull*. The government gave in. Not only did it allow 40 days' racing, but left it to the Jockey Club to fix the venues, subject only to approval by the War Office, Board of Trade and Ministry of Munitions. So Manchester, Stockton and Ayr got meetings as well as the southern courses.

VIII

Such selective treatment troubled hitherto docile enthusiasts for other sports. At the end of the 1917 season the editor of *Wisden* flew a kite for the resumption of cricket. 'There can be no doubt', he wrote, 'that as regards the propriety of playing cricket in war-time there was a great change of feeling last summer. People realised that with public boxing carried on to an extent not heard of before, and professional billiard matches played in the hottest weather, there was something illogical not to say absurd, in placing a ban on cricket.' He pointed out that crick-eters, unlike racing men, had no quarrel with authority. They had shut down their programme voluntarily and had every moral right to resume it. By this time people had 'come to regard the nightmare of war as a normal condition and cricket was felt to be as legitimate as any other recreation'.

Although the county championship had been suspended, and was unlikely to be resumed (a consequence in part of the public school spirit of its administrators and in part of its three-day pattern), cricket was enjoying a boom in the North of England with the Bradford League as its focal point. Early in the war the maver-ick S.F. Barnes had been signed by the Saltaire club and gates of thousands had rewarded this enterprise. Other clubs followed suit. Soon all had their stars, including Jack Hobbs, who was in munitions work until he joined the Royal Flying Corps. Keighley, with so many professionals that some had to play in the second team, was strong enough to have beaten any county side. George Gunn, Frank Wooley, J.N. Crawford, Cecil Parkin, Percy Holmes and Schofield Haigh were among the dozens of famous players Fred Root played against when he was invalided out of the army in 1916.[32]

Soccer and Rugby League also continued, if in a muted, regional fashion, to provide outlets for the war-weary and the munitions workers. Professional athlet-ics, more dependent on individual stars, continued only with difficulty. With Applegarth in the Army, Donaldson and his fellow-Australian Mears were the mainstay. Veterans came out of retirement and soldiers on leave, munition workers and the militarily unfit made up the numbers. But fields were thin, even for the handicap events, and big matches virtually disappeared.

As the war news grew worse escape became more precious. The autumn of 1917 brought the protracted agony of the second battle of Ypres: 300,000 were killed in the mud of Passchendaele. Disenchantment was widespread. The contrast between the escapism at home, which took the place of earlier innocent enthusiasm, and the horrors of the trenches, was hard for some gallant officers to bear. Siegfried Sassoon, having won the Military Cross, lost faith altogether.

I'd like to see a tank come down the stalls,
Lurching to rag-time tunes or 'Home Sweet Home', –
And there'd be no more jokes in Music Halls.

The effect of the Newbolt philosophy was seen in the casualty rates: officers lost their lives in the proportion of three to one from the ranks. Wilfred Owen was prompted to ask,

What passing bells for these who die as cattle?
Only the monstrous anger of the guns
Only the shuttering rifles' rapid rattle
Can patter out their hasty orisons.

But at a Harrow War Memorial meeting in 1917, General Sir Horace Smith-Dorrian was reassuring about 'the magnificent public school spirit, and the fact that the best material for leading troops came from those who had public school training, of which such as important part consists of games and sports'. In an essay published that year F.B. Malin wrote, 'What virtues can we reasonably suppose to be developed by games? First I should put physical courage... That it has been bred in the sons of England is attested by the fields of Flanders and the beaches of Gallipoli'.[33] And, with unintentional irony, a young man who had distinguished himself both scholastically and athletically, just before he himself made the supreme sacrifice, wrote, 'this war has shown the training of the playing fields of the public schools and the Varsities to be quite as good as that of the classroom; nay, as good? Why, far better, if training for the path of duty is the ideal end of education'.[34]

IX

Nineteen-seventeen had been a bad year. America's entry to the war in April produced no early evidence of its involvement. In Russia the Tsar had been overthrown in March and by the autumn the new Bolshevik government was out of the war. At sea Lloyd George had himself to take over the Admiralty for a spell to initiate a convoy system to protect the merchant fleet. On land the mud of Passchendaele was emblematic of British fortunes. The new tank corps, from which much had been hoped, had proved useless in the mud. When, belatedly, Haig gave it a chance on suitable ground, the relief of the victory at Cambrai in November was short-lived for there were no infantry reserves, no plans, to follow it up. The Labour leadership had talks with the new Soviet Union and the Party divided over whether to join the international peace movement.

By 1918 enduring the war had come to be associated in some minds with the possibility of losing it. The decision to allow 80 days' racing was less a sign of confidence in approaching victory than a safety-valve for growing dissatisfaction. There were plots and counterplots among the generals against Lloyd George and eventually the Prime Minister took personal charge of the War Office. Allied generals and politicians had their own differences: President Harding had to over-rule General Pershing. International operations were used as a cloak for domestic power-struggles and disunity undermined the theoretical comparative growth in Allied strength. However, desperation caused by the offensive mounted by the Germans in March 1918 at last forced the Allies to combine and they found a stalwart commander in Marshal Foch of France. With every man needed at the Front conscription in Britain was advanced to the age of 50. The railways were busy again, and the Jockey Club not only lost its extra days' concession but was once more restricted to Newmarket. The sacrifice was worthwhile, and the Allied advance began in August. Haig had at last learned how to deploy his tanks, and, used in short, sharp bursts along the whole front with some semblance of Allied co-ordination, they proved a war-winning weapon. By November the war was over, surprising the public when it ended as it had done when it started.

Everyone agreed that the world could never be the same again. Viewed from to-day's perspectives, the changes were perhaps less radical than they seemed at the time. For many who had survived them, the years of trench warfare put the Newbolt Code into perspective. Newbolt himself, after long years of battle with the law and literature, had his first and nearest experience of war in service at the Admiralty. He was knighted in 1915, at a time when, as we have seen, his words sustained many in their sterner duty. If the full-blooded invocation of 'Vitaï Lampada' now rang somewhat hollow, there were the more restrained sentiments of 'Clifton Chapel':

> To set the cause above renown;
> To love the game beyond the prize;
> To honour, while you strike him down
> The foe that comes with fearless eyes;
> To count the life of battle good,
> And dear the land that gave you birth,
> But dearer yet the brotherhood
> That binds the brave of all the earth.

Some fighting men needed, even so, a protective coat of cynicism to help them cope not only with the enemy but with the platitudes and fatuities of big-wigs back at base. England, home and beauty was a different world, where different standards applied. In the soldiers' code 'the Seven Deadly Sins ... were venial, so long as a man was courageous and a reasonably trustworthy colleague'.[35]

One post-war comment on how 'Play up! play up! and play the game!' stood the test of trench warfare was R.C. Sherriff's play, *Journey's End*. Its central character was the young Captain Stanhope, who, having gone out to Flanders straight from school, had quickly risen to command a company, and had been in the trenches for a year without a break. During this time the dashing public-school cricket captain had been transformed.

'He's a long way the best company commander we've got,' one colleague commented. 'Oh, he's a good chap, I know,' said another. 'But I never did see a youngster put away the whisky he does.' Stanhope was now admired in his off-duty hours, not for his cricket but for his ability to drink a whole bottle of Scotch in one hour 14 minutes, pick out his hat and walk home. He had forgone his last leave, ashamed to show himself in his father's country vicarage.

Stanhope's decline from original Newboltian heights was underlined by the presence in his command of Osborne, a no-longer young public schoolmaster, calm, wise, gentle, a reader of *Alice in Wonderland*, and suitably modest about his past achievements as a nigger international. Osborne, a recent recruit to the trenches, was, if concerned about Stanhope, yet sensitive to his charisma – 'I love that fellow' – and aware of his duty: 'I'd go to hell with him'. His dedication to the cause was, by that stage of the war, March 1918, strained to the point of gentle social remonstrance: 'They do send some funny people over here nowadays'. He had distinct opinions about the type of replacement the company needed: 'I hope we're lucky and get a youngster straight from school. They're the type that do best'.

Melodramatically, the new man, Raleigh, proved to be all too good an example of what Osborne had in mind. He had recently left Stanhope's old school, following admiringly in his footsteps ('He was skipper of rugger at Banford and kept cricket for the eleven. A jolly good bat, too.'), to the extent of engineering a posting to his company. His fellow subalterns, Osborne apart, were not from the same top social drawer. Hibbert was neurotic, terrified, prepared to feign illness to avoid danger. Trotter, a jollier plebeian, was a fat vulgarian, well-intentioned but limited.

The emblems of Trotter's vulgarity – aitchlessness and crude pronunciation, such as 'dooty' – are part of the social comedy that gives point to the heroic intensity of Stanhope's ordeal. Such nuances of speech as a source of class snobbery were largely an Edwardian invention. In earlier times the way the Welsh and the Irish spoke had provided broad nationalist jokes, but English regional accents were not intrinsically seen as emblems of class. Tennyson and Gladstone, in Victorian days, had been university men but had unashamedly spoken in regional accents. Shaw's *Pygmalion* reflected the change that took place in the Edwardian era. The war, as Sherriff illustrated, focused attention on this. 'Temporary gentlemen', like Hibbert and Trotter, were allowed into the officer class 'for the duration'. Northern plebeian recruits, however, often encountered for the first time, in the accents of their officers, the exaggerated drawl and other affectations of public school and Varsity speech that had become the fashion.

One Edwardian Varsity affectation was the substitution of '-er' for the proper word-ending. Some such coinages, like 'brekker' for breakfast, percolated into the language of the imitative, aspirant classes, and thence, via the newspapers and journals, into the language generally. Others, like the vogue name at Oxford for the Prince of Wales (the future Edward VIII), 'the Pragger', were mere curiosities. The world of sport, more conservative than the real world from which it was an escape, retained the best examples. The generic term for football was originally 'footer'. P.G. Wodehouse in his early school stories used it to mean what later generations would call 'rugger' because that was the kind of football his school played. In the post-war world the power of the turnstiles and, in consequence, of the class that filled Association football grounds, undermined such assumptions. Football came to mean Association football, and 'footer', if it were used at all, would nowadays be thought by most people to mean the Association Code. So even the most élitist would need to say 'rugger', if he wanted to avoid being misunderstood. 'Soccer' not only survived, it became standard English.

The Education Act of 1918, though reduced in its effectiveness by economic stringency which led to over-large classes and the abandonment of the progressive notion of day continuation schools, was an acknowledgement of the debt Britain owed, in winning the war, to the working classes. Democracy, inch by inch and hand-in-hand with commercialism and similar political expediencies, began to erode the assumptions of class. Soccer, for good or ill, was, after all, the national game.

Notes

1 Rudyard Kipling, *The Lesson* (London, 1902).
2 A.J.P. Taylor, *The First World War* (London, 1963).
3 See E.C. Potter, *Kings of the Court* (New York, 1963) and *The Davis Cup* (New York, 1969).
4 G.W. Hillyard, *Forty Years of First Class Tennis* (London, 1924).
5 A.J.P. Taylor, *English History 1914–1945* (Oxford, 1965).
6 Douglas Sutherland, *The Yellow Earl* (London, 1965).
7 'I see Lord Derby has given a hundred acres of his park to be broken up for Food Production,' he wrote to his agent in 1916, 'but that is the sort of thing he would do as he is entirely out for advertisemen...' Before long Lonsdale was making a similar gesture at Lowther. By then Derby was War Minister. The 'Derby Scheme' in which men of military age attested their willingness to serve, was a prelude to conscription. Single men were supposed to be called up first from the list of volunteers, but in order to bring this about it proved necessary to turn to compulsion.
8 Taylor, op. cit.
9 Rupert Brooke, 'The Soldier', in Francis T. Palgrave, *The Golden Treasury* (London: Macmillan, 1955), p. 433.
10 'Into Battle' was written by the Great War poet Julian Grenfell and published in *The Times* on the same day as his death at the Front was announced. See Derek Birley, *Playing the Game in International Studies in the History of Sport*, series editor J.A. Mangan published by Manchester University Press in 1995, p. 62.
11 Poems by John Bain in *The Malburian*, printed in full in J.A. Mangan, *Athleticism in the Victorian and Edwardian Public School* (Cambridge, 1981).
12 His death is still celebrated by an annual memorial match between the Barbarians and East Midlands.
13 Siegfried Sassoon, *Memoirs of a Foxhunting Man* (London, 1928).
14 Sutherland, op. cit.

15   *Bloodstock Breeder's Review*.
16   Wray Vamplew, *The Turf* (London, 1976).
17   David Frith, *The Golden Age of Cricket* (London, 1981).
18   Quoted in James Walvin, *The People's Game* (London, 1975).
19   *Athletic News*, 7 December 1914.
20   Quoted, Arthur Marwick, *The Deluge* (London, 1965).
21   *Wisden, 1917*.
22   Quoted, Walvin, op. cit.
23   Ibid.
24   Marie-Therese Eyquem, 'The Founder of the Modern Games', in Lord Killanin and John Rodda (eds), *The Olympic Games* (London, 1976), p. 68.
25   Known for short as DORA, and caricatured in the popular press as an interfering female busybody.
26   See D. Hayes, *Conscription Conflict* (London, 1949).
27   See Z. Steiner, 'Views of War', in *Moirae*, Vol. V (1980).
28   *Baily's Hunting Directory, 1918–1920*.
29   David A. Jamieson, *Powderhall Grounds and Pedestrianism* (Edinburgh, 1943).
30   Serving soldiers could not fight for money, so when Jimmy Wilde fought Joe Conn in 1918 it was for a purse of cut diamonds.
31   *Baily's Hunting Directory*, 1918–1920.
32   John Arlott, *Jack Hobbs* (London, 1981), and Fred Root, *A Cricket Pro's Lot* (London, 1937).
33   A.C. Benson (ed.), *Cambridge Essays*. Quoted, Mangan, op. cit.
34   Paul Jones, *War Letters of a Public Schoolboy*. Quoted, Mangan, op. cit.
35   Robert Graves and Alan Hodge, *The Long Weekend* (London, 1940).

Epilogue: rounding things off

Sport and middle-class culture: some issues of representation and identity before 1940

John Lowerson

In 2001 a small, enterprising English company issued a compact disc of 17 Victorian and Edwardian sporting songs, borrowing Newbolt's hackneyed exhortation, 'Play the Game', as the title.[1] With the notable exception of William Johnson Cory's and Algernon Drummond's 'Eton Boating Song' of 1878, it is doubtful whether the other pieces included were known to any but, and probably not even to many of, the most dedicated of sports historians. Whether 'Little Tommy went a fishing' or 'Captain Webb, the Champion Swimmer', they fall into the broad category of what the music historian Derek Scott has studied as the preserve of 'The Singing Bourgeois', and certainly seem to have been amongst the more ephemeral of them.[2] One, 'Our Football Supper', was written specifically for the music hall stage, and its description of a drunken riot broken up by the police would have debarred it from much domestic performance. Most of the rest would probably have been sung by semi-professionals brought in to provide genteel amusement at the end of an annual meeting, smoker or club dinner, to reinforce the much-employed local newspaper cliché of the period, 'The meeting ended in harmony', that is with musical entertainment designed to foster good feeling as much as the sentiment itself. Indeed the performers on the disc itself, including the formidable concert partnership of Ian and Jennifer Partridge, with the distinctly restrained backing of the Song and Supper Club, offer a portrait in sound of a sporting gentility which would have been noticeably at odds with the well-lubricated and rarely harmonized singing one would have expected from the average male audience at such an event when they joined in their favourite pieces.

The value of much of the disc's material lies in its selection from a very wide range of sources and, it may seem odd to claim, in the banality of much of

Originally published in *The International Journal of the History of Sport*, 2004, 21(1), pp. 34–49.
http://www.tandf.co.uk/journals

the words. Take the last two verses of the lauding of Captain Webb's cross-channel swim:

> Brave Captain Webb has made his fame,
> He's England's pride and glory;
> And many will repeat his name,
> And tell the wondrous story.
> Of how he fought against the sea,
> And battled with the billows;
> For twenty-two long hours swam he
> To gain the Calais pillows.
> [....Chorus....]
> At Dawley Captain Webb was bred,
> His age was twenty seven;
> And when along the waves he sped,
> Was fourteen stone eleven.
> And now my song comes to a close
> And still from here to zero;
> No greater swimmer England knows,
> Than our great Shropshire hero.[3]

Knowing Webb's weight seems remarkably irrelevant, except perhaps to the tall or over-built, hoping for some chance of sporting achievement in contrast with their being 'calorifically challenged'. But J.A. Mangan and a host of followers have taught historians in the last two decades to recognize both the ways in which heroism is socially constructed, and the means by which the values of a supposedly hegemonic educational elite were transmitted.[4] Few who were there will forget the expressions on the largely foreign audience's faces when a present-day English headmaster/historian sang some of the songs written by his subject, Thring of Uppingham, in a lecture on British public-school traditions during a sports history conference in Berlin.[5] Beyond the amusement and reconstruction, however, lies a number of questions that perhaps should be addressed rather more by sports historians as the work develops. The strength of the studies which have followed on the examples of Mangan, Mason and Holt, working in a British context but with a careful sense of international similarities and comparisons, and noted by the more general political and social historian Ross McKibbin, has been to foster 'sports history' as a vibrant sub-discipline given frequently to academic introspection.[6] But it has also encouraged at times approaches which are so sport-centred, using it as a collecting bowl for wider phenomena, that its own place as a form of cultural production is often divorced from parallel developments except where they are held to illuminate a moment within sports history. Sport was not quite the universal that we have helped it to appear, and some of the ways in which it might be understood have yet to be influenced by the analysis of other contemporary issues. Perhaps the strongest area where there has been an interplay has been in understanding the political role of sport. But we need to think about other ways in which some of its importance might be understood and accept the possibility that there was a significant element of cultural subordination in its development. Sport was usually a servant to weightier matters.

Musical mixtures

It is still probably the case that, whenever a new general book on a country or period appears, its index is checked by sports historians to see what it has to say about their concerns and, most probably, whether it has used their work. There is a gratifying increase in such acknowledgements but there is less evidence to be found in many sports historians' indices and footnotes of a flow coming the other way, despite concerns with class, gender and so on. This is most noticeable in terms of parallel investigations where such issues as consumption and the development of cultural forms and artefacts are concerned, now a booming part of historical enquiry and offering some significant insights. Hence beginning this chapter with music, often used as a reinforcement by sporting innovators who were singularly dependent on existing cultural mechanisms which also played many of the roles with which sport is identified, offering parallels of organization and concern as well as a frequently beneficial symbiosis. The music historian Trevor Herbert's study of Welsh nationalism and the choral tradition, together with the rather more comprehensive analysis by Gareth Williams, best known to sports historians for his studies of Rugby Union, have reminded their readers that competitive choral singing in South Wales from the 1870s fulfilled many of the same purposes as the eventual Welsh adoption of the supposedly English public-school version of football.[7] Others, such as Christina Bashford, have emphasized the Victorian development of forms of public listening etiquette and informed understanding during concerts, rather like good crowd behaviour at a match.[8]

Probably the most significant, and frequently controversial, study of the more general values surrounding organized and regulated sports' emergence in the late-nineteenth and early-twentieth centuries has been the American historian Peter Gay's literally monumental analysis of cultural history, *The Bourgeois Experience, Victoria to Freud*. In most of his volumes, covering sexuality, literature and so on in a pan-European context, there is virtually no mention of sport. The exception is Volume III, appropriately called *The Cultivation of Hatred*, where sport appears in the analysis of gender roles but also has a short section of its own, which in its breadth and incisiveness remains one of the best pieces of sustained analysis of sport in terms of culture and class yet written, certainly not superseded by anything that has appeared since its first publication in 1994.[9] Whilst recognizing the many positive virtues attached to sport by its proponents, both contemporary and scholarly, Gay reminds us of its intended primary purpose as a prophylactic against the possibility of disorder, from which expectation much of the apparatus that has come to surround it, honorifics, music and so on, can really only be seen as a sweetener for a not always welcomed pill. He discusses both the role of *English* innovation (he clearly does not understand golf) in a world of cultural free trade, the parallels with war which it was supposed to prevent as well as prepare for, the inherent contradictions in the ways it was taken up, the dislike within and without England at the behaviour of late Victorian soccer crowds, and points to a perhaps surprising German peacefulness in athletic exercises (*vide* Christiane Eisenberg's recent work) as against the increasingly militaristic French adoption of sporting practices, as well as the practical limits of amateurism.[10] Perhaps his most challenging contribution, one largely ignored by sports historians so far, is to discuss the cultural significance of the referee/umpire figure: 'this majestic authority, stands as a commentary on human nature, one the Victorian well understood'.[11] Behind this there lies a model of cultural pessimism, expressed perhaps as a social version of the doctrine of original sin which stands at odds with so many notions of improvement *per se*, yet which fits quite appropriately the style and aims of many of Mangan's headmasters. How much 'hatred' was effectively embodied in sport, class, national and personal?

Locking the history of sport into such contexts often involves constructing chronological and national backgrounds, which are then allowed to stand at some distance from narrative and analysis. What this approach ignores is the frequently subaltern role of sport in reinforcing other cultural forms and activities, and its instrumental adoption into those, as well as its borrowing from them. When the British general Morton retired in 1898, after long service in India, his farewell speech identified the 'manly' virtues usually expected from cricket as better developed in a setting that many subsequent students would have found astonishing as well as positively frivolous. He was talking to the Simla Amateur Dramatic Society, possibly the most elite amateur theatrical and operatic group in the British Empire. It was founded from an informal base in 1887, lasting until the British withdrawal in 1947, and was made up largely of the Viceregal household, the senior military people and civil servants, as well as selected merchants and professionals who gathered in the leading hill resort for the long summer retreat to relative coolness. There were lesser copies in the other hill towns, Ootacamund ('Ootie'), and so on. Avoiding the masculine focus of so much sports propaganda, in a gender-inclusive recognition of the role of the amateur stage, he said:

> I can confidently state that my best friends have been made on the cricket field and on the stage. There is in both, but especially in the latter, a spirit of true and a strong feeling of mutual sympathy which bind more closely than is usual in the ordinary avocations of life, and I know of no better place or condition for enabling a judgement to be formed of the character and qualities of an individual than associations with him or her during rehearsals or performances.[12]

The club, and many lesser copies in the Asian parts of the British Empire, were essentially multi-functional associations in which theatre and music used sport as a bonding ancillary, providing a seasonal or year-round meeting place in which the multi-talented, or at least interested, amateur was supposed to replicate much of the quality of country and suburban life back in Britain. In the same way, some elite amateur theatre groups on the eastern seaboard of the United States, such as the Savoy Company of Philadelphia which grew out of a 'cricket club' and the Blue Hill Troupe of Manhattan, both avowedly Anglophile, used tennis and golf to provide offstage bonding, and extend the possibilities for what described itself, in the latter case, as 'the most exclusive and successful matrimonial bureau in New York'.[13]

Bodies like this, including the wide range of late nineteenth-century country clubs which flowered in the States, attracted members from groups who were often already involved in other sports clubs, usually leadership of similar social-ranking.[14] However important they were in the development of the boom sports of lawn tennis and golf, those activities were essentially secondary to their associational role; the provision of athletic and intellectual skills as well as arcane language only strengthened the primary purposes further. They were rarely the primary purpose itself. Where sports fans organized themselves into groups essentially for play, they were able to use models which had permeated much of British society for some centuries; provincial life as discussed by Peter Clark had a powerful associational culture into which sport merely slotted without effecting a major transformation.[15] What it did do, in parallel with many other recreational activities such as music, was to extend the numbers of such bodies enormously and, through limited liability formation, to provide a much greater financial security by using mechanisms designed for commercial entrepreneurs.[16]

Similar issues emerge when one considers the great class and cultural barrier which has attracted so many historians of sport, the amateur/professional divide which has spanned British sporting experiences for at least a century. It is so thoroughly treated in the literature that it would be redundant to repeat much of that here, but the issues, not least of the 'shamateur', appeared in other booming recreational activities about the same time. The tensions focused not just on the question of aesthetic sensibilities as against the possibilities of commercial corruption, but also on the quintessential interdependence between professional and amateur in skill development. This was a clear cultural issue in the development of amateur musical activity, both in terms of orchestral players and singers, whether soloists or chorus. Cyril Ehrlich's major study of the piano opened up the realization of the wide extent of musical literacy in late Victorian England: in the 30 years before 1911, according to the census, the number of teachers of music in England and Wales almost doubled to some 47,000.[17] Many players and teachers were female, and they experienced many of the tensions over public or even group participation in music-making that they found in sport, since the groups often overlapped. The problems as to what was a suitable musical instrument that did not threaten femininity, piano or strings rather than the 'masculine' woodwind, brass or percussion, were fought out in a specialist and general press, as well as in local associations, just as they were in sporting parallels. The American historian of musical culture and women, Paula Gillett, has identified similar problems about the use of professional musicians playing alongside amateurs in terms easily understood by any sports historian, those of instrumental artisans with skills but limited understanding mixing with sensitive aesthetes with a proper sense of perspective.[18] Whilst there were few attempts to introduce a musical version of the Henley Rules, there was considerable worry about the local musical versions of W.G. Grace who appeared as soloists for any oratorio choir or operatic society that would pay their 'expenses'. Just as in sport, the pressures on such bodies matched those of teams and clubs who needed to make their numbers up from what was often a rather limited local pool of ability. For music societies there was an even greater pressure than that faced by many sportsmen – the licensing and associated costs of most public musical performances were so great, that a paying audience was necessary to cover the production costs. Sport and music shared other features in their attempts to legitimate participation in potentially frivolous activities: any financial surplus from performances, as with many amateur sporting groups, was usually given to charity. Amateur operatic groups, particularly in northern England, became well known before the First World War for supporting dedicated beds in local hospitals; it would be interesting to see if there any sporting similarities or whether such organizations as golf clubs fulfilled the claims of many of their critics that they were essentially resorts for the selfish. Two further points need to be made here – the membership of many of these bodies overlapped, and the musicians who entertained the proudly amateur sports groups' social events were often essentially shamateurs.[19]

Literary cultures

The tensions implicit in parallel organizational and skill developments between sport and other leisure activities need to be set in another context, which is to consider sport's place in a hierarchy of cultural legitimacy and expressions of taste, which was far more complex than either the supposedly inevitable opposition between 'aesthete' and 'hearty' or the simplification of social class identifiers. Beyond the occasional gesture in the direction of Foucault, few sports historians venture very far into the difficult undergrowth of cultural theory that surrounds the investigation of many parallel phenomena. Yet understanding the place of claims of legitimacy and purity in the hierarchy of socially acceptable games, especially for the middle classes of whatever country, does invite the consideration of such issues as the diffusion and restriction of supposedly elite activities, not least in terms of their representation. The words 'elite', 'popular' and 'mass' carry overtones that have yet to be fully worked out in sports history. In the usual fields of cultural history, these might be expressed as divided between 'Highbrow' and 'Lowbrow', the similarity of whose phrenological bases masks the time gap between their coinage – the former in the 1890s, the latter not long before the First World War. Using this categorization, it is deceptively simple to characterize most sports. Real Tennis is obviously highbrow, most of mature soccer – lowbrow, in terms of take-up and values attached, particularly where spectatorship rather than participation are concerned. But there are obviously chronological and social spectra containing sports at different points in their development; the placings within them will depend as much on the extent of diffusion at a given time as on the activity's ranking within social hierarchies.

Having said that, there is much about middle-class sporting culture in particular which sits uneasily within either grouping, and it is for this that a slightly later categorization, frequently used as derogatory, should be explored. 'Middlebrow' was coined in the mid-1920s but it is, with care as to anachronism, a useful container that can be applied from at least the 1880s. Most studies using it so far have tended to focus on literature, particularly the novel, seeing it as the preserve of women in particular; it may also be applied to the graphic and plastic arts and music.[20] The ascription is still some way from being accepted as a legitimating category in its own right, since it is usually regarded as a watered-down version of High Culture. Its use in recent years owes much to the influence of the late Pierre Bourdieu, whose French-based sociology has offered explanations of taste and activity that are usefully transferable if care is taken. For him, it was the experience of *la culture moyenne*, with a slightly broader applicability than 'middlebrow', used in the English translation, which explained much of the nature of modern bourgeois interaction.[21] By examining the tensions between absorption and modification of 'legitimate' High Culture into the middle-class world, he offered a way of understanding the development of self-legitimating bourgeois activities in ways that separated them both from threats from the elites and from the tides of working-class encroachment. My case here is that, by seeing much of the history of sport from the 1880s in such terms, we can understand some of the mechanics of growth and the ways in which various media of popularization, both formal and informal, were exploited in the process. Music was one such force, in which banality was often more effective than the expression of the aesthetic and moral sensibilities Mangan's elites fostered. Another would be literary representation.

Forget Newbolt for a while, although Patrick Howarth's 'Newbolt Man' features later, and turn to alternatives which were consumed, if not so readily memorized, to build up the acceptance of 'sporting' (meaning 'decent') behaviour through both comedy and adventures designed to be consumed by the sedentary or resting.[22] In both Howarth and the earlier study by Richard Usborne, there has been some consideration of the place of 'clubland heroes', but it was largely narrative, making little attempt at differentiation of representative types or to place them in more complex contexts of cultural production.[23] From the 1880s in particular, a number of relatively cheap works was aimed at a large, but not mass, audience in which sport featured as the reason for, or backdrop to, almost improbable adventures. Through the agencies of the circulating and new lending libraries, as well as those of some clubs, they filled out the developing world of middlebrow fiction but with some noticeable differences. Because of their themes, although 'romance' might feature occasionally, they were aimed just as much at a newly leisured male readership as at the usual female consumers of this burgeoning market, and they were suitable both for dreaming adolescents and for the more sedentary middle-aged; indeed, they were singularly non-age specific in their appeal. In common, they were perceived as being morally pure, a key point in their saleability. Because they verged occasionally on the frivolous, the very earnest might be less likely to read them than to consult practical handbooks. In his recent major study of the autodidact in British culture, *The Intellectual Life of the British Working Classes*, Jonathan Rose has pointed out that this significant part of the market thrived on the cheap literature of the late nineteenth century, but largely eschewed newly written books in favour of a supposedly elite canon of literature.[24] The heyday of new middlebrow writing was from the 1880s until the Second World War, much of it as fiction, but there was a significant input of works which were sporting autobiographies, usually of the more exotic or physically demanding kind, such as mountaineering, to be admired from afar rather than practised by the readers. The books of the engineering officer and climber Frank Smythe, for instance, on Alpine and Himalayan exploration between the wars, played a significant part in that group, as did their illustration with cheap photogravure.[25]

Floreat comoedia

The use of laughter as a means of popularizing new activities seems to have flowered in the later nineteenth century. Many popular sports histories have drawn heavily on cartoons, doggerel verse and printed versions of comic songs, usually without the music. It is probably a pity for us that the main corpus of the Gilbert and Sullivan musical comedies was completed before the sports boom came fully into its own. In their operettas, religion and politics were gently mocked in a way that reinforces their influence, but there was comparatively little about sport, although many will remember the Mikado's reference to 'elliptical billiard balls'.[26] More often it was songs throughout the entire spectrum of respectability in the music halls that made the sportsman or sports woman a jolly musical figure. Generally, however, the new generation of sports historians has been so concerned with the supposed seriousness of their subject that, unlike some other academic disciplines, it has eschewed the ability to laugh at a self which was so bound up in much of the new middle-class experience. Yet there was a constant flow of essentially middlebrow literary material that did precisely that. In travelogues and pseudo-journeys in particular, there was a rich field for comedy and self-deprecation by sportsmen. It was still possible in 2000 to purchase at Oslo airport, as well as local shops in Norway, a facsimile of the comic adventures of three Englishmen as they went shooting and fishing in the Norwegian Fjords – *Three in Norway by Two of Them*, first published in England in 1882.[27] And it was designed to be read as a vicarious experience by many more than the relatively privileged Britons for whom Norway was opening up as a sporting and tourist destination.

H.G. Wells produced an opportunistic piece when he published a book on the cycling adventures of a drapery salesman, *The Wheels of Chance*, in 1896. Probably much better known amongst contemporary semi-lampoons were the works of Jerome K. Jerome (1859–1927), actor, sportsman and writer, the improbable adventures of whose fictional trio, George, Harris and J provided *Three Men in a Boat* (1889) and *Three Men on the Bummel* (1900) with a rapid commercial success. These were not strictly about competitive sport as such, but used the new fashions to provide cameos of late Victorian enthusiasms framed with general social and national observations. And their expected readership was important: in what was a rather overstated case V.S. Pritchett observed in the 1950s, 'Jerome's humour is a response of the emerging lower middle class to the inconvenience of their situation. Their dreams have left a legacy of small comic defeat.'[28] The first of the books is the better known, as the three men and a dog navigate and camp along the upper Thames. Jerome, a keen tennis player and participant in winter sports in Switzerland, had much more ambivalent feelings about the colonization of the Thames for elite sports:

> It was King Edward who spoilt Henley Regatta. His coming turned it into a society function. Before that, it had been a happy, gay affair, simple and quiet. People came in craft of all sorts, and took an interest in the racing.[29]

By contrast *Bummel*, a slightly belated attempt to cash in on the cycling boom of the mid-1890s, was a less simply-happy book. After a brief comic voyage in a hired yacht along the East Anglian coast, which prejudiced the heroes against sailing forever, and worried about the risk of dampness consequent on a return to the river, they opted to cycle in the Black Forest. What followed was not just a series of misadventures but a steady exploration of German idiosyncrasies, ranging from the bizarreness of regional dialects, dealt with in a long and at times rather serious disquisition upon comparative schooling, to the fearful tidiness and order of public life: 'In Germany one breathes in love of order with the air, in Germany the babies beat time with their rattles.'[30] Minor officialdom and an over-enthusiasm for restaurants were castigated as national traits, as was the supposed indolence of the German student:

> He is not a sportsman, which is a pity, for he should make a good one. He plays football a little, bicycles still less; plays French billiards in stuffy cafés more. But generally speaking he, or the majority of him, lays out his time bummeling, beer drinking and fighting.[31]

The moral contrast with the assumed superiority of English public schoolboys and university students was left unspoken, but was nonetheless significant. When Jerome went on to discuss the militarism of the student societies, something at odds with his portrayal of idleness, the tone deepened, but it was the impression of an unthinking brutality fostered by them, and the likelihood of an inefficient soldiery resulting, that was being used to calm his readers' apprehensions as the Second Boer War raged. Duelling was portrayed as bizarre, an athletic culture to be despised. Jerome's only answer to the pending international crisis was to hope that, as German nationalism matured, it would take on some of the improving aspects that late Victorian Britain's sporting and cultural revolutions could offer it. Yet racial stereotypes, potential national condemnation and a sense of British sporting superiority floated just below the surface. There is indeed irony in

Pritchett's claims that this book was then adopted as a German school text to illustrate the vagaries of the English mind.[32]

Later spectators

This vein of comic writing survived the First World War, to generate laughter and offer one of the most affecting literary descriptions of English 'traditional' sport ever written. At first sight, the journalist A.G. Macdonell's *England Their England* (1933) was a product of post-war cynicism produced as an antidote to economic collapse.[33] Its hero, a gassed Scottish artillery officer called Donald Cameron, found himself drifting through the employment margins of post-war society, and collecting a series of ironic vignettes which could have only come to someone with 'the right connections', yet with the sharply useful eye of a national outsider. A country house weekend ran almost cheek by jowl with Home Counties golf of the ridiculously luxurious clubhouse variety, in which a canny Scottish professional recognized Cameron from his childhood; Cameron, who had not played since his youth, defeated the English middle classes easily. Foxhunting was ridiculed gently but redeemed by the presence of a formidable upper-class nurse whom Cameron remembered from a field hospital as a combination of extraordinary gentleness and an unashamed user of the racier language of the hunting field. The book's most loved, and oft referred to as well as filmed, part was Chapter 7, a lyrical description of a leisurely village cricket match between a scratch team drawn from the London literary world and a local side which employed almost every cliché of paternalistic bonding and bucolic independence. It was the comic account of a developing crescendo that rendered it a superb piece of action writing. Yet, beloved by schoolmasters and others for decades afterwards, it has remained remarkably ignored by scholars of sport.

Almost as ignored, without an overt comic element but replete with wry humour, have been the novels of John Buchan, whose popularity as a writer before the Second World War was considerable, yet he is singularly absent from the indices and footnotes of most students of sporting heroism. Through all his life of political and public service and his writings as a popular historian, Buchan kept up a stream of writing novels to pay for his lifestyle as a country squire, a role he entered into enthusiastically as a son of a Scottish manse. His historical novels and his modern adventures were largely informed by a knowledge of country sports acquired as a boy and young man, and the settings are often Scottish border territories and the Highlands, Ross-shire in particular.[34] These were not just stories for boys; at their heart were philosophies of life and action for grown men, who seem to have formed a substantial part of his readership. Buchan acknowledged his own love for Henry Newbolt's work and he offered a variety of heroes including a canny retired Glasgow grocer, Dickson McCunn, and a South African engineer, Richard Hannay, who ended up as a knighted general with a Cotswold estate.[35] They had gentlemanly patriotic and sporting values, but not the public school background often assumed to be an integral part of those. This was

Newbolt by other means, but Howarth's attempt to classify Buchan as a co-creator of 'Newbolt Man' is too simple; it ignores the considerable subtlety of much of Buchan's characterizations.[36] Probably his most significant creation, in sporting terms, was the man often claimed to have been Buchan's self-personification, Sir Edward Leithen, a self-proclaimed dry-as-dust lawyer and MP, Scottish by origin but practising in London and with an impeccable educational background, Eton and Oxford. With a group of aristocratic friends overlapping with those Buchan created for Hannay as that character grew English roots, he found himself drawn into adventures to resolve which the sporting skills of mountaineering, the grouse moor, deer forest and salmon and trout rivers were essential. The most philosophical of these, the final work written not long before the author's death, was *Sick Heart River* (1941), placed largely in Canada where the dying Leithen set out on a chivalric quest to find a missing man, and establish his own self-identity in the process.

Sport for Buchan demanded a balanced view of self and society; as he wrote of one of his relatively minor characters, 'Reggie was the very opposite of the hard-bitten sportsman; sport was for him only one of the amenities of life, a condiment which should not be taken by itself, but which in combination gave flavour to the dish.'[37] The best known and still emulated book of the Leithen series was *John MacNab* (1925) where the hero and two friends, bored by the civilized lives of London public service and clubland, set out to poach stags and salmon as a wager, enjoying the Spartan hospitality of another member of their social group. At the heart of the book was the virtue of using field craft and showing newish landowners in Scotland what 'good sportsmanship' really entailed, as a process of physical and spiritual healing which destroyed '*taedium vitae*. . . . a special kind of ennui'.[38] Even so, there was a somewhat surprising edge, especially for any reader who expected Buchan's values to be simple – Leithen and his friends took to their escapades because they felt so bored that ordinary sport had lost its attractions. A 'Macnab' has now passed into the language of Scottish field sports as something to be attempted legitimately by the sufficiently financially well-endowed and sportingly skilled.[39]

It would be easy to dismiss this as escapist literature set against the economic and international crises of the interwar years. Yet Buchan's novels of the period were on a totally different level from the drum-banging adventures of Sapper's 'Bulldog Drummond', whose thuggishness hardly fitted Newbolt's ideals, or the thrillers of Dornford Yates, although they did share the underlying assumptions that manliness could overcome the machinations of the more wicked members of the aristocracy and middle classes.[40] There is something of the Scottish teacher in his books; if the plots offered no great sophistication, they raised significant and often complicated moral dilemmas and offered codes with which to handle them. Their appeal lay in their availability as cheap copies before the paperback revolution, and in their describing sporting activities to which access was far removed, both geographically and economically, from the vast bulk of Buchan's readers. In that sense they used well-constructed middlebrow writing to continue a process of value implantation which was by no means limited to the public schools and their aping institutions, nor to the mass boys' stories discussed by George Orwell and Jeffrey Richards.[41] Buchan's reader was asked as much to search for self-meaning, like Leithen, as to enjoy a good yarn. His son William identified the audience for which his father wrote:

> Writers like my father, A.E.W. Mason or P.G. Wodehouse could count upon an educated public with seven and sixpence to spend, and space to store a growing collection. Educated that public certainly was, or anxious to be … educated and alert, and by no means uncritical.[42]

The idea, however, that the readership was made up only of buyers of new books does need substantial modification in light of the other means of access to books, libraries and so on, let alone the second-hand market operating in pennies identified by Jonathan Rose, but the key issue was the assumption that books spreading such values had educational as well as moral virtues and suited a continuing generation of essential autodidacts, however removed they might be from the aesthetic heights of the literary canon.[43]

The style of writing to which Buchan contributed so importantly, ended effectively with the Second World War, although it could still be found in rather minor post-war adventure stories, and must always have been in tension with the perceptions and marketing of mass values in spectator sports which grew so rapidly alongside it. Towards the end of his life he identified the problem in terms that have become familiar from other critics, when he wrote of a world dominated by new technologies:

> In such a world everyone would have leisure. But everyone would be restless, for there would be no spiritual discipline in life … their life would be largely a quest for amusement. The raffish existence led today by certain groups would here become the normal existence of large sections of society.[44]

Sport was one answer, a prophylactic once again.

Endgame

Beyond the moralizing, many of the essentials of British middle-class culture had become deeply rooted in its own transmogrification of forms designed initially for an elite. It went beyond Bourdieu's perception of creating an 'illegitimate' alternative form to one which overlapped with the 'legitimate', but could justify itself increasingly in self-referential terms. Put it another way – what happened when a public school educated aristocrat read Buchan? That is not easily answered but such a voyage into a description of one's own world aimed at a different audience indicates only too clearly that the abiding attraction of these genres was their extension of the love story into more masculine settings where the sexual was peripheral to other romances. They offered a portrayal and justification of sport that suggests that the popularity of the activity itself largely made sense as a relatively non-threatening exercise. The assumptions and artefacts of middlebrow culture usually reinforced safe and respectable values quite gently. There is much evidence available that leads one to assume that, for all its pretensions to strenuous effort and trumpeted moralities, much of sport did the same thing. It could be just as banal as so many of its representations but occasionally the best of the middlebrow experience raised it beyond that, to some genuine form of heroism, offering something rather more complicated than 'Newbolt Man's' vision of life.

Notes

Some of the ideas in this paper were generated by the symposium on Sport and History, held at the International Centre for the History of Sport and Culture at De Montfort University, Leicester, in October 2001, to whose organizers, I am grateful for being asked to contribute.

 1 Just Accord Music, CD JUSCD001, *Play The Game: Victorian and Edwardian Sporting Songs* (Tadworth, 2001).
 2 Derek Scott, *The Singing Bourgeois: Songs of the Victorian Drawing Room and Parlour* (Milton Keynes: Open University Press, 1989).
 3 CD JUSCD001, booklet, p. 27.
 4 R. Holt, J.A. Mangan and P. Lanfranchi (eds), *European Heroes: Myth, Identity, Sport* (London: Frank Cass, 1996).
 5 Malcolm Tozer, 'German Influences at a Victorian Public School', in A. Gounet, T. Nieuerth and G. Pfister (eds), *Welt der Spiele – Politische, Soziale und Padagogische Aspekte*, II (Sankt Augustin: Akademia Verlag, 1996), p. 89.
 6 Ross McKibbin, 'Class, Politics, Money; British Sport since the First World War', *Twentieth-Century British History*, 13, 2 (2002), 191ff.
 7 Trevor Herbert, 'Popular Nationalism; Griffith Rhys Jones ("Caradog") and the Welsh Choral Tradition', in Christina Bashford and Leanne Langley (eds), *Music and British Culture 1785–1914; Essays in Honour of Cyril Ehrlich* (Oxford: Oxford University Press, 2001), p. 225ff; Gareth Williams, *Valleys of Song; Music and Society in Wales 1840–1914* (Cardiff: University of Wales Press, 1998).
 8 Christina Bashford, 'John Ella and the Making of the Musical Union', in Bashford and Langley (eds), *Music and British Culture 1785–1914* (Oxford, 2000), p. 193ff.
 9 Peter Gay, 'The Cultivation of Hatred', in P. Gay (ed.), *The Bourgeois Experience, Victoria to Freud*, Vol. III (London: Norton, 1994), p. 434ff.
10 Christiane Eisenberg, *'English Sports' und Deutsche Burger; eine gesellschaftsgeschichte* (Paderborn: Schöningh, 1999), *passim*.
11 Gay, 'The Cultivation of Hatred', p. 446.
12 Edward Buck, *Simla Past and Present* (Calcutta: Tharker, Spring, 1904), p. 148.
13 William C. Ferguson Jr., *A History of the Savoy Company, 1901–1940* (Philadelphia: Savoy Company, 1940); *35th Anniversary of the Blue Hill Troupe, 1949–1959* (New York: J. Pierpont Morgan Library), p. 51.
14 Richard J. Moss, *Golf and the American Country Club* (Urbana: University of Illinois Press, 2001).
15 Peter Clark, *British Clubs and Societies 1500–1800; The Origins of an Associational World* (Oxford: Oxford University Press, 2000).

16 John Lowerson, 'Joint Stock Companies, Capital Formation and Suburban Leisure, 1880–1914', in W. Vamplew (ed.), *The Commercialisation of Leisure*, Proceedings of the Economics of Leisure Section, 8th International Economic History Congress, Budapest, 1982.

17 Cyril Ehrlich, *The Piano, A History* (Oxford: Oxford University Press, 1976, 1990), p. 77.

18 Paula Gillett, 'Ambivalent Friendships; Music-lovers, Amateurs and Professionals in the Late Nineteenth Century', in Bashford and Langley (eds), *Music and British Culture 1785–1914* (Oxford, 2000), p. 321ff.

19 John Lowerson, 'An Outbreak of Allodoxia? Operatic Amateurs and Middle-class Musical Taste Between the Wars', in Alan Kidd and Dave Nicholls (eds), *Gender, Civic Culture and Consumerism; Middle-class Identity in Britain 1800–1940* (Manchester: Manchester University Press, 1999), p. 198ff.

20 The best recent example of this is Janice A. Radway, *A Feeling for Books: The Book-Of-The-Month Club, Literary Taste, and Middle-class Desire* (Chapel Hill: University of Carolina Press, 1997).

21 Pierre Bourdieu, *La Distinction* (Paris, 1979), English translation, *Distinction* (London: Routledge and Kegan Paul, 1984) is the most general of his works on the theme.

22 Patrick Howarth, *Play Up and Play the Game: The Heroes of Popular Fiction* (London: Eyre Methuen, 1973), p. 14.

23 Richard Usborne, *Clubland Heroes* (London: Barrie and Jenkins, 1953, 1974).

24 Jonathan Rose, *The Intellectual Life of the British Working Classes* (New Haven: Yale, 2001), *passim*.

25 Very representative of his work are: Frank Smythe, *Kamet Conquered* (London: Hodder and Stoughton, 1932) and *The Spirit of the Hills* (London: Hodder and Stoughton, 1935, cheap edition, 1937).

26 The best recent study is Gayden Wren, *A Most Ingenious Paradox: The Art of Gilbert and Sullivan* (Oxford: Hodder and Stoughton, 2001), but sport plays little part in it.

27 J.A. Lees and W.J. Clutterbuck, *Three in Norway by Two of Them* (London: Longmans, 1882, Oslo: Tanum, 1968, 1995).

28 V.S. Pritchett, 'The Tin Openers', *New Statesman and Nation*, 15 June 1957, p. 783; I owe this reference and much more to John S. Batts, 'American Humor: the Mark of Twain on Jerome K. Jerome', in Jennifer A. Wagner-Lawlor (ed.), *The Victorian Comic Spirit: New Perspectives* (Aldershot: Palgrave, 2000), p. 91ff.

29 Jerome K. Jerome, *My Life and Times* (London: Hodder and Stoughton, 1926), p. 229.

30 Jerome K. Jerome, *Three Men on the Bummel* (Bristol: Arrowsmith [1900]; Harmondsworth: Penguin, 1983 edition), p. 96.

31 Ibid., p. 181.

32 Pritchett, 'The Tin Openers', 784.

33 A.G. Macdonell, *England, Their England* (London: Macmillan, 1933).

34 Janet Adam Smith, *John Buchan and His World* (London: Thames and Hudson, 1979), pp. 58 and 75; Andrew Lownie, *John Buchan, The Presbyterian Cavalier* (London: Constable, 1995), *passim*.

35 Hannay made his first appearance in *The 39 Steps* (Edinburgh: Blackwood, 1915); McCunn appears, *inter alia*, in *Huntingtower* (London: Hodder and Stoughton, 1922).

36 Howarth, *Play Up and Play the Game*, p. 142ff.

37 John Buchan, *The Gap in the Curtain* (London: Hodder and Stoughton [1932] 1935 edition), p. 173.

38 John Buchan, *John Macnab* (London: Hodder and Stoughton, 1925), p. 11.

39 A recent, rather different fictional attempt to rerun the adventure, with somewhat less socially elevated heroes, was Andrew Greig, *The Return of John Macnab* (London: Headline Review, 1996).

40 'Sapper' was Herman C. McNeile, see *Bulldog Drummond* (London: Hodder and Stoughton, 1920); 'Dornford Yates' was Cecil W. Mercer, see *Blind Corner* (London: Hodder and Stoughton, 1927); both had fought as officers in the First World War and are discussed, rather uncritically, in Usborne, *Clubland Heroes*.

41 George Orwell, 'Boys' Weeklies', in *Collected Essays, Journalism and Letters*, Vol. 1 (London: Secker and Warburg, 1968), p. 460ff; Jeffrey Richards, *Happiest Days: The Public Schools in English Fiction* (Manchester: Manchester University Press, 1988).

42 William Buchan, *John Buchan, A Memoir* (London: Hodder and Stoughton, 1942), p. 51.

43 Rose, *The Intellectual Life of the British Working Classes*, p. 230.

44 John Buchan, *Memory Hold The Door* (London: Hodder and Stoughton, 1940), p. 284.

Index